Iraq against the World

Iraq against the World

Saddam, America, and the Post-Cold War Order

SAMUEL HELFONT

OXFORD
UNIVERSITY PRESS

OXFORD
UNIVERSITY PRESS

Oxford University Press is a department of the University of Oxford. It furthers
the University's objective of excellence in research, scholarship, and education
by publishing worldwide. Oxford is a registered trade mark of Oxford University
Press in the UK and certain other countries.

Published in the United States of America by Oxford University Press
198 Madison Avenue, New York, NY 10016, United States of America.

CIP data is on file at the Library of Congress

ISBN 978-0-19-753015-3

DOI: 10.1093/oso/9780197530153.001.0001

Printed by Integrated Books International, United States of America

To Nadav, Edden, and Tally

Contents

Contents

Preface and Acknowledgments

Like many Americans in academia, think tanks, the military, diplomacy, and the intelligence community, Iraq has played an outsized role in my life. One of the driving questions behind my research is, why? How did a midsized country on the opposite side of the world come to dominate American foreign policy and the lives of so many Americans for almost thirty years? Plenty of people have attempted to answer this question from the American point of view. That type of American-centric approach to international history is all too common, but it is also distorting. For me, Middle Eastern history and Middle Eastern perspectives have filled in gaps and corrected the sometimes-glaring errors in narratives based strictly on Western sources. Along those lines, this book attempts to add an Iraqi perspective to broader histories of the post–Cold War. In doing so, I hope it also will help readers to understand how Iraq came to play such an outsized role in international history over the past three decades.

This book has its origins in research that I conducted for my previous book. While working in the Ba'thist archives at the Hoover Institution, I came across an organization that changed its name several times but usually went by something like the Iraqi Ba'th Party outside Iraq. I was intrigued. No one that I knew had heard about this organization and none of the scholarly literature on Iraq mentioned it. Yet, in the Iraqi regime's internal records, it played a prominent role. As I began reading this organization's files, I quickly came to realize that it was a central feature of Iraq's international strategies under Saddam Hussein's regime. Its records offered profound and unprecedented insights into Iraq's foreign policy, its worldview, and its clash with the international community in the final decade of the twentieth century. Several years of work with those files provided a core around which I built the narrative for this book. I have added additional layers of research from other American, British, and United Nations archives as well as from private papers, memoirs, and the popular press. The result, I hope, will contribute not just to Iraqi or American history, but to international and global histories of the post–Cold War more generally.

I owe many people and institutions a great debt for supporting me through the process of writing this book. First, and most importantly, I need to thank my family. I wrote much of this book in 2020 and 2021 during the outbreak of COVID-19. My wife, Tally, and I found ourselves secluded in a small, two-bedroom apartment with a preschooler, Nadav, and a first-grader, Edden. The situation was challenging to say the least. Tally was also holding down a full-time job, but the pandemic had lightened her workload considerably. She graciously took the lead with the boys to carve out time for me to write. Often, I would walk up the street to my mother's apartment, where she allowed me to set up an office in her guest room. The opportunity to write through the pandemic was a privilege many other scholars simply did not enjoy. Additionally, I am extremely lucky that Tally also possesses considerable background in Middle Eastern studies and American foreign policy. As such, she has been both my most important critic and my greatest supporter. She has read everything I have ever written, including multiple drafts of this book, and she has had to endure me droning on about the intricacies of Iraqi history over countless dinners, walks, and car rides. This book simply would not have been possible without Tally. I cannot thank her enough.

Outside my family, a number of people and institutions have been critical to the completion of this book. I began research for this project while still writing my dissertation under Bernard Haykel at Princeton University. Friends from Princeton like Aaron Rock-Singer, Simon Fuchs, and Cole Bunzel have remained an important network of support. Over the years I have also maintained a relationship with Tel Aviv University, where friends like Brandon Friedman, Joel Parker, Rachel Kantz-Feder, and Josh Krasna have been important sounding boards.

I really threw myself into this project during a three-year postdoc at the University of Pennsylvania in the International Relations Program headed by Walter McDougall. Other colleagues at Penn were excellent. Tomoharu Nishino accompanied me on three trips to the Middle East, two of which were to Iraq. Frank Plantan and Mark Castillo ensured I had all the resources I needed. Anna Viden and Mike Horowitz were always available if I needed to bounce ideas off someone.

While at Princeton and Penn, I was also a nonresident Senior Fellow at the Foreign Policy Research Institute, where I need to thank Alan Luxenberg, Barak Mendelsohn, Dom Tierney, Mike Nunan, Ron Granieri, and John Nagl for their friendship and support. I would also like to thank Cornell Overfield who was both my student at Penn and my intern at FPRI. He dedicated many months of research to this project. It would not have been the same without his enthusiasm and intellect.

I researched much of this book at Stanford University, where two institutions have been critical. The Abbasi Program in Islamic Studies provided a great deal of support. Its Director, Lisa Blaydes, deserves special thanks for her help through every stage of this project, including organizing a book workshop at the Abbasi Program in November 2021. At that workshop, I received valuable feedback from Alissa Walter, Ariel Ahram, Ruiheng Li, Shamiran Mako, David Patel, Larry Rubin, and Michael Brill, each of whom read and commented on my manuscript.

Also at Stanford I need to thank the Hoover Institution, which houses the Ba'th Party archives and has been generous with its support for many years. In particular, I have benefited from several summer workshops organized by Paul Gregory. Eric Waken, who directs the library and archive has bent over backward to accommodate my needs, including allowing me into the reading room during renovations. Haidar Hadi has been a tremendous help in deciphering the labyrinth of Iraqi holdings at Hoover, and Sarah Patton was always available to assist with my needs.

Since 2018, I have been Assistant Professor of Strategy and Policy at the Naval War College, but permanently in residence at the Naval Postgraduate School in Monterey. It would be hard to imagine a more collegial group of friends and colleagues (especially in academia!) than Mike Jones, Joyce Sampson, John Sheehan, Yvonne Chui, Craig Whiteside, Bob Tomlinson, Fred Drake, Jonathan Czarnecki, Misha Blocksome, Greg Reilly, and Karl Walling. Outside the Naval War College program, Chris Darton and Covell Meyskens of NPS's National Security Affairs Department have been great friends and have had to listen to me talk about this project incessantly for the past several years. While in Monterey, I also benefited from the insights of Don Stoker and an FPRI intern Tamara Milic. In the Strategy and Policy Department at the Naval War College itself, I have always relied on insights, feedback, and support from John Mauer, Scott Douglas, and Tim Hoyt.

Outside these institutions, I need to thank Marc Lynch, Ryan Evans, and Doyle Hodges for providing platforms for me to share my work and for offering invaluable feedback on it. Steve Coll and Mel Leffler, who are each working on their own books about Iraq, read and provided valuable comments on this book, as did Kate Tietzen-Wisdom and Daniel Chardell. Hal Brands helped with early framing of this work and commented on a copy of the book proposal. Although I already mentioned Michael Brill as a participant in the book workshop, he has done much more than that. He deserves special thanks for the constant and ongoing conversation we have had on Iraq.

I would like to thank everyone at Oxford University Press. This is the second book I have completed with Angela Chnapko as my editor and Alexcee Bechthold as the assistant editor. They have always been responsive to my needs and an absolute pleasure to work with.

Finally, while working on this project over the past few years, I have published some of my findings in the following articles and book chapter: "Saddam and the Islamists: The Ba'thist Regime's Instrumentalization of Religion in Foreign Affairs," *The Middle East Journal* 68, no. 3 (Summer 2014); "Authoritarianism beyond Borders: The Iraqi Ba'th Party as a Transnational Actor," *The Middle East Journal* 72, no. 2 (Spring 2018); "The Gulf War's Afterlife: Dilemmas, Missed Opportunities, and the Post-Cold War Order Undone," *Texas National Security Review* 4, no. 2 (Spring 2021); and "Catalyst of History: Francis Fukuyama, the Iraq War, and the Legacies of 1989 in the Middle East," in *The Long 1989: Decades of Global Revolution*, ed. Piotr Kosicki and Kyrill Kunakhovich (Central European University Press, 2019). I would like to thank the publishers for allowing me to draw upon and sometimes repeat arguments I made in those works throughout this book.

Introduction: Iraq and the World

"This is not, as Saddam Hussein would have it, the United States against Iraq. It is Iraq against the world."[1] George H. W. Bush spoke those words before a joint session of Congress on September 11, 1990. By invoking "the world," Bush was not referring simply to the large number of countries he was assembling into the Gulf War coalition. As he made clear in the speech, Bush saw the war as an opportunity to birth "a new world order." The Cold War was coming to an end, and in Bush's words, "a new world is struggling to be born, a world quite different from the one we've known. A world where the rule of law supplants the rule of the jungle." For its proponents, this new world would be the culmination of a centuries-old intellectual history rooted in utopian thinking about global peace and universal governance. It would be embedded in institutions of international law like the United Nations Security Council, which was designed to contain the might-makes-right calculations that had tortured the twentieth century.

The end of the Cold War marked a unique point in global history. It has been called a unipolar moment, *Pax Americana*, and even the "end of history."[2] One prominent analyst later described it as launching a period of "deep peace," fulfilling the biblical prophecy in which "nation shall not lift up sword against nation, neither shall they learn war no more."[3] Of course, not everyone was swept away by what one historian called the "millenarian expectations" of the period and that dissent is critical to this book.[4] Yet, whatever one makes of post–Cold War idealism, it was clear that after a decades-long struggle, the United States emerged as the undisputed leader of global politics; not just a great power, or even a superpower, but a "hyperpower."[5]

Bush had an unprecedented chance to shape the new world that he heralded in his speech to Congress, and he placed the recalcitrant regime in Iraq at the center of his strategy to do so. Following the Gulf War, Bush continued to rally international support for building a new world order based on his policies toward Iraq. He touted experimental tools such as international sanctions, weapons inspections, and no-fly zones, which he hoped a newly unified Security Council could use to enforce its resolutions and contain

Iraq against the World. Samuel Helfont, Oxford University Press. © Oxford University Press 2023.
DOI: 10.1093/oso/9780197530153.003.0001

Saddam. Many internationalists and peace activists shared Bush's aspirations and hoped that employing these tools would be an important step toward ending interstate war altogether.

This was "the world" that Bush invoked, and this book unearths the untold story of how Iraq confronted it throughout the 1990s and early 2000s. The book relies on American, United Nations, and British records, as well as years of research in Arabic-language Iraqi archives. The results highlight previously unknown Iraqi strategies, including the prominent use of influence operations and manipulative statesmanship. In exploring these strategies, the book traces Ba'thist operations around the globe—from the streets of New York and Stockholm, to the mosques of Pakistan and Saudi Arabia, and the halls of power in Paris and Moscow. In doing so, it highlights the limits of Bush's new world order. It also offers new insight into Iraq's attempts to influence the evolution of post–Cold War politics, the fallout of which continues to shape our world today.

Attempts to Influence the Post–Cold War World

Saddam's goals in confronting the post–Cold War world were clear. Iraq was being smothered under harsh UN sanctions and invasive weapons inspections; the Ba'thists wanted to end them while offering as few concessions as possible. Saddam saw these sanctions and inspections as tied to an emerging world order. Thus, he thought that breaking up the newly forming international system was the key to Iraq's salvation.

Following the Gulf War, Iraq's military and diplomatic options were limited. Instead, it developed deeply intertwined political and economic strategies to influence global politics. Until a UN "oil-for-food" program allowed the regime to begin selling its oil in 1996, economics remained an important but mostly latent force in Iraqi foreign policy. As such, in the early-to-mid-1990s, Ba'thist records highlight what Western analysts would call Baghdad's political "influence operations" and what the Iraqis called al-taharruk (literally, moving someone). These operations were far more extensive than anyone outside the Ba'thist regime understood. The Ba'th Party and the Iraqi Intelligence Service embedded themselves in Arab diasporas and worked from Iraqi embassies around the world. They attempted to shape political discourse in and among key states and they organized disparate constituents in foreign countries using a combination of moral and political persuasion.

By the mid-1990s and then even more so after the oil-for-food program went into effect in 1996, the Ba'thists incorporated economics into their influence campaigns. The political and economic aspects of Iraqi strategies reenforced one another. Party branches around the world and the Iraqi Intelligence Service identified actors who would assist the regime in circumventing or degrading sanctions. Iraq had one of the world's largest proven oil reserves, and as the United Nations' independent inquiry later noted, Saddam's regime "was willing to forego revenue from oil sales or to overpay for imports to reward or encourage certain foreign politicians, journalists, and businesses to exert influence in its favor, . . . especially in advocating a lifting of the sanctions."[6] Thus, politicians, states, and corporations benefited by supporting Iraq's strategic initiatives. At the same time, Ba'thists continued to amplify narratives around the world that emphasized the suffering of innocent Iraqis from international sanctions. Such narratives shaped media coverage about Iraq and provided political cover for those who stood to benefit economically from supporting Iraq. Therefore, while much has already been written about Iraq's manipulation of the oil-for-food program, previously unexplored Iraqi archives show how such economic operations were integrated into and dependent on broader political strategies.

The Ba'thists who carried out these operations were quite colorful and often corrupt. People like Huda Salih Mahdi Ammash, who the Western press dubbed "Mrs. Anthrax" and "Dr. Germ," coordinated with Iraqi intelligence officers who lived seemingly normal lives, running kebab shops in American suburbs while also spying on top secret military facilities. At their height, such Ba'thists operated organizations in over sixty countries. Outside Iraq, the Ba'thists were ideologically agile. They worked with people and groups that had little in common with the regime in Baghdad except for the fact that they opposed war and sanctions on Iraq. Thus, the Ba'thists worked covertly, using proxy organizations and disassociating with the Iraqi embassies "to provide cover for their [Ba'th] Party activities."[7] They courted people on both the political left and the right: academics, student organizations, militant Islamists, pacifists, liberal activists, and conservative isolationists. They found allies in the media and even among some mainstream politicians. Then, they attempted to bring these incongruent groups together into a loosely organized political force designed to achieve Iraq's strategic goals.[8]

Rethinking Iraqi Foreign Policy under Saddam

Ba'thist foreign policy focused on influencing politics in foreign states. While often neglected by diplomatic and military historians, this type of strategy has a long history. Political and military leaders have been using some form of influence operations since ancient times. As Sun Tzu famously argued, "to subdue the enemy without fighting is the acme of skill."[9] In Shakespeare's *Coriolanus*, the Roman general for whom the play is named touted his ability "to take in a town with gentle words."[10] However, the type of highly politicized approach to international strategy that typifies modern influence operations has its origins in the American and French Revolutions when the masses revolted against their leaders. As Lawrence Freedman notes, the realization that such uprisings were possible led to the emergence of "professional revolutionaries," who developed theories and tactics for fomenting unrest and mobilizing society toward political ends.[11] By the mid-nineteenth century, an early socialist leader in Russia named Alexander Herzen described the ideal professional revolutionary as someone possessing a "passion for propaganda, for agitation, for demagogy, if you like, to incessant activity in founding and organizing plots and conspiracies and establishing relations and in ascribing immense significance to them."[12] One would struggle to find better words to describe Iraqi Ba'thists operating around the world in the 1990s and early 2000s.

As these professional revolutionaries emerged, states quickly grasped the benefits of sponsoring and fomenting them among their adversaries. In World War I, the perfect storm of mass mobilization of European societies and new communication technology led to a bonanza of propaganda aimed both at domestic and foreign populations. After the war, European states institutionalized their influence operations, and their propaganda grew increasingly sophisticated.[13] The importance of influence operations paralleled what Hannah Arendt described as the rise of the age of "mass man," in which the downward push of political agency meant the masses could be manipulated to great political effect.[14] These developments reached their zenith in the Cold War when Soviet and American agents battled to destabilize each other's states from the inside out.[15] The father of America's Cold War containment strategy, George Kennan, developed what the Americans called "political warfare" in the 1940s and 1950s.[16] On the other side of the Iron Curtain, a former head of Soviet intelligence claimed influence operations, which the Russians termed "active measures," were "one of the most important functions of the KGB's foreign intelligence service."[17]

Influence operations are inherently difficult to study even many years after they occur. They are often covert or clandestine. Scholars only know the full extent of Soviet operations because a KGB archivist named Vasili Mitrokhin spent thirty years secretly copying files in handwritten notes which he stored under the floorboards of his dacha, and then defected with them to the United Kingdom in 1992.[18] By far the best archive of influence operations in the post–Cold War period comes from the Ba'th Party documents, which provide unprecedented insights into how a recent, illiberal, revisionist actor planned and executed its international operations.[19]

Strategies that rely on influence operations have been a consistent blind spot in international history. Some theories of international relations insist that power can only stem from material forces such as the military or economics. As such, Western analysts have often failed to recognize revolutionary political strategies and influence operations in international politics. George Kennan famously warned in his "long telegram" and "X" article that Western analysts who saw Stalin's Soviet Union simply as a military threat akin to Napoleon or Hitler had misinterpreted Moscow's worldview and its strategy. The Soviets, according to Kennan, had no intention of storming into Western Europe behind the Red Army. They expected to win the Cold War by attacking and undermining Western states politically.[20]

The same Western biases that Kennon criticized have also shaped the scholarship on Iraqi foreign policy under Saddam. Western analysts have tended to focus on what they think is important: the military, high diplomacy, and economics. Those *were* important elements of Iraqi power under Saddam—after all he used his oil wealth to build a large army, then to invade two of his neighbors, and he dreamed of leading Arab armies into Jerusalem. While not ignoring military officers and diplomats, this book puts more emphasis on political and economic elements of Iraqi strategy. Partly, this focus stems from the book's sources. Records from the Iraqi Intelligence Service and the Ba'th Party survived the 2003 war. The records from the Iraqi Foreign Ministry, which undoubtedly would have emphasized more traditional forms of diplomacy, did not.

However, even without relying on skewed sources, a careful study of Ba'thist Iraq would reveal that the military and traditional diplomacy were not the primary lenses through which Saddam viewed international politics. He was a populist and he attempted to achieve his goals by influencing the masses. Saddam owed his power to his place within a populist, self-described revolutionary political party. He did not rise through the ranks of the military or state security services. As one of his biographers noted, "for all the uniforms, titles, and honorary ranks . . . Saddam never had any military experience, had probably never read a military textbook, or even considered the finer points of strategy and tactics."[21] In fact, the Ba'thist regime that he ruled had a history of turbulent relations with the Iraqi military and other state institutions. A short-lived Ba'thist coup in Iraq had gone awry in 1963 when military officers turned against the party. Therefore, immediately after they took power in 1968, the Ba'thists purged Iraqi military and intelligence officers, replacing them with political activists who were loyal to the party. It should come as no surprise, then, that Saddam saw the party rather than the military as the source of his power, and throughout his life, he tended to view the world through the lens of its populist politics.

It was also no coincidence that many of what might be called quintessentially Saddamist institutions were described as "popular." When Saddam needed a loyal militia to defend his regime in the 1970s, he created the "Popular Army." When he wanted to mobilize international Arab support, he held the "Conference of the Popular Arab Forces." When he wanted to mobilize Islamic opinion, he organized the "Popular Islamic Conference." The word popular in these instances is a translation of the Arabic term sha'bi. It suggests something coming from the masses, unofficial, and of the people. And even Iraqi sources from outside the Ba'th Party show that when the regime engaged in international politics, it saw populist efforts as its natural source of strength. For example, when attempting to influence international Islamic opinion during the war with Iran, the Iraqis distinguished between official (rasmi) and popular (sha'bi) efforts. The Iraqis considered other states to be more adept in pursuing the official track; Saddam's regime focused on the populist track, which is why it organized the Popular Islamic Conference.[22] This view of the importance of popular mobilization in international politics was not limited to Islam and it remained an important part of Iraqi strategy until the end of Saddam's rule in 2003.[23]

Saddam's foreign policy was also influenced by a Middle Eastern geopolitical context in which conventional warfare and decisive battles have played a much smaller role in shaping states than they have in other regional systems, most notably in Europe. Since the nineteenth century, outside powers repeatedly intervened to prevent any Middle Eastern actor from achieving the type of decisive military victory necessary to become a great power.[24] Modern Middle Eastern states still had interests, but they have relied on influence operations and political warfare to achieve their goals. Throughout the middle decades of the twentieth century, radical Arab nationalists like the Ba'thists and Nasserists sponsored revolutionary parties across the region and filled international airwaves with their propaganda. Their adversaries returned the favor by supporting Islamists revolutionaries within their secular Arab republics.[25] Saddam exported these Middle Eastern strategies to the global arena.

Operational Influence, Strategic Influence, and World Order

This book's main contribution is its reconsideration of Ba'thist Iraq's foreign policy and its unearthing of previously unknown Iraqi strategies. However, a secondary and more speculative argument about the impact of those strategies on world order has important implications for international and global history. While most histories of the transition from Cold War to post–Cold War focus on Berlin, Eastern Europe, and Moscow, this book highlights how the post–Cold War was also negotiated, built, and ultimately undermined in Iraq. The book does not argue for a reduction in the significance of those other places in post–Cold War history. It simply attempts to place Iraq alongside them.[26] In doing so, it also upends the typical method of using Western archives to write histories of the Middle East. Instead, this book looks to Iraqi archives for insights into the histories of places like Russia, Western Europe, and the United States.

Internal Iraqi records contain thousands of pages on Ba'thist attempts to influence global politics. As such, describing Ba'thist strategies and operations is fairly straightforward. A more difficult but also more consequential question is: Were they successful? Answering that question requires distinguishing between what one might call operational level impacts and strategic level impacts. The former is fairly easy to analyze; the latter is more problematic.

On an operational level, the Ba'thists were successful when they were able to partner with the types of people and organizations that were necessary to execute their influence campaigns. They needed to work with and through foreign political parties, religious organizations, the media, unions, and so forth. Thus, measuring the effectiveness of Iraqi influence campaigns at this level is not too difficult: Either the Ba'thists found partners or they did not. Iraqi records make clear that throughout the 1990s and early 2000s, they were quite successful at this operational level.

In contrast to this rather straightforward analysis, determining whether the Ba'thists were able to transform operational gains into strategic impacts is more difficult and probably impossible. Success on the strategic level requires one to consider whether Ba'thist actions actually affected international politics in a way that aligned with Iraqi interests. The problem, as one scholar of Cold War influence operations has argued, is that influence operations work best when based on "existing conflicts and existing divisions."[27] Thus, separating their strategic effects from what would have occurred in their absence can be quite difficult.

States, organizations, and people act based on their interests and values. Iraqis could not change those fundamentals. However, this book asserts that Iraqi actions could affect policies and political decisions on the margins. That type of influence can still be quite important because political disputes are often won or lost on the margins. To take a more recent example, the well-documented Russian attempt to influence the 2016 American presidential election did not create the racial and postindustrial economic discontent that buoyed Donald Trump's campaign. If the Russians were successful in influencing the election—and as with other influence operations, that proposition is difficult to prove—they did so by amplifying and channeling this existing discontent. Theories that Moscow's actions affected the outcome of the election rest on the claim that Russian influence operations drove a tiny fraction of national voters to the polls who otherwise would not have voted. When concentrated in a few key states, these extra votes put Donald Trump in the White House and changed the trajectory of American politics.

Likewise, a group like the Muslim Brotherhood, or states like Russia and France, were poised to resist American hegemony in the 1990s. However, this book presents evidence that Iraq pushed these actors to contest the American-led order in a manner that significantly inflamed preexisting tensions. Moreover, Iraq was not necessarily going to be at the center of struggles between these actors and the United States. Baghdad's actions ensured that it would be. Thus, while Iraqis could not alter the fundamentals of international politics, this book makes a case that they were able to influence the *shape* and *scale* of post–Cold War tensions in a manner that had a lasting effect on the international system.

Much of this argument rests on Iraq's role in fracturing consensus at the United Nations Security Council. It is worth emphasizing that George H. W. Bush, not Saddam, put Iraq at the center of a new world order. As recent scholarship has shown, Saddam was clearly thinking about the end of the

Cold War when he invaded Kuwait, but there is little evidence to suggest that he had a broader plan to challenge post–Cold War politics on a global scale.[28] Nevertheless, following the Gulf War, Iraq stood almost alone against the international system that the United States attempted to impose. In the wake of the Cold War, the permanent members of the UN Security Council initially placed a high value on unity. Doing so gave them tremendous power in the newly cooperative international system. The Security Council's first action in this new phase was to demand painful concessions from Iraq during and after the Gulf Crisis. Thus, Iraq became a test case for a new global order. Rather than comply, Saddam adopted what political scientists would recognize as a classic "wedging" strategy to divide one's adversaries.[29] He attempted to lure states out of the coalition that had formed against him and to break the unity at the Security Council which underpinned it.

Beyond the Security Council, proponents of the post–Cold War order argued that a rules-based system could only operate through broad, collective action in global politics. Lesser powers had to see the American-led order as beneficial, or they would simply ignore the dictates of the Security Council.[30] The Ba'thist almost instinctually understood this reasoning and how to attack it. So, in addition to trying to divide the Security Council, Iraqis waged intense political battles for support among lesser powers in places like the Middle East and Western Europe.

Iraq's strategies undermined the type of liberal norms that were necessary for a rules-based international system to function.[31] Where leading states in the system committed to cooperation, the Iraqis sowed dissent; where these states committed to a rules-based system, the Iraqis enticed them to break the rules. In doing so, the Iraqis helped prevent these norms from crystalizing.[32]

Besides Iraq, other factors such as the Balkan wars, NATO expansion, failed humanitarian interventions, and disillusionment with economic globalization also undermined the post–Cold War system. Yet, because of the Gulf War, Iraq was entangled in the concepts of world order and even the idea of history itself in a way that, say, Somalia, was not. As such, the evolution of ideas about order and history in the post–Cold War period was disproportionately influenced by conflicts over Iraq.

The transformation of global politics that occurred over the last decade of Saddam's rule was stunning. In 1991, the world was united in its opposition to Iraqi belligerence. Ten years later, Iraq divided not only the world, but also Western allies such as the United States, France, and Germany. Moreover, tools such as sanctions, inspections, and no-fly zones, which had been heralded as humanitarian alternatives to war in the early 1990s, were considered extreme and unjust by much of the world a decade later. Again, Iraqi actions did not—and could not—create the fundamental tensions that drove this evolution. However, the Baʿthists could shape and exacerbate the way those tensions manifested, and they did so to lasting effect.

Baʿthist Iraq in History

Like the international order that Saddam hoped to challenge, Iraq had its own deep history that shaped its interaction with broader transnational trends. Though the intellectual power of Arab nationalism and Baʿthism were fading in the 1990s, they continued to provide an ideology and, just as importantly, a structure around which the Iraqi regime was organized. Likewise, the Cold War was over, but vestiges of Third Worldism and nonalignment lingered, eventually transforming into resistance against global American hegemony. The rise of Islamism in the last decades of the twentieth century filled the ideological void left by the end of the Cold War in shaping political debates across the Muslim World. Finally, mass migrations to the West from Iraq and the Arab World provided challenges for a closed authoritarian regime like Baʿthist Iraq, but they also provided new opportunities for Baghdad to influence international politics. These national, transnational, and international histories intersected as Iraq developed strategies to resist the dictates of the post–Cold War order.

Likewise, this book sits at the intersection of several streams of historical literature on Saddam's Iraq. Over the past decade, the historiography of Baʿthist Iraq has been revolutionized by an abundance of archival material that became available following the fall of Saddam's regime. Yet, clear divisions have emerged in this literature, largely based on the object of their study and the different type of Iraqi archives that they used. One group of historians has produced what Fanar Haddad called the "new generation" of archive-based studies relying on the millions of pages of Baʿth Party files at the Hoover Archives along with a wide range of other Arabic language sources to reconstruct the history of Saddam's Iraq.[33] Almost all the works in this category have focused on Iraq's domestic social and political history.[34]

Alongside these works, another stream of literature focusing on international history and strategic studies has emerged out of research with translated Iraqi state records.[35] Like the "new generation" of domestic histories just mentioned, these works on international and strategic studies have revolutionized what scholars know about Iraq. They have dissected critical issues like Iraqi weapons of mass destruction programs (or the lack thereof); they have provided deep insight into the decisions and ruling strategies of senior regime officials. Yet, these works have mostly been produced by generalists rather than Arabists. Therefore, they do not use the extensive but untranslated Ba'th Party records at the Hoover Archives. The latter files provide critical details on the development and execution of Iraq's international strategies. They enhance, and sometimes challenge much of the present literature on Iraq by shifting the focus away from what Western analysts consider traditional elements of power like the military and diplomacy, and instead point historians toward more politicized strategies, which as this book argues, were better aligned with Iraq's history and worldview.

In essence, then, the archive-based literature on Ba'thist Iraq falls into two rough categories: first, works that used a full range of Arabic sources—including the Ba'th Party records—but have focused mostly on domestic social and political history; second, works that deal mostly with international history and strategic studies, but have been limited to English language sources. *Iraq against the World* bridges the gap between these two literatures. Like the "new generation" of Iraqi histories, it will use a wide range of sources in an attempt to develop a rich and nuanced narrative on Iraqi social and political history. Yet, it will apply that approach to broader international and strategic issues that have, thus far, mostly been covered only by generalists lacking access to the full range of sources on Ba'thist Iraq.

The Book and Some Caveats

To investigate Iraq's place in international history, this book proceeds chronologically from Chapter 1, which lays out the necessary precursors about Iraq and the world, to Chapters 2 and 3 on the 1991 Gulf Crisis and its aftermath. In addition to providing details about some of Iraq's initial operational successes in gaining partners, the chapters also provide historical context for later chapters. The core of the book is found in Chapters 4 through 8 when Iraqi Ba'thists gained ever-increasing international support, ultimately leading to the breakdown of the UN Security Council's consensus on Iraq and the demise of the new world order. Chapter 9 deals with the fallout of that lost consensus, leading into the 2003 Iraq War. The book ends with a

Conclusion and Afterword that discusses the still-continuing fallout from Saddam's confrontation with the world.

This book toggles between social, global, and diplomatic history as well as between Iraqi and international lenses. As others have noted, some of the most interesting recent work in international history has examined interactions between state and nonstate actors, for example, discussing the intersection between states, international institutions, transnational religious movements, multinational corporations, and civil society.[36] This book attempts to continue along those lines. Doing so often requires a detailed discussion of the United States and its policies. However, some well-trodden American perspectives have been glossed over to make room for the Iraqi history this book provides for the first time.

As careful readers will have already noticed, the book also engages various theories of international relations. However, the book does not make an argument about an inherent or enduring nature of world order that exists outside of a historical context. Nor is it designed to create a social scientific model for how a particular type of state acts in a particular context. Saddam's whims often settled important policy decisions and this book makes no attempt to smooth them over or subordinate them to a logic about how this or that type of regime is supposed to act. Instead, the book spends considerable space providing the historical context of those decisions. That being said, Iraq was clearly an illiberal, authoritarian state trying to navigate a world which was growing increasingly hostile to authoritarianism. Thus, political scientists might find value in reading this book as a case study for how a state like Iraq tried to survive global transformations following the end of the Cold War. Additionally, as already mentioned, the book can be read as a recent case study on the use of influence operations in foreign policy.

A final caveat needs to be made regarding sources. The book relies on various American, British, and UN archives; collections of personal papers; English and Arabic language memoirs; and the popular press.[37] However, its most important sources are the internal records of Saddam's regime. Like all archival records, these have their idiosyncrasies, biases, and ethical dilemmas, which scholars need to consider.[38]

Moreover, while Iraqi files offer phenomenal details, they do not provide a complete picture. As already mentioned, the records of the Iraqi Foreign Ministry were destroyed. The vast majority of files that survived and that are relevant to this book fall into two discrete categories. The first consists of Iraqi state records that the American military confiscated in 2003. The

US Department of Defense selectively translated and released less than one hundred thousand pages from a collection which was estimated to include over one hundred million pages. The physical files were eventually returned to Iraq, but digital copies were available to scholars for a time through the now defunct Conflict Records Research Center at the National Defense University in Washington, DC.[39] These files contain valuable documents from the Iraqi Intelligence Service, the military, and transcripts of recordings from Saddam's closed-door meetings with his senior advisors. Some of these documents were published as collected volumes and are, therefore, still widely available.[40] The second set of records relevant to this book is the complete, untranslated archive of the Iraqi Ba'th Party Secretariat in Baghdad, which was captured by Iraqi dissidents in 2003 and eventually made its way to the Hoover Archives at Stanford University.[41] The original files have been returned to Iraq, but digital copies are still available to researchers. This archive includes somewhere in the range of ten million pages and provides by far the most detailed information about Iraqi politics under Saddam. Nevertheless, even this archive does not always paint a complete picture. It only contains the files that were maintained by the party secretariat. The details of everyday events were not always sent back to Baghdad, so the secretariat files sometimes only provide overviews and summaries of the activities of Ba'thist organizations operating around the world. Historians working with these files have access to tremendous amounts of information on some Ba'thist operations, but very little on others except for the fact that they occurred. The information available through the secretariate's files is more than enough to reconstruct Iraqi strategies and operations, but holes still exist.

1

Precursors

When the Iraqi Army marched into Kuwait on August 2, 1990, it sent shockwaves around the world. Iraqi troops unleashed an orgy of pillaging and violence as they transformed their previously sovereign southern neighbor into Iraq's nineteenth province. The resulting crisis put Baghdad at the center of global politics, where it remained for over a quarter century.

In many ways, Iraq's emergence as a central feature of international politics was strange. Iraq was a middling country in terms of size and human development; its population was not large; and its economy was overly dependent on oil. Iraq certainly was not the type of great power that traditionally dominated international history.

Historians of Iraq and the Middle East are quick to point out that while Saddam Hussein and Iraq entered popular consciousness in the West almost without warning in the summer of 1990, the Gulf Crisis had been building for some time. Most importantly, the Islamic revolution in Iran and then the long, bloody grind of the Iran–Iraq War increasingly pulled in outside powers and shaped regional politics.

Saddam also developed his populist and militantly revisionist approach to international relations long before the Gulf War. Thus, exploring the development of Iraq's international strategies prior to the Gulf War is critical for understanding Saddam's confrontation with the world throughout the 1990s. Iraq's lasting influence on international politics was at least partly due to the nature of Baghdad's approach to foreign affairs. While Iraq was no match for the United States militarily or economically during the Gulf War, Saddam's regime developed a highly politicized approach to international relations that the United States was ill-prepared to counter following the conflict.

Iraqis developed that approach to foreign relations in the 1980s. It was rooted in the history of Arab nationalism and the Baʻth Party, as well as global migrations in the postcolonial period and the rise of political Islam in the final decades of the twentieth century. These historical forces shaped Iraqi politics and foreign policy throughout Saddam's rule in Iraq. They were also catalysts for forging new Iraqi institutions and strategies, which would

Iraq against the World. Samuel Helfont, Oxford University Press. © Oxford University Press 2023.
DOI: 10.1093/oso/9780197530153.003.0002

confound Western states in the wake of the Gulf War and during the emergence of a post–Cold War period. Yet, a full understanding of the way that these events influenced Iraq's foreign relations has only become possible with the opening of the Iraqi archives.

Ba'thism and the Iraqi Ba'th Party

The Ba'th Party, which ruled Iraq from 1968 to 2003, provided the intellectual and institutional foundations for Iraqi politics under Saddam. The party was formed by the Syrian intellectual, Michel Aflaq, in the 1940s. Aflaq was born into a Christian family in Damascus in 1910. He became politically active while studying at the Sorbonne in Paris in the late 1920s and early 1930s, and he imbibed the radical trends on both the left and the right that dominated Europe during the period. By the time he returned to Syria in the mid-1930s, he was an active communist. Yet, he was also a staunch Arab nationalist, and he eventually abandoned the communist party due to its support of French colonialism in Syria.

Aflaq formed a political party, which he named the Ba'th, meaning "resurrection" or "renaissance." The name evoked the glories of the Arab-Islamic empires that ruled from the seventh to twelfth centuries. He mixed European romanticism and nationalism with indigenous Arab nationalist trends, calling for the Arab people to unite into a socialist, pan-Arab state powerful enough to throw off the yoke of imperialism.

In the 1930s and 1940s, Aflaq joined with like-minded activists such as Zaki al-Arsuzi and Salah al-Din al-Bitar. Together they carved out a space for Ba'thism in Syrian politics to the left of the large landowners and conservative religious leaders, but to the right of the communists. The Ba'thists support for socialism and revolution put them at odds with ruling elites in Syria. Yet, unlike the communists, Aflaq and others based their ideas on a mystical attachment to the nation rather than materialist economics. Moreover, Aflaq made clear that Ba'thists were believers in God, which separated them from the atheistic communists. Although he was Christian, he gave Islam pride of place. He interpreted Islam as an Arab religion for the Arab people, and he infused Ba'thism with Islamic symbolism. For example, he published his ideas in a collection of essays under the title *Fi Sabil al-Ba'th* (In the way of the Ba'th), which was a clear reference to the Islamic saying *fi sabil Allah* (in the way of Allah). Also, the Ba'th Party's slogan, "an eternal message (*risala*) for a single Arab nation (*umma*)," contained clear references to the Prophet Muhammad's message (*risala*) to the Muslim community (*umma*).

Aflaq and his followers joined with other Arab nationalists in Syria during the 1940s to form an expanded Ba'th Party. The Ba'thists adopted a clandestine hierarchical structure similar to that of underground revolutionary movements in Europe. They operated in secret cells which had limited contact with each other. Thus, they were able to hide their existence from state security services even if a Ba'thist was identified and tortured for information.

In adopting the structure of revolutionary European movements, the Ba'thists also laid the foundation for the Kafkaesque bureaucracy of the authoritarian states that emerged from that structure. Cells reported through a rigid party hierarchy to section commands, branch commands, and so on through banal party officials up to a National Command that sat at the pinnacle of the party. By the early 1950s, the party spread to other Arab states such as Iraq, Jordan, and Yemen. Under the party's pan-Arab ideology, each Arab state was merely a region in the broader Arab nation. As such, Regional Commands were responsible for Ba'th Party activities in places like Iraq, Jordan, or Syria, and they all reported to the National Command located in Damascus.

The Ba'th Party rode the post–World War II tide of Arab nationalism through the rough and tumble politics of the 1950s and 1960s in Syria. Syrian Ba'thists played key roles in the short-lived United Arab Republic (1958–1961), which combined Syria and Egypt into a single state. However, like other Syrians, they soon became disillusioned with Egyptian domination. After Syria broke away from Egypt, the party focused on gaining power in the various regions of the Arab World. Ba'thist military officers in Syria and Iraq staged coups which brought the party to power in both Damascus and Baghdad in 1963. Aflaq served as the Secretary General of the National Command which sat above the Regional Commands ruling both countries.

Far from stabilizing the Ba'th Party, the successful coups led to political infighting and discord. Ba'thist control of Iraq lasted less than a year. Ba'thist military officers who ruled Syria through the Regional Command chafed under the authority of Aflaq's National Command, which was supposed to control them but had no military or security forces to enforce its dictates. In 1966, Syrian military officers launched an internal party coup against the Damascus-based National Command and Aflaq fled into exile. He reestablished the National Command in Baghdad in 1968 following a second Ba'thist coup in Iraq. From that point forward, the Ba'th Party was split between a Baghdad-based faction that recognized Aflaq as the Secretary General and a Damascus-based faction that did not. The rivalry between these two factions was heated and continued for decades despite several attempts at reconciliation.

Saddam Hussein and the Iraqi Ba'th Party

The Iraqi Ba'th party was founded in the 1950s. After the leaders of the 1963 coup failed to consolidate power, a new faction led by Ahmed Hassan al-Bakr gained control of the party. In July 1968, al-Bakr and his young kinsman, Saddam Hussein, led another coup. This time they quickly solidified their power and were able to rule the country until the American-led invasion in 2003. Al-Bakr, a former general in the Iraqi Army, appointed himself the President of Iraq. Just as importantly, he became the Chairman of the newly formed Revolutionary Command Council, which ruled the country by dictate throughout the Ba'thist period.

Saddam was the muscle behind the Iraqi Ba'th Party's rise to power in 1968. Born in 1937 to an impoverished family outside the Sunni Arab city of Tikrit, Saddam's father died before his birth. His mother then married a man named Ibrahim al-Hassan. Although Saddam later denied it, most biographies of him describe his stepfather as a violent and abusive man.[1] When he was ten years old, Saddam fled his home to live with his uncle, Khairallah Talfah, in Baghdad. His uncle introduced him to hardline Arab nationalist politics. As a young man, Saddam was tall—well over six feet—and handsome. His well-tailored suits and wide shoulders gave him a presence that allowed him to dominate a room. His dashing appearance hid a violent streak, and he developed a reputation as a tough street fighter during the tumultuous political battles in post–World War II Iraq. He was accused of murdering a communist in Tikrit, and in 1959, at the age of 22, he attempted to assassinate Prime Minister Abd al-Karim Qasim, who had taken power through a military coup the previous year. Saddam was shot in the leg during the failed assassination attempt and fled to Syria. In Syria, the young Saddam met Aflaq and then moved to Cairo where he was heavily influenced by Gamal abd al-Nasser's pan-Arabism.[2]

Saddam returned to Iraq following the Ba'thist coup in 1963. When the Ba'thists were forced from power later that year, he decided against going back into exile. He was arrested in 1964 but escaped from prison two years later. In the run-up to the 1968 coup, Ahmed Hassan al-Bakr relied heavily on Saddam, eventually appointing him as Deputy Secretary of the Ba'th Party's Regional Command in Iraq. After the coup, Saddam also took the number two spot in the Revolutionary Command Council. He was only thirty-one years old.

Throughout the 1970s, Saddam gained increasing power. In 1972, he orchestrated a rapprochement with the Soviet Union after Ba'thist clashes with the Iraqi Communist Party had marred the relationship. That same year, Saddam spearheaded the nationalization of the British-owned Iraqi Petroleum Company and then used the revenues to implement ambitious development projects throughout the country. Saddam also took control of the security services. He sidelined his rivals in the party, often killing them or sending them into exile.

By the late 1970s, Saddam had taken de facto control over the Iraqi regime from his aging and ailing kinsman. In 1979, Saddam finally pushed al-Bakr aside in what some have speculated was a bloodless coup. Whatever the truth of such allegations, Saddam replaced him to become the President of Iraq, the Chairman of the Revolutionary Command Council, and the Secretary General of the Iraqi Ba'th Party. Aflaq had been an ally of Saddam's since moving to Iraq in 1968, and he remained the Secretary General of the Ba'th Party's National Command, which was also located in Baghdad. Officially, the Iraqi Regional Command, which Saddam controlled, was subordinate to Aflaq's National Command. In practice anyone in Iraq who questioned Saddam's absolute authority saw their life expectancy significantly reduced. Aflaq was not immune from that grim reality.

While Saddam's replacement of al-Bakr as the leader of Iraq was not violent, his early rule was filled with bloodshed and turmoil. Prior to Saddam's rise to the presidency, rumors swirled around Baghdad that factions within the regime were attempting to clip his power by uniting Iraq with the rival Ba'thist regime in Syria. Indications that al-Bakr was considering this plan provided the impetus for Saddam to force him from office. To Iraq's east, Iran was in the midst of an Islamic revolution that threatened to metastasize among Iraq's majority Shi'i population and inflame Sunni Islamists as well.

After securing his place at the top of the regime, Saddam moved quickly to address these threats. First, he called a now infamous meeting of the Iraqi Ba'th Party. The episode was preserved in a grainy video that Saddam made public soon after it occurred. As Saddam sat on a stage calmly smoking a cigar and staring at an auditorium filled with party members, a senior Ba'thist, who had been broken by torture, confessed to being involved in a Syrian plot against the Iraqi government. He read the names of dozens of co-conspirators aloud and as he did so, members of the regime's security service removed the offenders from the room. The accused pleaded for mercy and the remaining officials cried out terrified statements of loyalty to Saddam and to Iraq. After being dragged from the room, the accused were tried for treason. Some accounts state that Saddam ordered other senior Ba'thists to execute twenty-two of them personally, this way the entire regime leadership was implicated. Broader purges of the party and dozens more executions followed.[3] From that point on, Saddam's power in Iraq was absolute. He consolidated the Iraqi Ba'th Party under his rule and developed a highly personalized regime. Towering pictures of him appeared ubiquitously throughout the country and even the slightest indication of dissent among the population was met with harsh reprisals. People regularly disappeared; no one dared to ask what had happened to them. All information in the country was tightly controlled and the regime became increasingly despotic.

The Iran–Iraq War and Consolidated Tyranny

In 1980, Saddam launched an ill-fated war against the new Islamic regime in Iran. In 1979, the Islamic revolution to oust the Shah's regime in Tehran had decimated the Iranian military. At the same time, Iran's new leaders were attempting to spread their revolution to Iraq and overthrow the Ba'thist regime.[4] As such, Saddam had defensive reasons for launching the war, but he also saw opportunity to strike a weakened Iran.

The war allowed him to entrench his rule even further. He militarized and mobilized Iraqi society. Throughout the 1980s, the Army increased in size from 180,000 to over 800,000 men, with over a million more Iraqis in the reserve. That included approximately 75 percent of all Iraqi men between the ages of 18 and 34. By the end of the 1980s, Iraq had the fourth largest army in the world and the largest in the Middle East.[5]

Saddam also personally took control over the regime's religious policies. In addition to rooting out Iranian influence within Iraq's Shi'i institutions, he also cracked down on domestic forms of Islamism. He purged the venerated Shi'i seminaries in southern Iraq, executing a senior Iraqi cleric, Muhammad Baqir al-Sadr, and his sister, Bint al-Huda. Al-Sadr was closely connected to the Shi'i Islamist party, Da'wa, which had deep roots in southern Iraq and was influenced by al-Sadr's highly political, but modernist interpretation of Islam. Saddam's regime made membership in it a capital offense.[6]

The war with Iran ground on for eight years, leading to over a million casualties. It was waged on land, in the air, and at sea. In several incidents that caused little reaction at the time but would haunt the international community in the years after the war, the Iraqi military used chemical weapons against the Iranians as well as against its own restive Kurdish population. Kurds, which constitute around 20 percent of Iraqis are not Arabs and never fit neatly within the ethic nationalism of the Ba'thist regime. Many Kurds also had ties to Iran. During the war, the Iraqi military leveled countless Kurdish villages as part of a genocidal campaign the regime called al-Anfal. In a separate operation, it also gassed the Kurdish city of Halabja, indiscriminately slaughtering thousands of civilians. The attacks were led by Saddam's cousin, Ali Hassan al-Majid, who gained the moniker Chemical Ali.

The Iran–Iraq War was the largest conventional conflict since World War II and the largest war ever between two Third World states. It ended with neither side making any real gains. However, the war allowed Saddam to mobilize Iraqi society and to crush dissidents. Thus, Iraq emerged from the conflict as an almost complete autocracy.

The Iraqi Ba'th Party and the World

While Saddam consolidated his rule at home, he could not afford to ignore foreign affairs. Two of the main threats to the Iraqi regime in the 1980s had originated from Syria and Iran. Beyond Iraq's immediate neighbors, waves of Iraqis and other Arabs migrated to Western states. Large diaspora communities, including dissidents and political opposition parties, were organizing in foreign capitals. A repressive state like Saddam's Iraq, which strove to control all access to information, ignored such populations at its own peril.

The Ba'th Party was well-equipped to deal with foreign affairs. With Regional Commands in several Arab states, the party was by its nature transnational. Some of these Regional Commands, like those in Jordan, Yemen, and Sudan, were highly active. The party's National Command was designed to coordinate the activities of Ba'thists across these states so it generally handled international affairs. The National Command also contained a Bureau of Arabs outside the Homeland, which was responsible for the Arab diaspora around the world, including state officials on assignments overseas. From its headquarters in Baghdad, this Bureau created and attempted to control Arab student unions on college campuses in foreign countries, and to organize Arab diaspora communities. Ba'thists working for the Bureau overseas defended the Iraqi regime by silencing its dissidents and aiding its supporters. They also attempted to influence the politics and policies of the states in which they operated, and they courted and cooperated with local political parties and activists to increase support for Iraq.

The Bureau's status diminished significantly in 1982 when Saddam decided to separate Iraqi Ba'thsts from other non-Iraqi Ba'thists working abroad. This decision was imperceptible to those outside the mind-numbing expanse of Ba'thist bureaucracy, but it caused significant upheaval within the ridged and ideologically driven structure of the party. The regime maintained "embassy organizations," as the Iraqis called them, which in 1982 became responsible for all Iraqis outside Iraq. These embassy organizations reported to the Office of Organizations outside the Region in the Iraqi Regional Command rather than the Bureau of Arabs outside the Homeland in the Arab National Command. This shift in authority between two offices with clunky names buried deep in the party's bureaucracy had vast implications for Iraq's international strategies over the following decades.

The reason for separating the Iraqis from the rest of the Arabs remains unclear, but it was most likely related to Saddam's attempt to consolidate his power and to provide additional security measures for Iraq's international operations. The move put Iraqis rather than all Arabs at the center of Baghdad's international operations, and it allowed Saddam to manage them more directly. The regime conducted rigorous background investigations on Iraqis, which was impossible to do for non-Iraqis. Iraqis also had familial, financial, and professional ties to Iraq, which the regime could manipulate to ensure that they cooperated. If an Iraqi Ba'thist defected while working overseas, his family in Iraq might suffer the consequences. The same could not be said for non-Iraqis.

Another reason that Saddam may have decided to create a separate organization for Iraqis was the ballooning Iraqi diaspora. Like other Arabs, waves of Iraqis emigrated in the mid-twentieth century. The hardships associated with repression and war drove even more Iraqis from their country after Saddam's rise to power. The total number of Iraqis living abroad doubled in the 1980s from 500,000 to 1,000,000.[7] Even in the United States, which took considerable money and effort to reach, the population of Iraqis jumped by

40 percent to just under 45,000 during this period.[8] These Iraqis formed a critical mass that was large enough to operate independently from other Arabs for the first time. By the end of the decade, the bureau responsible for them was renamed from the "Office of Organizations outside the Region" to the "Bureau of Iraqis Outside the Region," reflecting the fact that an Iraqi diaspora community was coming into existence.[9]

Whatever the reason for the separation of Iraqis from other Arabs in the Ba'th Party's international operations, the move upset non-Iraqi Ba'thists. After all, as a pan-Arab ideology, Ba'thism was not supposed to distinguish between Iraqis and other Arabs. Yet, the non-Iraqi Arabs lost much of their access to the resources and power that flowed from party offices in Iraqi embassies. They complained that Iraqi embassies were taking "dangerous actions" by sidelining the party in a way that did "not reflect the original spirit of Ba'thism."[10] Of course, the embassies were not freezing out the party as a whole; they just shifted focus away from sections of it that did not fall under the Iraqi Regional Command, which Saddam controlled directly as the Secretary General. When the Iraqi Foreign Ministry asked several key ambassadors about the allegations from non-Iraqi Arabs, the ambassadors answered that they had excellent relations with the Ba'th Party, and that the relationship had even improved recently. The ambassadors' response was almost certainly true, but it reflected their relationship with Iraqi Ba'thists rather than non-Iraqi Arabs who fell under Aflaq's National Command.[11]

The non-Iraqi Arabs remained an important part of the Iraqi regime's strategies for engaging Arab diasporas. Baghdad even argued that there were some benefits to sidelining non-Iraqis. By revoking their diplomatic passports and cutting their ties with Iraqi embassies, the regime argued that it was actually "providing cover for their party activities." Thus, they could more easily carry out clandestine work that hid the hand of Baghdad in their operations. And indeed, while they lost much of their support, non-Iraqi Arabs continued to work on behalf of the Iraqi regime until 2003.[12]

The Ba'th Party in Iraqi Foreign Policy

After shifting the focus of the Ba'th Party's international operations to its Iraqi core, the regime in Baghdad began to employ the party more aggressively. In some ways the party's importance to Iraqi foreign policy rivaled or even surpassed the Foreign Ministry. It should not be forgotten that the source of Saddam's power in Iraq was the party. Unlike most Arab dictators, he did not rise through the ranks of the military or an intelligence service. He rose through the party, and it was to the party that he owed his position. Iraq's political history further solidified this relationship. The Ba'thist coup in 1963 was derailed by military officers. When the Ba'thists launched the 1968 coup, they made sure that the party rather than state institutions controlled the new regime. As such, Ba'thists treated state institutions such as the military and the Foreign Ministry with suspicion. Throughout the 1970s and 1980s, it subjected them to a process of what the regime called "Ba'thification" (*taba'ith*).[13]

Of course, senior Iraqi diplomats and ambassadors serving in important countries were often quite influential. As later chapters detail, their reports and activities were sometimes critical components of Iraqi foreign policy. If the records of the Iraqi Foreign Ministry had not been destroyed, they certainly would have provided even more details on the key functions they performed. However, there are also reasons to suspect that the Foreign Ministry was not as central to Iraqi foreign policy as one might assume.

Rather than filling the Foreign Ministry with loyalists, the regime regularly used it to exile untrusted senior officials by appointing them as ambassadors in some far-off capital. For example, the Ba'thists needed the assistance of a few key military officers for the 1968 coup. Abd al-Razzaq Said al-Naif was the deputy head of military intelligence prior to the coup and, in exchange for his cooperation, he demanded the post of Prime Minister in the new regime. The Ba'thists agreed, but soon after he assumed his new position, Saddam burst into his office, pointed a pistol at him, and escorted him to the airport. Al-Naif was put on a flight to Morocco, where he was appointed the Iraqi ambassador in Rabat.[14]

Similarly, Salah Omar al-Ali, Hardan al-Tikriti, and Salih Mahdi Ammash were all leaders in the 1968 coup that brought the Ba'th Party to power in Iraq. Each had a falling out with al-Bakr and Saddam in the years following the coup, and each was appointed ambassador in a foreign capital to get them out of Baghdad.[15] Saddam eventually had al-Tikriti assassinated. This pattern continued in later decades. When Saddam's half-brother Barzan al-Tikriti ran afoul of Saddam in the 1980s, he was appointed Iraqi Ambassador to the United Nations in Geneva. Saddam sent his son Uday to work with Barzan when he began causing problems for the regime in the 1990s.[16] During the Gulf Crisis, Iraq's Ambassador to the United States, Muhammad al-Mashat, claimed that he had fallen out of favor with the regime during the Iran-Iraq

War because he "was born a Shi'i." That fact did not stop him from being appointed to his post in Washington.[17] Throughout the Gulf Crisis, he received no guidance from Baghdad, and was forced to glean Iraqi policy by reading newspapers.[18] Clearly, the regime did not always see its diplomatic corps as a pillar of its international strategies.

An insightful example of the regime's early outlook toward the Foreign Ministry came from the case of Abd al-Malik Ahmad al-Yasin. During the 1968 coup, he was a midranking Ba'thist working in the Ministry of Education. He was from Tikrit, so he had close ties to Saddam and al-Bakr. However, after a quarrel with representatives of the Ba'th Party, he fled Iraq for Cairo. He used his connections with al-Bakr to return to Iraq and the Ministry of Education in 1969, but his dispute with the party made him too much of a risk to stay in that position. He was reassigned to the Foreign Ministry for a new job as a director general, which was a higher rank than his previous position. A year later, in 1970, he was appointed Iraqi Ambassador to Afghanistan. The regime deemed al-Yasin not trustworthy enough to work in education, so it moved him to the Foreign Ministry, at a higher level, and then appointed him as an ambassador![19]

Saddam's populism emphasized the politics of the masses rather than high-level diplomacy and the expansion of the Iraqi Ba'th Party abroad helped to fill the void left by his neglect of traditional diplomats. By the end of the 1980s, the Iraqi Ba'th Party had established branches in sixty-nine countries, and they played a leading role in Iraq's international strategies. Though, as will be discussed later, in the 1980s these overseas branches probably had little impact in achieving their primary mission of building support for Iraq during its war with Iran.

As the Ba'th Party expanded its operations around the world, it developed organizational structures that paralleled the party in Iraq. Under the Iraqi Regional Command, the party hierarchy in Iraq broke down into a bureau (*tanzim*), branch (*far'*), section (*shu'ba*), division (*firqa*), and finally, a cell (*khaliyya*). Most provinces and major cities in Iraq had their own branch command, which acted as a pillar for the entire system. The branch commands controlled most of the party's operations, and they kept records on people and activities within their areas of responsibility in Iraq. In the late 1980s, the party established a branch command for the Iraqi Ba'th Party outside of Iraq, as well as branch commands in each country in which it operated. Mirroring the party structure in Iraq, the branches overseas broke down into sections and divisions. In some cases, a section or division could be responsible for party operations in a major foreign city. It would report up to the branch command in the capital, which would report to Baghdad. Iraqi Ba'thists could join the party abroad, or if they were already Ba'thists, they could continue their party activities and rise through the party ranks.[20]

The Iraqi regime saw the party's political operations as distinct from diplomacy or intelligence. The party carried out what the Iraqis termed *al-taharruk* (literally: moving someone), and which Western analysts would call "influence operations." With the existing documents, it is nearly impossible to disentangle the relationship between Iraqi diplomats, intelligence officers, and party officials working abroad. Nevertheless, the regime's records make clear that Ba'thists working on behalf of the party overseas received their own appointments and reported back to Baghdad through party rather than diplomatic or intelligence channels. All Iraqis were required to treat the head of the party's branch command in a country "as if he is an officer in the Iraqi Intelligence Service," which made him beyond reproach.[21] The embassy staff, often including the ambassador himself, was forbidden from interfering with his work or even entering his office.[22] Yet, as later chapters will discuss, the regime sometimes deferred to the ambassador or the Foreign Ministry instead of the party organization in a country. Moreover, the head of the Ba'th Party was sometimes also a senior intelligence officer, diplomat, or even the ambassador. While it was clear in such cases that the official had two distinct roles and reported back to Baghdad through two distinct chains of command, the lines were clearly blurred.

Like other authoritarian leaders in the twentieth century, Saddam obsessed over gaining the loyalty of the youth and controlling women, and this phenomenon spilled over into Ba'thist operations abroad.[23] Aflaq's original articulation of Ba'thism mirrored other nationalist ideologies in the mid-twentieth century in its idealization of youth.[24] Moreover, college and secondary school students had helped found the Iraqi branch of the Ba'th Party in 1949 and 1950.[25] Once the Ba'thists came to power in 1968, they focused much of their attention on winning support from students and youth. They targeted schools and universities, rewriting textbooks as well as children's books. By 1976, Saddam stated that only Ba'thists were to be admitted to the teachers' college, and the regime attempted to mobilize university teachers by instituting "cultural guidance periods."[26] With this emphasis on youth and education, college enrolments skyrocketed from less than 9,000 in 1958 to more than 75,000 in 1975. Secondary school enrolment went from less than 74,000 to just under 500,000 in the same period.[27]

The National Union of Students and Youth of Iraq, which the Ba'th Party used to control students and youth in Iraq, also opened over a dozen branches outside Iraq.[28] As in Iraq, these student unions presented themselves as independent, but they were tightly controlled by the Ba'th Party. As the regime's records show, branches of the Iraqi Ba'th Party operating in each country "supervised" these unions and ensured their leaders were committed Ba'thists.[29] Like other elements of the party abroad these student unions reported on potential dissidents and organized political support for the Iraqi regime.[30]

Similarly, the Iraqi Ba'th Party extended the operations of the General Federation of Iraqi Women internationally, opening over a dozen branches abroad. As with the Iraqi student union, the Iraqis presented the General Federation of Iraqi Women as an independent association. It too was, in fact, tightly controlled by the party. The regime's approach to women was often contradictory.[31] Women in Iraq saw their status rise significantly during the Ba'thist period, especially in the early years. They attended universities at rates equal to and sometimes exceeding those of men; they were able to participate in economic and social sectors that had been closed to them previously;[32] and some women even took leadership positions in the Ba'th Party. Despite these real gains for Iraqi women, scholars of Iraq have pointed out that the regime often remained paternalistic in its approach to women and their role in society.[33]

This dichotomy extended to Iraqi women living outside of Iraq. Iraqi women could become senior leaders in Ba'th Party branches operating overseas.[34] In fact, as later chapters will show, one of the most influential Ba'thists in the regime's overseas operations was a woman named Huda Salih Mahdi Ammash. However, she was the only woman to rise to that level within the regime, and in many cases, the head of the General Federation of Iraqi Women's branches in foreign countries was simply the wife of the ambassador or another high-ranking man.[35] At times, women's roles were made explicit. For example, the branch of the federation in Syria was specifically designed for "the wives of the comrades and their daughters," and it "aimed at strengthening the bond of social relationships between the families of the comrades" rather than the political work that men carried out.[36]

The proliferation of party activities outside Iraq in the 1980s created a cadre of Iraqi Ba'thists who developed an expertise in international operations. Ba'thists were issued diplomatic passports. They cycled through positions outside Iraq and staff positions that dealt with foreign affairs in the party's secretariat back in Baghdad. In 1987, the regime established a special committee that was chaired by Saddam's cousin, Ali Hassan al-Majid, to vet and nominate Ba'thists for these sensitive positions.[37] Saddam was particularly concerned that foreign intelligence services, which he termed "preying apparatuses," would exploit Iraqi Ba'thists serving overseas to the detriment of the party and Iraqi national security.[38]

To mitigate these concerns, Baghdad kept its overseas party operatives on a short leash. All their activities were tightly controlled by the Bureau of Iraqis outside the Region within the Regional Command. Their primary mission of influencing foreign states required them to work with and through local political parties and organizations. However, they were not permitted to "establish any ties with any party or movement or political personality except under central guidance" from Baghdad. Party officials working abroad were instructed "to avoid individual interpretation (*ijtihad*)" in following directives and to request clarifications on any matter for which they had not received explicit instructions. The Ba'thist organizations operating abroad sent a steady stream of reports and request to Baghdad.

Despite its public commitments to party ideology, the regime remained quite pragmatic and agile in its overseas operations. Not all the parties with which the Ba'thists established contact were necessarily friendly or ideologically compatible with the regime in Iraq. For example, during the Iran-Iraq War, the regime worked with various hardline Sunni Islamists and Salafis who cooperated with Baghdad simply because they hated the Shi'i regime in Tehran. As long as a party or organization was willing to take a position that was beneficial to Iraq, the Ba'thists worked with it. In fact, Ba'thists working outside Iraq were ordered "not to dwell on intellectual discussions and conversations with regard to our party" because it might impede cooperation with such parties.[39]

Limitations on Iraqi Influence Operations in the 1980s

While, as the next section in this chapter will discuss, the Iraqis enjoyed some successes courting Islamic and Islamist actors in the 1980s, its broader influence campaigns enjoyed few operational or strategic successes during this period. Baghdad's alliances during the Iran–Iraq War were driven by fear of Iran's revolutionary Islamism. The new regime in Tehran thought it could spread its revolution across the Persian Gulf to Saudi Arabia and the other deeply conservative, pro-Western Gulf Arab monarchies. The pro-Western regime in Egypt, which had its own violent Islamist opposition was not pleased with the Iranian revolution either. None of these countries enjoyed friendly relations with Iraq prior to 1979, but the Iranian revolution brought them together to face the new threat. The same considerations increasingly led Washington and Baghdad to put their differences aside. The Americans wanted both sides to lose the war, but when the Iraqis appeared ready to buckle, Washington tilted toward Baghdad to prevent an Iranian victory. Baghdad and Washington reestablished diplomatic relations in 1984 and the United States provided increasing support to Baghdad throughout the remainder of the war.

While these geopolitical alignments aided Baghdad in its war against Iran, they undermined the Ba'th Party's attempts to court ideologicaly aligned partners. The Ba'thists presented themselves as revolutionary Arab nationalists, who opposed Western imperialism, Zionism, and reactionary forms of government like monarchy. Yet, throughout the 1980s, Baghdad found itself politically aligned with conservative Arab monarchies, an Egyptian regime that had just made peace with Israel, and the United States, which in their minds was the supreme symbol of neo-imperialism. Moreover, Iraq was fighting a truly revolutionary regime in Iran, which had impeccable anti-Western and anti-Zionists credentials.

Measuring the impact of influence operations is never easy. Often, they are most effective when they amplify existing political forces or convince people to take actions for which they are already inclined. During the Iran–Iraq War, Baghdad's alliances made its attempt to cooperate with likeminded revolutionaries almost impossible. The self-described radical groups that Ba'thists targeted looked skeptically at supporting a project so clearly aligned with American, Egyptian, and Saudi interests. On the strategic level, one has difficulty pointing to any important international actors who may have been influenced by the Ba'th Party's operations during this period. Of course, Iraq's geopolitical alignments transformed in the wake of the Gulf Crisis and, as later chapters will detail, the institutions and organizations that the Iraqi regime created in the 1980s provided a foundation on which Baghdad carried out much more effective overseas operations in the 1990s.

The failure of Ba'thist attempts to find likeminded partners in the 1980s did not mean that the party's other actions abroad were futile. The party branches abroad sent Baghdad a steady stream of reports on dissidents and on the Iraqi opposition in exile. The party secretariat sent these reports to the

Iraqi Intelligence Service, whose officers were ruthless and did not hesitate to carry out brazen acts of violence anywhere in the world. They were known to kidnap and kill Iraqis who spoke out against the regime overseas. In one case, an Iraqi living in Spain was called to the Iraqi embassy in Madrid and offered a cup of tea. After his first sip, the next thing he remembered was waking up in a prison back in Iraq.[40] Iraqi intelligence officers regularly assassinated dissidents. In 1988, they went on a global killing spree. Probably the most high-profile incidents occurred in London. In one widely reported case, two Iraqi agents slipped an odorless, tasteless, and colorless poison called thallium into the vodka of an Iraqi businessman named Abdullah Rahim Sharif Ali while meeting him for drinks at a popular restaurant. Another Iraqi, who had been a high-ranking Ba'thist, but had fallen out with the regime, was gunned down in the London streets.[41] As Amnesty International reported, these events were part of a larger wave in which Iraqi intelligence officers used thallium to kill forty dissidents in four months all around the world.[42]

Such operations were important for the Iraqi regime in the 1980s. As Baghdad became more and more dependent on Western support during its war with Iran, nettlesome dissidents who highlighted the brutal nature of the Ba'thist regime could hinder Western support. Assassinating some of the most prominent dissidents stoked fear in the majority, causing a veil of silence to fall over large parts of the Iraqi diaspora. It was no coincidence that Kanan Makiya, who later emerged as one of the most high-profile Iraqi dissidents, published his 1989 book *Republic of Fear* under the pseudonym Samir al-Khalil.[43] A campaign of terror prevented disaffected Iraqis from playing a spoiler role in the 1980s. However, perhaps more importantly, such operations established procedures and tactics that the Ba'thists would use as Iraq moved into the center of global politics in the 1990s. As such, they were a precursor to much more elaborate operations that would not only affect emigree Iraqis, but also international politics and possibly even world order.

Harnessing International Islam

The Ba'th Party was a product of the pan-Arab nationalism that dominated Middle Eastern politics in the mid-twentieth century. However, by the time Saddam rose to power in 1979, a different ideology, Islamism, was clearly making gains across the region. Although Saddam was deeply hostile to

Islamism and did not permit Islamist parties in Iraq, he attempted to harness the growing power of political Islam internationally.

Ba'thism possessed a positive outlook toward Islam and Saddam hoped to use Ba'thist reverence toward the religion to "neutralize" Islamist attacks on the Iraqi regime. Although the Ba'th Party's founder, Michel Aflaq was Christian, he imbedded a deep appreciation for Islam into his ideology. In the early years of the party, he made clear the party's veneration of Islam in essays such as "In Memory of the Arab Prophet" (*Dhikra al-Rasul al-'Arabi*) from 1943; "Our View of Religion" (*Nazratuna lil-Din*) from 1956; and "The Issue of Religion in the Arab Ba'th" (*Qadiyyat al-Din fi al-Ba'th al-'Arabi*) also from 1956.[44] The Ba'thists were not traditionalists. Aflaq insisted that Islam needed to be revived "spiritually, not in its form or letter."[45] Yet, Aflaq had always emphasized that "we believe in God."[46] He referred to Muhammad's preaching as "a heavenly message," and he described atheism as "evil."[47] For Aflaq and the Ba'thists, Islam was an Arab religion revealed to an Arab prophet for the Arab people. They considered its expansion in the 7th and 8th centuries to be an early example of an Arab revolution. Thus, despite Aflaq being born Christian, he claimed that Islam was the more appropriate religion for Arabs, and after his death in 1989, the Iraqi regime produced— questionable—evidence that he had secretly converted in 1980.[48]

The Ba'thists were clearly not Islamists. They did not want to root their state in Islamic law and they championed ethno-national rather than religious unity. When they came to power in Iraq and Syria, they crushed or exiled Islamist parties in both countries. Nevertheless, Saddam parroted Aflaq's reverence for Islam and rejection of atheism. In a highly publicized 1977 speech titled, "A View on Religion and Heritage," Saddam declared, "our Party . . . is always on the side of faith."[49] And in 1982, he included a long section on the party's devotion to Islam in the Central Report for the Nineth Regional Conference of the Iraqi Ba'th Party, which was the definitive statement on the party's ideology.[50]

Yet, the Iraqi regime had difficulty capitalizing on these ideas. Its reputation as a revolutionary regime hostile to both traditional and modern political Islam meant it had little experience working with any type of Islamic organizations. Unlike groups such as students or workers, the Ba'th Party did not have bureaus or offices devoted to Islamic outreach. Whether the Ba'thist were prepared or not, the Iranian revolution in 1979 and then the beginning of the Iran-Iraq War in 1980 left the regime in Baghdad vulnerable to Islamist critiques and made outreach to Islamic networks a critical national security requirement.

Fortunately for Baghdad, the same events that exposed Iraq to Islamic challenges also aligned it with other states that were willing and able to help it. The conservative regime in Saudi Araba had spent decades building networks of Islamic and Islamist actors across the Muslim World. While Riyadh and Baghdad were often bitter rivals in the 1960s and 1970s, the Iranian threat had brought them closer together. The Saudi monarchy was founded on an austere, sectarian, Sunni, interpretation of Islam known as Wahabism or Salafism. Yet, its oil-rich, eastern provinces were home to an oppressed Shi'i minority. The last thing Riyadh wanted to see was Iraq's majority Shi'i population overthrow the Ba'thist regime in an Iranian-style revolution. The Saudis would become the obvious next target.

The Saudis dispatched a former Syrian Prime Minister named Ma'ruf al-Dawalibi to aid Iraq in 1983. Al-Dawalibi was Saudi Arabia's top envoy for Islamic diplomacy. Born in Syria in 1909, he was drawn to Islamism and joined the Muslim Brotherhood.[51] His Islamist politics put him on the wrong side of the 1963 Ba'thist coup. Ironically, considering that the Saudis sent him to aid Iraq in 1983, his clashes with Aflaq in 1963 led to his arrest and then permanent exile in 1965.[52] Al-Dawalibi took refuge in Riyadh, where he and King Faisal Al Saud shared an aversion to Arab nationalist regimes, and the Saudis deployed him throughout the Muslim world to organize Islamic support for Saudi policy.[53] In a classic case of realpolitik, the Iraqis and Aflaq put aside their history and ideological animosity toward the Saudis and al-Dawalibi in the interests of security.

Al-Dawalibi brought a wide range of Islamic and Islamist actors to Baghdad from around the Muslim world for gatherings the Iraqi's called the "Popular Islamic Conferences." The first conference in 1983 hosted 280 participants from 50 countries. In 1985, al-Dawalibi organized a second conference with over 300 participants. An impressive list of religious officials, Islamic scholars, and activists attended, including former Ministers of Religious Affairs and Endowments from Morocco, Egypt, and Syria, as well as high-profile Salafis from Saudi Arabia and Deobandis from Pakistan. Other participants came from Africa, Southeast Asia, and even North America.[54] The conferences made Islamic legal arguments against the policies of the Iranian regime. Then they distributed their findings throughout the Muslim world. The Iraqis even translated the conference findings into Persian and used the Iraqi Ba'th Party's international branches to clandestinely spread them in Iran and among Iranians in the Gulf Arab states.[55]

In the latter half of the 1980s, the regime expanded these efforts, in its words, to "neutralize" Sunni Arab Islamists who had supported Iran, such as the Egyptian Muslim Brotherhood. The Iraqis continued to suppress any sign of Islamism at home, but they cooperated with non-Iraqi Islamists on issues of shared interests. Saddam despised Islamism but he thought Ba'thist views on Islam might be enough to "interact with them in a way that won't enable them to say to our faces that we are apostates."[56]

In 1987, the regime further expanded these efforts by creating the "Popular Islamic Conference Organization" with a permanent headquarters in Baghdad.[57] The Popular Islamic Conference Organization and its Gulf Arab backers then helped the Iraqis to create other Islamic institutions such as the Saddam University for Islamic Studies, through which Saddam could better control Iraqi Islam and reach out to potential supporters abroad. For example, the Iraqi regime required half the student body at the Saddam University for Islamic Studies to be non-Iraqis.[58] The regime provided scholarships for foreign "Islamic associations, organizations, and people, who are influential" with the purpose of "creating good supporters among Muslims who are sympathetic with our country."[59] A representative from the Ba'th Party secretariat suggested the university accept students who have not yet gone to a university so that the regime could better "build the loyalty of the students to Iraq and the Arab nation (*umma*)." He added that the Iraqis should target students in Africa and Southeast Asia because he believed that the Iranian regime also focused on them. Moreover, the Muslims in these regions were very "simple" and therefore "it is easy to influence them."[60] The regime used these foreign students to establish contacts and good relations with international Islamic and Islamist organizations around the world.

As later chapters will discuss, the Islamic networks that Iraq developed in the 1980s became a vital instrument for its foreign policy during the 1990s. The Popular Islamic Conference Organization spread throughout the Muslim world, opening local chapters, and providing a diplomatic channel between Baghdad and foreign capitals when official relations strained. Baghdad even issued diplomatic passports to Iraqi religious scholars associated with the Popular Islamic Conference Organization. The Iraqis used these networks to pressure other Middle Eastern states by fomenting unrest in their mosques and inciting protesters on their streets. Throughout the 1990s, such actions made it increasingly difficult for Arab and Muslim leaders to side with the United States against Iraq, even when they claimed in private that they wanted to.

Conclusion

The first decade of Saddam's rule in Iraq was bloody and tumultuous. He had inherited the ideology and institutions of the Ba'th Party, but he restructured them to meet the challenges created by mass migration and the rise of political Islam. Branches of the Iraqi regime spread throughout Arab and Muslim communities around the world to influence local and international politics. At home, Saddam created a highly personalized regime that became synonymous with violence and repression. He fought a grinding war with Iran, crushed his regime's opposition, and attempted to control all access to information in Iraq.

Had Saddam not invaded Kuwait in 1990, his rule would have remained infamous for its brutality, but it probably would have had little effect on broader trends in global and international history. When the Gulf Crisis put Iraq at the center of world politics, the events discussed in this chapter suddenly assumed a broader significance. The transnational institutions that the Iraqis built in the 1980s played a central role in Saddam's strategies during the Gulf Crisis and more importantly, after it. Western powers, and the United States in particular, had little understanding of these institutions or their capabilities. Hence, Western capitals struggled to respond.

2

The Gulf Crisis and the New World Order

In a seminal 1975 essay, Daniel Patrick Moynihan—the Harvard professor turned US Ambassador to the United Nations and then Senator from New York—famously described "The United States in Opposition" on the global stage.[1] The world seemed to be coalescing against the United States. Yet, far from heralding the end of American power, the mid-1970s marked a turning point in which Washington began to win over much of the world. Although it was difficult to perceive at the time, American-style neoliberalism slowly began to take hold and global opinion began to move toward the United States.

Similarly, during the Gulf Crisis in 1990–1991, Iraq also found itself at a low point—abandoned by its erstwhile patrons in Moscow and largely alone in the world of states. However, it was not the only international actor that was troubled by American dominance of a post-Cold War order. And just as the mid-1970s masked an underswell of pro-American sentiments, the Gulf Crisis brought Saddam to the fore of a nascent, largely bottom-up global resistance against what Bush called the "new world order."

Throughout the previous century, internationalists had developed new tools such as international sanctions and weapons inspections to manage global security. The end of the Cold War created a cooperative environment at the UN Security Council for the first time and thus made testing these new tools possible. American leaders hoped that they would not only help to end Iraqi aggression, but also to solidify Washington's position at the top of a new post–Cold War order. While this new world order proved popular among diplomats at the United Nations, Iraq's new position in global politics corresponded almost perfectly with Ba'thist narratives about resistance to imperialism and Western hegemony. As a result, Iraq's international operations began to gain new allies and its propaganda began to reach new audiences. Iraqi gains among the global opposition to American hegemony could not stop the American-led onslaught in the Gulf War. However, the crisis helped Iraq to create alliances and working relationships that it would

Iraq against the World. Samuel Helfont, Oxford University Press. © Oxford University Press 2023.
DOI: 10.1093/oso/9780197530153.003.0003

use to challenge the post–Cold War international system in the years following the Gulf Crisis.

A New World Order?

Myriad justifications coalesced to prompt Iraqi forces to invade its oil-rich neighbor, Kuwait, on August 2, 1990. Iraqi leaders throughout the twentieth century considered Kuwait an Iraqi province that British imperialists had illegitimately separated from the rest of the country.[2] Likewise, Saddam insisted that "Kuwait is Iraq" and that it had been "stolen."[3] He blamed imperialist skullduggery for not only depriving Iraq of significant oil reserves, but also of Kuwait's deep-water ports and unfettered access to the sea.

Many Iraqis considered the Kuwaitis smug and uppity. For these Iraqis, their southern neighbors had no cultural or political history, they had made no contributions to civilization, and they did not deserve their riches. As Saddam stated in a closed-door meeting with his advisors: "Who do they think they are? They think they are better than any other Arab country and they look down on everybody else."[4] A telling sign of Saddam's view of Kuwaitis can be seen in one of his plans for pacifying them in the days after the Iraqi invasion. "I know the Kuwaiti society and I know what type of corruption and luxury this society lives in," he stated. "We need to have a party to provide their youth heroin; we should order a party to supply them with drugs."[5] For Saddam, like many Iraqis, the Kuwaitis had no desires beyond the base pleasures of a *nouveau riche*. Such people had no right to rule themselves.

Saddam believed he had waged the long and bitter war with Iran in the 1980s on behalf of all Arabs, including the Kuwaitis. Indeed, Gulf Arab states such as Kuwait had felt threatened by the Iranian revolution and they funded Iraq's war efforts. Saddam insisted that these rich Gulf states had agreed to bankroll the war, but after the threat had passed, they "changed their minds" and demanded repayment.[6] Despite Iraqi protests, Kuwait refused to forgive the loans following the war and Iraq struggled to repay them as it attempted to rebuild. To make matters worse, Saddam accused Kuwait of slant drilling into Iraqi oil wells, and flooding the market with oil, which kept prices low and cut into Iraqi profits.[7]

The Ba'th Party that ruled Iraq was founded on the idea of unifying the Arab nation. In Ba'thist imaginations, a conservative monarchy like Kuwait was just the type of reactionary state that radical pan-Arabism was sup-posed to devour. In the confrontation that followed Iraq's invasion of Kuwait, Saddam believed revolutionary "flags will be hoisted from the Arab Maghreb [Western Arab countries] to the Arab Mashreq [Eastern Arab countries]." His background as a Ba'thist had conditioned him to see mass politics as the key to uniting the Arab World around Iraqi leadership, and as he told his advisers on August 7, he felt the Arab masses would "watch us and see whether we are strong or weak."[8]

Finally, as some recent, innovative scholarship has pointed out, all of these events occurred within an evolving system of international politics that coincided with the end of the Cold War. Saddam felt threatened by some of the international and regional trends, especially a weakened Soviet Union, and he hoped to exploit the instability of global politics for Iraq's benefit.[9]

Some Western analysts have suggested the United States unwittingly greenlighted Iraqi actions when just prior to the invasion, US Ambassador April Glaspie told Saddam that the United States had "no opinion on your Arab-Arab conflicts, such as your dispute with Kuwait."[10] The argument that Glaspei unintentionally encouraged Iraqi aggression corresponded well with social scientific theories about deterrence, but there is little evidence to support the claim that her meeting had any effect on Iraqi actions. As then Iraqi Foreign Minister Tariq Aziz later noted, "Ambassador Glaspie met Saddam and didn't say anything unusual. She didn't say anything that can be interpreted as encouraging the invasion, to be fair."[11] Senior US officials, including President Bush and National Security advisor Brent Scowcroft as well as independent diplomatic historians have noted that Glaspie's lan-guage in the meeting was mundane and standard. It did not provide Saddam with a signal and as Aziz noted, the Iraqis did not feel they received one.[12] Even if Glaspie had threated American retaliation for an Iraqi invasion, it probably would not have changed Iraqi calculations. Saddam already ex-pected a confrontation with the United States, but he felt he could weather the consequences. "I mean, what will they do?" he asked rhetorically, be-fore providing the answer, "All they can do is bring their airplanes and start bombing: boom, boom, boom, boom, boom, boom. So what? Nothing will happen, we will give them hell. Give me one instance when an airplane has settled any situation."[13] Moreover, Saddam believed the United States could not stomach casualties. Once Americans began to die, he presumed, polit-ical pressure and the need to return Kuwaiti oil to the market would force the Americans to find an arrangement with Iraq.[14] For this combination of reasons, Saddam felt the invasion of Kuwait was a just and viable policy.

In addition to sending the Iraqi military into Kuwait, Saddam also exported his repressive politics. To rule the new province, Saddam appointed his cousin, Ali Hassan al-Majid, who had gained the nickname, Chemical Ali, for gassing Iraqi Kurds in the 1980s. Prior to the invasion, al-Majid made clear he intended to apply the same levels of violence to Kuwait's 700,000 citizens, and 1.5 million foreign residents. As he told Saddam, "I do not want it to be like . . . any other of our provinces. We are interested in its position and what is under its ground. We do not want its people."[15] Saddam issued direct orders to kill anyone who resisted Iraqi rule and to exile their families. If Kuwaitis refused to allow Iraqis to enter their homes, Iraqi security forces were to arrest the entire family and burn the home down in front of them. Some prisoners were also executed in front of their homes to serve as a warning to others. Likewise, when religious leaders preached against Iraq in a mosque, soldiers were ordered to hang them in front of the congregation.[16]

Iraqi actions ran against the grain of global politics. The Cold War was coming to an end. A year prior, in 1989, the political scientist Francis Fukuyama famously declared the "End of History" on the pages of *The National Interest*. Fukuyama channeled the German philosopher G. W. F. Hegel, who argued that history evolved as a dialectic to correct for contradictions in political systems.[17] For Fukuyama, the victory of liberal democracy in the Cold War resolved the last of these contradictions and put an end to this dialectic evolution. Thus, the philosophical concept of History (with a capital H) had ended.[18]

Fukuyama struck a chord with his readership because his arguments articulated a broader sentiment that was already widely held in the late 1980s and early 1990s. John Mueller's influential 1989 book, *Retreat from Doomsday*, documented a centuries-long intellectual process that had transformed war. According to Mueller, war was initially a celebrated activity that people— especially nobles—conducted for adventure, excitement, and enjoyment. In the age of enlightenment, it was relegated to a necessary evil. Then, increasingly in the twentieth century, war became altogether illegitimate.[19] Similarly, the noted military historian, John Keegan discussed a repugnance for war that had slowly emerged over the previous 2000 years as Western society began to value "the sanctity of human life, respect for rights of the individual, tolerance of minority opinion, acceptance of the free vote, accountability of the executive to representative institutions and everything else that is meant by the rule of law, democracy and the Judeo-Christian ethic."[20] In early 1991, the doyen of Cold War studies, John Gaddis, penned an essay titled, "Toward the Post–Cold War World," in which he argued that the Cold War was being replaced by a "contest between forces of integration and fragmentation."[21] The forces of integration, he argued, included the "combination of easy communications, unprecedented prosperity and freedom from war" along with the fact that "ideas now flow more freely" and "ultimately worked to undermine the legitimacy of authoritarianism itself."[22] These ideas were part of a broader wave of humanitarianism that crept into Cold War diplomacy when it was included in the 1975 Helsinki agreement of the Conference on Security and Cooperation in Europe. Following the agreement Washington increasingly found the language of human rights to be an important tool in its competition with Moscow, and as recent scholarship has argued, it played an important role ending the Cold War.[23] Iraq's behavior challenged these ideas. Nothing about Saddam's regime indicated an end of history, the rise of humanitarianism, or the demise of authoritarianism and war.

Thus, countering Iraqi belligerence presented an opportunity for the Bush administration to ride the tide of global history and shape it in accordance with American interests. However, not everyone in the Bush administration saw this opportunity right away. The sentiment at the first US National Security Council meeting following Iraq's invasion of Kuwait was, "Hey, too bad about Kuwait, but it's just a gas station, and who cares whether the sign says Sinclair or Exxon? Anyway, what can we do? Doesn't Iraq have the Middle East's largest army and aren't we a long way from the scene?"[24] Secretary of Defense Dick Cheney thought the world needed Kuwaiti oil, but not Kuwait. In that sense, whether Iraq or Kuwait sold the oil on the open market did not really affect American interests. The Chairman of the Joint Chiefs of Staff, General Colin Powell, did not think the United States should "go to war over Kuwait." At one point he even asked, "Does anybody really care about Kuwait?" Administration officials attempted to separate Kuwait from other, more important regional security issues like protecting Washington's much larger, oil-rich ally, Saudi Arabia. As Director of the Office of Management and Budget, Richard Darman argued, "There is a distinction between what to do to defend Saudi Arabia and to liberate Kuwait." And then, "There is a chance to defend Saudi Arabia if we do all that's possible. On liberating Kuwait, I sense it's not viable."[25]

Bush and his National Security Advisor, Brent Scowcroft, were not satisfied with this discussion. They worried that it focused too much "on the price of oil" and on regional security. More importantly, it failed to grasp the opportunity that Iraq had presented them. As Scowcroft noted, such discussions treated Iraq's invasion as "the crisis *du jour*" rather than "the major crisis of our time." He was more concerned about "the ramifications [. . .] on the emerging post-Cold World order."[26] A week later, Bush decided that America would respond militarily. He made clear that the issue at stake, and the justification for American action, was global order. "What we're doing is going to chart the future of the world for the next hundred years," he proclaimed. "It's that big."[27]

Bush is often described as an international realist. He was cautious in international affairs, and he understood the dangers of ignoring the realities of power.[28] Yet, the idealism embedded in his response to the Gulf Crisis also aligned well with aspects of his broader worldview. Bush came of age as a Navy pilot in the Second World War. The war taught him the dangers of appeasing someone like Saddam, whom he portrayed as the embodiment of evil. And while it is easy to write off Bush's repeated comparisons of Saddam to Hitler as pure opportunism, there is no evidence that he was insincere. Typical of Bush's background among the privileged New England elite, he held a deep belief in the righteousness of America and American democracy. In fact, Bush proceeded Fukuyama in arguing that liberal democracy had superseded all other political systems when he made the claim in his January 1989 inaugural address. Indeed, as one prominent historian of Bush's diplomacy has argued, "Bush believed the stream of history flowed toward an inevitable democratic end."[29]

If Bush needed a reminder of the stakes in the Gulf Crisis, the end of the Cold War provided it. He had spent the months just prior to Iraq's invasion of Kuwait dealing with German unification—an issue which had been at the center of world order since the nineteenth century. The question of German unity, and with it the problems of appeasing dictators and unchecked aggression, were at the fore of his mind when Iraqi troops poured into Kuwait on August 2. German unification was just one part of ending the Cold War, and Bush's interactions with Moscow also clearly bled into his thoughts about Iraq. On September 9, 1990, Bush met Soviet President Mikhail Gorbachev in Finland. Bush told him, "I think there is an opportunity to have develop out of this tragedy [in the Gulf] a new world order."[30] After some discussion, Gorbachev agreed.[31]

Two days later, on September 11, Bush delivered a widely publicized address to Congress in which he fully embraced the utopian rhetoric of the end of history. He linked the conclusion of the Cold War, his recent meeting with Gorbachev, and the Gulf Crisis, explaining that the "crisis in the Persian Gulf, as grave as it is, also offers a rare opportunity to move toward an historic period of cooperation." He stated explicitly that a "new world order" was one of the objectives of the coming conflict, and that the crisis would birth "a new era—freer from the threat of terror, stronger in the pursuit of justice, and more secure in the quest for peace. An era in which the nations of the world, East and West, North and South, can prosper and live in harmony." This was no ordinary foreign policy venture. As Bush explained, "a hundred generations have searched for this elusive path to peace, while a thousand wars raged across the span of human endeavor." Yet, the coming conflict in the Persian Gulf would finally put within reach a "world in which nations recognize the shared responsibility for freedom and justice. A world where the strong respect the rights of the weak." Bush's new world order promised that even in international affairs, the "rule of law" could supplant "the rule of the jungle." In such a world, the might-makes-right calculations of previous eras would be replaced by a rules-based system that was imbedded in international institutions like the United Nations.[32]

For more cynical observers, Bush's discussion of a liberal world order seemed quaint or even intentionally misleading. As previously mentioned, Bush's foreign policy was typically depicted as realist rather than liberal, and as late as 1989, Bush oversaw the American invasion of Panama in the face of strong opposition at the United Nations.[33] Moreover, the classified, official objectives that Bush provided to the military for the Gulf Crisis in August 1990 and for the Gulf War in January 1991 did not mention a liberal international order or the post–Cold War.[34] Thus, skeptical analysts and even some senior Bush Administration officials felt that too much was made of the new world order concept. Instead, they have tended to see less idealistic considerations about power, oil, and regional security as the main drivers of the Gulf War and they have written off the new world order as little more than rhetoric.[35]

Whatever Bush's personal commitments to liberal internationalism, his idealistic language solidified his diplomatic efforts to build a coalition for war with Iraq. The Saudis quicky requested American assistance and the US military deployed to the Arabian Peninsula, right in the heart of the Islamic World. Bush, Scowcroft, and Secretary of State James Baker built a wide coalition of states. The thawing Cold War offered new opportunities and Moscow supported Washington's diplomatic efforts against its erstwhile client in Baghdad. Thus, in addition to NATO allies and pro-Western Middle Eastern states, some Warsaw Pact states such as Poland, Czechoslovakia, and Hungary, as well as traditionally anti-Western states like Syria joined the American-led coalition.

The United States pushed through a string of binding resolutions at the UN Security Council, some of which invoked Chapter VII of the UN Charter to apply sanctions on Iraq. This was a watershed moment in international history. Sanctions have long been an element of statecraft. However, the idea of enforcing international law and global order through sanctions had its origins in the nineteenth century, when peace activists searched for alternatives to war.[36] The concept was incorporated into notions of collective security that were codified following the devastation of the World Wars and the failure of the League of Nations. At the center of the post-World War II order was the United Nations, which established an international legal regime designed to replace aggressive war all together. Most importantly, the UN Charter included Chapter VII, which gave the United Nations the power to enforce its resolutions—and uphold international law—through sanctions and, if need be, military action.[37]

Yet, Cold War rivalries created a zero-sum game that prevented the United Nations from playing the role its founders had anticipated. The Security Council had only explicitly invoked Chapter VII of the charter twice during the Cold War. The first was the fluke case of Korea in 1950, when the Soviet representatives temporarily boycotted the Security Council, and the remaining members voted to authorize military force. The second was the case of Rhodesia in 1966. The government of Rhodesia had declared independence from the British to preserve the rule of a white minority over the black majority. The Security Council voted to reject Rhodesia's declaration of independence and, for the first time in history, imposed sanctions on it.[38] Everyone agreed that Rhodesia was a repugnant, racist regime, but it was too minor an issue to shape world order or to influence international ideas about war and peace.

In addition to the bi-polar deadlock at the Security Council during the Cold War, the expansion of UN membership in the 1950s and 1960s meant non-Western states began to dominate the UN's General Assembly and its other institutions. Many of these new member-states were openly critical of American policies. In light of the deadlock at the Security Council and animosity in the General Assembly, American attitudes toward internationalism and the United Nations declined precipitously in the 1960s and early 1970s.[39]

Yet, below the surface, global trends began to shift back in America's favor beginning in the 1970s. As a combination of neo-liberal economic policies and democratization swept through East Asia and Latin America in the 1970s and 1980s, more and more governments began to see the United States as a model for political freedom and economic success. Eventually, this wave spread to Eastern Europe, washing away communist regimes from Berlin to Moscow.[40]

Iraq's invasion of Kuwait presented the United States with an opportunity to further these liberal trends by empowering the Security Council to carry out its intended mission. As the historian Paul Kennedy has argued, the Gulf Crisis was "the perfect example of what the [UN] planners of 1944–45 contemplated" in enforcing international law.[41] Many international stakeholders were enamored by the possibility of a new world order based on such principles. The century-long push to rethink war and peace seemed finally to be bearing fruit. This broad support was necessary because, as Bush told world leaders in private conversations, "sanctions have failed in the past because countries did not stand together in enforcing them."[42] As such, Secretary of State Baker told world leaders that "Iraq's unprovoked invasion and continued occupation of Kuwait is a political test for how the post-Cold War order will work."[43] And he made clear "what is at stake: Shaping the post-cold war world and whether there will be basic civilized ground rules of behavior."[44]

Javier Pérez de Cuéllar, the UN Secretary General at the time, called the manner and the scale in which the Security Council employed Chapter VII in the Gulf Crisis "unprecedented" and a demonstration of the United Nations' potential. Other important international actors tended to agree. For the vote tightening sanctions on Iraq in September 1990, thirteen foreign ministers from the fifteen members of the Security Council personally represented their states. The meeting included the foreign ministers from all five permanent members, and thus marked only the third time in history that the foreign ministers from all five permanent members had attended.[45]

Such enthusiastic support for the American approach at the United Nations was at least partly driven by the millenarian hopes of the new world order. In private meetings, foreign leaders told Bush that they saw US actions at the United Nations as part of "a major trend in history" in which the transformation of Soviet-American relations allowed the world to stand up against aggression.[46]

Secretary General Pérez de Cuéllar argued that the employment of Chapter VII in the Gulf Crisis, showed "that the way of enforcement is qualitatively different from the way of war" in that "it strives to minimize undeserved suf-fering."[47] Many others looked beyond the Gulf Crisis and saw the new world order as "an unprecedented expansion of the UN's responsibility and powers in the humanitarian realm."[48] As such, very early on, the Gulf Crisis emerged as an attempt to shape the nature of warfare and world order based on a new style of international politics that was more liberal and more humane. This new world order cast the United States as the undisputed leader of the inter-national system, and it empowered the United Nations to uphold the order, taking much of the burden from Washington. Americans were riding high.

Iraq in Opposition

The success of American diplomacy during the Gulf Crisis put pressure on Iraq's international operations. Several states closed Iraqi embassies and consulates.[49] Even when the embassies continued to function, Iraqis with ties to the regime came under suspicion and were sometimes deported. For example, Iraqi Ba'thists reported that Pakistani intelligence officers tapped their phones and bugged their homes. A car from the Pakistani intelligence service was almost permanently parked outside the Iraqi embassy.[50] At one point, the Pakistani Foreign Ministry summoned the Iraqi ambassador and warned him to stay within the "boundaries of diplomatic work."[51] Similar restrictions were put on the Iraqi embassies in Western states such as the United States, the United Kingdom, and France. The movements of Iraqi diplomats were severely restricted, and the British deported forty senior Ba'thists, including the military attaché and nine other military officers.[52]

Iraqi operations on university campuses also came under sharp scru-tiny. In the United Kingdom, the head of the Iraqi student union, who was studying statistics at the University of London, received a very polite letter stating, "Dear Sir, The Secretary of State has decided that your departure from the United Kingdom would be conductive to the public good for reasons of national security." He was given eight days to leave, or he would be arrested.[53] Other Iraqi students studying sensitive subjects like nuclear physics were asked not to continue their courses.[54]

Likewise, the French began monitoring Iraqi students and looking for any connections to the Ba'th Party or the Iraqi regime. If any suspicious infor-mation was uncovered, the government canceled the student's university registration.[55] One Iraqi working toward a PhD in Theater at the Sorbonne

reported that when Iraq invaded Kuwait, Iraqi students "intensified our political and informational activities in France." He and his comrades "held
demonstrations and gatherings to assist our fighting country and its beloved president," and they "executed a wide campaign to distribute tens of
thousands of publications and proclamations." As a result of his "intense influence activities," French counterintelligence agents raided his home and
arrested him in front of his family.[56] The deportations of Iraqi students like
him became such a problem that the regime began compiling a file on them.
It eventually reached 750 pages and included cases from around the world.[57]
With the student leaders being rounded up, the Ba'th Party organizations
working out of the embassies had to take direct control over the Iraqi student
unions.[58]

The breakdown of Ba'thist and particularly student networks abroad
hurt Iraqi influence operations significantly. People associated with Iraqi
student unions were accused of being "spies for Saddam," and many Iraqi
students began to keep their distance.[59] One regime report in October 1990
complained that demonstrations in some countries were "not on the level
that was requested when compared with the large number of Iraqis, and especially [Iraqi] students in these states."[60] However, an even bigger problem
for Baghdad was that foreign states were attempting to turn Iraqis against
the Ba'thist regime. Western states such as France and the United Kingdom
began to pressure Iraqi students to apply for political asylum. Iraqis were
offered money, housing, and the ability to continue their studies. All they had
to do was cooperate with local security services.[61]

Defection was a real concern for the Iraqis. Numerous Iraqi Ba'thists living
abroad decided not to return to Iraq. Probably, the most high-profile defector
was the Iraqi Ambassador to the United States, Muhammad al-Mashat. Born
in 1935, al-Mashat became a committed Ba'thist early in life.[62] However,
Saddam's violent rise to power made him nervous, and al-Mashat began to
put aside money in case he had to defect one day. He held several important
diplomatic posts throughout the 1980s, leading to his appointment as the
ambassador in Washington in 1989. The Gulf Crisis convinced him that the
regime in Baghdad was irredeemable. When the Washington embassy was
closed in January 1991, the Foreign Ministry booked him a flight to Vienna,
where he was supposed to arrange follow-on travel to Iraq. He boarded
the flight to Austria, but he had no intention of returning to Iraq. This put
him and his family in a precarious position. If Iraqi intelligence officers in
Vienna learned of his plan to defect, they would have assassinated him. He

thought the American CIA was also trying to recruit him. One day a man with an American accent who simply went by the name "Jones," called his hotel room, asked to meet, and offered Green Cards to him and his family. Al-Mashat eventually received an offer to "retire" in Canada, where he became a permanent resident.[63]

The al-Mashat affair, as it was called in Canada, was a significant problem for the Ba'thists, and as later chapters detail, defections continued to haunt the regime throughout the 1990s. Yet, despite these very real setbacks, the regime also made important international gains during the Gulf Crisis. The conflict inflamed the passions of many Arab nationalists and Islamists. Even those wary of Iraqi aggression were more incensed about the prospect of an American-led attack on an Arab-Muslim state.

Mobilizing Allies

Beginning almost immediately after the Iraqi invasion on August 2, Baghdad sent a steady stream of instructions to Iraqi Ba'thists outside Iraq. The regime ordered them to use all their connections and capabilities to mobilize the Iraqi, Arab, Islamic, and foreign masses. They were to work through local parties and unions, as well as political, humanitarian, cultural, and social leaders to hold "angry demonstrations" against "America, the Zionists, and their allies among the bloodsucking (*masasi dima*') peoples who are cooperating with them." The Ba'th Party told its followers to hold sit-ins and gatherings at religious sites, UN offices, humanitarian organizations, and any other influential place in their areas.[64] Ba'thists abroad were to arrange statements of support from local allies for Saddam and for "the free government of Kuwait," which was an Iraqi creation Baghdad tried to present as an indigenous Kuwaiti initiative.[65]

At this operational level, initial Iraqi actions achieved some limited effects, mostly among populations that had traditionally been supportive of the regime in Baghdad. On August 7, less than a week after the invasion, King Hassan of Morocco warned Bush that "Iraqi recruiting offices have been opened in Mauritania." And that "they have 500 recruits already."[66] Large, pro-Saddam demonstrations took place in several Jordanian cities.[67] By September, several international Arab student unions met in Jordan to announce "the formation of a brigade to strike at American interests if the United States carries out any aggressive acts against Iraq." In an obvious exaggeration, they claimed, "scores of organizations and hundreds of thousands of Arabs are ready to volunteer."[68] In Sudan, the Khartoum Student Union denounced the "terrorizing of the Iraqi state by foreign imperialist posturing." Similarly, the Khartoum University Student Union sent a message to Saddam, praising him for defending the Arab and Islamic world from "the stain of imperialist hegemony."[69] The second week of August, over 200,000 Sudanese participated in a march to support Iraq.[70]

In other areas of the world, Ba'thists used different ideas and networks to mobilize support. For example, in majority Catholic states throughout the developing world, Iraqis worked through Catholic centers and Catholic social justice movements.[71] Additionally, the regime used Christians it had co-opted in Iraq to garner support abroad among international Christian organizations.[72]

The Iraqis tailored their operations to reach new audiences. In the United States, for example, Ba'thist cells used slogans such as: "Why sacrifice the sons of America for the sake of the families of corrupt dictators." And, "We do not want another Vietnam." They criticized the "oil sheikhs," and argued, "It is not possible to compare the blood of Americans with the price of oil."[73]

While popular American narratives of the Gulf War present it as enjoying wide public support, much of that sentiment was slow to develop. In fact, the war was quite controversial in the months between the Iraqi invasion of Kuwait and the beginning of American-led operations against Iraq in January 1991. The vote to authorize the war only passed the Senate by five votes and large majorities of Democrats voted against it in both chambers of Congress. The Iraqi slogans tapped into popular American antiwar sentiments. In Washington, DC, estimates of between 75,000 to 125,000 demonstrators attended an antiwar protest. Hundreds of thousands more protesters attended other events around the country. Although it is impossible to measure their impact, Iraqi Ba'thists secretly helped to organize some of these demonstrations and their slogans were echoed by the crowds. Thus, Baghdad saw some operational successes in their influence campaign. If nothing else, the Ba'thists were finding likeminded partners.[74] However, they were unable to translate these successes into the type of strategic impact that would affect the outcome of the war.

In Western Europe similar protests occurred. Over 200,000 protesters mobilized across Germany. The United Kingdom and France, both key members of the Gulf War coalition, saw their capitals flooded with tens of thousands of protesters. The European protests were led by leftists, trade unions, environmentalists, and peace activists.[75]

In this wave of antiwar sentiment, the political ground shifted under the Iraqi diaspora. The results set the stage and opened opportunities for Iraqi influence operations throughout the rest of the decade. Iraq had one of the Middle East's largest communist parties in the mid-twentieth century, but successive Arab nationalist regimes had crushed it, exiling many of its members to places like Stockholm and London. In the 1980s, these Iraqi dissidents had been an important part of leftist coalitions, especially when Western governments were supporting Baghdad in the Iran-Iraq War. As the British writer, Nick Cohen stated, "When I went to leftish meetings in the late Eighties, I heard that Iraq encapsulated all the loathsome hypocrisy of the supposedly 'democratic' West. Here was a blighted land ruled by a terrible regime that followed the example of European dictatorships of the Thirties."[76] Yet as antiwar movements began to focus on an American war with Iraq, Iraqi critics of the regime became inconvenient at best. Kanan Makiya, for example, was an Iraqi exile with a Trotskyist background. He wrote a scathing portrait of Saddam's regime under the pseudonym Samir al-Khalil. Doing so made him a darling in the late 1980s among some circles of Western intelligentsia who opposed American support for Iraq.[77] The Iraqi invasion of Kuwait turned him into a pariah among the same circles. His supporters became his critics when he called for the overthrow of Saddam, and Western leaders employed his arguments to justify war.

The shifting politics among Iraqi and Arab diasporas was perhaps best exemplified by the standard-bearer of Arab critique, Edward Said. The real villains of the Gulf Crisis for Said were Saddam's enemies—the United States of course, but also Kuwait, whose leaders he correctly stated, respected "neither human rights nor the priorities of their own people."[78] The Kuwaitis, Said claimed, were "viewed by most Arabs as flawed, complicit in oil production geared not to Arab requirements but to American needs, powerless to object when American support of Israel exhibited permissiveness and hypocrisy."[79] Said was too sophisticated to become a supporter of Saddam, whom he denounced as an "appalling dictator."[80] However, at times, he was overly forgiving. "Iraq's case against Kuwait," he insisted, "was given no hearing, thereby ensuring the need for war." In a bizarre incident, he cited a discredited US Army War College study, which was written as Washington was aiding Baghdad in the Iran–Iraq War and which attempted to sow doubt about the well-established fact that the Iraqi regime gassed its own Kurdish civilians. Said claimed that the failure of the Western media to reference this study highlighted its anti-Iraqi bias.[81] An Army War College study that papered over the crimes of an abhorrent, American-supported, Arab dictatorship was just the type of work that Said was famous for eviscerating. The fact that he was referencing it positively just a few years after it was written shows the fickleness of political alignments. Said became a harsh critic of Iraqi dissidents like Makiya, whom he accused of being a native informant and shill for Western warmongers.[82] In leftist coalitions across the West, people like Makiya were replaced by Iraqis who—sometimes unknown to their fellow travelers—worked directly for the regime in Baghdad.[83]

Islam in the Gulf Crisis

The most successful Iraqi outreach, by far, was to Middle Eastern and particularly Islamic organizations. In August, Baghdad instructed Ba'thists working outside Iraq to pay particular attention to Muslim majority states. The regime directed them to use slogans such as "do not give precedence to the infidels over the believers," and to highlight that the Prophet Muhammad said to "expel the hypocrites (*mushtarakin*) from the Arab Peninsula."[84] The Ba'th Party's efforts to use Islam were aided by other elements of the regime and Saddam's personal interventions.

On August 10 and then again on September 5, Saddam gave speeches in which he invoked Islamic symbols, sometimes militantly. He appealed to Arab and Muslim masses, arguing "Your turn has come to show your values and to highlight the meanings of the message of Islam in which you believe and which you practice."[85] Saddam also altered the Iraqi flag, writing the Islamic call, *Allah Akbar* (God is Greatest) on it in his own handwriting.

The Iraqi military joined with the Ministry of Endowments and Religious Affairs to produce propaganda designed to "raise the emotions of hatred and hostility of all Muslims against [the Saudis and their Western allies]." It stressed "the Islamic holy sites are being violated by foreign forces that entered the holy land and the desecration of the *Kaaba* and the Prophet's grave." In doing so, the regime hoped to "emphasize jihad for God's sake to expel the American invaders and their allies."[86]

The various components of the regime worked in concert. As the historian Jeremy Long observed, when Saddam discussed Islam and jihad, "the Popular Islamic Conference, the National Assembly, 'Holy Mecca Radio' (a clandestine Iraqi broadcast aimed at Saudi troops), and Abdullah Fadil, the Iraqi minister of [Endowments and] Religious Affairs, immediately gave parallel and equally vigorous calls to holy war." And of course, "The news media carried the same message without deviation, writing editorials that squared exactly with what the regime had said and done."[87]

Much of Iraqi rhetoric relied on Ba'thist interpretations of Islam.[88] Saddam's speeches, for example, addressed the Arabs and discussed Islam as an Arab religion. Behind the scenes, senior Iraqi officials remained skeptical and even derisive about both traditional Islam and Islamism. Yet, while they derided the "huge turban" of one of their supporters they saw on television, they were happy that he was "inciting the audience against the United States and explaining Iraq's position."[89] The regime kept its critiques private. In public it relied on the Ba'th Party's respect for Islam and its championing of issues such as the Palestinian cause that most Muslims supported. In doing so, Saddam was able to court Islamic and Islamist activists abroad.

The Popular Islamic Conference Organization was at the center of Iraqi efforts to win Muslim support. As discussed in Chapter 1, the Saudis had helped Iraq to recruit international Islamic activists for the Popular Islamic Conferences that were held in Baghdad during the Iran-Iraq War. The Iraqis continued to build those networks with and without Saudi support through the rest of the 1980s. For example, the largest foreign contingents to the Popular Islamic Conferences in the early 1980s were from Pakistan, and Iraqi Ba'thists entrenched themselves in Pakistani religious networks.[90] Their reports back to Baghdad stated that in Pakistan, these religious actors were even more important than the politicians. During the Gulf Crisis, Iraqis held seminars with prominent Sunni religious scholars and distributed their propaganda around the country.[91] A Sunni group, Jamiat-ul-Ulama-i-Islam Pakistan, offered to send medical doctors and Mujahideen to Iraq "to fight the American aggression in the event of war."[92] The Ba'thists were even able to convince a prominent Shi'i cleric, with the rank of *Hojjat al-Islam*, in Pakistan to issue a fatwa and distribute 100 copies among Pakistani Shi'is.[93]

Similar operations occurred around the Muslim world. In January 1991, just days before the UN deadline for Iraq's withdrawal from Kuwait, Saddam convened a Popular Islamic Conference in Baghdad in which he called for Muslims to declare jihad if Iraq was attacked.[94]

The Saudis were incensed that Iraq was attacking Saudi Arabia with the conference that the Saudis had founded. They held their own Popular Islamic Conference in Mecca on the same days as the Iraqi conference. The Saudis attracted delegates representing officially recognized Islamic organizations in states like Egypt, Morocco, and Syria, who supported Riyadh in the Gulf

Crisis. Participants in the Meccan conference included prominent Saudi scholars, the Egyptian Sheikh of al-Azhar, heads of Saudi sponsored international Islamic organizations such as the Muslim World League, and importantly, Ma'ruf al-Dawalibi, who had created the conference in the early 1980s and continued to serve as the chairman of its executive committee. After years of remaining quiet about the ideology and people who had exiled him from his Syrian homeland, al-Dawalibi was finally able to speak freely about Aflaq's Ba'thism as an "idiotic philosophy."[95]

In contrast to its Saudi counterpart, the Popular Islamic Conference in Iraq attracted representatives of Islamic movements that were not state-sanctioned. Most importantly, representatives of Islamist opposition parties flocked to Baghdad from many of the states that supported Saudi Arabia. Saddam depicted the conflict in terms of good versus evil and Arab-Muslims versus infidels. He used Ba'thized Islamic idiom to link the American presence on the Arabian Peninsula with the Israeli occupation of Jerusalem in a master antiimperialist narrative tailored to appeal to Islamists.

Many Islamists were initially unsure how to respond to Iraq's invasion of Kuwait and this episode helps to demonstrate how Iraqi actions could affect international politics. An American-led attack on an Arab-Muslim country was repugnant for Islamists and most were inclined to oppose it, especially if their authoritarian leaders in places like Egypt or Syria supported it. Nevertheless, Islamists remained hesitant at first. Many of them received significant financial support from Gulf Arabs. Plus, had Iraq not just invaded a fellow Arab Muslim state? And it was hard to hide the atrocities that the Iraqis were committing in Kuwait. Had Saddam and the Ba'thists been militantly secular or unwelcoming to Islamists, groups like the Muslim Brotherhood may have stayed on the side-lines. Yet, Saddam said all the right things and did all he could to welcome Islamist support from abroad even if he remained intolerant of Iraqi Islamism at home. These actions appear to have had an effect. By the time the war began in January 1991, many Islamists across the region abandoned their earlier reluctance and became some of Saddam's most ardent supporters.[96]

In Egypt, for example, the Muslim Brotherhood had called for a withdrawal of Iraqi troops from Kuwait in the immediate aftermath of the invasion. However, as Gehad Auda has argued, "Once Iraq began to rely heavily on Islamic propaganda and Saddam began to project himself as a reborn Muslim, they came to see the invasion as an expression of hostility between two Islamic forces."[97] By January 1991, the Egyptian Brotherhood made clear where its loyalties lied when it sent its delegation—as part of the Egyptian Labor Party—to the Popular Islamic Conference in Baghdad rather than Mecca.[98]

Likewise, the Jordanian Muslim Brotherhood had initially opposed Iraq's invasion of Kuwait. However, pro-Saddam sentiments swept the country, especially among the large Palestinian population. Once the Saudis invited US troops to deploy to the Arabian Peninsula, the Jordanian Brotherhood moved clearly into the pro-Iraq camp.[99] An Iraqi intelligence report in November 1990 even claimed that members of the Jordanian Muslim Brotherhood were "smuggling weapons to Saudi Arabia" for "commando operations against US forces and its allies."[100]

The crisis inflamed other militant Islamists from around the Muslim world. In Pakistan, a Lahore-based group called the Armed Battalions Revolutionary Party penned and distributed an "Open Letter to President George Bush" in English. It began, "We the people of Pakistan and soldiers of Islam have been helplessly watching you pork eating kafirs [infidels] running our country by proxy through purchased agents and traitors." Continuing in a similar tone, it argued, "You have infected our pure Muslim society by introducing drug and gun culture through your paid CIA agents. You have made our youth as impotent as your dirty Chicago Gangsters." And then,

> You pig eaters have desecrated the holy land of MECCA and MADINA by sending your troops infected with AIDS and VD to be stationed in Saudi Arabia. Your unwilling mercenary troops are now ogling at Muslim women with evil eyes to outrage their modesty like you dogs of war did in Vietnam, where your bastards are still growing up.[101]

They "denounced Iraq for swallowing up Kuwait" but insisted that the United States was committing "a crime against humanity and the Muslims." Then they demanded that Washington close its embassy in Pakistan or they would burn it down as Islamists had done in the early 1980s.[102]

War

By early January 1991, George H. W. Bush had assembled the largest international coalition since World War II. Over 500,000 American troops joined hundreds of thousands of their coalition partners around the Arabian

Peninsula. A UN Security Council resolution gave Iraq until January 15, 1991 to withdraw its forces from Kuwait. If Baghdad refused, the resolution authorized the use of force. A week prior to the deadline, the US Congress endorsed the Security Council resolution with its own authorization to use military force.

Iraqis watched nervously from encampments in Kuwait and from head-quarters in Baghdad. Saddam attempted a few last-minute diplomatic moves to delay the onslaught. He tried to tie the Iraqi occupation of Kuwait to the Israeli occupation of Palestinian territories, insisting that Iraq would withdraw its forces if Israel would do the same. Baghdad worked through Moscow on a proposal to delay the American-led attack for the promise of Iraqi cooperation and the redeployment of its troops to Iraq. Additionally, Iraqi Foreign Minister Tariq Aziz met US Secretary of State James Baker in Switzerland to see if any arrangement could be made.[103]

The Bush administration quashed most of these efforts. Baker only met Aziz to give the impression that military action was a last resort, but the op-tics were helpful. For example, the Egyptian ambassador to the United States later wrote to Baker that he "particularly appreciated your [Baker's] efforts to bring about the Iraqi withdrawal from Kuwait through diplomacy so as to avoid a war that inevitably would have its human and material toll."[104] Despite such diplomatic posturing, by January, war was the only option for the Americans. The logistics of deploying hundreds of thousands of troops to the region were extremely complex, and providing them food, water, and shelter in the middle a desert was a herculean task. That many people could only be maintained on the Arabian Peninsula for a few months. Then they would be forced to redeploy. Moreover, in 1991, the Islamic holy month of Ramadan began in March. The implications of launching an attack once it started were unclear and possibly prohibitive. Thus, the United States could not allow Iraqi diplomacy to delay the war.

Iraqi efforts to stop the war were largely inept. Later in the decade, Saddam learned to bring the world to the edge of war and then pull back at the last minute. In doing so, he split the coalitions forming against him and made attacks on his forces difficult politically. Had Saddam withdrawn his troops from Kuwait but kept them mobilized on the Iraqi side of the borders, he would have put the United States and its coalition partners in an impossible situation. Yet, Saddam did not seem to recognize the opportunity.

Instead, the Ba'thist regime often turned to strategies that were more aligned with Saddam's populist instincts. In an early example of the type of tactic Saddam would use with devastating effectiveness following the war, he attempted to drive a wedge into French-American relations. The Iraqi regime thought France might side with it in the Gulf Crisis, or at least attempt to stop a war.[105] At the start of the crisis, the Iraqi regime took foreign workers in Iraq as hostages. When Baker visited Paris to discuss the coalition's strategy, Iraq released the 327 French workers. The move was meant to raise American suspicions that France had broken with the coalition to negotiate its own deal with Baghdad. When France denied the allegations, the Iraqis leaked details about a secret meeting that senior Iraqis had held with French officials on the matter. The event did raise doubts about France's commitments in Washington, but it did not ultimately undermine the coalition.[106]

Baghdad also hoped that Ba'thists operating abroad could organize large global protests from January 13 to January 15. Their goal was to make it politically difficult for Western states to launch a war.[107] Additionally, Iraq's militant propaganda about jihad and foreign desecration of the holy sites on the Arabian Peninsula was designed to prevent Arab states from being able to host Western militaries.[108] Ultimately, these efforts were unsuccessful during the Gulf Crisis, but they foreshadowed more effective campaigns following the war.

More directly, the regime carried out sabotage and assassination missions in the hope of crippling the coalition. The Iraqi Intelligence Service had a secretive detachment called Unit 999, which executed covert and clandestine operations in Saudi Arabia and the Gulf Arab states.[109] They collected information on coalition military personnel, installations, and their disposition. They also attempted to assassinate members of the exiled Kuwaiti royal family.[110]

For all the operational successes the Iraqis had in recruiting new partners, they were unable to create the type of strategic impacts that could stop the war. On January 17, 1991 the American-led coalition began air strikes. Coalition aircraft quickly gained control of the air and unleashed a destructive strategic bombing campaign. After a month of punishing attacks from the air, the coalition launched a ground campaign on February 24. Iraq's military capabilities proved as inept as its diplomacy. By the time the ground war began, Iraqi soldiers were demoralized. They surrendered by the thousands to any coalition members they could find.

The Iraqi military only took offensive action against the coalition in two areas. First and most effectively, it used SCUD missiles to target coalition forces as well as Israel, which was not in the coalition. Second, it launched an ill-fated ground offensive to take the Saudi town of Kafji. Both operations confounded Western military officers, who were trained in accordance with a Clausewitzian rationality that suggests tactical actions combine to form operations, which are part of a strategy to achieve a political objective.

By contrast, Iraqi actions were designed as spectacles meant to rally political support for Iraq. The Iraqis hoped the SCUD attacks would provoke an Israeli response and that Arab states such as Saudi Arabia and Syria would balk at finding themselves on the same side of the conflict as the Jewish state. Tellingly, some of the SCUDS fired at Israel were a variant the Iraqis called *Hijara al-Sijil* (stone from dry clay) because they contained concrete warheads.[111] Western analysts concocted all sorts of explanations for why Iraqis would employ such warheads. An Iraqi general later revealed that Saddam wanted to mimic the rocks that Palestinians were hurling at their Israeli occupiers in the First Intifada.[112] In other words, the SCUDS were symbolic; they were a political show. The Iraqi attack on al-Khafji was similarly erratic. Iraqi commanders felt that being on the offensive was operationally sound. They hoped to spark an early ground war and felt that, if successful, al-Khafji could lead to other operations. However, the plan was never incorporated into a broader strategy. One gets the sense that Saddam just wanted to strike and that doing so would somehow stir the passions of his supporters.[113]

Western military leaders focused on military objectives. They had trouble understanding Iraqi actions that were more performative than operational. The commander of the coalition forces, US Army General Norman Schwarzkopf later wrote that he was "perplexed" by the Iraqi attack on al-Khafji and that "it defied military logic."[114] Similarly, the coalition's military leadership saw the Iraqi SCUD attacks as militarily ineffective, so they did not take them seriously. Civilian leaders in the Bush administration, who were much more attuned to the potential political consequences of attacks on Israel, had to strongarm the military into targeting Iraq's mobile SCUD launchers. After making clear how important the SCUDS were, Secretary of Defense Dick Cheney uncharacteristically "exploded" in one of his morning briefings when he was told that only 30 sorties had been sent on anti-SCUD missions. "Come on we've got to get this together," he berated the military leadership.[115]

Saddam Discovers a New Narrative

From the operational perspective of the military, the main problem the American-led coalition faced was that it performed too well. The ground war consisted of a two-pronged attack. The US Marines and allied Arab forces pushed straight into Kuwait. The main coalition force conducted a "left hook" through the Iraqi desert to the west and then north of Kuwait. This left hook was designed to seal off the Iraqi military's escape from Kuwait. However, the Marines faced far less resistance than they anticipated, and they pushed the Iraqi forces out of Kuwait before the left hook sealed off the escape routes. Air power destroyed the fleeing Iraqis and the left hook eventually moved close enough to engage the main Iraqi forces—though in a major blunder, the coalition failed to destroy Iraq's Republican Guard.

In most ways, the Gulf War was a disaster for Iraq. Its military, economy, and society were largely incapacitated. Widescale uprisings erupted across Iraq following the war, threatening Saddam's rule. In the Kurdish dominated north and the Shi'i Arab south, whole provinces broke free from Baghdad's control. The regime only regained control in southern Iraq by launching a brutal campaign of repression. In the north, the regime never recaptured Kurdistan.

Despite these setbacks, the regime's survival in the face of what it called "the aggression of the 30 [states]," led Saddam to claim a victory of sorts. Later in 1991, Saddam looked back on the Gulf Crisis and noted, "this war, however, was beneficial for us."[116] As astounding as such a claim sounds, one must remember that Saddam interpreted power through the lens of mass politics. In the months after its invasion of Kuwait, Iraq knitted together a network of supporters among Islamists, Third World critics of American hegemony, and loose anti-war coalitions of leftists, far right isolationists, and other political activists in the West.

During the Gulf War itself, Saddam shifted the narrative that Iraq presented to potential allies. Prior to the beginning of the Gulf War in January 1991, the Ba'thists presented themselves as powerful and able to stand up to Western aggression. Saddam thought that as long as Iraq appeared strong, the masses would flock to support him. He changed his outlook when the coalition bombed the al-'Amiriyah bunker in Baghdad during the height of the Gulf War air campaign. The Americans mistakenly thought it was a military command center. It was actually an air-raid shelter and the bombing killed hundreds of Iraqi civilians.

Condemnations of American actions poured in from all over the world. The Soviet Union and China expressed dismay, and the Soviet press used the event to call into question the legitimacy of the war itself.[117] Arab supporters of Saddam, such as the Palestinian leader, Yasser Arafat and King Hussein of Jordan criticized the "heinous" attack.[118] Even coalition members like Spain,

Italy, and Sweden denounced the bombing, and Spain attempted to force the Security Council to end the war.[119] In the wake of these critiques, Washington ordered the US Air Force to end its bombing campaign in Baghdad and to focus on strictly military targets outside of populated areas.[120] As such, international political pressure did more to curtail coalition military operations than any Iraqi anti-aircraft system.

The al-'Amiriyah incident taught Saddam the power of weakness. As one American journalist working in Iraq at the time observed, prior to al-'Amiriyah, the Iraqi regime tried to hide civilian casualties in an attempt to project strength. After the bombing, the regime went to great pains to highlight Iraqi casualties. Saddam realized that the narrative of a weak and helpless Iraq being bullied by a neo-imperialist superpower was much more effective than a narrative of a strong Iraq standing up to the United States.[121]

The attack on al-'Amiriyah was part of a broad and needlessly destructive strategic bombing campaign targeting Iraqi infrastructure and essential systems deep inside Iraq. Post-war academic assessments have argued that strategic bombing in Iraq was largely ineffective and that the air campaign would have been equally successful in expelling Iraqi forces from Kuwait had it restricted its targets to the Iraqi military and command-and-control systems.[122] Yet, while it lacked any real strategic utility, the bombing of Iraqi infrastructure and vital systems contributed significantly to a humanitarian crisis. Even the largely sympathetic Gulf War Air Power Survey, which the US Air Force commissioned following the conflict, acknowledged the targeting and widespread damage done to power plants as well as the "damage to other, less critical, components such as gantry cranes, warehouses, petroleum-storage tanks, and water-conditioning systems." Without access to electricity and clean water, Iraqis suffered from disease and malnutrition following the end of the war. As the survey recognized, the "the bombing of electric power had 'contributed to' 70,000–90,000 postwar civilian deaths."[123]

In light of this onslaught, Iraqis and their sympathizers around the world began to contrast the destruction in Iraq with the broader political project that justified the war. As one Iraqi intellectual recorded in her diary after twenty days of bombing: "Bush says, we make war to have peace. Such nonsense. What a destructive peace this is. A new world order? I call it disorder."[124] A few days later, she simply wrote, "Killing is the new world order."[125] That Iraqis had to suffer to prop up an international order designed to alleviate suffering was exactly the type of Hegelian contradiction that Fukuyama claimed the end of the Cold War had resolved in his "End of

History" essay. Saddam quickly recognized the political power that existed in the gap between the justification for the war and the conduct of war.

This realization formed the core of Iraq's political strategy to break up the US-led coalition that was attempting to enforce sanctions and inspections in Iraq as part of the Gulf War's cease fire agreement. The regime preserved the al-'Amiriyah bunker, transforming it into a museum, and immediately following the war, the Iraqis used the excesses of the conflict to highlight the contradictions in the emerging international system. Because of the coalition's "interest in human rights," the Iraqis argued, "thousands of Iraqi children face death, deformity and vagrancy."[126] There was enough truth in such claims to be taken seriously by global audiences.

Conclusion

The Gulf Crisis was not simply a regional war to expel Iraqi forces from Kuwait. It was an important global moment marking the transition from the Cold War to the post-Cold War, and it was where George H. W. Bush planted the flag of his new world order. Yet, despite what seemed like a quick decisive victory for the coalition, the heady rhetoric of Bush and his allies did not match the destructive reality on the ground in Iraq. This disparity gave Saddam ammunition for a heavily politicized strategy which American leaders had trouble understanding during the war and which plagued them in the years ahead.

3

Triumph and Despair After the Gulf War

In the spring of 1991, as coalition troops were returning to their home countries, Iraq's "Child Welfare Committee" produced a glossy blue booklet in both English and Arabic. It was titled "The New World Order and the Disaster of the Iraqi Children."[1] The booklet contained page after page of gut-wrenching pictures and statistics showcasing the suffering of Iraqi children. Like all effective propaganda, this booklet played on existing anxieties and political tensions. The new world order, which Bush claimed was an objective of the Gulf War, promised a more humane international system. Yet, the war created an acute humanitarian crisis in Iraq, which the international community repeatedly failed to resolve.

This Janus-faced outcome produced conflicting trends in post–Cold War international politics. On one hand, America and its allies were triumphant. When Bush released his administration's National Security Strategy in the summer of 1991, he titled the preface "A New World Order."[2] The United States and its partners attempted to solidify their gains and to liberalize the international order even further than they had prior to the war. On the other hand, the unaddressed despair in Iraq began to gnaw at the cohesion of the international community.[3] While the trend toward despair eventually overtook and drowned out the wave of optimism, that result was neither obvious nor inevitable in the immediate aftermath of the war.

As the title of the glossy blue pamphlet suggested, Saddam and his Ba'thists understood that they could exploit the gap between the promises of the new world order and the despair of innocent Iraqis. However, Saddam's regime was in shambles. If it were going to seize the political opportunities provided by these contradictions, the Ba'thists would have to rebuild their operations both at home and abroad. Thus, this chapter first outlines the tensions running through international politics in the wake of the Gulf War, and then highlights Iraqi attempts to develop strategies, policies, and institutions to exploit those tensions. Later chapters discuss how Saddam's regime carried out its strategies around the world.

Iraq against the World. Samuel Helfont, Oxford University Press. © Oxford University Press 2023.
DOI: 10.1093/oso/9780197530153.003.0004

Triumphalism and Expansion of the New World Order

As the guns fell silent in Iraq, senior statesmen at the United Nations were in a self-congratulatory mood. The Gulf War had exceeded all expectations. The coalition easily defeated the vaunted Iraqi military and did so with little loss of life—at least among coalition partners. Several members of the UN Security Council wanted to use the victory to cement a new, post–Cold War order that could hold rogue states accountable. Thus, the conflict's ceasefire agreement became the longest and most detailed UN Security Council resolution in history. It included, among other things, demands for reparations, weapons inspections, the renouncement of terrorism, and a plan for restoring peace to the region. Boutros Boutros-Ghali, who was appointed the UN Secretary General at the end of 1991, argued that the resolution "sent the United Nations into uncharted territory in many areas." It had to define the border between Iraq and Kuwait, and to ensure Iraqi cooperation with the International Atomic Energy Agency (IAEA) and the UN Special Commission (UNSCOM), the latter of which the ceasefire set up to ensure that Iraq disarmed in compliance with the resolution.[4]

These expanded functions for the United Nations promised a truly new order. During Security Council deliberations about the ceasefire agreement on April 3, 1991, the British Ambassador to the United Nations claimed the war was "of far greater and of far more positive significance for all countries in the world, and for [the UN] as a whole, than the many regional conflicts with which we have tried to grapple over recent decades." The conflict, he averred, "marked a clear, firm and effective determination of the world community not to allow the law of the jungle to overcome the rule of law."[5] In a sign of the times, the Soviet representative agreed, arguing that the conflict was "a serious test of the soundness of the new thinking, the new system of international relations." The United Nations, he continued, "has passed that test and demonstrated that a considerable path has been travelled between the Cold War and the new system of international relations."[6] The American representative provided an even more soaring statement: "This resolution is unique and historic. It fulfills the hope of mankind to make the United Nations an instrument of peace and stability."[7]

Not everyone used such heady language to describe the war. The French, for example, prioritized an effective ceasefire and "re-establishing regional security."[8] Their representative at the Security Council avoided the grand rhetoric about world order that his colleagues espoused. Other states were equally coy in their statements, but only Cuba voted against the resolution and a triumphal mood permeated much of the discussion.[9]

Two days later, on April 5, the Security Council met again to discuss a resolution that had the potential to push its mandate, and thus aspects of the post–Cold War order, in a radical direction. The Security Council was designed explicitly to deal with issues of international peace and security. It did not have a mandate to interfere in the domestic affairs of sovereign states, even in the case of egregious human rights violations. Yet, several states referred Iraqi attempts to quell its post–Gulf War uprisings to the Security Council.

The uprisings stemmed directly from the Gulf War. In the final days of the conflict, President Bush suggested that the "Iraqi people" and the "Iraqi military" should "take matters into their own hands and force Saddam Hussein, the dictator, to step aside."[10] This message was broadcast into Iraq by Voice of America. The impact of Bush's words has been disputed, but whatever the cause, the Iraqi people rose up in a mass rebellion against the Ba'thist regime immediately following the war. The insurrection was particularly potent in the Kurdish north and the Shi'i Arab south.

At the ceasefire negotiations, Iraqis received permission to fly helicopters because many of the bridges and roads in the country were destroyed. Saddam used these helicopters along with his elite Republic Guard divisions, which had survived the war despite American intentions, to rain terror on the uprising in southern Iraq. Whole towns were demolished, important Shi'i shrines were badly damaged, and the bodies literally piled up in the streets of southern Iraqi cities.[11] In the north, over one million Kurds fled their homes in the fear that Saddam would repeat the genocidal campaign his regime waged against them in the late 1980s. The Kurds made their way to the mountains or to dilapidated camps along the Turkish and Iranian borders. Their situation further enflamed an already dire humanitarian crisis in Iraq at the end of the war.[12]

The Security Council was designed explicity to address international peace and security rather than domestic matters. Baghdad argued that its treatment of the Kurds was a domestic issue and thus outside the purview of the Security Council. However, Turkey insisted that the resulting refugees who were flowing across its border constituted a breach of international peace and security. Therefore, addressing this issue was within the Security Council's mandate. This reasoning became the official justification for a Security Council resolution, but some states clearly saw the council's actions as opening the door, for better or worse, to the inclusion of humanitarian issues on the council's agenda. Bush's pre–Gulf War speech introducing the new world order hinted that its scope went well beyond international security when it referenced "human decency" and referred to the new order as "freer from the threat of terror, stronger in the pursuit of justice."[13] Several western European states, which were not on the Security Council, asked to join the April 5 meeting on Iraqi repression. They did so explicitly to promote this humanitarian approach to international order. The French representative summed up the sentiment of these Western European states, claiming, "the Security Council [. . .] would have been remiss in its task had it stood idly by, without reacting to the massacre of entire populations, the exterminations of civilians, including women and children."[14]

Other states were not pleased about the Security Council adopting human rights violations as a part of its mandate and saw in this resolution something more than an attempt to mitigate refugee flows. Cuba, Yemen, and Zimbabwe voted against the resolution. The Chinese made clear they did not consider it appropriate for the Security Council to deal with this issue. However, the end of the Cold War and the emergence of the Security Council as a functioning body to regulate global affairs required unity of the council's five permanent members. Breaking with other members on the issue would have undermined that unity. Thus, Beijing abstained rather than veto a resolution to which it clearly objected.

The United States, the United Kingdom, and France used this resolution to launch an operation in northern Iraq to protect the Kurds. The Russians supported the operation, but behind closed doors they expressed some reservations to Bush about encroachments on Iraq's territorial integrity.[15] What became known in the United States as Operation Provide Comfort began simply as a humanitarian mission to deliver food, medicine, and shelter for Kurdish refugees in Iraq. One of the goals was to keep these refugees out of Turkey—a NATO ally—which had a long and troubled history with its own Kurds and certainly did not want to see millions more pouring across its borders. Provide Comfort quickly became a military operation to protect the Kurds from the Iraqi military. The United States, the United Kingdom, and France used the resolution to justify a no-fly zone over northern Iraq, which was not mentioned in the text of the resolution and was a clear violation of Iraqi sovereignty. As the Kurds fought the Iraqi military on the ground, the Americans, British, and French provided air cover. The resulting Kurdish autonomous zone in northern Iraq functioned as a de facto independent state until the fall of Saddam's regime in 2003.

Throughout 1991 and 1992, diplomats continued to spar over human rights in Iraq, the appropriateness of the Security Council addressing them, and the implications for world order. Washington, London, and Paris pressed for more expansive interpretations of Security Council resolutions. They initially received a great deal of support among some non-Western states as well. In a March 1992 meeting, the representative of the Russian Federation, which had taken the Soviet seat on the council, explicitly invoked "human rights," and denounced "the repressive policy of the Iraqi authorities with regard to the civilian population of the country."[16]

This push for an expanded interpretation of the resolution was indicative of trends in the United Nations as a whole. When the Egyptian diplomat, Boutros Boutros-Ghali was elected UN Secretary General in late 1991, he assumed the position with a mandate for reform and expansion. His plan, *An Agenda for Peace*, which he presented in 1992, built on the perceived successes in the Gulf War. It proposed a much more activist Security Council that had the tools, including a UN military force, to enforce resolutions and keep peace around the world.[17] Such bold plans were not always feasible, but the Security Council was clearly interested in supporting his efforts. Four weeks into his tenure, the council held an unprecedented meeting where member states were represented for the first time in history by their heads of state or heads of government. Because the United Kingdom held the rotating presidency of the council, the British Prime Minister, John Major, presided over the meeting and called it "a turning point in the world and at the United Nations."[18] President Bush, who represented the United States at the meeting, made clear that he saw Saddam's Iraq as a central problem for the world as it moved forward into this bold new territory.[19]

In August 1992, several Western states attempted to blur the lines of the Security Council's mandate even further by inviting the Rapporteur from the UN's Human Rights Council, Max van der Stoel, to brief the council on the situation in Iraq. Privately, van der Stoel had told Boutros Boutros-Ghali that "the human rights situation in Iraq" was "one of the worst since World War II." He pressed to have the Security Council do more.[20] China, India, and several other members of the Security Council saw his intervention as an attempt to integrate the work of the Human Rights Council into the Security Council, and they objected forcefully. As a compromise, van der Stoel was permitted to address the Security Council but in a private capacity rather than as an official representative of the Human Right Council.[21]

Nevertheless, the Security Council was clearly taking human rights much more seriously than it had in the past, and some states candidly discussed their desire to integrate humanitarianism into the international order. Austria, for example, constantly reminded other members of the Security Council that issues surrounding Iraq had implications far beyond Iraqi borders. As the Austrian representative stated in August 1992, "let me make one thing absolutely clear. Austria's aim in participating in this debate is of a principled nature, not confined to matters related merely to Iraq. Humanitarian and human rights questions are important for peace and stability equally in all parts of the world."[22] Indeed, as a former Canadian ambassador to the United Nations has argued, Iraq became a test case and a precedent for addressing post–Cold War humanitarian crises in places like Somalia, the Balkans, and Haiti.[23]

At the end of August 1992, the United States, the United Kingdom, and France expanded their humanitarian-come-military operations in Iraq considerably by launching a no-fly zone over southern Iraq. China and several other members of the Security Council objected, but Washington, London, and Paris did not ask for a resolution. Instead, they justified their actions within a broad interpretation of the original April 1991 resolution that recognized the need to address refugee flows stemming from repression in Iraq.

In these early years of the post–Cold War era, the Security Council valued cooperation, especially among the five permanent members. It is worth noting that in the first two years following the Gulf War, China was the only real dissenter on Security Council actions in Iraq. The Communist regime in China had not gone through the same political transition as the Soviet Union, and it was still uneasy with a Western-dominated, liberal world order. Yet, Beijing had not yet built up the military and economic power that it gained in the twenty-first century, and it was still recovering from the political isolation that followed its violent crackdown on Tiananmen Square protests in 1989. Iraq was not one of China's primary concerns.[24] As such, Beijing simply abstained rather than veto resolutions because it did not want to be isolated further outside the emerging world order. Saddam noted the Chinese stance, quipping, "the whole world is taking orders" from the United States.[25]

Moscow and Paris were enthusiastic supporters of sanctions and weapons inspections. They formed a block with Washington and London sometimes referred to as the "P5 minus China," clearly excluding Beijing from policymaking among the five permanent members of the Security Council.[26] In stark contrast to the positions that they took later in the decade, in 1991 and 1992, France and Russia focused their condemnations on Saddam's regime, blaming it rather than the United States or the United Nations for the continued plight of the Iraqi people and for defying international law. As the French representative on the council argued in March 1992,

> My Government cannot today accept an easing or lifting of sanctions. Nor does it accept the theory that if Iraq complies with 50 percent, 70 percent or 80 percent of the Security Council resolutions the Council must lift the sanctions by a similar proportion [. . .] a resolution is not divisible; it must be implemented in full, not according to the proportion that is to the liking of the Iraqi authorities.[27]

The Russians took an equally hard line against Iraq, often echoing the same arguments made by the United States, the United Kingdom, and Austria. After criticizing Baghdad's human rights violations and repressive policies in March 1992, the Russian representative at the council made clear that for Iraq to "return to the international community as a full-fledged member" it "must immediately and fully implement all of the Council's demands."[28]

The mood at the United Nations and the stakes for its Iraq policy were perhaps best summarized by the Swedish diplomat, Rolf Ekéus, who directed weapons inspections in Iraq. During a private conversation with Boutros-Ghali, he asserted that "it would be risky for the United Nations if it allowed decisions taken under Chapter VII of the Charter to remain unimplemented." He saw "a growing respect for the United Nations" in "many important quarters," and he thought "this derived in part" from the work of the inspectors in Iraq. He claimed their success in Iraq "could be a great asset" for the United Nations, but if they "gave up half-way, there could be a very serious backlash."[29] These were the risks and rewards that put Iraq firmly at the center of international history throughout the rest of the decade.

Seeds of Disorder

Despite these trends toward a more cooperative and liberal post–Cold War international system, the aftermath of the Gulf War also sowed the seeds of discord at the Security Council and even among Western allies. Soon after the war, reports began to emerge that cast a shadow over the coalition's accomplishments in Iraq. The American military had downplayed much of the damage that strategic bombing caused in Iraq. However, when a UN team led by Under-Secretary General Martti Ahtisaari visited the country in March 1991, it was shocked by the level of destruction. As its report claimed, "nothing that we had seen or read had quite prepared us for the particular form of devastation which has now befallen the country." The team argued that the war "wrought near-apocalyptic results upon the economic infrastructure of what had been, until January 1991, a rather highly urbanized and mechanized society."[30] *The New York Times* wrote that the report's findings "seemed to be at odds with allied military officials' insistence that the damage in Iraq was largely confined to military sites and transportation links."[31]

Further complicating matters, when the Security Council met to vote on the ceasefire agreement, coalition troops had already left Iraq. Thus, the only option for enforcing Iraqi compliance with intrusive elements of the agreement was to leave economic sanctions in place. Yet these sanctions hurt the Iraqi population just as much—if not more—as the Iraqi regime. Under-Secretary General Ahtisaari's team recommended an immediate end to the embargo on Iraq to prevent "imminent catastrophe."[32]

Some of the Security Council member-states that strongly supported continuing sanctions on Iraq were also disturbed by Under-Secretary General Ahtisaari's findings and uncomfortable with the suffering that sanctions imposed on Iraqi civilians. Even some Western states that were important coalition members and the core of Bush's new world order were skittish. During the meeting to approve the ceasefire, the French representative at the Security Council cited Ahtisaari's report. Despite France's support for sanctions, the French ambassador argued, "The necessary goal of the restoration of lasting peace in the Gulf should not involve measures that are unnecessarily punitive or vindictive against the Iraqi people. It would be unjust if they were held responsible for the actions of their leader."[33]

For the United States, ending sanctions without full Iraqi compliance was unthinkable. The Bush administration had transformed Iraq into a symbol for the international system that it wanted to build. For members of the Bush administration, like many internationalists before them, UN sanctions were meant to replace aggressive war as the means to solve international disputes. As such it was imperative for the United States to demonstrate that sanctions could compel Iraq to abide by UN resolutions. If the Security Council could not enforce its resolutions, the post–Cold War system would devolve from the rule of law to the might-makes-right calculations that had devastated the twentieth century.

The tension between the United States and some of its international partners only grew worse in the spring and summer of 1991. In May, a team of medical and legal experts from Harvard University visited Iraq and completed a peer-reviewed study. They came to largely the same conclusion as the previous UN team, estimating that "at least 170,000 Iraqi children under five years of age are likely to die from epidemic diseases unless the situation in Iraqi changes dramatically for the better."[34] As the report showed, 9,000 homes were destroyed and over 70,000 people were left homeless. Coalition bombing damaged or destroyed seventeen of Iraq's twenty power plants. Of the seventeen that were damaged, eleven were deemed unrepairable. The report concluded that "most means of modern life support have been destroyed or rendered tenuous."[35] Again, there was a gap between these finding and what the American military had briefed during the conflict. In June 1991, the *Washington Post* reported that "The strategic bombing of Iraq, described in wartime briefings as a campaign against Baghdad's offensive military capabilities, now appears to have been broader in its purposes and selection of targets."[36]

By June 1991, tensions began to mount in the Security Council over how to address the humanitarian situation in Iraq. The United States and the United Kingdom saw Saddam as the major impediment to positive change in Iraq. Following the war, Bush insisted that the only way to proceed in Iraq was without Saddam. As Bush told the German foreign minister Hans Dietrich Genscher on March 1, "With all of the atrocities and the damage he has done to the environment, it will be impossible for us to do anything constructive with Iraq as long as he is there."[37] Baker echoed this sentiment in April when he told his European counterparts that "No one—I repeat no one—should conduct any normal business with an Iraqi government headed by Saddam." And in contrast to statements about using sanctions to force Iraq into compliance, Baker insisted that "We must never normalize relations with an Iraqi government controlled by Saddam. And it means that UN sanctions must not be relaxed so long as Saddam remains in power."[38]

In May, Bush signed a "presidential finding" directing the CIA to "create the conditions" for removing Saddam from power; in other words, to foment a coup or uprising.[39] American plans for the Gulf War—including Bush's classified orders to the military in National Security Directive 54—did not list regime change as a required objective. Nevertheless, the war raised expectations about

Saddam's demise. Some national security staffers at the White House argued that simply expelling Iraqi troops from Kuwait while leaving Iraq's regime and its industrial capacity in place was untenable. Secretary of Defense Dick Cheney later admitted that the US military had Saddam in its crosshairs from the first day of the conflict.[40] Bush himself claimed to have "miscalculated" in his assumption "that Saddam could not survive a humiliating defeat." He lamented that Saddam remained in power following the war and later stated that the United States "could have done more" to weaken his regime and ensure he did not survive.[41] In retrospect, it seems clear that the Bush administration felt uneasy about using the American military to march on Baghdad and overthrow Saddam. However, Bush and his advisers wanted regime change and assumed it would take place through either a precision strike or internal Iraqi actions. These sentiments carried over to the postwar period, with Washington wanting to solve the compliance-versus-humanitarianism dilemma by removing Saddam from power.[42]

Other states at the Security Council were uncomfortable with this approach. The United Nations had never approved regime change and the American demand for it seemed like a heavy-handed shift toward unilateralism. Concerns over the humanitarian situation and violations of Iraqi sovereignty pushed China, India, Yemen, and Cuba to press for easing the sanctions.[43] This divergence at the Security Council began a process that eventually shattered its post–Cold War unity.

Despite these disagreements, the United States was committed to working through the United Nations. To avoid a standoff at the Security Council over Iraq in the summer of 1991, member states needed to find a formula that would address the humanitarian situation in Iraq but would not allow the regime to skirt binding resolutions and rearm. The UN Secretary General had appointed senior UN statesman Prince Sadruddin Aga Khan to be his Executive Delegate for the humanitarian crisis in Iraq. In July, Sadruddin returned from Iraq with a detailed report on the scale of the problem as well as recommendations for addressing it within existing Security Council resolutions. The "impact of the sanctions" he argued "had been, and remains, very substantial on the economy and living conditions of [Iraq's] civilian population."[44] Iraq was only able to generate 25 percent of the electrical power it had prior to the war.[45] Iraqis lacked access to clean water, raw sewage was flowing in the streets of some cities, and outbreaks of typhoid and cholera had already occurred.[46] Additionally, sanctions had led to food shortages and threatened to "cause massive starvation throughout the country."[47]

The biggest impediment to addressing the humanitarian crisis in Iraq was financial. The report surveyed critical sectors of Iraqi society (agriculture, medicine, water, electricity, etc.) to estimate their needs. Even the most minimal, short-term effort required tens of billions of dollars. The only state capable of financing Iraqi reconstruction was Iraq. Money from its oil provided the potential to rebuild the country, but UN sanctions prevented Baghdad from selling its oil or importing the materials it needed.

Sadruddin's report highlighted that existing resolutions permitted exceptions for Iraqi exports and imports to ensure the Iraqi government had "adequate financial resources" to procure "essential civilian needs." This exception could easily include oil exports and imports of critical goods for reconstruction. However, such exceptions required approval by the Sanctions Committee that the Security Council had established to oversee the sanctions.[48]

To make certain that Baghdad used oil revenue to address Iraq's humanitarian crisis rather than for other illicit purposes like rearming, the report argued that existing monitoring mechanisms could easily be expanded "to provide adequate information on the destination and use of the goods in question." All money would flow through banks in the United States and as the report detailed, "commercial transactions relating to the export of oil and the import of the above-mentioned goods and services" would be "sufficiently transparent at the international level to allow adequate controls with respect to their shipment and entry into Iraq."[49] Before leaving Iraq, Sadruddin received Iraqi assurances that it would acquiesce to this plan and its monitoring mechanisms.[50]

This proposal was designed to meet the needs of the Iraqi people while maintaining the security architecture to prevent Iraq from rearming in violation of Security Council resolutions. It also left weapons inspections and more targeted sanctions against the regime in place. In practice, the proposal separated humanitarian issues from international security. The report received enthusiastic support among a majority of the Security Council members. In early August, India lauded its "useful suggestions," claiming they made "evident that the humanitarian objectives we aim at can be achieved with simple and yet effective arrangements for observation and regular reporting."[51] China made clear that it strongly backed the report's "sound recommendations."[52]

The United States was less enthusiastic. Washington was not happy that Saddam had survived the war and it still viewed him as the primary impediment to a cooperative, post–Gulf War Iraq. While the Bush administration could not muster enough support at the United Nations to demand Saddam's removal, it did not want him to reconsolidate his power. By giving Baghdad the ability to sell its oil and provide services for the Iraqi population, this report's recommendations provided Saddam the means to resolidify his rule. Thus, Washington led a minority effort at the Security Council to block the implementation of the report's recommendations.

Instead, Washington backed a separate plan in which the United Nations would manage the sale of Iraqi oil and use the proceeds to deliver food and essential supplies to Iraqis. Like, Sadruddin's proposal, this "oil-for-food" arrangement provided humanitarian relief to the Iraqi population while limiting Iraq's ability to divert money to illicit programs. However, it cut the regime in Baghdad out of the process. States that had backed Sadruddin's proposal also backed this plan, though several of them voiced reservations about American unilateralism in blocking what they perceived to be a better formula. China, India, and several smaller states worried that the American-backed program would not provide enough humanitarian aid and that it excessively encroached on Iraqi sovereignty.[53]

The American-backed oil-for-food program easily passed a Security Council vote, but it immediately ran into a major problem. The resolution assumed that Saddam cared more about the Iraqi people than he did about his own power. That assumption proved incorrect, and he rejected the program even in the face of a humanitarian catastrophe. Despite considerable efforts by senior UN officials, including Secretary General Boutros Boutros-Ghali, Saddam continued to reject the resolution as a violation of Iraqi sovereignty.[54] Boutros-Ghali eventually concluded that "the suffering of the Iraqi people was in [Saddam's] interest because it undermined international support for sanctions against his regime."[55]

With Saddam's refusal to cooperate, the United States and its allies—including, for the time being, France and Russia—blamed him rather than the sanctions for the humanitarian situation. Over the next year, the Security Council's five permanent members along with the majority of the ten nonpermanent members remained unified in blaming Iraq for not cooperating with the oil-for-food program. Yet Saddam had managed to put them in an impossible position of maintaining sanctions that were slowly starving the Iraqi people.

Postwar Challenges for Saddam

While statesmen around the world were struggling to birth a new world order, Saddam's Ba'thists were devising plans to destroy it, and thus to free Baghdad from the yoke of sanctions, inspections, and no-fly zones. Doing so would not be easy. Throughout 1991, Saddam received a barrage of negative reports from the Iraqi Intelligence Service and Ba'th Party organizations around the world. The Ba'thists were clearly losing the political fight to shape international narratives. Saddam's half brother, Barzan al-Tikriti, was both the Iraqi Ambassador and head of the Iraqi Ba'th Party in Switzerland. His regular reports on the state of politics in Europe were not pleasant for Baghdad. Barzan stated that the Western European press depicted Iraq as a retrograde state, and radio broadcast from European capitals were picked up by "hostile" news agencies like *Sawt al-Kuwait* in the Arab World.[56] Moreover, as Barzan reported, Iraqi and Arab intellectuals in Europe were calling for Saddam to surrender power to save Iraq from destruction.[57]

Many of the intellectuals that Barzan mentioned were organizing under the umbrella of the Iraqi National Congress (INC), which was the first attempt to bring disparate groups of Iraqi Arabs, Kurds, Sunnis, Shi'is, Islamists, liberals, monarchists, and communists together. They met in London and plotted strategies for a post-Ba'thist Iraq. As Baghdad was well aware and as became public later, the United States was supporting the INC in the hope that it could be used to oust Saddam from power.[58] The INC's efforts were undermined by the inevitable ideological, religious, and ethnic tensions inherent in bringing such a diverse group together. As one of the INC's liberal-leftist leaders, Kanan Makiya, lamented, the collective could not even agree on the simple statement that "people have rights for no other reason than that they exist as individual human beings."[59] Instead, the assorted factions insisted on pushing their religious and ethnic agendas. Complicating matters further, the INC's leader, Ahmed Chalabi, was corrupt and liable to shift loyalties depending on his audience. Yet, despite all its problems, the formation of a viable American-sponsored opposition in exile was a real threat to the Iraqi regime.

Iraqi dissidents and other opponents of the Ba'thist regime tried to capitalize on Saddam's moment of weakness. Chalabi maintained a global network, and the Iraqi Ba'thists tracked his actions across the Middle East.[60] Elsewhere states hostile to Iraq continued to apply political pressure on the Ba'thist regime. In Indonesia, the Saudi and Egyptian embassies distributed anti-Iraqi literature.[61] Similar publications appeared in African mosques and on Western college campuses.[62] Examples of opposition newspapers and "hostile" stories in the press poured in from around the world. Ba'thists abroad reported on an Iraqi citizen who was recruited by French intelligence while he was living in Algeria. He was then sent to infiltrate the Iraqi population in Yemen, which had a pro-Iraq regime and a seat on the UN Security Council.[63] Reports on similar operations inundated the party secretariat in Baghdad.

Iraqis faced a number of obstacles in responding to these threats. Many of the means that Ba'thist relied on had been disrupted in the aftermath of the Gulf War. For example, while Ba'thists living abroad often received direct guidance and orders from the party secretariat, they also relied heavily on official Iraqi newspapers—especially the party's paper, al-Thawra—for official narratives of day-to-day events. Thus, these newspapers were essential for providing political guidance as well as material to influence local actors. Because of the embargo on Iraq, Baghdad could not send the newspapers to Iraqi embassies to be distributed around the world. The Ba'th Party office responsible for operations outside Iraq recommended using Jordan, which had not joined the coalition against Iraq in the Gulf War and maintained good ties with Baghdad following the conflict, as a waystation from where they could distribute the newspapers globally.[64] Even that plan proved problematic because the Iraqis could not find an international airline willing to cooperate with them in violation of the sanctions regime. Eventually, the secretariat in Baghdad was forced to compile a fact sheet covering the main news and commentary from Iraqi papers and then send it to the embassies through diplomatic channels. While this solution was practical, it left Iraqis outside Iraq with far less guidance and political material than they were accustomed.[65]

The Iraqi embassies and Ba'th Party offices that were responsible for tracking the droves of defectors were in disarray. Some embassies had been closed and many Ba'thists had been deported. The lack of resources and political pressure on Iraqis who continued to work for the regime often created suspicions about who may have been compromised by deep-pocketed local security services. In the United States, for example, the embassy in Washington closed in January 1991, leaving behind a small office containing the section for Iraqi interests. It only had three full-time employees along with some local helpers. The three employees did not like each other, and the head of the office, an Iraqi diplomat named Khalad Jaafar Shwish, was suspected of working with the FBI. Moreover, he was accused of drinking too much wine, not doing enough work, and secretly planning to defect to Canada.[66] The office was unable to track the large number of Iraqi students studying in the United States and many of them were disregarding policies about returning to Iraq following their graduations.[67]

Because informal familial networks permeated the Ba'th Party's rank and file, when one Iraqi defected or came under suspicion, the effects cascaded across Iraq's global operations. Thus, when a Commander (*muqaddam*) in the Iraqi Navy fled with his family to Italy, it torpedoed the career of his brother who had recently been nominated to serve as first secretary in the Iraqi embassy in Malaysia.[68] Another Iraqi ambassador had his career threatened when his son, an Iraqi Ba'thist studying at the American University in Washington, DC, was accused of "attending hostile meetings" as well as "criticizing the party and the ruling leadership." Some also suspected him of "drug use and acquiring debts."[69] As the compounding effects of such problems rippled through Ba'thist networks following the Gulf War, the Iraqis struggled to influence international politics.

Saddam Picks up the Pieces

Despite the difficulties that Iraqi Ba'thists faced, they were able to slowly rebuild and expand their efforts in the two years following the Gulf War. The devastation and suffering that the war wrought—and that continued sanctions exacerbated—provided the foundation of a powerful Iraqi narrative for challenging America's post–Cold War plans. The Iraqis seized on reports from Harvard and the United Nations that detailed the damage in Iraq caused by war and sanctions. As already mentioned, they made a high profile museum out of the al-'Amiriya bunker, where the Americans had killed hundreds of Iraqi civilians during the height of the Gulf War air campaign.

The regime in Baghdad also produced pamphlets and flyers that Ba'thists distributed through both overt and covert networks around the world. Disturbing pictures of agonizing Iraqi children filled their pages. As one smartly produced booklet proclaimed, "Thousands of Iraqi children" will die "as a result of the aggressive bombing, which lasted for 43 days and covered most of the Iraqi cities." The Iraqis painted America and its Western allies as hypocrites: "some of the aggressive countries, while alleging respect of human rights, insist on continuing the sanctions even though the reasons for its imposition are no longer valid." And, "The upholders of human rights bombed al-'Amiriyah shelter, causing the death of hundreds of children, women and elderly."[70]

To take full advantage of this narrative, the regime needed to overhaul its institutions and policies both at home and abroad. By early autumn 1991, several parts of the regime began to regroup and to plan future operations. On September 11, 1991, exactly one year after Bush's new world order speech, the Iraqi Intelligence Service created a plan to ensure the American-led order failed. Iraqi intelligence officers proposed a regime-wide committee for influence operations as well as for recruiting foreign agents and mobilizing foreign supporters.[71] At the same time, the Ba'th Party office responsible for foreign relations began compiling lists of associations, organizations, and people in key states that had "active, important connections with their governments." The Iraqis looked for people with "a clear position against the war and against the unjust economic embargo."[72] The results of these efforts are discussed in later chapters, but here it is important to note that this plan along with the Iraqi Intelligence Service's recommendations formed the basis for new institutions and policies that guided Iraq's international operations through the rest of the 1990s.

Based on the recommendations from the party and the Iraqi Intelligence Service, Saddam's Presidential Diwan formed a new committee in December 1991. It was chaired by Nizar Hamdun, who was one of Saddam's most trusted advisors. Hamdun had helped guide Saddam through his tremulous relationship with Syria and the Syrian Ba'th Party in the 1970s.[73] Then, he became Iraq's first ambassador to Washington when the two countries reestablished diplomatic relations in 1984. Later in the 1990s, Hamdun would return to the United States as the Iraqi Ambassador to the United Nations, where he had the rare ability to criticize Saddam and his regime without suffering any consequences.[74] Hamdun's appointment at the head of the committee to develop the regime's influence campaign signaled its importance to everyone. Senior representatives from several Ba'th Party bureaus, the Ministry of Foreign Affairs, the Iraqi Intelligence Service, the Ministry of Culture and Information, the Ministry of Endowments and Religious Affairs, the Ministry of Health, and the Organization of Friendship, Peace, and Solidarity also sat as permanent members of the committee.[75]

The composition of the committee indicated its scope as well as Iraq's strategy. The Ministry of Health's presence showed the important political leverage that Iraq's humanitarian crisis provided for Baghdad's international operations. The representation of Ministry of Endowments and Religious Affairs highlighted the role of international Islamic networks. The Organization of Friendship, Peace, and Solidarity was a cover organization that worked with foreign nongovernmental organizations. It cooperated closely with Ba'thist organizations outside Iraq, but the regime used it when Baghdad wanted to conceal its role in those relationships.

In March 1992, the Iraqi Ba'th Party bureau responsible for foreign operations developed actionable plans. They formed a committee "to understand and influence [foreign] populations, parties, movements, organizations, and people" in "political, intellectual, and religious" fields. They cooperated closely with the Arab (non-Iraqi) Ba'th Party as well as the Organization of Friendship, Peace, and Solidarity. One of their main tasks was to arrange trips for Iraqis to travel abroad so they could discuss the effects of the Gulf War—or as they called it, the aggression of the thirty states—on Iraqi infrastructure, industry, health, and economy. Working through local actors who had positive views of Iraq, they planned meetings, seminars, and conferences showing "the danger of continuing the criminal siege."[76]

In addition to sending delegations abroad, the party wanted to bring sympathetic visitors to Iraq. Ba'thist organizations outside Iraq coordinated with local embassies to ensure that only people who were likely to reenforce the regime's political narratives were recruited or offered visas to visit Iraq.[77] Such trips were sensitive because the regime wanted to ensure that foreign visitors returned to their home countries parroting the regime's account of Iraq's valiant efforts to overcome an American-imposed humanitarian crisis.

The picture of Iraq that the regime provided to foreign visitors needed to be carefully curated. In March 1992, at the same time as the party was creating a committee to facilitate trips abroad for Iraqi delegations, it created a separate committee to gain the "maximum benefit from the visits of foreign delegations" to Iraq. This committee coordinated with different parts of the regime to ensure that all the appropriate agencies and offices cooperated during these visits. The Ba'thists were particularly keen on gaining full media coverage. They also wanted to give foreign delegations the impression they were meeting people and organizations independent from the regime. Yet, the Ba'th Party committee organized the meetings with supposedly unaligned Iraqis and made certain they echoed the official narratives. The regime went as far as to coordinate with these supposedly independent people and organizations so that none of them repeated what had been said in a previous meeting. They all had their script and they had to stick to it.[78]

Mobilizing Iraqi Society

As these actions demonstrated, an important part of the regime's influence operations abroad depended on mobilizing Iraqi society domestically. Since the regime had come to power in 1968, it had implemented a ruling strategy called "Ba'thification" (tab'ith), in which it attempted to penetrate all aspects of society and to transform them from independent or civil actors into instruments of Ba'thist power. The regime preferred not to destroy civil and social institutions in Iraq. Instead Ba'thists infiltrated them, hollowed them out, and converted them into political tools. Women's organizations, student groups, trade unions, and ethnic associations were all Ba'thized during the 1970s and 1980s. The Ba'th Party then incorporated them into its institutions behind closed doors, but continued to present them as independent representations of Iraqi society in public. Having done so, the regime used these Ba'thized sectors of Iraqi society to show that it not only received acquiescence of the Iraqi population, but active support.[79]

During the 1980s, the regime began to mobilize these elements of Iraqi society in pursuit of international goals. When news of the Iran Contra scandal leaked, showing that the United States sold Israeli weapons to the Iranians, Saddam's worst conspiratorial fears were confirmed.[80] The scandal was one of the few instances during the Iran-Iraq War that fitted Ba'thist narratives about an Imperialist-Zionist-Iranian assault on Iraq. As such, Saddam not only used his normal, diplomatic, party, and intelligence services to capitalize on the scandal, he also mobilized trade unions and agricultural workers in Iraq. They reached out to their foreign counterparts, hoping to gain popular support for Iraq internationally.[81]

Following the Gulf War, Ba'thist political narratives similarly aligned with the real policies and inclinations of other international actors. Again, Saddam mobilized all elements of Iraqi society as part of his international strategy. In an attempt to "provoke humanitarian feelings" toward Iraq in January 1992, an internal regime report claimed that popular organizations and unions "are called more than at any other time in the past" to play an "active role" influencing their counterparts in other countries and through them, to affect "general global opinion and pressure decision makers to lift the criminal siege."[82]

The Union of Iraqi Artists reached out in English to its counterparts across the world. "Dear Artists, Dear Creators of Beauty Everywhere in the World," its appeal began. It then claimed "the economic blockade unjustly imposed on Iraq" kept food and medicine from the Iraqi people and innocent Iraqi children. It also hurt Iraqi artists in the "first cradle of human civilization." The Iraqi artists called for their counterparts across the globe to "raise their voices" against blockading a people which had "built its civilization on the blood of martyrs and is standing up today to build what war inhumanly destroyed."[83]

Other Iraqis took even more proactive steps. For example, the "Iraqi Agricultural Engineers Syndicate" held a conference in December 1991. They invited their foreign counterparts to Iraq ostensibly to discuss industry issues but also to highlight how Iraqi agriculture was suffering under the sanctions regime.[84]

Mobilizing Students and Youth

In the immediate aftermath of the Gulf War, the Ba'thist were perhaps most active in mobilizing Iraqi students and youth. This focus aligned with the regime's ideological commitments as well as the new international networks that the regime had established. Following the conflict, Saddam stressed "operations to recruit [students] to the ranks of the party" and his regime's strategic plans emphasized that a commitment to students and youth was a basis of party activities. The regime felt it could not succeed in the future if it did not win their support.[85]

Considering these ideological commitments, one should not be surprised that even in the aftermath of war, the National Union of Iraqi Students was well-organized, and that it was staffed by some of the most capable regime officials. As mentioned in previous chapters, it had expanded its operations overseas in the 1980s creating over a dozen branches abroad. Following the Gulf War, the student union began regrouping and planning for the long struggle ahead. Recognizing that Iraqi students were defecting in high numbers, the regime began offering special incentives to ensure their loyalty and to incentivize their return to Iraq. The regime exempted them from certain taxes, provided special stipends, and guaranteed them a job upon their return home.[86]

The Iraqi student union produced "work plans" to confront the "evil aggression and blockade."[87] Similar to strategy and policy documents one might find on a Western military staff, the work plans for the National Union of Iraqi Students laid out policy objectives and then the strategies to achieve them.[88] The three policy objectives in a December 1991 plan were: first, to expose the crimes of the NATO, Zionist, American aggression against the Iraqi people; second, to "mobilize the masses inside and outside [of Iraq] against the criminal economic siege and to form a force that can apply pressure for lifting it"; and third, "to form a counter-front to the policy of Zionist, imperial, aggression and work on developing it."[89]

When discussing strategies to achieve those objectives, the plan divided the student union's activities into three categories: headquarters activities, domestic activities, and activities abroad. The section on activities abroad was longer than the other two sections combined, showing the importance of international students for the regime. The three types of activities were connected and mutually reenforcing. The headquarters in Baghdad organized the union and created literature and proclamations based on the activities of the domestic student union. For example, domestic branches of the union organized Iraqi student protests, which provided fodder for the propaganda that the headquarters produced. Then, the Iraqi students abroad used the propaganda to win support internationally.[90] They also recruited delegations to visit Iraq with the hope of demonstrating the disastrous effects of war and sanctions.[91]

The Iraqi students calibrated their approaches depending on the audience. They used less ideological language to target groups with which they had no ties. For example, they sent New Year and holiday cards to all student and youth organizations they could find, as well as to international human rights organizations and the heads of state around the world. The cards appealed for the "unification of world and humanistic conscience" in opposing "the crimes of America and its allies."[92] At times, the cards were quite blunt: "We hope that you, while celebrating the New Year will remember the blockade has caused death to more than 75 thousand people." The student union arranged for one hundred students from every province in Iraq to send cards to the heads of state in countries with a seat on the UN Security Council, and the union had student survivors of al-'Amariya bunker send messages around the world. All this material was produced in Arabic as well as the relevant foreign languages.[93]

Similarly, the Iraqi regime also emphasized youth organizations, and the Ba'th Party secretariat controlled the Federation of Iraqi Youth. Baghdad used this federation in the same way as the Iraqi student union. The Federation of Iraqi Youth reached out to its counterparts around the world as well as to political leaders. They employed similar imagery of suffering Iraqi children and blunt language to shock their fellow youth organizations into action. For example, the federation's holiday cards in December 1991 reminded their foreign counterparts that "while you are celebrating Christmas and New Year . . . there are thousands of people in Iraq who are sick with no medicine and hungry with no food." Then the Iraqi youth requested the recipients of the cards to "please make your voices louder in order to lift the unjust sanctions against Iraq."[94]

The Ba'th Party secretariat in Baghdad tracked the Iraqi student and youth organizations' extensive correspondences with their counterparts and political leaders in the fall and winter of 1991–1992.[95] The secretariat also tracked the results of these operations as reports poured in from all over the world. In Hong Kong, the Asian Students Association wrote to the Security Council's Sanction Committee in the name of 26 student organizations across Asia. It requested that the United Nations "immediately cancel the blockade on Iraq." The association emphasized that war and the continuation of the blockade harmed the children and the people of Iraq.[96] The Asian Student Association also agreed to visit Iraq. They planned a trip for January 1992 as part of a "campaign to relieve sanctions on Iraq." The delegation wanted to report about the situation, as well as take pictures and videos that they could distribute to the Asian Student Association's members.[97]

In London, Iraqi students participated in a protest and march demanding the lifting of the embargo on Iraq.[98] The National Union of Algerian Students held a large solidarity gathering with Iraqi students. They were joined by the Palestinian Ambassador to Algeria, as well as representatives from Arab organizations, the Egyptian National Front, and other Algerian and Arab organizations. In Cuba and Brazil, the Iraqis held protests with local student groups and elicited proclamations from their leaders.[99]

In India, which was serving on the Security Council, the All India Muslim Youth and Students Council claimed to have "organized more than 100 [anti-American] demonstrations, seminars, symposium and public meetings at the US Embassy, the British Embassy, Jama Masjid, Boat Club, Parliament House, and UN office."[100] Iraqi Ba'thists sent newspaper clippings back to Baghdad showing the coverage these activities generated in the Indian press.[101] Across the world, similar events occurred. Messages of solidarity and promises of cooperation poured in from places as disparate as Mauritius, Spain, South Africa, Austria, France, Pakistan, and Morocco.[102]

Iraqi students and youth rooted their arguments in humanitarianism and attempted to provoke global sympathy for the plight of innocent Iraqi children. They published proclamations commemorating the anniversary of the Universal Declaration of Human Rights and linking it to the situation in Iraq.[103] They also sent the reports from Sadruddin Aga Khan and Harvard University to allied student organizations outside Iraq, requesting that "in light of our previous cooperation," that they use these sources "to publish articles in newspapers, and in local and student journals."[104]

Of course, not all Iraqi student outreach was successful. The letters, proclamations, and messages from Iraqi students and their foreign counterparts to political leaders were often ignored or met with strong disapproval. In response to a letter from the Unions and Organizations of Arab Students and Youth in India, the British Foreign and Commonwealth Office wrote that it was "deeply concerned about the difficulties faced by the civilian population in Iraq and have been paying close attention to reports on the humanitarian situation there." However, it continued, "We have said many times that our quarrel is not with the Iraqi people but with Saddam Hussein and his regime." It stated that in response to Sadruddin's proposal, the international community organized "a massive aid programme" for Iraq. The United Kingdom itself had committed 62 million pounds. "Sadly, however, the Iraqi Government has not yet given its agreement to these arrangements."[105]

Foreign student and youth organizations also sometimes rejected Iraqi efforts to influence them. For example, in January 1992, Iraqis planned to send delegates to the 16th World Student Union conference in Cyprus. The Iraqi students had allies within the organization, and they hoped to shape its final proclamation to gain even more support.[106] Yet, at the conference, the Iraqis had their membership frozen. The conference leadership said that the Iraqi union was part of the ruling party and thus part of a nondemocratic regime that was guilty of human rights abuses.[107]

Despite such setbacks, the Iraqis made huge gains on college campuses and in student unions around the world. Student and youth activists did not often impact their states' policies directly. However, their determined and unrelenting campaign to ease sanctions on Iraq played an important role in shaping political narratives in their countries. Student and youth activists represented some of the first real pushback against the emerging world order. Bush sold his Iraq policy as an essential part of a post–Cold War strategy to unite the world under an idealistic, liberal order. Senior statesmen around the world affirmed the idea at the United Nations and Security Council in particular. However, international students and youth provided an initial indicator that the idealism of high politics was rather thin. All was not as well in global politics as it appeared in the halls of power.

Conclusion

The Gulf War and its aftermath demarcated the lines of confrontation between Iraq and the world. For the time being, the world was united against Saddam's regime, but cracks had begun to develop in global opinion over the appropriate way to address Iraq's humanitarian crisis. Saddam knew Iraqi suffering was one of his most important political weapons. He planned to use it to weaken the resolve of his adversaries and break up the coalition that had aligned against him. Doing so required significant institutional reforms at home and the reconsideration of policy and strategy abroad. As the next chapters demonstrate, Iraq carried its strategies to the far ends of the earth. The strategies and policies that this chapter discusses helped lure important states out of the American-led order; then later in the 1990s, Iraq combined narratives of suffering with more traditional economic and geopolitical pressure to great effect.

4

Building Networks in the West, 1991–2

As the Ba'thists recovered from the Gulf War, they schemed to gain allies, find sympathizers, or simply to present their message to foreign audiences in every far-flung corner of the world. In most cases, Iraqi Ba'thists abroad hoped to influence the decisions of foreign policymakers by creating bottom-up political pressure.

The regime's international operations were made simpler by the clear, all-encompassing objective of ending sanctions while acquiescing as little as possible to violations of Iraqi sovereignty such as weapons inspections. No competing policies or mixed goals muddied the waters. The Iraqis knew exactly what they wanted, and they were relentless in their pursuit of it. Of course, they applied different tactics depending on where they worked. In some places local politicians and officials were sympathetic and cooperative. In other places, the Ba'thists faced hostility and repression. Iraqis had options in predominantly Muslim societies that did not exist in the West. In some countries, human rights were important; in other countries they were not. The Iraqis adapted their tactics accordingly.

In North America and Europe, as this chapter discusses, humanitarianism and the suffering of innocent Iraqis provided a wedge that Iraqi Ba'thists could use to sow discord between people and their leaders. As Western populations became aware of dire conditions in Iraq, they began to question more force-fully the logic of international sanctions on the country. The Ba'thists under-stood this dynamic very well and they did everything they could to amplify and accelerate it. In the two years following the Gulf War, they achieved some successes in the West on the operational level. In other words, they were able to attract and partner with people and organizations who shared their desire to end sanctions in Iraq and who were willing to work toward that goal. Often the Ba'thists operated clandestinely to hide their connections with Baghdad. There is little evidence they impacted the foreign policies of Western states in this period, but their successes in attracting partners and building networks became an important foundation for Iraqi actions later in the decade.

Iraq against the World. Samuel Helfont, Oxford University Press. © Oxford University Press 2023.
DOI: 10.1093/oso/9780197530153.003.0005

The United States

In the unipolar post-Cold War world, the biggest prize in any international strategy was the United States. Iraqi operations there were even more important because New York was home to the United Nations. However, America presented a particularly unwelcoming environment for Ba'thists. In an internal memo in December 1991, Iraqi Foreign Minister Tariq Aziz averred that influence operations in the United States were impeded by American narratives of the Gulf War that painted Saddam as a villain and the Ba'thists as an outlaw regime. Moreover, as 1991 turned to 1992, Aziz claimed that the American presidential election campaigns would inflame these narratives and further hinder Iraqi efforts.[1] Aziz played an outsized role in Baghdad's foreign policy throughout Saddam's rule. Perhaps because he was a Christian—his original name was Mikhail Yuhanna before he Arabized it—the regime considered him to have special insight into Western politics. Whether or not that was true, his warning about the difficulties the regime would face in the United States proved right.

Nevertheless, the United States was too important to ignore, and the Iraqis had some important assets in the country that they could exploit. The Iraqi embassy in Washington had closed in January 1991, but Iraq maintained a small interest section that operated out of the Algerian embassy. More importantly, the Iraqi mission at the United Nations in New York remained open. Both provided the Iraqis with important footholds from which they could run operations. The Ba'th Party also relied on some of its most adept members to run its American campaigns. The head of the party in the United States was Sameer al-Nima, who also served as Iraq's Deputy Chief of Mission and sometimes the *chargé d'affaires* at the United Nations. After the fall of the regime in 2003, an Iraqi diplomat claimed that al-Nima was, in fact, an officer in the Iraqi Intelligence Service.[2] When he was not making what the American press described as "defiant" statements at the Security Council, internal Iraqi documents show that he ran networks of Ba'thists throughout the country.[3]

Al-Nima coordinated Ba'thist cells in places like Michigan, New Jersey, and California, which had large Iraqi and Arab diasporas, as well as on college campuses around the country.[4] Ba'th Party operatives and Iraqi students intersected with networks of Iraqi intelligence officers who also spread through Arab diaspora communities across the country. To take just one example, Saubhe Jassim al-Dellemy came from Iraq to the United States to study in the 1980s. The Ba'th Party paid his tuition and living expenses. Once he finished his studies he decided to stay in the United States, but he continued to work for the party and received regular payments from the regime. Following the American invasion of Iraq in 2003, the US Department of Justice captured Iraqi records showing that he also "secretly worked as an agent of the Iraqi Intelligence Service." Operating under the code name, Adam, al-Dellemy recruited agents, attempted to influence American political narratives, and collected information on the American military. He ran a kebab restaurant in Maryland where Iraqi intelligence officers regularly met. It provided a perfect location to collect information on sensitive nearby facilities such as Fort Meade and the National Security Agency. As the Department of Justice alleged, and internal Ba'th Party documents confirm, al-Dellemy also spied on other Iraqis, reporting back on opposition activities and even on his fellow Ba'thists when they were suspected of having met with the FBI.[5]

The number of Iraqi Ba'thists who operated in the United States in the 1990s is difficult to determine, but it was certainly in the dozens and probably in the hundreds. Like al-Dellemy, they not only promoted political narratives that were helpful in ending sanctions, but they also acted as the regime's eyes and ears on the ground. Ba'thists in America sent Baghdad a stream of reports about Iraqi expatriates and on dissidents like Kanan Makiya, who had taken a faculty position at Brandeis University in Massachusetts and emerged as one of the leaders of the Iraqi opposition in exile.[6]

In Baghdad, the party official responsible for American operations was a remarkable woman named Huda Salih Mahdi Ammash. She was the daughter of Salih Mahdi Ammash, who was one of the leaders of the 1968 coup that brought the Ba'thist to power in Iraq. The elder Ammash served as Iraqi Vice President but fell out of favor with Saddam. He was sent into pseudo-exile as an ambassador in the Soviet Union and other European countries. He died in Finland in 1985. Huda Ammash pursued an education in science. After graduating from Baghdad University, she studied microbiology, earning a MA from Texas Christian University, and then a PhD from the University of Missouri in 1983. After returning to Iraq, she became one of the country's leading experts in microbiology. Suspicions about her involvement in Iraqi biological weapons program led the Western press to dub her "Dr. Germ," "Mrs. Anthrax," and "Chemical Sally."[7] She rose through the ranks of the regime, ultimately becoming the only woman to serve on the Regional Command, which was the highest decision making body in the

Iraqi Ba'th Party. In 2003, she was also the only woman included in the famous deck of playing cards that the occupying American forces created to
depict the most wanted members of the former regime.

In Baghdad following the Gulf War, the familiarity with American culture
and politics that she had gained in graduate school proved invaluable. She
became the official responsible for the United States within the Ba'th Party's
bureau for international operations. In a party bureaucracy filled with ba-
nality and inertia, her memos regularly popped with creativity and flare. Her
goal was to "create a popular stream" within American society that had the
"power to pressure decision makers to lift the criminal siege on our beloved
Iraq." To do so, she wanted to recruit—wittingly or unwittingly—well-known
Americans "whose voices" were "heard by the largest number of people."[8]
This became the measure for success for Iraqis in the years immediately following the Gulf War.

Initially, Huda Ammash and the Baghdad-based Ba'thists created plans to
target prominent Americans directly, but little evidence exists to suggest that
these early efforts were successful. The Iraqis in the United States achieved
much better results once they learned to work with and through sympathetic
American groups that had developed organically. However, examining the
regime's early efforts offers valuable insight into Ba'thist tactics and strategy.

The first instinct of Iraqis like Huda Ammash and Sameer al-Nima was
to cooperate with American cultural leaders and prominent politicians who
had opposed the Gulf War or who had shown sympathy for Iraqi suffering
in its aftermath. The Ba'thists did not care about party affiliations or political stance as long as an individual or organization could be useful in lifting
sanctions. Thus, Ba'thists targeted people like Gary Hart, who had run for
president as a Democrat, and Patrick Buchanan who had run as a Republican.
The Ba'thists also pursued cultural figures such as the singer John Denver and
the actress Vanessa Redgrave.[9] Even when these people did not cooperate
willingly, Ba'thists attempted to amplify statements they made that criticized
American policy. Thus, for example, when the American country-folk singer
Kris Kristofferson spoke out against the Gulf War and sanctions, Huda
Ammash noticed he was a "top tier" artist with millions of fans in America
and around the world. Ba'thists in the United States worked "to increase the
prominence of [his] activities toward lifting the siege on Iraq." They also
obtained his address and contact information. Then they arranged for Iraqi
artists and organizations whose connections to the regime were concealed to
reach out to him.[10] Measuring the impact of Iraqi influence on Kristofferson

is difficult. Despite invitations, he does not appear to have visited Iraq. Yet, he continued to speak out against American policy toward Iraq and later even wrote a song titled, "The Circle," about Layla al-Attar, a prominent Iraqi artist who was killed in an American missile strike in 1993.[11]

Some Iraqi operations attempted to compromise American politicians and even members of Congress. For example, Sameer al-Nima ran an operation in which he intercepted UN mail by what he termed "special means." The Iraqis were primarily interested in learning who supported them and who opposed them. In early 1992, Huda Ammash noticed that a number of people who sent messages protesting sanctions to the head of the Security Council's Sanctions Committee quoted US Representative Henry B. Gonzalez of Texas. After doing some research, she realized that Gonzalez had been a vocal critic of the Gulf War and that he had introduced legislation in the House of Representatives to end sanctions. Gonzalez was using the issue to gain national attention and possibly to launch a presidential run. Ammash also noticed that he was from Texas which had oil companies connected to Iraq. In one of her typically bold plans, she suggested finding a way to use these connections to influence him, most likely by having the oil companies push pro-Iraq policies. At minimum, she thought Iraqis could benefit from his election campaign and the media attention surrounding it.[12]

Gonzalez was a Democrat and his objection to sanctions ended when Bush, who was a Republican, lost the election later in 1992. As such, the Iraqi efforts to court Gonzalez ended abruptly. Nevertheless, Ammash's tactic of combining influence operations, oil money, and political interests to target policymakers in key positions was a precursor to the work she performed later in the decade once Iraq agreed to a modified version of the UN's oil-for-food program.

Working through Local Organizations

The Ba'thist were much more successful when they worked through nongovernmental organizations (NGOs) and humanitarian groups that had developed organically in the United States to fight sanctions. Scholars of strategy have shown that when states attempt to impose strategies on complex social environments they often fail. By contrasts, strategies that move within existing political currents have been much more successful.[13] The history of Iraqi influence operations support this theory. When Ba'thists created plans in Baghdad, for example to recruit celebrities or politicians, they produced few results. There is little evidence that Baghdad's attempt to directly influence people like Patrick Buchanan, John Denver, Kris Kristofferson, or Henry Gonzalez helped to spread Ba'thist political narratives any more than if the Iraqis had taken no action at all. Yet, when indigenous American groups formed on their own, they were much more deeply imbedded in American society and the Ba'thists were able to either cooperate with them or to amplify their work to great effect. Many of these NGOs were small and on the surface they might seem insignificant. Yet, like small embers, if they were introduced into the right environment, and stoked properly, they spread quickly.

For example, one of the many NGOs that sprang up in the United States to address the humanitarian situation in Iraq following the Gulf War was the American-Iraqi Friendship Federation. A group of prominent Iraqi-Americans founded it in 1991 to support their families and friends, who were suffering horribly under the twin plight of sanctions and a repressive regime. The Federation was incorporated at the home of one of its founders, Dr. Ali Hossaini, in Virginia.[14] Hossaini's background was typical of the Federation's leadership. He was born in Basra in 1928, and then immigrated to the United States in the early 1950s. He became a leading medical doctor and a founding member of the Virginia Arab American Democratic Caucus as well as a founding board member of the Islamic Center of Virginia. The Arab American Institute later awarded him its "Lifetime Achievement Award."[15] Iraqis of similar stature joined chapters of the organization as they opened in diaspora communities around the country. Doctors, businessmen, and academics all joined. Several of them had significant means at their disposal. For example, members of the Sinaam family, which owned many of the grocery stores in the Detroit area and had close ties to Congress, became enthusiastic members.[16]

The founding charter of the American-Iraqi Friendship Federation made clear that its purpose was to "foster understanding between the people of the United States and the people of Iraq." Considering the dire humanitarian situation in Iraq, it focused much of its efforts on providing aid to people in Iraq and working to lift the UN sanctions. To those ends, it collected donations and medicine to send to Iraq. It also attempted "to obtain and provide information to the Congress of the United States and the general public."[17] Its bylaws stated explicitly that it would "not align itself with any political party in Iraq and will not permit the society to be politically exploited by any individual or group."[18]

Despite these non-political commitments, by the beginning of 1992 the Ba'thists noticed that the federation had successfully collected and delivered large quantities of medicine to Iraq. It had also held an art exhibition on Iraqi children suffering under sanctions, sent letters to political leaders, and organized a charity night to collect donations for Iraqis. Ba'thists in the United States reported that the federation was apolitical. However, it did seek to lift sanctions on Iraq, and that was good enough. Abd al-Haqq Isma'il al-Khaldi, who worked at the Iraqi Interest Section in Washington DC and ran Ba'th Party operations in the area, ordered Ba'thists "to join [the American-Iraqi Friendship Federation] and to work within its ranks to ensure that it continues to hold its positions, and to seek to guide it and [to have it continue to work] in matters that serve our goals."[19]

On February 23, Ba'thists helped the Federation hold a fundraiser for Iraqi children at the George Washington University. The event featured an art exhibit about Iraq and several speakers, including one from the Harvard team that had visited the country in the wake of the Gulf War. The Ba'thists reported that some of the attendees were "highly influential." Among them was the attorney-activist Faye Williams, who was famously detained with 200 other women in the Arabian Sea as they attempted to sail to Iraq to disrupt the Gulf War. Later, in 1995, she helped organized the Million Man March in Washington.[20]

In an attempt to conceal the Iraqi regime's cooperation with the American-Iraqi Friendship Federation, the Ba'thists worked through their Organization of Friendship, Peace, and Solidarity, which they presented as a nongovernmental organization. In March 1992, representatives from the Organization of Friendship, Peace, and Solidarity met with the leadership of the American-Iraqi Friendship Federation and the two sides signed an agreement to cooperate for the next three years. The agreement included a commitment to carry out "activities with the goal of continuously informing the media and American public opinion" about the situation in Iraq. The two sides also agreed "to exchange publications and pictures," hold a conference, and to produce exhibits "of photographs and children's drawings in a number of American states as well as other annual activities that match American society."[21] For the Ba'thists, cooperation with the Federation provided grassroots support for their influence operations. It gave them access to money as well as prominent politicians, businessmen, and activists. The Ba'thists were also able to ensure the Federation's work aligned with Baghdad's strategy. For the Iraqi-Americans in the Federation, cooperation with the Ba'thists was necessary to carry out their humanitarian work. Delivering medicine, funneling money to sick Iraqi children, and obtaining material necessary to raise awareness about the humanitarian situation all required access to Iraq and the acquiescence of the regime.

While the Ba'thists signed an agreement with the American-Iraqi Friendship Federation, they also employed other, less official models of cooperation with other groups. At times they found it useful to keep their relationships with NGOs informal and easily denied by all sides. For example, the Committee to Save Iraqi Children was formed in the wake of the Gulf War. The Ba'thists played no part in creating this organization, but the Committee to Save the Iraqi Children produced literature remarkably similar to the propaganda emanating from Baghdad. The Committee's pamphlets included disturbing pictures of suffering Iraqi children and underscored the dire humanitarian situation in Iraq. To highlight the plight of Iraqi children, the Committee also brought sick Iraqi children to the United States for medical treatment and published op-eds in American newspapers. The Committee was affiliated with the Washington DC-based Schiller Institute, through which it reached wider groups of antiglobalization activists including a robust network of doctors, religious leaders, and academics. In calling for the end of sanctions on humanitarian ground, the Committee was essentially doing Iraq's work for it. As an independent organization, it was doing so without the taint that accompanied operations clearly originating in Baghdad.

As al-Nima reported back to Baghdad, Ba'thists in the United States facilitated and amplified the Committee's work. They also channeled it toward strategic ends. The Ba'thists worked through one of the Committee's founders, the German-American writer Muriel Mirak-Weissbach. Whether Mirak-Weissbach knew she was working with Ba'thists or whether the Iraqis were working undercover remains unclear. In one meeting, the two sides discussed "organizing a campaign for pressuring the UN Sanctions Committee to isolate the American and British position." They hoped to accomplish this by "sending continuous messages directly to members of the [Sanction] Committee that are accompanied by studies and newspaper articles." They also agreed that the Committee to Save Iraqi Children would relay its messages to the UN Security Council through "its branches in Germany and through the government of Germany, as well as through other states in Europe and their governments." Both sides agreed to continue their contacts and to evaluate the results of their efforts as they proceeded.[22]

By cooperating with organizations such as the Committee to Save the Children of Iraq, the Ba'thists not only gained a partner in producing propaganda, they also gained channels through which to influence other governments. Moreover, they were able to recruit—sometimes unwittingly—the type of prominent Americans that Huda Ammash targeted. For example, the former heavyweight boxing champion, Muhammad Ali, chaired the Committee to Save the Children of Iraq's chapter in Richmond Virginia and he held charity dinners for the organization.[23] There is no evidence to suggest that Ali knew that Ba'thists were supporting the Committee or facilitating its work. Similarly, there is no reason to believe that he had any sympathies for Saddam or the Ba'thist regime. Nevertheless, his mission to lift sanctions overlapped with Baghdad's policy and any work he did to help the Iraqi children necessarily supported the Iraqi regime.

Ba'thists in the United States integrated into and amplified numerous other organizations and events designed to highlight the plight of Iraqis and to pressure policymakers to end sanctions. Ramsey Clark served as the US Attorney General during the Johnson administration in the late 1960s, and then became a prominent political activist. He was a vocal opponent of the Gulf War and of the continued sanctions after it. In the early 1990s, he became an important ally of the Iraqi regime in the United States. On February 29, 1992, Ba'thists in the United States supported a high-profile mock war crimes trial that he held at the Martin Luther King School in Manhattan. In a public spectacle, Clark tried and found guilty President Bush, Vice President Quayle, Secretary of Defense Cheney, General Powell, and General Schwarzkopf. According to Iraqi estimates, over 1,500 people attended, including 80 reporters. The Ba'thists were not pleased with the muted reaction the event received in the American press, but they felt it resonated with humanitarian organizations and received wide coverage in the European press.[24]

Throughout the spring and summer of 1992, Iraqi Ba'thists in the United States continued to rebuild their networks and launch ever-expanding operations. In July, they reconstituted the National Student Union of Iraqis in America. It was controlled by Abd al-Haqq Isma'il al-Khaldi, the Ba'thist leader who worked at the Iraqi Interest Section in Washington.[25] Iraqi students could then begin to organize on campuses. In New York and Washington, Iraqi delegations held parties and gatherings that attracted increasing numbers of sympathetic diplomats and activists. The Ba'thists used their connections with NGOs in the United States to bring disparate people and organizations together to support lifting sanctions. By August 1992, for example, the Ba'thists had helped build the "National Network to Lift Economic Sanctions against Iraq." A small sampling of the network's wide ranging membership, included the American Friends Service Committee, the Council for the National Interest, the Washington Peace Center, the American-Arab Anti-discrimination Committee, the Jewish Peace Fellowship, Unitarian-Universalists Association, numerous groups supporting the Palestinian cause, feminist organizations, and liberal Christian movements.[26] Like other advocates of lifting sanctions, many of these organizations had little sympathy for Saddam or his regime, but in practice, their humanitarian concerns overlapped perfectly with Baghdad's desire to escape UN dictates.

At the strategic level, Iraqi attempts to influence American policy in 1991 and 1992 largely failed. As Tariq Aziz had predicted, the political landscape was too hostile to Saddam and his regime. Yet, by amplifying the work of sympathetic organizations in the United States, the Ba'thists built important networks and ever so subtly began to shift public discourse about Iraq. The resulting cracks in support for what had been an extremely popular policy in the immediate aftermath of the Gulf War laid the groundwork for future operations in the country.

Influencing the United Nations

Because the United Nations was located in New York, Ba'thist operations in the United States were often directed at influencing it as well as American policymakers. At first, Ba'thists in the United States targeted UN officials indirectly by planting stories in the press, publishing proclamations, and highlighting scientific studies about the humanitarian situation in Iraq. Yet, by the spring of 1992, Sameer al-Nima reported to Huda Ammash that these efforts were "not achieving the direct benefits that are desired."[27] Members of the Sanctions Committee did not have time to follow the news closely and Iraqi attempts to follow-up with them often showed that they were unaware of reports in the press supporting Iraq's position. That situation was intolerable. As al-Nima wrote in April 1992, "the unfortunate truth is that the work of the Sanctions Committee will continue for a long period from now. We need to apply continuous pressure [. . .] and we cannot be satisfied with media efforts only."[28]

He suggested that Ba'thists ensure sympathetic organizations send their materials directly to members of the Sanctions Committee in addition to presenting them in the media. This shift to a more direct approach in targeting the Sanctions Committee was a fantastic example of how the regime learned and adapted. The crude stereotype of an inflexible totalitarian regime was simply not accurate. Ba'thist officials like al-Nima were free to point out when a tactic or strategy did not work and the regime supported their efforts to reassess and adapt.

As mentioned above, al-Nima had developed a scheme to intercept UN mail by what he termed "special means" (shakl khas). It is unclear what these means were, but the regime treated the information they produced as extremely sensitive. The Iraqis used it to identify people and organizations that, in their words, were playing a "voluntary role" in combating "the criminal embargo."[29] Thus, for example, Ba'thists in New York collected, and Huda Ammash's staff in Baghdad analyzed messages that were sent to the Austrian diplomat, Peter Feller, who chaired the Sanctions Committee. In the United States, letters came from organizations such as the Green Party in California, the New York Branch of the Young Women's Christian Association, the Celtic Network (which included twelve different organizations), a study group from Harvard, the Fellowship for Reconciliation, and the Woman's Professional Network, among others.[30]

Letters protesting sanctions also poured in from organizations in Europe, Asia, and Africa. The Iraqis tracked the name of each and their country of origin. In Norway alone, sixty-eight separate organizations sent letters of protest to the committee. Others came from the Lawyers Union in Japan, the Committee for Opposing the Gulf War at Leuven University in Belgium, the German Kultur des Friedens, a Malaysian antinuclear weapons organization, the Islamic Party of Somalia, the Australian Peace Committee, and so forth.[31]

The regime used these messages to plant stories in the press. The Ba'thists also collected the addresses and contact information of the organizations sending these messages. They then attempted to "create a link with them" through Ba'th Party organizations in their countries, "or even better [to work] through popular and professional channels" that disguised the role of the regime.[32] Such campaigns helped the Ba'thists to develop important relationships and connections. The resulting networks created a foundation for Iraqi influence operations throughout the rest of the 1990s.

Western Europe

In 1991 and 1992, Baghdad approached political operations in Europe much the same way as it approached them in North America, and it achieved the same type of results. Ba'thists enjoyed important successes in identifying and linking people and groups that shared the regime's goals. These actions laid the foundation for future operations that would affect the foreign policies of European states later in the decade, but that type of strategic impact was generally absent in the years immediately following the Gulf War.

Like in the United States, many European countries had enthusiastically supported the Gulf War and saw Saddam as the head of a brutal, totalitarian regime that was responsible for serial human rights abuses. Yet, in some ways, Europe provided a more welcoming target for influence operations than the United States. Sympathy for Iraqi suffering was generally higher among European populations, and some European states had long, friendly histories with Baghdad prior to the Gulf Crisis.

France was a particularly enticing target. In December 1991, Iraq's Foreign Minister, Tariq Aziz had warned about the difficulties of influencing the United States. At the same time, he argued that in France, "perhaps the conditions for influence operations are more favorable." Prior to the Gulf War, France had supported Iraq, selling it arms and even aiding its nuclear project despite clear indications that the Ba'thists would militarize it. France had a veto at the Security Council, and while it was highly critical of the Iraqi regime following the war, its statements at the council were much more sympathetic to Iraqi suffering than its Western counterparts. The French representative on the council had argued that "it would be unjust if [the Iraqi people] were held responsible for the actions of their leader."[33] Moreover, unlike some of its fellow council members, France avoided the heady language of world order and a new international system when discussing the Gulf War. Instead, its representative prioritized instituting an effective ceasefire and "re-establishing regional security."[34] As such, French policy on Iraq was less tied to broader interests and it could be much more flexible.

Aziz suggested that Abd al-Razzaq al-Hashami lead the effort to influence France. Al-Hashami was a graduate of Boston University and in 1974, he participated in a delegation to France to negotiate the purchase of nuclear reactors. He had served as a diplomat and a senior advisor to Saddam. He understood Western, and particularly French politics well.[35] Similar to their efforts in the United States, the Ba'thists hoped to work through French nongovernmental organizations, such as Mothers against War and the local chapter of Green Peace.[36] In a sign of the potential the Ba'thists thought existed in France, Iraqi Vice President Taha Yassin Ramadan created a special committee in 1992 specifically for "political and media" work in "mobilizing the masses" of France. It included senior representatives from all the Iraqi and Arab bureaus of the Ba'th Party that dealt with foreign affairs.[37] As later chapters detail, the instincts of senior Ba'thists about France proved prescient. Over the course of the 1990s, Paris moved steadily from Washington's camp to holding a position much more favorable to Baghdad.

Across the English Channel, the United Kingdom was another important target for Iraqi influence operations. Like the United States and France, the United Kingdom had a veto at the Security Council. That in itself made British politics important. The United Kingdom was also home to the largest and most influential Iraqi diaspora community in the Western world. British universities were often the first choice for Iraqi students, and London was the home of the main Iraqi opposition groups in exile.

As they did elsewhere, Ba'thists in the United Kingdom organized marches, distributed political posters, and published pamphlets. They also allied with sympathetic local actors who would support their narrative about international sanctions and suffering Iraqi children.[38] Like other Western governments attempting to fight back against the activities of Ba'thists, London often found itself facing a dilemma. If it intervened to stop Iraqi activities, especially among students and youth, the British appeared callous and could push independent students further into Iraqi arms. If the British government did not intervene, the Iraqis would continue to organize and gain support. For example, an Iraqi student attempted to attend a meeting for World Youth Council, which was held in London in December 1991. However, the British refused to provide him a visa. Baghdad sent other Iraqi students who were already in the United Kingdom to attend instead. The surrogate Iraqis rallied the support of the other attendees around the fact that Britain had blocked Iraq's official delegation. The meeting expressed regret that the British had refused to allow an Iraqi student to attend. All the members of the conference except a representative from Denmark expressed sympathy with Iraq and the Iraqi people in the face of the embargo.[39] For the British government, there was no good solution to this problem. They clearly understood the student delegate was acting as an agent of the Iraqi regime, and had they allowed him to attend, he would have attempted to organize actions against the British government. However, refusing him a visa only aided his mission.

The Ba'thists in the United Kingdom also carried out more traditional espionage. They forwarded Baghdad information about British operations in Northern Iraq. They also closely tracked the Iraqi opposition and even nonpolitical organization such as the Khu'i Foundation, which the regime in Baghdad considered hostile because it insisted on remaining apolitical instead of supporting Saddam.[40]

The existence of a large Iraqi population in the United Kingdom consumed much of the time of Ba'thists in the country. Thus, while they did carry out influence operations, their reports from London show that Ba'thists were equally concerned with American and British operations targeting Iraqis in the country. The United States openly courted members of the Iraqi opposition in London and one Ba'thist report lamented that British intelligence was "exploiting the living conditions and material needs" of Iraqis. The British offered them work, forgiveness of their student loans, and political asylum. As of June 15, 1992, one Ba'thist report read, "British intelligence has effectively carried out influence operations on all Iraqi students currently in Britain."[41] As a result, another report claimed, "a large percentage" of them had no desire to return to Iraq.[42]

As the 1990s continued, Iraqi groups in the United Kingdom increasingly schemed to overthrow the regime in Baghdad. They began working closely with American and British officials and they went on to play important roles in the run-up to the 2003 war as well as in post-2003 Iraq. In the years following the Gulf War, the fight over the loyalty of these Iraqis in Britain and the fate of the opposition groups based there became a center of gravity in the global struggle between Washington and Baghdad.

Austria was also an important state for Ba'thist operations. It served on the Security Council in the early 1990s. Although it was not a permanent member and it did not have a veto, it chaired the Sanctions Committee, which gave it an important voice on Iraqi policy. Vienna had been a crossroad between East and West during the Cold War and it remained a hub of activity for Ba'thists and the Iraqi Intelligence Service even prior to the Gulf Crisis.[43] Thus, like the United Kingdom and France, Austria became a prime target for Iraqi operations.

Ba'thists in Austria organized conferences and festivals that showcased the damage that international sanctions inflicted on Iraq. As elsewhere, sometimes Iraqi Ba'thists directly organized these events.[44] Other times they worked with and through local groups. One such festival was organized by the Arab Committee of Austria. Some of the official slogans of the festival were, "Lift the economic blockade on the children of Iraq" and "How long will the children of Iraq be without milk?"[45] These events attracted a wide range of political activists and Austrian academics. Faculty from the political science department at the University of Vienna were frequent attendees.

Ba'thists also courted local politicians. For example, in a meeting with Marijana Grandits, who was a member of the Austrian parliament and the spokeswoman for the Austrian Green Party's committee on foreign relations, they arranged the visit of an Iraqi Ba'th Party delegation from Baghdad.[46] The fact that Grandits was a member of the Green Party was no coincidence. The Green movement across Europe and North America was filling the void in left wing politics created by the demise of Marxist groups in the post–Cold War world. As environmentalism became politicized, the Green movement took what it understood as firm antiimperialist positions. Thus, they became some of the most vocal critics of American and Western foreign policy. As one Danish environmental activists explained to the Ba'thists in their correspondences, "We are ourselves in the process of realizing the interconnectedness of environmental conservation with social, political and cultural aspects." He noted his movement's "distress" with "the immoral conduct of the American armed forces," and claimed, "we are deeply concerned with the misinformation of the public by the American media giants."[47] As the Green movement continued to gain more support in the 1990s, it offered the Iraqis an opening into mainstream European politics.

Conclusion

Western Europe and North America were the liberal core around which post-Cold War politics was supposed to be built. Their institutions and political values were supposed to radiate out to the rest of the world until the entire globe fell under the umbrella of the new world order. Yet, within Western politics, humanitarian impulses and the ability to organize freely opened the door for dissent. As the Iraqi Ba'thists learned to navigate this political landscape, they built important networks and amplified voices that were beneficial to Baghdad. This process was subtle at first, but by the end of the decade, it would become impossible to ignore.

5

Toward Influencing Policy in non-Western World, 1991–2

Similar to their operations in the West, Ba'thists spent the first few years regrouping in the non-Western world. They searched for sympathetic people and organizations with whom they could partner, and they began to launch some preliminary operations. In non-Western states, however, Iraqi Ba'thists received much more support than they did in the West. While the ruling regimes in these states may not have supported Saddam, his appeal for solidarity, and his opposition to Western hegemony tapped into existing sentiments that were popular among non-Western and post-colonial populations. For all his faults in the eyes of these populations, Saddam was one of the only leaders to stand up for popular anti-imperialist and anti-Zionist principles. Saddam had launched missiles at Israel and remained uncompromising in the face of an overwhelming, American-led onslaught. His willingness to stand steadfast and defend his principles earned him a grudging respect among peoples who had long hoped that their own leaders would resist what they saw as neo-imperialism emanating from places like Washington, New York, and London.

For these reasons, important people and organizations in many non-Western states were poised to support policies that aligned with Iraqi interests and that resisted an American-dominated new world order. It is not surprising, therefore, that as early as 1992, the political positions of some important non-Western states began to shift. Ba'thists recognized that potential. They designed their operations to further exacerbate emerging tensions and to ensure that Iraq, as a political issue, was at the center of those debates.

Russia

One of Iraq's most important Iraqi targets in the non-Western world was Russia. The end of the Cold War, and then Moscow's support for the Gulf

Iraq against the World. Samuel Helfont, Oxford University Press. © Oxford University Press 2023.
DOI: 10.1093/oso/9780197530153.003.0006

War, had left Iraqi Ba'thists in Russia distraught. The Soviet Union had balanced American power and was an important Iraqi ally until the end of the Cold War. Then Moscow sided with Bush in the Gulf War and recognized the war's role in birthing a new, post–Cold War system of international relations. As Russia emerged from the Soviet Union in 1991, it initially embraced American attempts to use policies toward Iraq to forge the new world order. As the Soviet representative at the United Nations stated during discussions about the Gulf War's ceasefire resolution, the Security Council's approach toward Iraq demonstrated "that a considerable path has been travelled between the Cold War and the new system of international relations." And, he made clear that he believed the way that the Council handled the conflict demonstrated "the soundness of the new thinking."[1]

The Iraqi Ambassador in Moscow lamented that following the Gulf War, the Soviets and then the Russians took a position on the Security Council that was exactly "in accordance with the American view." He claimed "political decisions in Russia" were "under American influence and the Jewish-Zionist Lobby."[2] In early 1992, Iraqi diplomats and Ba'thists in Russia pressed their case, but their normal tactics fell flat. They attempted to arrange numerous meetings and phone calls with the Russian Foreign Minister and the Minister of External Economic Relations. The Iraqis followed phone calls with written notes, but to no avail. They also reached out to the Russian-Iraqi Cooperation Committee, which had been one of the main bodies for bilateral ties, but while members of the committee met with their Iraqi counterparts, the outcome was not satisfying. "Despite many promises," the Iraqis reported back to Baghdad, the Russian side could not produce any results. Instead, the Russians deflected Iraqi attempts to pin them down by claiming that "their positions were unsettled" and that they were not responsible for determining the Russian position at the Security Council.[3]

At the end of January 1992, the Iraqis urgently tried to arrange a visit for a delegation from the Iraqi parliament. The Iraqis said they could come at any time that was suitable to the Russians, but the Russian parliamentarians deflected, claiming that they were very busy. At the end of May, the Russians excused themselves through diplomatic channels from receiving the Iraqi Foreign Minister during a visit to Moscow. In August, the Iraqi parliament invited a delegation from the Russian parliament to visit Baghdad and to "discover the truth directly, and to refute the foreign and American claims" but the Russian parliament "did not respond to any invitation."[4]

Nevertheless, some Ba'thists sensed that not everyone in the Russian government was fully behind Moscow's policies in Iraq.[5] Later in 1992, the Iraqis adopted a new, indirect approach to tease out supporters. The Iraqi ambassador in Moscow reported that after being stonewalled by Russian President Boris Yeltsin's administration, "we were forced to extend an invitation to the opposition in parliament [to visit Iraq]." Unlike the Russian leadership, the opposition "responded with enthusiasm" and "when the delegation returned [to Russia] it undertook numerous activities inside and outside of parliament." According to the Iraqi ambassador, the Russian opposition "explained the truth of the situation in Iraq, it defended the Iraqi view, and it demanded that the Russian government change its position on Iraq and work towards lifting the economic blockade." The Iraqi ambassador continued, "wide circles of the Russian people are beginning to understand the just Iraqi position, and to feel that the Russian position toward Iraq is an error." Russian policies toward Iraq, he argued, "especially intensify the nationalist opposition in its activities inside parliament and the people's conferences, in the media, and in demonstrations."[6]

Whether Iraqi influence operations impacted national policies, and therefore the post–Cold War order, is an important question in this book. Yet, given the nature of influence operations the question is almost impossible to answer definitively. Iraqi actions in Russia offer an opportunity to make a case for how and why the Iraqis did have an effect. Iraqi records suggest the Ba'thists helped transform Moscow's policy on Iraq into a wedge issue that isolated the ruling coalition. Communists and hardline nationalists in Russia were inclined to push back against Moscow's pro-Western, post–Cold War foreign policy even without Ba'thist prodding, but Iraqi machinations and Baghdad's ability to create opportunities spurred these Russians to turn those inclinations into actions. In doing so, the Ba'thists ensured that Iraq would become an important issue in Russian politics for years to come. By the end of 1992, Iraqi records assert that pressure from the opposition forced the Russian government to change its approach. Yeltsin's government realized that continuing to spurn Iraq would cost it political support at home. Instead of ignoring or deflecting Iraqi outreach, the Russian Foreign Ministry eventually decided to send a senior delegation to Baghdad for political discussions with the Iraqi Foreign Ministry. The Iraqi ambassador in Moscow thought this marked a positive shift in the Russian approach toward Iraq.[7]

As later chapters demonstrate, the Iraqi ambassador was correct. The end of 1992 marked the beginning of a process in which the gap between Russian and American approaches toward Iraq widened and ultimately became unreconcilable. Throughout the remainder of the 1990s, Iraq was an open wound in the relationship between Moscow and Washington, driving the two sides apart and spoiling the cooperative norms that had characterized their relationship at the UN Security Council during the immediate aftermath of the Cold War.

The breakdown in Russian-American relations was one of the main causes for a breakdown in a cooperative, rules-based, post–Cold War system. There were, of course, many intervening reasons for this rift that had nothing to do with Ba'thist actions. Yet, Iraq's role in the breakdown of the Russian-American relationship has often been overlooked. The literature on the souring of the once hopeful relationship between Moscow and Washington in the 1990s normally points to disputes in the Balkans and later NATO expansion as the main causes. Iraq is at best a sideshow or collateral damage.

These other events were clearly important. The Russians had long seen themselves as protectors of the Serbs. One only needs to consider the origins of World War I to see how deep and important those ties were. When NATO intervened in the Balkans against the Serbs and without a UN resolution, the Russians saw American and Western actions as a violation of post-Cold War norms in which military action was rooted in Security Council approvals. Moreover, the Russians believed that in exchange for their acquiescence on German unification, George H. W. Bush had promised them that NATO would not expand further into Eastern Europe.[8] The Russians claimed NATO's eventual expansion and its operations in the Balkans were a direct threat to their sphere of influence and these factors stunted the cooperative norms that were developing between Moscow and Washington in the post–Cold War period.

Nevertheless, on closer examination, Iraq played as important, and in some ways an even more important role as these other issues in spoiling the bilateral relationship. As Iraqi records demonstrate, the Ba'thists turned the tide in Moscow in 1992. That was prior to the Balkan crisis or NATO expansion. Thus, these later issues could not have caused animosity about the former. Moreover, as later chapters will discuss, American CIA reports from the 1993 Balkan conflict asserted that disagreements about Iraq were affecting Russian outlook toward American policy in the Balkans, not the other way around. As such, one could argue that because of Iraq, the fallout from the Balkan crisis was more toxic than it would have otherwise been. Finally, when diplomatic ties broke down later in the decade, and Russia recalled its ambassador to Washington, it did so over disagreements about Iraq, not the Balkans or NATO expansion. As such, already in 1992, one can see the beginnings of the long-term consequences that Iraqi actions had on the post–Cold War international system. Iraq certainly was not the sole cause of the Russian-American rupture, but its actions ensured that Moscow's disagreements with Washington occurred earlier and were more intense than they otherwise would have been. In that sense, Iraq undoubtably contributed as much if not more than these other oft-cited issues to the declining relationship.

The Middle East and the Muslim World

Similar to the situation in Russia, the Ba'thists found willing partners and an inviting political landscape in much of the Middle East and the Muslim world, even in the immediate aftermath of the Gulf War. No majority Muslim state had a permanent seat on the UN Security Council and there are no great powers in the Middle East. Thus, support for Iraq in the Islamic world was only capable of challenging the unity of the Security Council indirectly. However, for the international system to isolate Iraq, Middle Eastern states had to cooperate with Security Council dictates. Moreover, Western powers like the United States, the United Kingdom, and France closely watched popular opinion in the Middle East. Muslim and Arab support was an important marker of legitimacy for international policies during the Gulf War and the Western powers did not want to lose that.

Yet Baghdad was perhaps most successful finding allies in the Muslim world. Saddam's ability to defy the United States, his championing of Arabism and Islam, and his anti-Zionism earned him widespread respect, especially in the Middle East where some believed the United States had attacked Iraq to defend Israel. The Popular Front for the Liberation of Palestine discussed "the interrelationship (al-'alaqat al-mutabadilah) between the Gulf Crisis and the Intifada," which Palestinians waged against Israel in the late 1980s and early 1990s. For many in the Middle East, both conflicts were fought against the connected phenomena of neo-imperialism and Zionism. This was an important part of Saddam's master narrative, and it was being developed and promoted by the Palestinians themselves.[9]

Such support did not mean that the Ba'thists faced no opposition in the Muslim world. Iraqis working for the regime throughout the Islamic world sent Baghdad a steady stream of reports on the obstacles they faced. Hostile newspapers were distributed in mosques among the Muslim minority in Kenya. A Ba'thist who was working for the Iraqi Intelligence Service under the cover of a bank employee in Abu Dhabi was arrested and then disappeared into the murky Emirati security system. The hostile Libyan regime was recruiting Iraqis with advanced degrees. And so on and so on.[10] The Ba'thists fought back aggressively, particularly against the regimes in Kuwait, Saudi Arabia, and Egypt. For example, the Iraqis tried to undermine or possibly even overthrow the Kuwaiti regime after the 1991 war through a secret strategy to cooperate with Kuwaiti "religious groups" that "reject the foreign presence in Kuwait."[11]

Despite the hostility emanating from some pro-Western states, Ba'thists working in the Muslim world reported numerous successes. They fanned out, searching for potential allies, and solidifying existing relationships. They sent Baghdad lists of people, parties, and organizations who could help the regime. The Office for Foreign Relations in the party secretariat tracked these potential allies and develop outreach strategies. Many of them bore fruit almost immediately. From Indonesia, to Pakistan, to Morocco, Ba'thists held meetings with local sympathizers, spread propaganda, and organized demonstrations.[12]

Unlike in the West, Ba'thists working in the Muslim world in the wake of the Gulf War were able to gain support from people and organizations who had real power in their respective states. In Malaysia, the Ba'thists helped organize "The Iraqi-Malaysian Committee for Saving Iraqi Children." They then held a seminar that was opened by Sati Hasma—the influential wife of the Malaysian Prime Minister, who served continuously from 1981 to 2003. On the sidelines, Malaysians told Iraqis that their government was beginning to lean toward Iraq on the issue of lifting the embargo.[13] Iraqi Ba'thists in Chad arranged a delegation of two senior Chadian officials to visit Iraq.[14] In Tunisia, they brought a delegation of 63 Tunisian students, youths, workers, farmers, and government employees to Iraq as representatives of the ruling Democratic Constitutional Assembly. The delegation traveled around Iraq, saw the effects of strategic bombing, and met with Iraqi students in a show of solidarity.[15] Not to be outdone, the Tunisian opposition hosted three sick Iraqi children and paid for their treatment in Tunis. Despite public statements about humanitarianism, internal Ba'thist documents reveal that the primary reason for sending the children there was "to dismantle the siege on our fighting country."[16]

These and similar activities throughout the Muslim world in 1991 and 1992 showed that despite Iraq's isolation at the United Nations, the Ba'thists were still welcomed in many places. As the events also highlighted, relations between Baghdad and foreign regimes were often conducted through party channels. The embassies and diplomats played important roles in Iraqi foreign relations, but often, the Ba'th Party organizations in these countries reached out to foreign leaders directly and arranged the visits of official delegations.

The Iraqis also relied on Muslim solidarity to mobilize Muslim minorities in non-Muslim states. Throughout the 1990s, the Ba'thists targeted Muslim minorities in Europe and the United States, but in the immediate aftermath of the Gulf War, one of its first operations was among Indian Muslims.

In the early 1990s, India had one of the rotating seats on the UN Security Council. India and Iraq were two of the most ardent supporters of the nonaligned movement during the Cold War. The Indians attempted to circumvent sanctions in the Gulf Crisis by delivering food to Iraq.[17] Then, in Security Council discussions after the Gulf War, India frequently spoke on behalf of the nonaligned movement to press for resolutions that were more lenient toward Baghdad.[18]

These factors made India an ideal target for Iraqi influence operations. Sameer al-Nima, who served both as the head of the Iraqi Ba'th Party in America and as the Iraqi *chargé d'affaires* at the United Nations, asserted that Iraqis should work through local nongovernmental organization to inflame "rage" in India about the situation in Iraq. If channeled through Indian diplomats, he hoped this rage could influence the Security Council.[19] Iraqi Ba'thists and the branch of the National Union of Iraqi students in India integrated with numerous sympathetic Indian organizations. However, Muslim organizations such as the All India Muslim Youth and Students Council were clearly the most active and zealous supporters of Iraq. Using material produced by the Harvard team that visited Iraq, the Ba'thists worked through these organizations to spread propaganda, hold demonstrations, and even organize a hunger strike to raise awareness about the humanitarian situation in Iraq.[20]

Popular Islamic Conference

Iraqi efforts in the Muslim world were aided by institutions that the regime had built in the 1980s to court Islamic and Islamist organizations. The most important of these institutions was the Popular Islamic Conference, which the Gulf Arab states had helped Iraq create to fend off religious attacks from Iran. To the consternation of the Gulf Arab regimes, Saddam turned the Popular Islamic Conference against them during the Gulf War. The Iraqis were particularly successful in prying away Islamists who had previously relied on Gulf Arab sponsorship. Saddam's championing of Arab-Islamic causes and his mix of anti-Western and anti-Zionist bombast proved too much to resist. By the end of the conflict, many of the Muslim world's Islamist movements openly supported Iraq, and Baghdad wanted to build on that momentum.

In June 1991, the Popular Islamic Conference held an emergency meeting in Baghdad with delegates from across the Muslim world. The Iraqi Minister of Endowments and Religious Affairs Abdullah Fadil told the assembled participants that it was "necessary to coordinate action among Islamic organisations, societies and unions." He called on Arabs and Muslims "to work hard and put pressure on international organisations so that the unjust economic blockade imposed on Iraq's Muslim Arab people would be lifted."[21] On the second day of the conference, Iraqi Vice President Taha Yasin Ramadan met Yasin Umar al-Imam, who was one of the founding leaders of the ruling National Islamic Front in Sudan. Ramadan explained to him that the American-Zionist-NATO "conspiracy against Iraq was a conspiracy against all the Arabs" but that the Arab masses would rise up to "abort the evildoers' intentions and their despicable designs." According to the Iraqi press, al-Imam "praised the brave militancy of the Iraqi people and their leadership, describing it as a source of pride for the Arabs."[22] The conference's executive committee released a closing statement affirming that "the continuation of the siege and the boycott constituted a flagrant violation of Islamic law," and it repeated its support for the Palestinian intifada, linking the two issues.[23]

The June Popular Islamic Conference set the tone and outlined the mission for its continuing efforts throughout the 1990s. The conference regularly brought together influential delegates from around the Muslim world with the explicit purpose of organizing a unified Islamic front against UN sanctions on Iraq. As later chapters will detail, the Popular Islamic Conference expanded considerably throughout the following decade. It opened branches around the world, carrying out diplomacy and organizing Islamist oppositions in states that opposed Saddam's regime.

The Jordanian Outlet

Within the Middle East, Ba'thist influence operations helped to cement geo-political relationships with states such as Jordan and Qatar, which were vital to Iraq's survival. The relationship between both these states and Iraq shows the difficulty of cementing a post–Cold War order without the full compli-ance of minor but geopolitically important states. Of these relationships, Jordan was perhaps the most critical.

Iraq and Jordan shared a border and they had deep historical ties. Both states emerged out of the Ottoman Empire as key sites of Arab nationalism. Following World War I, they were ruled by two brothers, Faisal in Iraq and Abdullah in Jordan. The Iraqis overthrew their monarchy in 1958, and the two states found themselves on opposite sides of the Arab Cold War in the 1960s. However, Amman and Baghdad became deeply intertwined politically and economically in the 1980s. The Iran–Iraq war shut down Iraqi outlets to the Persian Gulf. To compensate, Iraq developed the land route through Jordan to the port of Aqaba on the Red Sea. Jordan was a small country with few nat-ural resources. As such, it received scant foreign investment. Once it became the conduit for its much richer, and much more populous neighbor, money began to pour in. Outside investors refurbished its port facilities as well as other transportation infrastructure and factories. Jordanian exports to Iraq increased from $168 million to $212.3 million per year between 1985 and 1989. By the end of the decade, the Iraqi market accounted for one quarter of all Jordanian exports and bilateral trade reached almost one billion dollars per year.[24]

Iraq, and Saddam in particular, also had significant political influence in Jordan. Half of the Jordanian population was of Palestinian origin.[25] Saddam's championing of the Palestinian cause, showcased in the Gulf War when he fired SCUD missiles at Israel, made him a hero to much of the Jordanian population. Moreover, large populations of Iraqis lived in Jordan and Arab nationalism was popular there. Thus, in addition to Iraqi Ba'thists, the Jordanian Ba'th Party was quite active and maintained its own Regional Command that reported to the National Command in Baghdad.

For all these reasons, Jordan's King Hussein had difficulty opposing Saddam, and Jordan was the only pro-Western state in the region not to sup-port the American-led efforts to isolate Iraq during the Gulf Crisis. In fact, the Jordanians at first refused to abide by UN sanctions on Iraq. They were even-tually compelled to do so when the US Navy blockaded Aqaba. Following the

Gulf War, in May 1991, Jordan informed the UN Sanctions Committee that it was importing Iraqi oil. This was a violation of UN resolutions, and the committee "took note" of the information. However, the committee also realized that Jordan was dependent on Iraqi oil and that it had no other choice, so it took no actions against Amman. Nevertheless, international experts were concerned that Aqaba and then the land route through Jordan provided a conduit for Iraq to import banned military equipment and luxury goods. Thus, from 1990 to 1994, the United Nations mandated that all goods entering Jordan through the port of Aqaba be subject to inspection by a UN authorized Maritime Interception Force.[26]

With Iraq under sanctions, Jordan remained its main outlet to the broader world. If Iraqis needed to ship materials or travel, they regularly went through Jordan. Often, Iraqis traveled to Jordan in person to arrange visas for foreign travel and Royal Jordanian Airlines became a surrogate Iraqi carrier.

As one might imagine, Saddam and the Iraqi Ba'thists devoted considerable time and effort to ensure that Jordan continued to play this role. In addition to using economic leverage against Amman, the Ba'thists believed that shaping Jordanian politics in a way that maintained popular support for Saddam was critical. In 1991, Saddam donated three million dollars to a "housing fund" for Jordanian reporters and editors. This was an obvious attempt to buy good coverage in the Jordanian press.[27] Iraqi Ba'thists in Jordan worked closely with Jordanian unions and professional organizations. Jordan's Chamber of Industry became a particularly powerful force for promoting Iraqi interests. Iraqi Ba'thists also arranged public, pro-Iraq demonstrations as well as trips to Iraq for Jordanian doctors, students, and activists so they could witness firsthand the devastation that war and sanctions were causing.[28]

The importance of Jordan to Baghdad can be seen clearly in Iraqi archives. Jordan became a hub for Iraqi Ba'thists operating throughout the Middle East and it had the only cultural attaché at an embassy in the region.[29] Iraqi Ba'thists in Jordan were the regime's eyes and ears on the ground. They spied on their counterparts just as they did elsewhere.[30] Yet, while issues in other states may have merited a memo and a page or two of discussion in the party secretariat, discussions about problems in Jordan often stretched on for dozens of pages and included input from senior officials including Saddam himself.[31]

Jordan also played an important role in Iraqi strategies to influence other states. Thus, when Iraqi Ba'thists around the world worked through local organizations to ship medicine to Iraq, attend a conference, or distribute literature, they had to go through Jordan, and often worked with Royal Jordanian Airlines.[32] Iraqis also used their relationships with people and organizations in Jordan to influence senior statesman at the United Nations or the international press. In an indirect way, by keeping Jordanian politics oriented in the right direction, Iraqis also ensured that Jordanian leaders, such as the widely respected King Hussein, highlighted Iraq's preferred narrative about the damage sanctions were inflicting on innocent Iraqis.[33]

Jordanian-Iraqi relations waned throughout the 1990s, especially after Jordan signed a peace deal with Israel. By the end of the decade, King Hussein was a harsh critic of Saddam, and the United States military began operating from Jordanian territory. However, Baghdad continued to use its influence with the Jordanian population to pressure the Jordanian monarchy from below. The king was never able to break away from Iraq completely and Jordan remained an important outlet for an isolated Iraq until Saddam's demise in 2003.[34]

The Qatari Foothold in the Gulf

Qatar also proved an important geopolitical foothold for Iraq, although it could not help Iraq to circumvent the UN embargo. Qatar was too small, its foreign trade was closely tied to Dubai, and the US Navy plied the waters that separated it from Iraq.[35] Nevertheless, its location on the Arabian Peninsula and its membership in the Gulf alliance structures made it an important target for Iraqi operations. Just as importantly, if not more so, Qatar's politics were conducive to Iraqi influence.

During the Gulf Crisis, most Gulf Arab states broke ties with Baghdad and closed Iraqi missions in their territories. On the eastern shore of the Gulf, Iraqi ties with Iran had never fully recovered from eight years of war in the 1980s. As such, Iraq was largely frozen out of regional politics in the Persian Gulf during and after the Gulf Crisis. At the same time, geopolitics in the Gulf were shifting. For much of the Cold War, the United States had relied on the twin pillars of Iran and Saudi Arabia to ensure stability and thus the free flow of oil to global markets. Following the Iranian revolution, Washington supported Iraq just enough to halt Tehran's bid for hegemony in the Gulf. With the Gulf Crisis, that strategy was no longer viable. Instead, the United States hoped to build the capacity of Saudi Arabia and the Gulf Arab monarchies to balance Iranian and Iraqi power. That project required time, and until it could be completed, the United States needed to play a much more hands-on role in Gulf security.[36]

The Iraqis paid close attention to these developments, always searching for ways to influence them. Not all Gulf Arab states were equally hostile toward Iraq, even in the wake of the Gulf War. The Gulf Cooperation Council (GCC) was a regional alliance consisting of Saudi Arabia, Kuwait, Qatar, Bahrain, the United Arab Emirates, and Oman. Formed in 1981, it was the basis for Gulf Arab economic, diplomatic, and military cooperation. Yet, despite external displays of solidarity, Oman and Qatar did not join the other GCC states in breaking diplomatic ties with Baghdad during the crisis. Following the war, Qatar proved a particularly valuable foothold for the Iraqis in Gulf affairs.

As Iraqi reports indicate, Qatar had not been as enthusiastic as some of its neighbors about the Gulf War. In the early 1990s, Qatar had not yet gained the political influence it enjoys in the twenty-first century as leader in producing both liquified natural gas and pan-Arab media, but its location on the Arabian Peninsula and in the heart of the Persian Gulf made it important to Iraq. Tensions between Doha and Riyadh had existed for decades, and Qatar was initially hesitant to allow American or other Western troops on its territory. Qatari leaders only did so because of Saudi pressure and out of a sense of solidarity following a meeting of the Gulf Cooperation Council in September 1990.[37] Even then, Qatar did not take any actions to enforce the UN sanctions on Iraq, and it did not carry out a deliberate media campaign against Iraq except in response to disparaging comments Tariq Aziz made about Qatar. Following the Gulf War, Iraqis in Doha reported that Qatar had stopped broadcasting hostile programs and even took Iraq's side in some regional disputes with Turkey and Israel.

Throughout 1991, the Iraqi ambassador continued to meet with Qatari officials of all ranks, and despite their public statements, they were often quite sympathetic to Baghdad behind closed doors. The Qatari Foreign Minister spoke to the Iraqis about the need to end differences among the Arabs by bringing together Arab states that were sympathetic with Iraq.[38] No less than the Qatari Crown Prince suggested that if Baghdad were savvy, it could use the Arab media to "solidify a unified Arab position" against non-Arab attacks on Iraq.[39]

This generally welcoming environment gave the Ba'thists an outpost in the Persian Gulf. Qatar became an intermediary in secret talks between the Iraqi regime and Washington later in the decade.[40] It also provided a foothold from which the Ba'thists could keep abreast of political and cultural trends in the region. Then, they could design influence operations accordingly.

For all the successes of the Gulf War, the conflict created political problems throughout the Gulf Arab states. The Iraqis noticed that after the war, critiques of family rule and tribal politics increased. The younger generation wanted to modernize.[41] The Iraqi ambassador in Qatar reported that Arab intellectuals from the Gulf felt that calling on the West to defend them "opened the way for neo-imperialism under the cover of international law and the new world order."[42] He assessed that Gulf populations were becoming more sympathetic to Iraq following the Gulf War because they realized that the United States and its Western allies were increasingly dominating the region, and because Gulf Arabs linked Western power with Zionism.[43] In other words, while Gulf Arabs felt they had a duty to fight the war against Iraq, they also recognized that the war created a pseudo-Western occupation in parts of the Arab World. Any mention of occupation was necessarily tinged with critiques of Zionism, which many Arabs assumed the United States was in the region to defend.

Islamist opposition in Gulf States was particularly intense in the wake of the war. For example, Ba'thist organizations in Qatar reported on a prominent imam in Saudi Arabia who denounced the influence of Christians and Jews on Middle Eastern politics to the 3,000 attendees at his mosque.[44] Even in Qatar itself, where Ba'thists described the Islamist movement as "weak and limited," Egyptian and Palestinian preachers at Doha's most prominent mosque (Umar bin Khitab) criticized "support for the foreign infidels" during the Friday sermons.[45] These sentiments offered an opening for Iraq to stir up trouble for the Gulf Arab states and to make it difficult for them to provide bases from which Western coalitions could attack Iraq. As later chapters demonstrate, the Iraqis did exactly that.

In addition to aiding influence operations, the Iraqi presence in Qatar also provided traditional diplomatic and military intelligence. The Ba'thists tracked a steady stream of visits by senior American State Department and Defense Department officials to Gulf Arab States following the war. The Iraqis must not have been pleased to watch Qatar and other Gulf States agree to American plans to build a network of military bases, or to see how the Gulf Arab states facilitated American efforts to establish a lasting presence in the region. Nevertheless, Iraqi Ba'thists clearly had good sources within the Qatari political leadership. The Iraqis often received detailed descriptions about sensitive agreements and private meetings.[46] The Iraqis in Qatar also tracked high level talks about political and security cooperation between the GCC and states such as Egypt and Syria.[47]

Just as importantly, Iraqis in Qatar reported on problems within the GCC that Baghdad could exploit. Unresolved border disputes existed between several states. Their economies were overly reliant on oil and foreign workers, who caused all sorts of political and social problems. Moreover, while the GCC was meant to be a political, economic, and security union, the various member states maintained independent foreign policies and were unable to build a common defense force or even sign agreements for internal security. Instead, they depended on the United States and the West.[48]

As early as 1991, the Iraqi ambassador in Qatar provided a set of recommendations outlining the ways Iraq could use these weaknesses to subvert Western and particularly American military operations against Iraq. By supporting the opposition, pumping the region full of propaganda, and generally sowing discord, the Ba'thists made cooperation with Washington increasingly difficult for Gulf Arab rulers. As later chapters will show, these rulers slowly but steadily restricted what the United States was able to do from their territories. In private they told American leaders that while they would like to support American initiatives in the region, and specifically operations against Iraq, they could not ignore the domestic political consequences. Iraqi Ba'thists played no small part in creating that reality.

Conclusion

Iraq found the political landscape in places like Russia and the Middle East ripe for influence. In addition to simply building networks and amplifying narratives that aligned with its interests, as it did in the West, a case can be made that Iraq was able to influence the policies of several non-Western states.

Iraqi influence was not simply a matter of ideas. Geography was also its ally. Iraq's geopolitical position nestled deep in the non-Western world provided it with a protective cushion that helped mitigate the attacks emanating from the heartlands of the new world order in the West. The United States and its Western allies were never able to completely isolate Iraq from its neighbors. Baghdad preserved important land routes connecting it to the wider world. It also maintained a foothold in the Persian Gulf. Despite what some proponents of a globalized and interconnected post–Cold War had theorized, these geographical factors proved difficult even for superpowers like the United States to overcome. As the decade continued, Saddam used his ability to influence regional politics to increasingly improve Iraq's geostrategic position. Saddam would use the inroads described in this chapter to frustrate American attempts to isolate Iraq economically or to launch punitive military strikes against it.

The results not only affected regional politics; they often had broader, global implications. Russia had a permanent seat and a veto on the UN Security Council. In the Middle East, Washington viewed its actions in Iraq as upholding Security Council resolutions and thus the international law at the heart of the post–Cold War order. When, as later chapters describe, Saddam's influence on regional politics impeded American actions in Iraq, the consequences reverberated throughout the global order.

6

Courting Clinton

Bill Clinton, who defeated George H. W. Bush in the November 1992 presidential election, contrasted starkly with his predecessor. Bush was the closest thing America had to an aristocrat. His father was a successful businessman-turned-Senator in New England. Bush attended prestigious preparatory schools, then Yale, where he was a member of the elite secret society, Skull and Bones. Clinton, by contrast, was born into a poor, broken family deep in the American South. Bush, a member of the so-called greatest generation, had volunteered for the Navy in World War II, where he distinguished himself as a pilot in the Pacific. Clinton, a baby boomer, had protested the Vietnam War and avoided the draft. Bush was known for his foreign policy prowess. He served as the head of the US mission in China, the US Ambassador to the United Nations, and the Director of the CIA. By contrast, Clinton won the presidency by arguing that the Cold War was over, and America should focus its efforts at home. His unofficial campaign slogan was "it's the economy, stupid." Despite these fundamental differences, Clinton faced many of the same challenges as Bush when dealing with Iraq.

Because of his shift toward domestic priorities, some scholars have argued that Clinton's foreign policy lacked a grand strategy.[1] There is some truth in such claims. Early in his presidency, Clinton focused on domestic affairs, his administration was undisciplined, and nothing like the Cold War existed to organize America's international strategy. Yet, such arguments can be overstated. The Clinton administration had a clear "theory about how to produce security for itself," which is one of the most common definitions of grand strategy.[2] In its first year, the administration committed to the "enlargement of the world's free community of market democracies."[3] This became the basis of its first National Security Strategy, which it released under the title of "Engagement and Enlargement" in 1994. Clinton and his top national security advisors believed that the

Iraq against the World. Samuel Helfont, Oxford University Press. © Oxford University Press 2023.
DOI: 10.1093/oso/9780197530153.003.0007

more liberal, democratic, and capitalist the world became, the more secure and prosperous America would be. The United States was the sole super-power. The Clinton administration made clear that it would act to secure American interests, but it also acknowledged that the best way to do so was through a multilateral framework and international institutions. As such, Clinton blended a commitment to liberal institutionalism with the strategy of liberal hegemony that his predecessor had adopted at the end of the Cold War. At the heart of this approach was the United Nations, through which Clinton wanted to solidify a liberal post–Cold War order. Clinton imme-diately demonstrated the central place of the United Nations in his foreign policy when he appointed one of his most trusted advisors, Madeleine Albright, as the US Ambassador to it. He elevated her position to a Cabinet post, calling it "one of the most critical foreign policy positions" in his administration.[4]

This liberal approach to foreign policy put the Clinton administra-tion at odds with what it called "backlash states" such as Iraq.[5] As Albright explained, the Clinton administration arranged states into a hierarchy. At the top were liberal, free-market democracies. In the middle were countries that the United States wanted to help transition toward liberal, free market democracy. At the bottom were states like Iraq, which were ruled by irre-deemable regimes and needed to be contained until they were eventually discarded into the dustbin of history.[6] Some in the Clinton administration, like Secretary of State Warren Christopher, initially considered states like Iraq to be unimportant and did not want to devote much attention to them.[7] Yet, as Albright came to realize, Saddam was "not just another dictator."[8] In hindsight, she lamented, Iraq was the most persistent foreign policy chal-lenge that the Clinton administration faced and the worst problem the pre-vious administration had left behind.[9]

The arc of Clinton's approach to Iraq in the early years of his administration—from neglect to open hostility—also defined Baghdad's approach to Clinton. Baghdad's initial optimism about Clinton quickly faded into resentment and then antagonism. In response to these shifts, the Ba'thists launched sustained and increasingly successful operations to undermine Clinton's policies. As this chapter details, the slow but relentless press of Iraqi operations challenged Clinton's relationship with the international community during the mid-1990s. The post–Cold War order began to show its first cracks.

Courting Clinton

Saddam and his senior advisors initially struggled to understand the Clinton administration's outlook. When Saddam met in private with his advisors on the day after Clinton's election, Tariq Aziz argued that Clinton "has not taken a specific stand toward us" and Aziz recommended that Iraq should not take a "negative stand" toward him, at least in public.[10]

There were, of course, limits to what Saddam was willing to do. He disliked that Iraq was expected to show restraint: "Actually, it is Clinton who is supposed to be willing to carefully handle the relationship with us in a way where *we* don't get upset with him," he told his advisors in the meeting. "Why is it only he who gets upset with us? Why doesn't he carefully handle his demeanor?" After all, Saddam argued, Clinton was "part of a state that assaulted us and is still assaulting us."[11]

Nevertheless, Saddam recognized that "if we accept peace with him just because he says, 'Hi' and we say 'Hi' back, this, in itself, is a big improvement."[12] Then in a similar meeting on January 13, 1993—a week prior to Clinton's inauguration—Saddam made clear, "I believe that during [Clinton's] reign, a change will occur" and Saddam brushed aside Clinton's criticism of the Iraqi regime as public posturing.[13]

Perhaps projecting his own highly personalistic politics onto the United States, Saddam assumed that Clinton not only represented a new administration, but also a new regime, and that the new administration would be hostile to its predecessor. As will be discussed shortly, the Iraqis even manufactured a military confrontation with the outgoing Bush administration in January 1993 and then attempted to assassinate Bush in the spring. One might see such aggressive actions as counterproductive for Iraqi outreach to Washington. However, politics in Baghdad was a blood sport and leaders typically did not mind if a third party knocked off their rivals. Thus, the Ba'thists likely did not see attacking Bush as an impediment to courting Clinton.

In Saddam's self-centered view of the world, he and some of his senior advisors even interpreted the American election as a referendum on Bush's approach to Iraq.[14] As such, Baghdad saw Clinton's defeat of Bush as an outstanding opportunity to reset its relationship with Washington and to escape international isolation.

Three weeks after the American election in November 1992, Baghdad sent a cable to all Ba'thist organizations operating in over sixty countries. The cable ordered them to "urge all people, organizations, unions, associations, political parties" as well as anyone else who had "political, popular, and professional influence" in their respective countries to convince Clinton to turn "a new page when dealing with Iraq."[15] In December 1992, Baghdad followed up with more specific instructions. Party organizations across the globe were told to focus on three tasks in particular: First, "hold solidarity activities with the people of Iraq" that influence local politics and the media; Second, hold meetings with "ambassadors from the aggressor states" (it named America, Britain, and France). Ba'thists were to rely on arguments about international law and human rights to convince them to end the embargo on Iraq. They were to emphasize that 1993 could be a year of peace; Third, Ba'thists were to arrange for letters to be sent to President Clinton, members of Congress, the US Secretary of State, and their like.[16]

These cables elicited responses from around the world. From London, England, to Dhaka, Bangladesh, Iraqis reported on myriad efforts by their local allies to contact Clinton and influence the incoming administration's policies on Iraq.[17] At times, the Iraqis were able to enlist allies with considerable influence. In addition to the normal nongovernmental organizations in India, they convinced "a number of members of Indian Parliament" to write Clinton, asking him to lift "the economic siege on Iraq and to lessen the suffering of the Iraqi people."[18] In Greece, Iraqi Ba'thists met with a range of officials and organized three letters to Clinton. The first was signed by 50 people including a retired major general, a famous female writer, and the Deputy Head of the Union of Greek Lawyers, who was a former Member of Parliament. The second letter came from "diverse sections of Greek society," and the third from members of the Arab diaspora in Greece.[19]

In the United States itself, Iraqi Ba'thists worked through the Council of Lebanese American Organizations (CLAO). According to Iraqi sources, CLAO was active in 40 American states as well as its Washington, DC headquarters. Even more importantly, it had direct contact with Clinton, and the Iraqis thought they could use their ties to CLAO to influence him.[20]

The Iraqis also tried to contact Clinton through Oscar Wyatt, who was the founder of Houston-based petroleum and energy firm, Coastal Corporation. Wyatt worked with the Iraqi-American, Samir Vincent, and both were later arrested on charges of operating as illegal agents of the Iraqi regime and corruption of the oil-for-food program.[21] Tariq Aziz provided them a letter to deliver to Clinton on behalf of the regime, which, the Iraqis hoped, would help establish a better relationship. As an Iraqi official told Saddam behind closed doors, "Samir and Oscar are very optimistic."[22]

Some senior Iraqi officials recognized that seizing this opportunity required changing the way the regime operated. At times, these suggestions caused internal friction. Huda Ammash, the Iraqi official responsible for Ba'thist operations in the United States, clashed with the Iraqi Minister of Culture and Information about how Iraqi newspapers were depicting Clinton in the immediate wake of his election. In November 1992, she wrote a memo criticizing Iraqi newspaper articles that discussed Bill and Hillary Clinton in negative terms. She wrote that Clinton was not clearly hostile toward Iraq and that such articles could be seen as a "provocation." She recommended "not to write negative headlines such as this in our newspapers at least for the time being."[23]

More significantly, in early 1993, the bureau responsible for Iraqi operations abroad circulated a long report full of unprecedented recommendations for courting Clinton and breaking Iraq's international isolation. Iraq and the United States shared interests in "balancing Iran strategically" and in relation to oil, the report stated. These interests could form the basis of a new relationship during the Clinton administration. However, it added, Iraq must "keep up with modern times." The report discussed the need to address human rights violations in the country and even to introduce some democratic reforms.[24] This was not the first or last time that the Iraqi regime spoke about the need for democratization, and one should read such documents with a healthy dose of skepticism.[25] Saddam ruled a brutal, tyrannical regime. It was not on the cusp of becoming a liberal democracy. Indeed, the report's authors clarified that they had "intense reservations" about most forms of democracy and that Western-style democracy was neither good nor viable for Iraq.

Nevertheless, Clinton's liberal approach to foreign policy seemed to reflect an increasingly dominant trend in international politics. Thus, the report stated, "it is not hidden from the [regime's] leadership that the global orientation is marching toward the realization of democratic practices." The report suggested the Iraqi parliament discuss the formation of committees representing all slices of society and then arrange "free elections" for these committees in which all Iraqis could participate. The report argued that, in the immediate wake of the Gulf War, the regime could not take these steps without giving the impression that it was succumbing to internal and international pressures. Such an impression would have empowered the regime's adversaries. However, that time had passed. While the report recommended that the regime proceed with "extreme caution," it made clear that calls for democratic reforms would "resonate globally." In taking such actions, the regime could cooperate with "concerned global organizations" at the United Nations and in the United States to improve Iraq's international status.[26]

As one might expect, not all regime officials supported these reforms. Some were particularly concerned that the report suggested Ba'thists may lose some of their privileges, and other elements of the plan were debated throughout 1993 within the regime.[27]

To change Iraq's image in Clinton's America, Ba'thists also launched a campaign to influence the American and international press. In addition to pushing local allies to publish stories that were favorable to Baghdad, Ba'thists also attempted to recruit American journalists to visit Iraq, but only if the Iraqis were convinced that the journalists would publish what Baghdad considered the right type of stories. Ba'thists relied on local party organizations and their allies to vet potential visitors. As the journalist Quil Lawrence stated, he could not get a visa to Iraq until he signed on with a group called "voices in the wilderness" which was an anti-sanctions organization with close ties to the Ba'thists. As Lawrence recalled, "They put me on their list and my visa magically appeared."[28]

The most important operation that Ba'thists carried out to influence the American media in the wake of Clinton's election was bringing the journalist Jon Alpert to Iraq in January 1993 to interview Saddam. Alpert had reported from Iraq during the Gulf War. His work highlighted the damage from the American strategic bombing campaign, and it undermined the official US narrative about a clean and precise war. He wanted to return to Iraq in 1992, but he had difficulty obtaining a visa. Former US Attorney General Ramsey Clark, who was one of the harshest American critics of sanctions, and an Iraqi-American name Abdul Kadir al-Kaysi, who had close ties to the Ba'thists, heard about his attempts and intervened with the regime on his behalf.

Clark and al-Kaysi worked with Alpert to craft a request to travel to Iraq and interview Saddam. Knowing that the regime was interested in reaching a wide American audience, they wrote a request on letterhead from the cable network, HBO, with which Alpert had recently worked. They also made sure to include language showing that they intended to present the regime in a favorable manner. "As you know" they wrote, "there has been a constant campaign to vilify you. This propaganda enables the continued assault on your country," and "Recent developments make it clear that the American Government will continue to pick at the open wound between our two countries so that it will not heal."[29] The letter was sent through the Ba'th Party organization in the United States to Baghdad and then through the secretariate to Saddam. Throughout the process, Ba'thists endorsed the request, noting that HBO was one of the most prominent networks in the United States and that the interview would reach a large audience.[30]

In January 1993, just as Clinton was preparing to take office, Alpert traveled to Baghdad and interviewed Saddam. Iraqis also took him on a tour of the country to highlight the suffering of the Iraqi people under sanctions. Alpert visited a children's hospital and in addition to his interview with Saddam, his program showed graphic footage of children who were dying for lack of medicine and bandages. This fitted exactly into Ba'thist narratives about innocent Iraqis suffering under the embargo. Moreover, as Alpert showed, the sanctions were not working. Iraqis were not losing their resolve or questioning their support for Saddam.

The interview and footage made a significant impact in many places around the world. In Europe, Alpert's program received considerable attention. However, in the United States itself, the program was not televised until after the 2003 war—over a decade after it had been recorded. The HBO letterhead that Alpert had used was left over from a previous project. Though he clearly attempted to give the Iraqis the impression that HBO would air the footage, he did not have an agreement with the network. Neither HBO nor any other American television station agreed to run his program, probably because it was too uncritical and at times had the feel of propaganda. The Ba'thists were clearly upset at having been led astray, and Saddam did not agree to be interviewed by another American until 2003 when he spoke with Dan Rather.[31]

Operations in America

The Iraqi regime had other problems in the United States as well. The American political landscape was clearly hostile. The Ba'thists in the United States argued that the country was under "indirect Zionist control."[32] They were convinced that they were being targeted by the FBI and other security services. They were reluctant to communicate, even through diplomatic channels.[33] Huda Ammash was concerned that Iraqi students in the United

States were a security risk. They faced financial difficulties because Iraq did not have enough money to cover their stipends and benefits. Moreover, when the embassy closed, they lost even more support. As such, the students were vulnerable and could be recruited by American intelligence.[34] Other Iraqis in America faced similar problems. Even at the Iraqi Interest Section in Washington, DC, which was the official diplomatic mission, one guard reported that he was approached by a white skinned, blue-eyed American who spoke Arabic and tried to recruit him by saying that he could help him and his family through the hard times in Iraq.[35] Many Ba'thists working in the country were suspected of generally delinquent behavior. They drank too much, used drugs, and gambled.[36] The son of a Ba'thist who worked as a translator in Iraq's permanent mission to the United Nations was arrested for possessing an unlicensed firearm. He was released on bail and fled to Iraq to escape trial.[37] The resulting disruptions impeded Ba'thist efforts to coordinate across the country. Ba'thists operating around the United States claimed that they were being wasted because they lacked strong organizational connections.[38]

Even for the Iraqi regime, tracking Ba'thist activity in the United States was challenging. The American landscape was filled with spies, crime, and corruption. Agents and double agents permeated the Iraqi diaspora community, and it was nearly impossible to differentiate them. Perhaps the best example of this phenomenon was Abdul Kadir al-Kaysi, who had helped bring Jon Alpert to Iraq in early 1993.

Al-Kaysi was close to Ramsey Clark and participated in numerous high-profile activities to break the sanctions throughout the 1990s. Yet, while the Iraqi regime was eager to benefit from his work, it struggled to pin down his status within the Ba'th Party, his loyalty to the regime, and even his true identity. Among Iraqis in the United States, he went by the name Keduri. Some reports on him said he had been in the United States since the 1970s, but others claimed he was a veteran of the Iran–Iraq War, which took place in the 1980s. Most reports assumed he was Iraqi, but at least one report stated that he was dismissed from his work at Iraq's UN mission when it "Iraqized" its staff.[39] Some reports claimed he had been arrested in Detroit for smuggling weapons to Iraq, and that he strongly supported Iraq during the Gulf War, collecting donations and carrying out information operations.[40] Others said he was "hesitant and cowardly" during the Gulf War.[41] Some reports claimed he was a Ba'thist in good standing and referred to him as comrade.[42] Others said he had been a Ba'thist but that his affiliation with the party had lapsed.[43]

Several reports suspected him of disloyalty. He asked strange and intrusive questions, and he traveled to Iraq even though he did not have the money to do so.[44] These activities, according to one report, "put him in doubt," and "the prevailing position on him among the [Iraqi/Arab] community in New York and New Jersey is that he has connections to American security services."[45] Nevertheless, shady figures like Keduri were at the very heart of Iraqi operations in the United States.

Like the Soviet Union during the Cold War, which planted stories in the Russian language press among diaspora communities in New York City, a favorite tactic of Iraqi Ba'thists in the United States was to filter information up through the Arab American press to mainstream media outlets.[46] The Ba'thists in the United States worked with the Arab American Press Guild based in Los Angeles.[47] They also published their own Arabic newspapers, such as Al-Tahaddi, which was written by Ba'thist youth in Southern California.[48] As with other elements of their strategy, the Ba'thists were most successful when they amplified or boosted the work of existing media outlets which were sympathetic to Iraq. For example, the Arabic language monthly, Al-Watan, was published by an Islamist, Palestinian-American activist named Nizam al-Mahdawi. In 1993, Ba'thists in the United States thought the paper's anti-Saudi stance was useful and al-Nima reported that they were "cooperating" with al-Mahdawi. However, al-Nima was skeptical that the paper was financially viable, and he feared that it would not remain in print. Therefore, the Ba'thists bought 100 copies of three different monthly editions of the paper and distributed them throughout the Arab-American community.[49] Whether or not the Ba'thist intervention was critical to the paper's survival is difficult to discern, but Mahdawi continued to print al-Watan into the twenty-first century.[50]

· Ba'thists in the United States also spied on the Iraqi opposition. They regularly sent hostile newspapers and videos to Baghdad. When Kanan Makiya and other exiled Iraqi intellectuals met at Princeton University in 1994 to discuss a constitution for a post-Saddam Iraq, the Ba'thists provided details on the participants.[51] The Ba'thists also tracked the thousands of Iraqi refugees who flowed into the United States in the early 1990s as a result of the Gulf War and its aftermath. They settled in the Washington, DC suburbs; Richmond, Virginia; Louisville, Kentucky; Baltimore, Maryland; Nashville, Tennessee; and Detroit, Michigan. Baghdad assumed that most of these refugees were hostile, and it set up organizations across the country to monitor them.[52]

Of course, most Ba'thist operations in the United States attempted to identify and coopt allies in the fight against sanctions. In March 1993, Ba'thists compiled a twenty-six page list containing hundreds of American nongovernmental organizations they hoped to court. They targeted various humanitarian activists, religious groups, and Muslim advocacy organizations such as the Council on American-Islamic Relations (CAIR). The Ba'thists also listed less obvious but potentially useful organizations such as Rotary International, the United Way, the International Studies Association, and the Trilateral Commission, as well as some completely random groups like the National Association of Realtors and the International Senior Citizens Association.[53]

Of course, the Ba'thists had the best relationships with groups that were founded to support Iraqi-American relations or to address the humanitarian crisis in Iraq. For example, a group of Iraqis in the United States created the Iraqi Babylon Committee in 1993 "to strengthen ties between members of the community, to aid them, and to defend their rights in the United States." According to its founding documents, it also wanted "to strengthen spiritual ties with their homeland," and "to work on informing American public opinion about Iraqi issues – especially the conditions of the current embargo and seeking to end it." One of its founding members was Abdul Kadir al-Kaysi, also known as Keduri.[54]

The Iraqi Babylon Committee depicted itself as an independent representative of Iraqi-American civil society. It organized antisanctions demonstrations at the UN Headquarters in New York, and it corresponded with political leaders in the United States as well as European leaders like the Pope, Russian President Boris Yeltsin, and French President François Mitterrand. Although it was founded without the support of the Iraqi regime, the Iraq Babylon Committee quickly began coordinating with the Iraqi Ba'th Party organization in the United States and Iraq's Organization of Friendship, Peace, and Solidarity, which the regime used as a front to hide its relationships with nongovernmental organizations.[55]

The Iraqi Babylon Committee's letters to political leaders offered the standard arguments about Iraqi suffering and the inhumane sanctions. The Committee joined the campaign to influence Clinton. One of its letters pointed out that Iraqi suffering was "a direct result of the US-led embargo, imposed by President Bush in 1991." Then in the hope of driving a wedge between the two administrations, a letter stated, "we reach out to you as president with a new regime and different views than the former president."[56]

Groups like the Iraqi Babylon Committee were successful in presenting themselves as representatives of Iraqi-American civil society and their outreach elicited responses from American and world leaders who did not want to appear callus to Iraqi suffering. These responses provided important intelligence to the regime in Baghdad. For example, in March 1993, a group called the Iraqi-American Cultural Society wrote to Clinton expressing its concern about sanctions and the suffering they caused in Iraq. The letter appealed to Clinton "to personally intervene to facilitate the lifting, or at least, alleviating, the economic embargo."[57] Clinton had been in office less than two months, and his policies were not yet settled. He simply responded that "I welcome your thoughts and promise they will be carefully considered. I appreciate your taking the time to let me know how you feel."[58] The Iraqi-American Cultural Society was deeply embedded in the network of Ba'thist-backed organizations in the United States and Clinton's response was dutifully reported back to Baghdad.[59]

A year later, the Iraqi Babylon Committee had a quite different exchange with both Bill and Hillary Clinton. In response to a holiday card highlighting Iraqi plight, the First Lady's Director of Communications wrote, "The suffering of the Iraqi people is due, regrettably, to the policies of the government in Baghdad and its refusal to abide by United Nations resolutions." The response continued, "The international community and our own country have worked hard so that food and medicine are available to those in need in Iraq, but the regime in Baghdad has not permitted all of those supplies to reach the people who need them."[60] Bill Clinton responded personally with a similar message. Then, he added that Saddam was being investigated for "crimes against humanity, including genocide." Clinton stated that he intended "to see that Saddam Hussein and his regime are held fully responsible for the bloodshed in Kuwait and Iraq."[61]

The Iraqi regime, including Saddam himself, was keenly interested in these exchanges and the information they provided about the evolution of American policy. Whatever illusions the Ba'thists may have held about Clinton being a harbinger of change were clearly dispelled by 1994. In truth, while the Clinton administration, like all administrations, took some time to develop its policies fully, it never considered altering course on Iraq. The Iraqis completely misjudged the implications of American election and Clinton's outlook toward Bush. A change of administrations did not mean a change in policy and certainly not a new political regime.

From the very beginning, the new administration in Washington indicated that it intended to continue its predecessor's approach to foreign policy issues such as Iraq.[62] Prior to his inauguration in January 1993, President-elect Clinton sent a private emissary to deliver an "unofficial message" to Saudi Arabia, reassuring Riyadh that American policy in the Gulf and toward Iraq would remain the same.[63] In the spring of 1993, Secretary of State Warren Christopher, stated explicitly that "concerning Iraq, President Clinton has clearly reaffirmed the continuity of our policy."[64] Internally, the administration was divided about how much attention to give Iraq, but as CIA analyst and National Security Council staffer, Kenneth Pollak, claimed, "there was a consensus [. . .] that Saddam was evil."[65]

Clinton's Response

Iraqi misperceptions about Clinton led to several missteps. In the week prior to Clinton's inauguration on January 20, 1993, Iraq provoked a confrontation by deploying surface-to air missiles to the southern no-fly zone. The US military already had its hands full. Revelations about atrocities in the Balkans led to calls in the American media for a no-fly zone similar to what had been imposed on Iraq. A crisis was also escalating in Somalia and the US military was deploying an aircraft carrier and up to 30,000 troops there.[66] Despite these other commitments and potential commitments, the United States, the United Kingdom, and France responded to Saddam's provocations with airstrikes in Iraq. Foreshadowing events that would plague the international system throughout the late 1990s and early 2000s, the United States and its allies argued that existing UN Security Council resolutions gave them the authority to use force against Saddam. Therefore, they did not return to the Security Council to request authorization for the strikes. Noticeably missing from the small coalition that responded were any Arab states. Saudi Arabia was the only state in the region that allowed flights originating from its territory. Turkey refused to permit flights from its air bases despite a request from President Bush. Ankara claimed that recent massacres of Muslims in the Balkans made supporting attacks on Iraq difficult politically.[67] The British recognized such statements as a harbinger of "fragile" Arab and Turkish support for operations against Iraq, and London warned that more would have to be done to shore up their backing in the future.[68]

After several days of punishing allied attacks, Iraq unilaterally declared a ceasefire and withdrew its missile systems on January 19. Clinton was inaugurated on January 20, and the Iraqis claimed their decision to end the confrontation represented "gesture of goodwill" to the new president.[69] Because the Iraqis assumed a deep chasm existed between Bush and Clinton politically, they underestimated the negative effects of this small clash on the incoming administration.

The same Iraqi misperception led Baghdad to make an even graver error later in the spring of 1993, when the Iraqi Intelligence Service attempted to assassinate former president Bush. The US Ambassador to the United Nations, Madeleine Albright, had served in her seat for less than three months and this was her first real interaction with the Iraqis. Because the American response came on a weekend, she called on her Iraqi counterpart, Nizar Hamdun, at his home in Manhattan. He clearly did not know the reason for her visit and politely invited her for tea, asking, "So what brings you here today?" Albright responded, "Well, I'm here to tell you we are bombing your country because you tried to assassinate former President Bush." Handun exploded in anger and Albright feared she might not make it out of his residence.[70] Thus began her long, rocky relationship with the Iraqi delegation at the United Nations.

The United States responded, this time completely alone, with a missile strike on the Iraqi Intelligence Service's headquarters in Baghdad. In a nod to multilateralism, Albright briefed the Security Council about the operation and the American justification, which she claimed was an act of self-defense and therefore did not require UN authorization. Russia and the Western powers backed Washington, but the non-aligned states of Cape Verde, Djibouti, Pakistan, and Venezuela, who occupied rotating seats on the Security Council, delivered a joint statement that was far from supportive of the American operation. They expressed their "concern" with Iraqi actions. However, they claimed to "deeply regret the loss of life" caused by the American attack and they urged "restraint by all states." Moreover, they declared that Security Council resolutions should be "implemented in a non-discriminatory manner," which was a clear gesture to Iraq's assertion that it was being singled out. China followed the nonaligned states with a similar statement about the need to resolve disagreements peacefully.[71] These were some of the first outward signs that the world was no longer as united over Iraq as it had been only a few years earlier.

Even as skepticism about American and UN policy grew, changing the international approach to Iraq without American acquiescence was nearly impossible. The resolution instituting sanctions was designed so that it needed to be rescinded rather than renewed. In other words, as long as the Security Council did not act, the sanctions would remain in place. Therefore, permanent members like the United States and the United Kingdom could veto any attempt to end sanctions.

Washington and London remained steadfast in their approach. They simply did not trust Iraq. In the wake of the Gulf War, Western intelligence agencies reported that Iraqi programs to produce weapons of mass destruction were far more advanced than they had understood. In the spring and summer of 1991, Iraq lied about its weapons programs and then blocked, coerced, and derailed UN inspectors, leading to armed confrontations. Baghdad clearly signaled that it was going to fight implementation of the ceasefire agreement every step of the way. As the French diplomat, Pascal Teixeria da Sailva, stated, the ceasefire agreement and its accompanying UN resolution assumed that "Iraq declares, discloses and provides evidence" then the UN inspectors "verify." This approach required "not only Iraq's acceptance of the rules, but also Iraq's active cooperation." Yet, da Sailva continued, "Iraq never abided by its obligations in good faith." Instead, Baghdad adopted "the reverse logic." UN inspectors would search, then the Iraqis would explain whatever they found.[72] Technically, the inspectors had the right to go anywhere they judged appropriate. However, as one of the lead inspectors, Charles Duelfer, noted, the inspectors worked in a "defeated nation—not an occupied country." As such, "rights on paper were not necessarily enforceable in practice."[73]

American officials, first in the Bush administration and then in the Clinton administration assumed Iraq was acting in bad faith. This assumption continued even in 1994 when the Iraqis began to cooperate with UN inspectors. As next chapter discusses, some members of the UN Security Council pushed to alter the sanctions and inspections regime in light of Iraqi cooperation in 1994, but this effort was undercut in 1995, when Hussein Kamel, who was one of the regime's senior officials and Saddam's son-in-law, defected to Jordan with information on Iraq's efforts to deceive UN inspectors even further. Saddam was forced to turn over troves of documents his regime had hidden and to reveal previously unacknowledged parts of its weapons programs.

After the fall of the regime in 2003, investigators trying to discover what happened to Iraq's weapons of mass destruction programs concluded that Iraq had destroyed most of them following the Gulf War in 1991. Then, the regime dismantled the remainder, which it had attempted to conceal, following the Hussein Kamel affair in 1995. American and British bombings later in the 1990s destroyed whatever illicit weapons infrastructure was left.[74]

A growing literature has emerged to explain why America and other Western states failed to recognize that Iraq had indeed given up its weapons programs. In 2006, the CIA assessed that its "analysts . . . did not go far enough in accounting for how greatly Western and Iraqi thought differ."[75] American analysts focused almost exclusively on finding Iraqi weapons and did not consider how inspections also put the regime's survival at risk in ways that had nothing to do with illicit weapons. Thus, Iraqi officials sometimes blocked inspections or deflected requests out of concerns about internal security and coup-proofing.[76]

Moreover, Iraq's attempts to conceal certain aspects of its weapons programs in the early 1990s hindered its attempts to come clean later in the decade. The more Iraq revealed about its programs in 1994 and 1995, the more the UN inspectors saw that Iraq had previously tried to deceive them. Each revelation made the inspectors even more certain that Iraq was not cooperating fully. As one perceptive analysis recently concluded, Iraqi leadership found itself in a "cheater's dilemma." In other words, Iraqi cooperation with UN inspectors sometimes made lifting of sanctions less likely and thus disincentivized it.[77]

In addition to problems with inspections, the Americans also saw the Ba'thists as ruling a brutal regime that had launched two devastating wars against its neighbors and that was guilty of deplorable human rights abuses, including genocide against its own people. Thus, Washington dug in its heels and demanded full compliance with the most far-reaching interpretations of UN resolutions before it would consider lifting sanctions.

Clinton developed a policy on Iraq that essentially mirrored the approach of his predecessor. His administration dodged taking any responsibility for the humanitarian crisis in Iraq by pointing to the oil-for-food resolution that the Bush administration had sponsored in August 1991. "Iraq refuses to comply with these resolutions," one set of National Security Council talking points asserted in 1994, "because the regime would prefer the Iraqi people to suffer."[78]

Like Bush, the Clinton administration also struggled with developing a policy on regime change. Publicly, the Clinton administration introduced a policy of dual containment aimed at both Iraq and Iran, but behind closed doors, it almost immediately adopted a policy of regime change. Already in February 1993, internal administration documents stated, "We believe that in the long term, the security and stability of Iraq depends on the creation of a democratic, representative government within the confines of

Iraq's current borders." It hoped that the exiled Iraqi opposition in the Iraqi National Congress could shepherd that process.[79] Clinton also reauthorized Bush's "presidential finding" directing the CIA to "create the conditions" for removing Saddam from power and by 1994, that policy was being implemented from secret bases in northern Iraq.[80] In 1996, Secretary of Defense William Perry announced publicly that the United States was cooperating with several Arab states to precipitate Saddam's demise.[81] In 1997, Secretary of State Madeleine Albright stated, "We do not agree with the nations who argue that if Iraq complies with its obligations concerning weapons of mass destruction, sanctions should be lifted."[82] In 1998, President Clinton signed the Iraq Liberation Act, which had passed unanimously in the Senate and that made regime change the official policy of the United States government. Essentially, Clinton opted for regime change, but had no viable strategy to carry it out. However, this policy gave Iraq little incentive to reform. As Saddam repeatedly argued to his advisors, "We can have sanctions with inspectors or sanctions without inspectors; which do you want?"[83]

The Ba'thists could not ignore the very real threat posed by American sponsorship of the Iraqi opposition and their combined attempts to overthrow Saddam. Of course, the regime cracked down on any potential dissident at home, but that was not enough to address a threat that was imbedded in transnational networks of the Iraqi diaspora. The Iraqi regime established a special program designed to carry out "bombings" and "assassinations" targeting Iraqi exiles around the world. They paid particular attention to dissidents in Europe and Iran. Of the fifty students who attended a special Iraqi Intelligence Service school for these operations, the top ten graduates were sent to the United Kingdom and Europe; the next ten were sent to Iran.[84] Often the Iraqi operations against exiled dissidents were quite elaborate. In one case, an Iraqi Kurd who lived in Baghdad fled to Kurdistan after a fist fight with his neighbor who worked for the Iraqi Intelligence Service. While in Kurdistan, he worked as a bodyguard for the Iraqi banker-turned-dissident, Ahmad Chalabi. However, after a general amnesty was announced, the Kurd returned to Baghdad. When the regime discovered what he had been doing in Kurdistan, it employed him as a double agent in an ultimately unsuccessful attempt to assassinate Chalabi in London.[85]

As these spy-games played out across the globe, the world slowly grew frustrated with the American approach and the resulting sanctions and suffering in Iraq. Even some of Washington's most important allies started to rethink their policies, and Baghdad was well-aware of the shifting political tides. When the Iraqi Babylon Committee wrote Clinton, it received a cold response. When it wrote French President François Mitterrand in 1994, he responded with a handwritten note stating that Iraqi suffering strongly impacted him. Huda Ammash noted his positive response and circulated it throughout the regime.[86]

Even parts of the American political landscape were shifting underneath Clinton. George H. W. Bush developed his Iraq policy against the backdrop of a euphoric moment in global history. The end of the Cold War, and with it, discussions about the end of history and a new world order, provided an important context for the American approach toward Iraq in 1990. In the first years of the Clinton administration, the intellectual pendulum had reached its apogee and began to swing in the other direction. Americans were still both triumphal about the end of the Cold War and hopeful about the future.[87] However, configuring a new world order in America's image was proving more difficult than they anticipated. Efforts to bring humanitarian relief to Somalia ended with the killing of American soldiers in 1993, and Clinton quickly abandoned the operation. The breakup of Yugoslavia awakened age-old geopolitical schisms and ethnic hatred in the Balkans. Then, the United Nations found itself ill-equipped and unable to stop a genocide in Rwanda.

Public intellectuals also began to push back against what they saw as messianic post–Cold War dreams of a liberal world order and global peace. Harvard's Samuel Huntington wrote the influential "Clash of Civilizations" article in 1993 as a response to Fukuyama's end of history thesis. In 1994, Henry Kissinger published his magnum opus, *Diplomacy*. It began and ended with chapters that critiqued the idealism of the new world order, and throughout the book, dreamers like Napoleon III were defeated by practitioners of *realpolitik* like Otto von Bismarck.[88] At the same time, soaring discussions of history and the grand evolution of the human condition faded from diplomacy in the mid-1990s. A 1993 *Time* magazine article on Boutros Boutros-Ghali described his expansive peace keeping missions as "stymied, even rejected" and it stated that "his ambitions to help shape the architecture of a new world order have run into trouble."[89] Similarly, conversations between statesmen at the Security Council began to revert to mundane legalities or the practicalities of agreements and enforcement.

As the euphoria of the new world order waned, punishing sanctions on Iraq to enforce it made less sense. Right on cue, a *New York Times* editorial in the summer of 1994 argued that "Iraq paid a heavy price for defying a series of Security Council resolutions" including the "devastating economic sanctions, which remain in effect to this day." The editorial concluded that "the Administration's position is misguided, putting domestic political posturing ahead of the problem of containing Iraq's military power most effectively."[90] Thus, even in the United States, cracks in the once solid support for Iraq policy began to form. These widening fissures would plague Clinton, and then George W. Bush throughout the rest of the 1990s and the early 2000s.

Conclusion

Clinton inherited a world infused with hope—so much so that he initially felt he could shift his focus from international to domestic affairs. He and his administration learned very quickly that the age-old hatreds and geopolitical rivalries did not cease with the end of the Cold War. The dreams of a new world order began to strain in Africa, the Balkans, and the Middle East. As this reality set in, Clinton adjusted. In some places, like Somalia, he abandoned ongoing humanitarian operations when they turned bloody. In Rwanda, his administration failed to prevent a genocide. Such approaches could not work in Iraq. Clinton's predecessor had put the American strategies toward the Ba'thist regime at the center of the post–Cold War order. To Baghdad's surprise and frustration, the United States could not simply walk away from Iraq. Too much was at stake.

As this reality set in, the Ba'thists launched a sustained political campaign in the United States to undermine Clinton's policies and to delegitimize American approaches toward the post-Cold War order, which centered on Iraq. Clearly, Iraqi manipulation did not drive events in Europe, Africa, and elsewhere. However, these events helped create political openings which Ba'thists could use to gain new allies and partners. Baghdad also attempted to aggravate and shape emerging tensions in the American-led order. As the decade wore on, the political rifts over Iraq discussed in this chapter expanded considerably. Clinton found himself consumed with multiple crises in Iraq and waning support at home. These challenges only increased as Baghdad expanded its operations around the world.

7

A Turning Point for the New World Order

Historians of World War I Germany, which also suffered from a punishing embargo, have discussed "the criminalization of everyday life."[1] Rations did not provide enough food, and people relied on the black market to survive. A similar phenomenon was evident in mid-1990s Iraq. As the embargo continued to pulverize Iraqi society, the economic and humanitarian situation descended to a point that was unacceptable both to the Iraqis and to the international community. Between 1990 and 1995, food prices had increased by 4,000 percent. The price of basic commodities sometimes doubled in a single week. Civil servants, who had set salaries, made the equivalent of four US dollars a month.[2] There were ubiquitous reports of ordinary Iraqis "selling their gold and furniture," and of poor families who were "giving children to orphanages." Some Iraqis were even reported to be "selling their internal organs for hard currency."[3] Food and basic goods were rationed but that did not alleviate the problems. At the same time, the black market flourished and those with connections to the regime emerged as a new class for whom "money [was] no object."[4]

These realities on the ground in Iraq clashed with the idealistic promises of the new world order. As Iraqis slipped further into despair, the world grew impatient with Washington. Policies and approaches that seemed reasonable as temporary measures in the immediate aftermath of the Gulf War became more difficult to justify as the years passed. Saddam could sense that the global mood was shifting, and he used every means at his disposal to facilitate and encourage these trends. In many places, Baghdad attempted to move from building networks and partnerships to influencing national policies and weakening the world order that was containing Iraq.

By 1996, these efforts seemed to pay off. France and Russia changed course and the consensus on Iraq between the five permanent members of the Security Council finally broke down. Whether this breakdown was inevitable or caused by Iraqi actions is impossible to tell. However, the Iraqis certainly saw it as a validation of their efforts, which gained new momentum and opened fresh possibilities.

Iraq against the World. Samuel Helfont, Oxford University Press. © Oxford University Press 2023.
DOI: 10.1093/oso/9780197530153.003.0008

France and Western Europe

As the United States was doubling down on its Iraq policy, Paris and Baghdad made small steps toward reestablishing formal ties. When Clinton took office in January 1993, France was still firmly in the Western camp. It participated in the air strikes when Iraq moved its surface-to-air missiles into the southern no-fly zone, and behind closed doors, it promoted a unified position on Iraq among Paris, London, and Washington as the three permanent Western members of the Security Council.[5] Yet throughout the mid-1990s, French interests and Iraqi influence operations began to separate Paris from Washington and London.

Like all successful influence operations, Iraqi attempts to lure France out of the American-dominated order in the mid-1990s played on existing tensions and worked within already-present political trends. Even the most optimistic voices of the new world order recognized that it produced winners and losers. The *New York Times* foreign affairs columnist, Thomas Friedman, was probably the most prominent chronicler of economic globalization that accompanied the post–Cold War order in the 1990s, but even he discussed it as a struggle between a "Lexus," representing economic and technical advancement, and an "olive tree," representing what he saw as age-old forces like nationalism and tribalism that stood in the way of progress. In his influential book, *The Lexus and the Olive Tree*, Friedman advised his readers to "buy Taiwan, hold Italy, and sell France."[6] According to Friedman, France was ill-suited for the economic globalization of America's new world order. It should come as no surprise that French foreign minister Hubert Védrine popularized the term hyperpower in the late 1990s as a critique of all-encompassing American prowess which seemed to leave former great powers like France prostrate before American supremacy.[7] France's dissatisfaction about its position within international politics provided Iraq with openings to channel and amplify French angst in a way that created daylight between the policies of Paris and Washington toward Iraq.

In July 1993, the Quai d'Orsay officially received two Iraqi officials, and in September, Baghdad opened an Iraqi Interest Section at the Moroccan Embassy in Paris. A month later, the Iraqi regime's top foreign policy official, Deputy Prime Minister Tariq Aziz, visited Paris for what he claimed was medical treatment. However, his real purpose was to meet French officials to discuss reestablishing relations with Iraq. Iraq owed France four billion dollars, but repayment required lifting the sanctions. To further entice Paris,

Baghdad began negotiating with French oil companies about developing Iraq's southern oil fields once the embargo was finished.[8]

These contacts deepened in 1994, when several French business and parliamentary delegations visited Iraq. By March 1994, France began pushing hard to end sanctions on Iraq.[9] In September 1994, Tariq Aziz met officially with French Foreign Minister Alain Juppé. In cables, American diplomats complained that the French were causing "enormous difficulties" over Iraq at the United Nations and that America's policy on Iraq was increasingly impairing bilateral relations between the United States and France.[10]

Iraqi influence operations attempted to drive a wedge between French and American policies. Iraqi Ba'thists worked through French nongovernmental organizations and through influential people who the Iraqis had courted over several decades. The Iraqi French Friendship Association, which was founded in the 1980s, was reestablished in 1994. It was coordinated by Giles Munier, who had participated in solidarity and commercial activities with Baghdad since the 1970s. The association also included several former French ambassadors to Iraq. In 1995, Marc Bonnefous, an influential former head of the North Africa and Middle East desk at the Quai d'Orsay, began to preside over the organization's public relations and lobbying campaign to end Iraqi sanctions. In 1996, Jeanou Lacaze, who had been the Chief of Staff of the French armed forces and served as a member of parliament, formed a parallel commercial lobbying group. He had close ties to the former Iraqi General Amer Rashid, who served as Iraq's Oil Minister in the 1990s.[11]

Several similar groups, in what the historian of French diplomacy David Styan called a "shadowy field" of Ba'thist-linked organizations, emerged during this period. As Styan argued, these groups facilitated "media coverage of Iraqi affairs" and "were partly responsible for far greater awareness among the French press and public of the humanitarian impact of sanctions upon Iraqis."[12]

In internal documents, officials from Clinton's National Security Council claimed that the French were "motivated by commercial interests to preposition themselves to dominate the post-sanctions market in Iraq."[13] However, despite these clear material interests, Paris was reluctant to break publicly with its Western allies at the United Nations over Iraq. Flouting liberal post–Cold War norms in favor of pandering to a brutal dictatorship for financial gain would be hard to sell politically in France. Thus, Paris continued to vote with Washington at the Security Council, and the meeting between Juppé and Aziz occurred in New York at the annual meeting of the UN General

Assembly rather than in Paris. The latter could have angered the Americans.[14] For the relationship to proceed further, French leaders needed to make a moral as well as a material argument to the French people. Ba'thist influence operations were designed to foster and intensify just such arguments about Iraqi suffering.

The election of Jacques Chirac as French president in 1995 accelerated Paris's movement away from the American position on Iraq. Chirac had a long history of close ties to Baghdad. He had helped supply the Iraqis with arms and nuclear technology in previous decades. Just as importantly, he was a Gaullist, who was uncomfortable with American hegemony and disapproved of Washington's increasing unilateralism in the 1990s. Baghdad hoped the new president would transform Iraq's fate. The Iraqis congratulated him in a cable that expressed their desire to revive "relations between our countries on the same base and with the same vitality" as before.[15]

Chirac almost immediately began to alter French policy toward Iraq. He considered the American interpretation of UN resolutions to be excessive and he thought that demanding Iraq meet all requirements before any sanctions were lifted was impractical. Earlier in the decade, Paris had been in lockstep with Washington on this issue. In March 1992, the French representative at the Security Council rejected "the theory that if Iraq complies with 50 per cent, 70 per cent or 80 per cent of the Security Council resolutions the Council must lift the sanctions by a similar proportion." The French government had insisted that "a resolution is not divisible; it must be implemented in full, not according to the proportion that is to the liking of the Iraqi authorities."[16] However, in 1995, Chirac felt that approach had failed. For Iraq to make progress, he believed, it needed to see a "light at the end of the tunnel." Thus, the United Nations needed to lift sanctions incrementally as Iraq made progress in meeting Security Council demands.[17]

Following Chirac's election, Tariq Aziz declared that Iraq was giving French businesses a privileged position and a wave of French companies rushed to make deals with Baghdad in 1995 and 1996. By April 1996, Chirac broke with the United States, openly declaring that the time had come to welcome Iraq back into the international community.[18]

The extent that France's changing policies can be attributed to Iraqi actions is impossible to know. Clearly, Paris was poised to move away from Washington and may have done so without any help from Baghdad. Yet when considering how Iraqi actions impacted French thinking, it is worth considering a counterfactual. Had Baghdad frozen out French companies as punishment for Paris's Gulf War policies, or abandoned French politics as a lost cause, it is difficult to see France incurring the cost of breaking with Washington. Instead, by creating a nexus of economic interest, political support, and humanitarian imperatives, one could reasonably argue that the Ba'thists helped transform French inclinations into French actions. If nothing else, Baghdad's actions probably prodded Paris to break with Washington earlier and more intensely than it would have otherwise.

In addition to great powers like France, a new world order required the acquiescence of lesser powers as well. If these states failed to abide by UN resolutions, the system simply would not work. Additionally, both Baghdad and Washington saw these middle and lesser powers as providing legitimacy in global politics. Thus, Ba'thists ran influence operations across Western Europe. From Germany to Spain, Iraqis working for the regime attempted to overcome at times intense hostility and to paint themselves as the victims of American neo-imperialist policies.

Examining Iraqi operations in Sweden provides a granular look at how the Ba'thists dealt with these political challenges during the period. In the spring of 1993, the Ba'thists began with a cleareyed assessment. Iraqi-Swedish relations were in crisis. Large numbers from the Kurdish and Islamist opposition from Iraq lived in Sweden. They received "generous" aid from the Swedish government, nongovernmental organizations, as well as the Americans and the Gulf Arab states. The Iraqi opposition had significant influence on Swedish politics. The Ba'thists claimed that Kurds in Sweden drummed up hype over the Halabja incident, in which the Iraqi military gassed the Kurdish population. Then, in July 1990, Iraq executed an Iraqi Swede who Baghdad accused of espionage, but who the Swedes said was a reporter. Finally, Iraq had arrested and continued to hold three other Swedish citizens who had entered Iraq illegally through Kuwait.

According to the Ba'thists, these events were blown out of proportion by the hostile Swedish media, which followed the lead of "the Zionist, American media" because it was controlled by the "known, Jewish, Bonnier family." Thus, the Swedish press depicted Iraq as an "abnormal" country that could not coexist peacefully with the community of modern, developed states.

Moreover, the Swedish government was headed by the pro-American Moderate Party. During the Gulf Crisis, Sweden expelled six Iraqi diplomats including the *chargé d'affaires*. The Prime Minister had met with the American president, the Secretary of Defense, and senior intelligence officials. Swedish intelligence continued to closely monitor the Iraqi embassy and it regularly detained or interrogated people who visited it.[19]

These Iraqi views are confirmed in American records. In internal correspondences, the Bush administration had praised Swedish Prime Minister Carl Bildt, who it claimed had overseen "a quiet revolution" instituting "market-oriented reforms based on privatization and lower taxes" and in foreign affairs, had moved "Sweden away from neutrality and pet Third World causes, and into the European mainstream."[20]

Bildt considered Iraq a pariah and he thought that holding Saddam's regime accountable was vital to building a liberal post–Cold War order. As he told UN Secretary General Boutros Boutros-Ghali during a private conversation in 1992, "operations in Iraq had enhanced the United Nations' prestige; they had demonstrated that, in the context of the 'new world order', the [United Nations] could achieve results." In response, Boutros-Ghali made clear that such statements raised the stakes for Iraq in international politics. "But we cannot fail, or we shall lose our credibility," Boutros-Ghali replied, "the high expectations prevailing today create this danger."[21]

Despite Swedish attitudes toward Iraq and the importance that the Swedish government afforded the issue for world order, the Ba'thists saw a political opening in Stockholm. Bildt's government was in crisis and the Iraqis thought that a new government would be elected soon. If so, a window of opportunity presented itself to change Stockholm's position on Iraq. The Iraqi regime created a special committee to address the situation in Sweden. Noting that Swedes were more willing to work with nongovernmental organizations than official representatives of the regime, the Ba'thists hid their relationship with Baghdad. Instead, they worked through proxies who presented themselves as representing the "innocent sons of the people of Iraq."[22] They carried out a wave of operations targeting members of the Swedish Parliament, writers, intellectuals, and media personalities. However, they hit a wall of resistance. Many Swedes considered the Ba'thist regime barbaric and the fact that Iraq continued to hold three Swedish citizens as prisoners made cooperation almost impossible.[23]

The Ba'thists reassessed and then developed the type of shrewd plan that typified their influence operations around the world during this period. Working through the Union of Arab Geologists, the Ba'thists secretly contacted the Swedish Dag Hammarskjöld Foundation, which had close ties to the government and was influential on matters of international policy. Behind closed doors the two sides negotiated the release of the Swedish prisoners in exchange for Sweden sending humanitarian aid to Iraq. This aid by itself was a symbolic victory for Saddam. It highlighted Iraqi suffering and undermined the effects of the embargo. Baghdad also pushed to "exploit" the agreement further by arranging for Swedish journalists to travel to Iraq for the release of the prisoners. While in Iraq, the regime exposed the reporters to the humanitarian crisis that the country faced under sanctions. Following the return of the prisoners and the journalists to Sweden, the Ba'thists arranged another wave of influence operations carried out by unions and professional organizations, which could hide any connection to the regime in Baghdad or the Iraqi embassy in Stockholm.[24] By the time the center-right Moderate Party was defeated by the Swedish Social Democrats in 1994, Sweden was poised to move away from Washington's policy on Iraq. As later chapters will detail, it did exactly that.

Russia

In the mid-1990s, Moscow split with Washington even faster and more forcefully than Paris had. When Clinton came to office, his administration was, at least at first, closely aligned with the French. Russia, by contrast, had already turned against American policy on Iraq. As US intelligence reports from the time demonstrate, the American-British-French air strikes in Iraq just prior to Clinton's inauguration "caught Russia—and others—by surprise."[25] The "domestic reaction" in Russia was extremely hostile to the attack. Moscow believed that it was "not adequately consulted" and it began to seriously question "Western attempts to manage UN-authorized military actions independently." As the American intelligence community reported, these sentiments not only affected Russian-American relations on the issue of Iraq; they also influenced Moscow's perceptions of Washington's actions during the emerging conflict in the Balkans. Yeltsin began pairing the two issues and "accused the US of dictating to the international community on Iraq and Yugoslavia." As such, American intelligence reports suggested, Russia was taking a harder line in the Balkans "because of domestic reaction to the latest [American-led] military actions against Iraq."[26]

The Iraqis followed political developments in Russia carefully.[27] Even more so than in France, Russian political winds were shifting against the American-led post–Cold War order. By the mid-1990s, Russians realized that the new world order and globalization had failed to bring the economic prosperity and political stability that had been promised. Disputes with the West over the Balkans and NATO expansion inflamed these sentiments even further. The Ba'thists seized on the resulting skepticism about pro-Western politics. By mid-1993, Iraqi Ba'thists could count on the support of every major political party in Russia—from the Christian Democrats to the Communists to the Liberal Democrats and everyone in between. According to Iraqi sources, the Ba'thists developed close relationships with the leaders from each party. They all "agreed repeatedly" to aid Saddam and his regime. Many of them visited Iraq to show their support.[28] Baghdad developed particularly close ties to Vladimir Zhirinovsky, who emerged in the early 1990s as Boris Yeltsin's main rival, and whose Liberal Democrats received a plurality of votes in the 1993 election for the Russian Duma. Zhirinovsky personally sent letters of protest against the January 1993 air strikes in Iraq to leaders in Washington, London, and Paris. Similarly, the anti-Yeltsin coalition of communists and hardline nationalists that organized under the National Salvation Front announced its support for Iraq during the confrontation.[29]

Through much of 1993, the Russian government attempted to sustain two incompatible policies. On one hand, it wanted to support Iraq. On the other, it wanted to maintain its relationship with the United States and preserve the cooperative post–Cold War order. At times these competing priorities split politicians and ministries within the government. On August 5, 1993, for example, the Russian Ministry of Foreign Economic Relations signed joint-cooperation agreements in Baghdad on economics, trade, science, and technology. Two days later, the Russian Ministry of Foreign Affairs declared the agreements "inoperational."[30] Similarly, some Russians were pushing Iraq to abide by UN resolutions and to cooperate with weapons inspectors. However, the head of Iraqi Military Intelligence, Wafiq Samarrai, told UN inspectors after he defected in 1994, that the Iraqi Intelligence Service was paying other Russian officials for information that allowed Baghdad to sidestep the inspections.[31]

Baghdad enticed Moscow by signing billions of dollars-worth of contracts with Russian companies that would be fulfilled after sanctions were lifted. By September 1994, this economic pressure, along with Ba'thist influence operations and outreach to Russian leaders, helped to dispel the ambiguity in Russia's Iraq policy. The Russians and Iraqis created a joint committee "to discuss methods of developing the bilateral economic relations and projects," and Moscow began to demand the lifting of sanctions on Iraq.[32]

The changing Russian position, and Iraq's influence on it, was demonstrated most clearly during a standoff in October 1994 between Iraq on one side and the Gulf Arabs and their Western allies on the other. Iraq manufactured the crisis. Once Baghdad realized that its outreach to the Clinton administration was in vein, the Ba'thists reluctantly began to cooperate with UN inspectors and agreed, finally, to recognize Kuwait as a sovereign state within the UN-demarcated borders. Yet, by October 1994, it became clear that the UN inspectors were still not recommending that the Security Council lift sanctions, and that Washington and London were determined to keep them in place. Saddam found himself in a dilemma. He worried that the sanctions regime was becoming normalized. Despite what Baghdad considered as positive developments in Russia, Iraq was fading to the background of international politics. Indeed, Iraq had fallen off the agenda at the UN Security Council.[33] When Russian Foreign Minister Andrei Kozyrev met Secretary General Boutros Boutros-Ghali on October 5 to discuss the priorities of Russian foreign policy, he spoke at length about the Balkans, Azerbaijan and Armenia, Tajikistan, and even Russian personnel issues at the United Nations, but he did not mention Iraq.[34] The Ba'thists needed to find a way to force Iraq back into global consciousness. As Saddam told his advisers in a closed-door meeting, "if the sanctions are not lifted in the upcoming round . . . then we have to proceed to crisis. And this crisis might create new horizons where the political environment will be more conducive."[35]

To recenter Iraq in global politics, Saddam deployed his elite Republican Guard near the Kuwaiti border on October 7. It was a clear provocation. The United States immediately deployed a blocking force to Kuwait. By October 10, Iraq shot to the top of the Security Council's agenda.[36]

Savvily, the Iraqis called on the Russians to mediate. In doing so, Baghdad empowered its sympathizers in Moscow to play a more prominent role negotiating international policy on Iraq. After a meeting on October 13 in Baghdad, Saddam and Russian Foreign Minister Kozyrev issued a joint communique, which was forwarded to the Security Council. "To prevent an escalation of the tension" and to facilitate "the lifting of the sanctions against Iraq" the communique recommended that after Iraq recognized Kuwaiti sovereignty, the United Nations would transition to a long-term program for monitoring Iraqi weapons programs. The new program would include a six-month "test period," after which sanctions would end.[37]

This communique set up a confrontation between the Russians and the Americans at the United Nations. Once Iraq redeployed its forces away from

Kuwait and the crisis dissipated, the Security Council met to discuss a way forward. Tariq Aziz and Russian Foreign Minister Kozyrev flew to New York to represent their respective states personally at a Security Council meeting on October 17. The Russians adopted a diplomatic but clearly confrontational tone at the meeting. If Iraq agreed to abide by UN resolutions, Kozyrev asserted, "the Security Council must be ready to take 'Yes' for an answer."[38]

To the dismay of the Americans and their allies, Kozyrev also used his presense at the meeting to call for "corrections" in the manner that the Security Council applied sanctions more generally. "Thought must be given," he argued, "to laying down clear humanitarian limits in determining sanctions." He was also clearly frustrated that the Security Council had set up sanctions in a way that Washington could veto lifting them. Instead, Russia and others felt a more logical arrangement was to have sanctions expire if there were not an affirmative vote to continue them.[39]

Voicing such concerns openly at the Security Council was a clear break with the norms of unity. For example, France held many of the same views as Russia, but in public, it coordinated its statements with the United States and other Western allies. Following the Russian statements at the Security Council, the French representative simply stated "We are very aware of the suffering endured by the Iraqi population, and we deplore the fact that its Government has never wished to take advantage of the possibilities offered it under [UN] resolutions."[40] In a show of the power of norms to shape behavior, even Russia, after voicing its concerns, voted with the other permanent members of the Security Council on the resolution condemning Iraq.[41]

This episode provides excellent insight into how Iraqi actions shaped the post–Cold War system. Moscow had let Iraq slip from its priorities. Moreover, when Russian Foreign Minister Kozyrev met with Boutros-Ghali just prior to Iraq's deployment of troops to the Kuwaiti border, he made clear that he hoped to find ways to improve Russian-American relations.[42] Instead, Iraq provoked a crisis and then used its allies in Moscow to position Russia in opposition to the United States. During the crisis the Russians not only backed Baghdad, they tested norms of unity by challenging the United States openly at the Security Council. They also questioned the validity of UN sanctions on Iraq, which had been hailed as a harbinger of a new era in international politics and a held up as a pilar of the post–Cold War order. There is no reason to believe that Russia would have taken such provocative positions during this period without Iraqi prodding and manipulation.

The Ba'thists helped solidify Moscow's retreat from Washington as well as its own previous positions on Iraq. As late as March 1992, Russia had placed all the blame for Iraqi suffering on the Iraqi regime and insisted that for Iraq to "return to the international community as a full-fledged member" it "must immediately and fully implement all of the Council's demands."[43] In the October 1994 crisis, Russia blamed the sanctions for Iraqi suffering and argued that if Baghdad took steps toward meeting the Security Council's demands, the Security Council should begin to lift sanctions incrementally.

These trends gathered momentum following the crisis. Later in October, Russia upgraded its diplomatic relations with Iraq, sending an ambassador to serve in Baghdad for the first time since the Gulf War.[44] By March of 1995, Russia's Deputy Foreign Minister, Victor Bosolikov, traveled to Baghdad and in private meetings, signaled Moscow's "intent to sell Iraq weapons and aid it in developing its military industry."[45] Clearly, Russian policy had shifted.

The Middle East and the Muslim World

Outside Europe, the Iraqis continued their deliberate push to win popular support throughout the Middle East, the Muslim World, and within developing states more broadly. As in earlier periods the Ba'thists remained highly active in Arab states, Pakistan, and among other potentially sympathetic populations around the world. However, when global politics shifted, the Ba'thists opened new fronts as well. Most prominently, as membership of the UN Security Council rotated, Baghdad adjusted its operations accordingly. Thus, for example, the small state of Djibouti was largely unimportant to the Iraqis until it took a nonpermanent seat on the Council from 1992 to 1993. At that point, Ba'thists almost immediately filed a string of reports covering all aspects of Djiboutian politics and on Djiboutian political parties as well as suggestions for how to make inroads into them.[46]

Turkey also emerged as an important target for the Iraqis in the mid-1990s. Like the Gulf Arab states, Turkey's long border with Iraq made it critical for enforcing an embargo. If Ankara was not proactive in enforcing Security Council resolutions, Iraq could smuggle its oil onto the international market, making UN sanctions ineffective. Turkey was also a vital node in Western attacks on Iraq, which at least theoretically, were carried out to enforce UN resolutions. American, British, and French air forces relied on

Turkey's Incirlik Air Base, and humanitarian aid to Iraqi Kurdistan flowed through Turkey.

In the immediate aftermath of the Gulf War, Ankara and Baghdad had clashed. Ankara blamed Baghdad for driving tens of thousands of desperate Kurds to the Turkish border. Baghdad accused Ankara of violating Iraqi sovereignty, including military incursions to attack the Turkish Kurdistan Workers Party (PKK), which had set up camps in northern Iraq. Yet, the two countries had been important trade partners prior to the war and the Turks were losing several billion US dollars in trade every year due to the embargo. A pipeline exporting Iraqi oil to Western markets ran through Turkey. Its closure alone cost Ankara between 600 and 700 million dollars a year. To quell Turkish angst, the Gulf Arabs compensated Ankara three to four billion dollars a year, but this did not cover all the lost revenue. As the decade wore on, Baghdad and Ankara began to realize that they shared an interest in ending the embargo on Iraq. The Ba'thists stepped up their operations in Turkey in 1993 and the two governments began to jointly pressure the United Nations to clear the pipeline for operation in January 1994.[47]

Elsewhere around the Middle East and Muslim World, the Ba'thists continued to spread propaganda and look for ways to influence governments. They brought delegations of sympathizers and potential sympathizers to Iraq. One of their favorite tactics was to collect medicine for Iraqi hospitals and have foreign allies sponsor sick Iraqi children to receive medical treatment outside Iraq. The regime's documents record internal criticism when such operations did not receive the hoped-for media coverage, and the Ba'thists adjusted accordingly. These internal critiques also lay bare the regime's motives. In public, Ba'thists concentrated their attention on the poor, suffering Iraqi children. However, internal reports focused almost exclusively on the amount of media coverage these operations received. The fate of the sick Iraqi children who were sent abroad for treatment was almost never mentioned.[48]

The Popular Islamic Conference Organization also continued to meet and reach out to explicitly Islamic actors around the world. In 1994, the regime revamped the organization, appointing Abd al-Razzaq al-Sa'di as its Secretary General—a position he held for the remainder of the decade. Al-Sa'di came from an important Sunni scholarly family in Iraq's al-Anbar Province. His brother, Abd al-Malik al-Sa'di, was perhaps the country's most prominent Sunni Islamic scholar. The regime granted Abd al-Razzaq al-Sa'di a diplomatic passport and he traveled throughout the Muslim World and among the Muslim diaspora in Europe.

His ability to blend religion and politics aided the Ba'thists tremendously. As a religious scholar, al-Sa'di could more easily visit states where Iraqi diplomats were unwelcome, such as Saudi Arabia, Iran, or the United Kingdom. Yet as a representative of the regime, he met senior officials and discussed high politics during his visits. In Saudi Arabia his role was particularly important. Baghdad did not maintain diplomatic relations with Riyadh. However, al-Sa'di and other representatives of the Popular Islamic Conference Organization regularly traveled to the headquarters of the Organization of the Islamic Conference in Jedda where they held discussions with Saudis. At times al-Sa'di conducted missions that one would normally associated with more traditional diplomats. After visiting representatives of the local Muslim community in Russia, he met the director general of the Russian oil company Bashneft. They concluded an agreement on "exchanging specialists and high school professors as well as exchanging gas and oil processing technologies."[49] These were not the type of negotiations one would expect from a religious leader.

As the Secretary General of the Popular Islamic Conference Organization, al-Sa'di's primary mission was to organize international Islamic activists to create bottom-up political pressure to end sanctions on Iraq. In 1995, the conference elected a twenty-five-member executive council of influential Islamic leaders from around the world. The Secretary General was al-Sa'di. The Chairman was the Jordanian cleric, Ali al-Faqir, who had served as the Jordanian Minister of Religious Endowments and then the First Deputy Speaker of the Jordanian Parliament. The Deputy Chairman was Yasin Umar al-Imam, who had helped found the ruling National Islamic Front in Sudan. Other prominent Islamic leaders made up the remaining members. Louis Farrakhan, the head of the Nation of Islam, represented the United States. While attending the meeting of the executive committee in September 1995, Farrakhan was organizing the Million Man March in Washington, DC. The march assembled the leading African American and civil rights organizations in the country to bring hundreds of thousands of black men together on the National Mall in October 1995. Farrakhan was at the height of his influence, and he would remain an important pro-Iraq voice in the United States for the remainder of Saddam's rule.[50]

The Popular Islamic Conference Organization's operations were mostly overt. The Ba'thist regime designed them to present Muslims around the world with an image of a pro-Iraq Islamic consensus. Baghdad relied on the Iraqi Intelligence Service to run other covert and clandestine operations among Islamic actors. The regime's goal was to use these dissidents to create costs for foreign states which might cooperate with the United States against Iraq. Throughout the mid-1990s, Iraqi intelligence officers worked closely with the Sudanese regime to contact and coordinate with Saudi dissidents. The Iraqis recruited Saudis from across the ideological spectrum, including the Shi'i Saudi Hezbollah, although Baghdad was concerned that it might be a front for Iranian intelligence.[51]

At times, the Iraqis brought disparate Saudi groups together. For example, the Saudi dissident Mohammad al-Massari was a prominent Islamist in London. The Iraqis worked through the Sudanese to contact him and then to coordinate anti-Saudi operations with him. The Iraqis also put him in contact with Ahmad Khudair Al-Zahrani, who had served as a Saudi diplomat at the embassy in Washington. When al-Zahrani defected, the United States refused to offer him asylum. Iraq stepped in to provide him and his family Iraqi passports under false names. When he arrived in Iraq in 1995, he immediately began coordinating with the Iraqi Intelligence Service and the Iraqis created links that would not have existed otherwise between him and other members of the Islamist Saudi opposition.[52]

In retrospect, the most prominent contact the Iraqis made through their Sudanese partners was Osama bin Laden. The brief relationship would come back to haunt Saddam in the buildup to the 2003 Iraq War as the George W. Bush administration looked to tie the Ba'thist regime to al-Qaida. The Iraqis listed bin Laden as the head of a Saudi dissident group called the "Reform and Advise Committee" which was based in Sudan. The Iraqis contacted him through the deputy head of the Sudanese National Islamic Front, Ibrahim al-Sanusi, who traveled to Baghdad in December 1994. In a meeting with Saddam's son Uday and the Director of the Iraqi Intelligence Service, al-Sanusi said that bin Laden was "reserved and afraid to be depicted by his enemies as an agent of Iraq."[53] Nevertheless, the two sides were willing to work toward the common purpose of undermining the regime in Riyadh. Saddam was informed about the discussion a few days later, and in January 1995, he approved the Iraqi Intelligence Service's trip to visit bin Laden in Sudan. The meeting occurred on February 19. Bin Laden requested the Iraqis broadcast the sermons of the dissident Saudi Islamist, Salman al-Awdah, from Iraq into Saudi Arabia. Bin Laden also suggested the two sides "perform joint operations against the foreign forces in the land of Hijaz." In March

1995, Saddam approved the broadcasts. The Iraqi Intelligence Service said it was "left to develop the relationship and the cooperation between the two sides to see what other doors of cooperation and agreement open." However, international pressure on Khartoum forced bin Laden to move from Sudan to Afghanistan in 1996. The Iraqis claimed to be in touch with him through the Sudanese, but the relationship seems to have ended and no more operations were planned.[54] Iraqi tactics like this posed a real threat to Saudi Arabia and made Riyadh reticent to support American actions in Iraq.

Iraqi outreach to Islamists was aided to some extent by a National Faith Campaign that Saddam launched in 1993. The regime increased religious education and built mosques across the country. Ironically, Saddam used the Faith Campaign within Iraq to crush Islamism in favor of a theologically generic, Arab nationalist interpretation of the religion. Its key institutions, such as the Saddam University of Islamic Studies, which graduated its first class the same month the Faith Campaign began, were created explicitly to undermine "the intellectual campaign and creed of Islamists."[55] The university banned Islamist literature from groups like the Muslim Brotherhood even for reference purposes, and the regime's records contain thousands of pages in which it attempted to root out any Islamist influence in Iraqi society. The mosques it built and the religious education it provided were simply tools for doing so.[56]

Of course, Saddam also added his own despotic flare to the campaign. In Baghdad, he built the enormous "Mother of all Battles Mosque," which had minarets shaped like Scud Missiles around its perimeter and then more four minarets shaped like AK-47 machine guns closer to the mosque's dome. The outer minarets were 37 meters high, and the four inner minarets stood at 28 meters. Together the numbers involved (4-28-37) denote Saddam's birthday. Inside the mosque, Saddam ensconced an ornate Qur'an written in his own blood.[57] By building mosques, however unorthodox, as well as increasing Islamic symbols and education at home, the regime could portray itself to potential foreign allies as a champion of Islam.

Of course, the dissonance between the regime's foreign and domestic policies often created friction. The Ba'thists lamented that the foreign Islamists they supported sometimes exploited their good relationship with the regime to spread Islamist literature inside Iraq.[58] Iraqi leaders often found navigating these relationships difficult. For example, Louis Farrakhan was one of Saddam's most enthusiastic and influential supporters in the United States, but when his name came up in a closed-door meeting, Saddam sneered, "By God, I do not like them. I do not like those who engage in politics under the guise of religion. I don't trust them."[59]

The superficiality of the regime's support for Islamism abroad can also be seen in how it quickly dispensed with Islamist or even Islamic rhetoric when courting non-Muslims. In 1993, the same year that Saddam launched his National Faith Campaign, Iraqi Ba'thists also created the Nonaligned Student and Youth Organization (NASYO). It was an international organization designed to fill the void left by communist and Soviet-backed student and youth organizations that lost power at the end of the Cold War. NASYO was headquartered in Baghdad and was controlled by the Ba'th Party with the help of the Iraqi Intelligence Service. It played a central role in the regime's attempt to organize international students, and later in the decade, Huda Ammash took direct control of it. Yet, despite the Faith Campaign in Iraq and Baghdad's outreach to foreign Islamists, NASYO's official motto was "A Secular International NGO at the Service of Humanity."[60] Islamists considered the term "secular" to be a dirty word and the humanistic motto rejected Islamist particularism. Clearly, the regime employed different tactics depending on the audience.

1996 Missile Strikes Expose Differences

The gradual breakdown in international support for the American approach to Iraq was laid bare during American-British missile strikes on Iraq in September 1996. The crisis grew out of a Kurdish civil war in northern Iraq. Once the Iraqi Kurds gained *de facto* autonomy following the Gulf War, the Patriotic Union of Kurdistan (PUK), led by Jalal Talabani almost immediately began a struggle for power and influence with Masoud Barzani's Kurdish Democratic Party (KDP). Each side maintained its own militia of Peshmerga fighters and the two factions engaged in an on-again-off-again conflict—often backed by various regional capitals—throughout the 1970s, 1980s, and early 1990s. Once northern Iraq was liberated from Ba'thist control and protected by an American-led no-fly zone, self-rule presented the two sides with possibility of real power for the first time. The heightened stakes and the lack of checks on their power by Baghdad led to increased tensions.[61]

The United States worked closely with all sides as it set up intelligence operations in northern Iraq and plotted to overthrow the regime in Baghdad.

The Ba'thist had their own spies in Kurdistan and they were well aware of American operations.[62] In the summer of 1996, an opportunity for Baghdad to address several problems at once appeared, and the Ba'thists quickly seized it.

The Kurdish conflict erupted into a civil war in the summer of 1996, and PUK forces advanced toward the KDP held capital of Iraqi Kurdistan, Irbil. Facing humiliation and defeat, Barzani did the unthinkable. He asked Saddam to send the Iraqi army to help him repel the PUK. Barzani's call to Baghdad came less than a decade after that same Iraqi army had carried out a genocidal campaign called al-Anfal against the Kurds. The Iraqi military had gassed the Kurdish city of Halabja and attempted to ethnically cleanse key areas like Kirkuk, replacing local Kurds with Arabs from southern Iraq. Hundreds of Kurdish villages were destroyed, and thousands of Kurdish civilians were massacred.[63] Barzani's decision to invite the Iraqi military back into Kurdish held territory outraged the PUK and outsiders like the Americans, who were assisting the Kurds in their fight against the Iraqi regime.

The United States was committed to protecting the Kurdish population, weakening the Iraqi military, and protecting its own intelligence assets in northern Iraq. As such, it decided to launch what it called Operation Desert Strike in September 1996 to compel an Iraqi retreat. However, regional and international politics were shifting in ways that constrained American actions.

Iraqi influence operations created significant difficulties for Middle Eastern leaders. Populations throughout the region were adopting Saddam's narrative, portraying Iraq as a victim of Western neo-imperialism. Local leaders began to distance themselves from the United States even as they privately told American officials that they agreed with, and wanted to support, American policies in Iraq. It simply was not politically viable for them to do so.[64]

When the US military attempted to launch the operation in 1996, Turkey, Jordan, and Saudi Arabia denied American requests to use their bases. As an American Air Force officer later reported, this rejection occurred "even though the strikes were already planned and ready for execution."[65] Without the use of those air bases, the American military had to rely on aircraft carriers in the Persian Gulf and long-range bombers based in Guam. The carrier-based aircraft did not have the range to carry out sustained operations in northern Iraq and the heavy bombers were ill-equipped for more nimble close air support missions that would be necessary to repel Iraqi ground forces. Instead, the United States was forced to launch less effective cruise missile strikes on Baghdad in the hope of deterring the regime's actions in northern Iraq. The results were far from conclusive.[66]

International support for American actions was also evaporating outside the Middle East. As UN Secretary General Boutros Boutros-Ghali commented, Saddam "found precisely the point that would create differences of opinion within the international community." Iraqi actions were "just outside the coverage of the Security Council resolutions but just inside the line where the United States would have to react or lose face."[67] France, Spain, Russia, and China condemned the missile strikes.[68] Russia described the attack as "inappropriate and unacceptable."[69] Its Foreign Minister, Yevgeny Primakov, condemned Washington, without mentioning it by name, accusing it of attempting to establish a hegemonic order in which there was "only one superpower in the world that could dictate its terms to others."[70] For the first time since the Gulf War, the Russians threatened to veto an American-backed resolution condemning Iraq at the Security Council. Washington and London were forced to withdraw their resolution and proceed without it.[71]

Just as important for the American-led coalition, and eventually for world order, Paris finally broke with Washington over the attack. Not only did France decline to participate in the strikes with the United States and the United Kingdom, but when the United States expanded the southern no-fly zone during the operation, the French Air Force pulled out of the coalition enforcing it. Eventually the French rejoined the coalition flying over southern Iraq, but only within the original boundaries, and as it turned out, only temporarily. France quit the coalition enforcing the northern no-fly zone at the end of the year and then then southern no-fly zone in 1998.

The French covered their rupture with the Americans in diplomatic niceties to preserve the appearance of Western unity. They used the change in designation of the northern no-fly zone from Operation Provide Comfort to Operation Northern Watch to withdraw from it. In doing so, Paris claimed that it was not pulling out of an operation but refusing to join a new one. Despite the semantics, there was no denying that the French were abandoning their erstwhile partners.

French posturing could not fully hide the growing rift between Paris and Washington. In addition to seeing Washington's approach in Iraq as counterproductive, Chirac also considered US policy toward Iraq as an opportunity to restore France's influence in the region at America's expense. In April of 1996, he gave a high-profile speech in Cairo in which he touted France's "Arab" policy as an alternative to American domination. In it he highlighted French differences with the US over Iraqi sanctions.[72]

Chirac's strategy tapped into growing disillusionment with American policies in Iraq throughout the Middle East. Arab resolve was evaporating. Kuwait was the only Arab state to support the American-led strikes publicly in 1996.[73] Several Arab governments showed an increasing willingness to co-operate with Saddam. Even Syria, which had long been one of Iraq's most relentless nemeses, condemned the American-led strikes. The Arab press reported that Syrian President Hafez al-Assad met with Saddam and while a full diplomatic breakthrough did not occur, the two regimes agreed on important steps such as water-sharing and the exchange of officials.[74]

Conclusion

For Saddam and his regime, the inroads that Ba'thists made in political systems around the world marked important political gains. Paris's divergence with Washington, as well as shifting attitudes in Russia and the Middle East highlighted an important turning point and a new direction in global politics. The once unified American-led coalition was breaking apart. As a result, norms of unity and cooperation that underpinned the anti-Iraq coalition at the Security Council were melting. These trends would grow even more profound in the coming years and would eventually entice Saddam to challenge the system more directly.

8

Breaking Isolation

In 1911, the British naval theorist, Sir Julian Corbett, observed that a blockade "can only work by a process of exhaustion." Thus, "its effects must always be slow, and so galling both to our own commercial community and to neutrals, that the tendency is always to accept terms of peace that are far from conclusive."[1] The UN embargo on Iraq was the late-twentieth century equivalent to the naval blockade of Corbett's time. As Corbett would have predicted, the effects of the embargo proved slow to influence Saddam. They indeed proved galling to commercial interests and to neutral parties, and they would ultimately force the United States, at least temporarily, to accept terms of peace that were far from conclusive.

In addition to a grinding economic embargo, Iraq also faced invasive weapons inspections. With the defection of Hussein Kamel, the Iraqi regime gave up the last of its documentation on its weapon of mass destruction. There was nothing else it could turn over to inspectors, but considering Iraq's previous deceptions, the international community simply did not believe Baghdad. Iraq refused to detail the denial and deception program it had previously used against the inspectors because doing so would have exposed other state secrets, and it would have likely created more doubts about Iraqi intentions. As such, Saddam saw little reason to think that the inspections or sanctions would ever end.

Saddam needed to alleviate Iraq's financial situation, meet some of his population's humanitarian needs, and regain some semblance of the sovereignty that the inspections and sanctions had eroded. At the heart of Iraq's problems as well as their solutions was America's relationship with its allies and partners, especially at the Security Council. Those relationships had already hit a turning point in the mid-1990s. Then, the passage of a viable oil-for-food program provided Saddam powerful economic weapons to pry these alliances apart even further and create even more space to pursue Iraqi interests.

Iraq against the World. Samuel Helfont, Oxford University Press. © Oxford University Press 2023.
DOI: 10.1093/oso/9780197530153.003.0009

Oil-for-Food

By the mid-1990s, the United States was torn between two competing impulses. Gary Sick, who had served on President Jimmy Carter's National Security Council staff and remained one of the most influential American voices on Middle East policy, summed up the sentiment in the journal *Survival*. On one hand, he argued, "There is very little debate in the US about the desirability—even the necessity—of maintaining strict sanctions against Saddam Hussein's government." On the other hand, "There is considerable sympathy in the US for the plight of the Iraqi people."[2]

This dichotomy setup American officials for political failures. Most infamously, in 1996, the host of the popular television show, *60 Minutes*, asked Madeleine Albright: Was "the price worth it" when a "half million children have died" in Iraq because of American policy? Albright responded, "I think this is a very hard choice, but the price—we think the price is worth it."[3] She later stated that she regretted the comment.[4] Nevertheless, her words reflected a genuine sentiment that increasingly isolated the United States from much of the international community.

Elsewhere, once-staunch American allies increasingly found the US approach to Iraq untenable. Washington had already lost Russia and France. Other important states were headed in the same direction. In February 1995, press reports discussed Spanish and Brazilian attempts to end sanctions.[5] During Security Council discussions in April 1995, the Italian representative at stated, "Frankly, an Iraqi child who looks at us from our television screens, with his big eyes made even larger by famine and disease, is no different from a child in Somalia or any other country whom we rush to aid."[6] Something clearly had to change.

In 1995, Washington and London made what a former Canadian Ambassador to the United Nations called "rare concessions to Baghdad" on the oil-for-food program.[7] Iraq had rejected the original incarnation of the program in 1991. Over the years, Baghdad held out, arguing that it had no problem with UN monitors, but "as a sovereign country," Iraq could not accept some other authority "to impose on us the way we feed our people."[8] The revised plan in 1995 made Baghdad responsible for distributing the food and humanitarian aid in the country. That had been a key component of a plan that the United States blocked in the summer of 1991 prior to sponsoring its own oil-for-food resolution. At the time, Washington balked at allowing the Ba'thists to use the program to reassert their power, but by 1995, Saddam had worn down American resolve. In another major concession, the new formula allowed Iraq to choose the contractors to which it would sell its oil and to negotiate the conditions with them directly.[9] The latter concession permitted Iraq to manipulate the program for considerable political and financial gains.

Even with these incentives, the Iraqis were at first reluctant to agree to the new plan. In a closed-door meeting, Saddam said he feared that accepting the agreement would create a sustainable status quo. He did not want to "lose the focus of the security council" while sanctions remained in place and the Kurdish regions remained outside of Baghdad's control.[10] Nevertheless, the new plan had numerous advantages. Saddam was particularly concerned about controlling Iraqi resources and this plan allowed for that. Some mundane and practical matters also sweetened the deal. The Iraqi Minister of Trade told Saddam that the deal would allow Iraq to import goods through the Persian Gulf rather than by the land route from Jordan. Doing so would rescue Iraqi ports from dilapidation, allowing them to remain functional for future operation once sanctions were eventually lifted. Trade deals could be renegotiated much more easily than infrastructure and ports could be rebuilt.[11]

Saddam also felt boxed in. The Iraqi economy had sunk to a catastrophic state with no end in sight. Saddam did not believe that the inspections were genuine attempts to rid Iraq of illicit weapons. As he told his advisors, "we destroyed everything they asked us to."[12] As such, Iraq could not do anything to lift the siege and as Saddam stated, "there is not a chance on the horizon for it to end, no one can say that it will be over in a year, or six months."[13]

Iraq reluctantly agreed to the 1995 oil-for-food resolution, yet the implementation was delayed several times. First, the Iraqis dragged their feet. Then, in 1996, the Iraqi military's intervention in the Kurdish civil war and the American-British attacks led Washington to block the program for several more months. Finally, at the end of 1996, it went into effect.

Buying Influence

The oil-for-food program offered the Ba'thists tremendous power to shape international politics. Baghdad's corruption of the program developed over several phases, each with different tactics and goals. As discussed in next chapter, the regime eventually tried to benefit financially through illicit kickbacks. However, Saddam initially used the program simply for political gain. As a UN-sponsored independent inquiry into the program found, "the government of Saddam Hussein was willing to forego revenue from oil sales or to overpay for imports to reward or encourage certain foreign politicians, journalists, and businesses to exert influence in its favor, most especially in advocating a lifting of the sanctions."[14]

The Iraqi regime created a "Command Council" headed by Vice President Taha Yassin Ramadan and including Deputy Prime Minister Tariq Aziz, as well as the Minister of Oil and Minister of Finance. The Council was responsible for identifying politically influential people, companies, and states that could help Iraq, especially at the United Nations. Then, in an attempt either to influence their future behavior or reward previous actions, the regime provided them lucrative contracts for Iraqi oil. As one internal Iraqi report stated, "These contracts" were "intended to be an economic weapon."[15]

For the Iraqi strategy to work, the regime needed to find people and companies that were willing to trade influence for oil. Thus, Ba'thists who had spent the previous decade embedding themselves in the political landscapes of influential states provided the foundation on which the regime conducted its oil-for-food scheme. Such operations needed to be discrete. The Iraqis established front companies, sometimes in Jordan, and they often created proxy firms in Iraq through which they could work. Much of the process was controlled by senior officials on the Command Council and the Iraqi Intelligence Service. At times, even the Ba'thists working abroad to identify potential targets for the regime to exploit did not fully understand the system.[16]

Nevertheless, the Ba'thists applied the hard-won lessons and experience they had gained over the years to manipulate the oil-for-food program. Huda Ammash, who had led the Iraqi efforts to influence America, expanded her role to cover Europe as well. She traveled to key states and personally aided the efforts of Ba'thists working there. For example, on a trip to Spain in 1999, she worked with local Ba'thists to determine "Iraq's connection with a number of Spanish oil companies that have influence on Spanish political decisions because of their great leverage over politicians."[17] When she returned to Baghdad, she provided the regime information about "important and influential companies" in Spain that had money invested in Iraqi projects which had been suspended because of sanctions. She recommended "that an invitation be extended to these companies to aid or facilitate Iraq either directly or indirectly." She believed that "promises that Iraq will settle its debt" would entice them to work with "influential people who are known to the Iraqi embassy in Madrid." In doing so, they could "help to open these outlets on the Spanish economy and then on political decisions."[18]

Other Iraqi Ba'thists, who had worked in the hostile and enigmatic political landscape of the United States, also expanded their operations internationally. Shakir al-Khafaji was a naturalized American citizen with a degree in architecture from the New York Institute of Technology. He was the director of the office of former US Attorney General Ramsey Clark, who was one of the most prominent pro-Iraq voices in the United States. Al-Khafaji also worked closely with Abdul Kadir al-Kaysi—also known as Keduri. Like Keduri, who was discussed in Chapter 6, al-Khafaji had many detractors and the regime struggled to pin down his loyalties.

On one hand, some internal reports claimed he was a veteran of the Iran-Iraq War and a senior Ba'thist in good standing. Apparently, he had done important work with Ramsey Clark on behalf of the regime during the Gulf War. He led the Ba'th Party organization among the Arab community, including students in New York and he carried out operations behalf of the Iraqi Ambassador to the United Nations.[19]

On the other hand, Saubhe Jassim Al-Dellemy—the Iraqi Ba'thist who ran intelligence operations out of a kebab restaurant in Maryland and who was later arrested in the United States for working as an illegal foreign agent[20]—claimed al-Khafaji had "suspicious connections" with unscrupulous members of the Iraqi-American community, one of whom had been killed in 1992 while working with drug gangs. Other reports accused him of cursing the Ba'th Party in front of the wife of another Ba'thist, and of running poker games out of a number of homes, including his own. The head of the Ba'th Party in the United States, Sameer al-Nima, also reported that al-Khafaji falsely claimed to be a spokesman on behalf of the Iraqi embassy at the United Nations and to be the head of the party organization in Detroit. Al-Nima conceded that al-Khafaji had numerous enemies within the Iraqi-American community and thus reports about him were "not always objective." However, al-Nima continued, "trusted sources in New Jersey" confirmed "some of this negative information." And likewise, in 1993, al-Nima personally attested to the fact that al-Khafaji did not currently have any connections with the party.[21]

Despite such reports, by the end of the decade, al-Khafaji managed to work himself into the middle of Iraq's international oil-for-food schemes. He facilitated contracts on behalf of the regime with the energy companies Italtech and Bayoil. The latter, which was American, amused Iraq's Minister of Oil, who "enjoyed the irony of a United States company indirectly assisting in the financing of Iraq's lobbying effort against the sanctions."[22] As one might expect from al-Khafaji's background, people who dealt with him in these shady deals were often left with unexpected debts and with al-Khafaji nowhere to be found.[23]

Nevertheless, al-Khafaji also participated in some successful operations. For example, in the late 1990s, Iraq courted South Africa intensely. The South African President, Thabo Mbeki not only led South Africa's ruling party, but he was also the Chair of the Nonaligned Movement and the Chairman of the African Union.[24] Iraq ran influence operations in the country, staging protests against sanctions and making political alliances with local actors.[25] Tariq Aziz asked al-Khafaji to facilitate Iraq's relationship with South Africa by granting oil contracts to Sandi Majali and Rodney Hemphill. The former was an advisor to President Mbeki and the latter was a South African businessman who ran the Montega Trading corporation. Al-Khafaji traveled with both men to Baghdad, where after several days of meetings, Majali was awarded a contract for two million barrels of Iraqi oil, which he used Montega Trading to purchase.[26]

The United Nations' oil-for-food inquiry highlighted al-Khafaji's courting of Majali as an example of the "exploitation of the symbiotic relationship between a country's closely aligned political and business figures and the Government of Iraq."[27] Majali, the inquiry stated, became "very involved in strengthening ties between South Africa and Iraq." He led various high-level delegations representing business and energy firms, and he held discussions aimed at strengthening ties between South Africa's ruling African National Congress party and the Iraq Ba'th Party. Majali stated explicitly that a "joint effort" between the African National Congress and the Iraqi Ba'th Party "will add a lot of value towards achieving the common political objectives" and "will result in an effective strategy geared towards campaigning for the lifting of sanctions."[28]

Al-Khafaji's courting of Majali was part of a broader operation targeting South Africa in the late 1990s and the early 2000s. Throughout the oil-for-food program, Iraq actively developed business and political ties to South Africa. In November 1999, South Africa's Deputy Foreign Minister Aziz Pahad traveled to Iraq at the head of a delegation of thirty South African companies representing oil, electricity, and other sectors. One of the goals was "to expose South African businesses with already established interests in the so-called 'oil-for-food' programme . . . to the processes involved in winning such UN-approved contracts."[29] Within a week of Pahad's return home, Iraq established an embassy in the South African capital of Pretoria. In 2001, Iraq accredited its ambassador there, using funds which had previously been frozen. For the remainder of the Iraqi regime's time in power, its leaders, including Saddam, made clear to their South African counterparts that they would "observe special care" to ensure that economic, technical, and scientific relations with South Africa benefited from the political support that South Africa provided Iraq.[30]

The Iraqis also targeted other states in which they had well-established Ba'thist networks. In Austria, the Iraqis pursued the far-right politician, Joerg Haider and his Freiheits Partei Öesterreichs (FPÖ). Following the fall of the Iraqi regime, a scandal erupted in Austria over the revelations that the FPÖ-associated Iraqi-Austrian Society "concluded lucrative oil deals with the Iraqi dictator." According to Iraqi documents, the society sold their oil to a UAE-based company that was controlled by Iraqi Vice President Taha Yassin Ramadan.[31]

In the United Kingdom, the Iraqis targeted the far-left Member of Parliament, George Galloway. In the late 1990s, he was one of the most forceful British opponents of sanctions. Though the extent that he benefited financially remains unclear, the UN oil-for-food inquiry asserted that a "total of over 18 million barrels of oil were allocated either directly in the name of George Galloway ... or in the name of one of his associates ... to support Mr. Galloway's campaign against the sanctions."[32]

Early in the oil-for-food program, as the UN inquiry noted, the most important factor for determining who to target "was influencing foreign policy and international public opinion in favor of ending sanctions against Iraq." As such, Iraq favored companies and people in states that Tariq Aziz described as "friendly."[33] Initially, the Iraqis hoped to influence American policy, but they quickly realized that the United States would not change course. As such, the main Iraqi effort focused on Russia, China, France, and Italy. The latter had a large energy sector and occupied one of the rotating seats on the Security Council in the late 1990s. Taha Yassin Ramadan took responsibility for Russia and China, and Tariq Aziz did the same for France and Italy.[34]

Of these states, investigations later revealed that the Russian government was most explicitly linked to the oil-for-food scheme. Moscow took an "active role in coordinating the activities of Russian companies" that participated in the program. Tariq Aziz had "almost weekly" meetings with the Russian ambassador in Baghdad. Also, in addition to the major oil companies, contracts were also allocated to Russian political figures like the heads of the Liberal Democratic Party and the Communist Party, which were helping Iraq to shape Russian policy and break sanctions.[35] The leader of the Liberal Democratic Party, Vladimir Zhirinovsky, who was one of Iraq's first and most forceful allies in post-communist Russia, received an allocation of 73 million barrels, which he could sell for a significant personal profit.[36]

Like Russia, the Iraqis saw France as a "friend," and French companies were second only to the Russians in the amount of oil Baghdad allocated them. Yet, the relationship between the French government was less direct. The Iraqis relied on French companies and influential elder statesmen to lobby the French government instead of providing contracts directly to French leaders. Yet, as the Iraqi Minister of Oil stated, "at times there was a direct correlation between an increase in oil allocations and the extent of a beneficiary's anti-sanctions activities."[37]

The most noteworthy French case was that of Jean-Bernard Mérimée. He had served as France's representative at the Security Council from 1991 through 1995, including periods as the Council's President, a position which rotated among the representatives. This put him at the Security Council when the more conciliatory version of the oil-for-food program was renegotiated and adopted in 1995. He advocated for lifting the sanctions and the Iraqi Oil Minister praised France's "positive and important role" to pass the resolution during his tenure.[38] In 1998, Mérimée retired from the French Ministry of Foreign Affairs. From 1999 until 2002, he served in various senior posts at the United Nations under Secretary General Kofi Annan. During this later period, Iraq allocated him six million barrels of oil on which he made 165,725 US dollars in commissions. In 2005, he admitted in French court that it was a bribe.[39]

In addition to Mérimée, several other senior French statesmen were implicated. The French courts also convicted the French oil company Total of taking bribes from Iraq between 1996 and 2003, and they fined the Swiss company Vitol. Over a dozen more French corporations were dragged into court in the decade following Saddam's downfall and the release of the UN oil-for-food inquiry.[40] These people and corporations had an immense impact on French policy toward Iraq in the late 1990s and early 2000s. At Iraq's behest, they helped to drive a wedge between Washington and Paris.

The End of Inspections

By 1997, Iraq found itself at a crossroad. As discussed previously, Saddam did not think Iraq could satisfy the UN weapons inspectors. After all, he reasoned, Iraq had already given up or destroyed all its illicit weapons. Any new revelation about defunct programs was likely to delay the end of sanctions rather than alleviate them.[41] With the United States increasingly signaling that it would block any move to end sanctions until a new regime came to power in Iraq, Saddam had little incentive to cooperate.[42]

In addition to these disincentives, Saddam also felt increasingly comfortable with Iraq's geopolitical position. He had been prying France and Russia away from the American-led faction on the Security Council for several years. The American-British missile strikes on Iraq in 1996 finally brought to the surface tensions that had been simmering between Washington and its erstwhile supporters in Paris and Moscow. Then the oil-for-food program, which went into effect at the end of 1996, gave Iraq the political and economic tools to keep the Security Council divided.

In 1997, the lack of incentive to cooperate and the political leverage Iraq had gained led Saddam to challenge the UN weapons inspections and sanctions more forcefully. In the spring, Iraq requested 50 million US dollars that had been frozen in Gulf Arab states to finance Iraqi pilgrims participating in the *hajj* to Mecca. Baghdad never took the necessary steps to recover the money; it preferred to let the impression that the pilgrims were being blocked stain Iraq's adversaries. Then, without gaining the required clearance from the Sanctions Committee, Iraq flew a plane of elderly pilgrims to Saudi Arabia. The flight was clearly designed to challenge restrictions on Iraqi sovereignty in a way that regional Arab leaders could not oppose politically. By flying through Jordanian and Saudi airspace, Iraq essentially dared each of those states to stop the flight. Saddam knew that neither wanted to deal with the political backlash they would face. The Security Council noted its displeasure that Iraq did not make a formal request for the flight, but it stopped short of condemning it. By violating UN restrictions without being punished, the episode was a clear political victory for Saddam.[43]

In the summer of 1997, Iraq began restricting or delaying the inspectors' access to sensitive sites such as the offices of its Special Security Organization and presidential palaces. Saddam thought the insistence on inspecting palaces to be ridiculous and probably in bad faith. Storing weapons of mass destruction in a palace would have put the regime's leadership at risk. Such weapons would be stored deep in the desert if Iraq had them.[44]

In response to Iraq banning some inspections, Washington and London wanted to impose further sanctions that restricted the travel of regime officials. However, when they brought the matter to the Security Council, they quickly learned the extent that American and British standing had diminished. The Russians and others negotiated the resolution down to a threat of sanctions, rather than actually imposing them. Even then, France and China clearly disliked it. Stalwart American allies like Egypt, which had a rotating seat on the council, stated that it was "opposed to any measures that might increase tensions in the region."[45] Cairo worried about Iraq's ability to foment unrest on Egyptian streets, as would indeed occur a year later. In the end, China, Egypt, France, Kenya, and Russia abstained from the watered-down resolution. The abstentions allowed it to pass, but the vote was a major blow to the United States and to the unity of the Security Council on Iraq. It also marked a turning point among the five permanent members. Beginning with that resolution, two clear voting blocs emerged. China, Russia, and France consistently banded together to oppose the United States and the United Kingdom. France's position in what was otherwise a non-Western grouping perturbed other Western diplomats.[46]

Saddam saw the vote as a major defeat for the United States and an indication of the Security Council's evolving alignments. He pushed to further exacerbate the divisions. As early as 1992, Saddam had told Tariq Aziz in a private meeting that regarding inspectors, "our core demand is that we want neutral people whom we will agree upon." At the time, Saddam favored Chines and Indian inspectors.[47] By 1997, the group of nationalities that Saddam trusted had expanded considerably. Saddam simply wanted to exclude American and British inspectors, who he claimed, posed a threat to Iraqi security. To isolate the United States, Iraq announced that it would no longer allow Americans to participate in inspections. It was an overreach. The Security Council voted unanimously to condemn Iraq and it imposed sanctions restricting the travel of Iraqi officials. In response, Iraq expelled the remaining inspectors.[48]

The United States deployed an additional aircraft carrier, the USS George Washington, to the Persian Gulf in anticipation of a confrontation. Yet, unlike in the Gulf Crisis seven years earlier, Saddam realized that the international community was uniting against him, and he backed down. Russia helped Iraq to negotiate a compromise that allowed American inspectors to return in exchange for a promise that the inspection teams would be reviewed and reformed.[49]

Even with Russian mediation, Iraq's actions strained the Russian-American relationship. Clinton understood the importance of his relationship with Moscow for the post–Cold War order and he worked hard to maintain a cordial rapport with Russian President Boris Yeltsin.[50] However, in November 1997, Clinton sent him an eyes-only message to follow up on a phone call. In it, he complained, "Frankly, I was a bit disappointed that your delegation at the UN felt it necessary to question the validity of [the UN inspectors]'s findings." He then pivoted to more diplomatic language, claiming that if Iraq cooperated, "the council should be able to explore ways to get more humanitarian aid to the Iraqi people, something I strongly support."[51]

Yet, the damage was clearly done. British Prime Minister Tony Blair sent Clinton a cable emphasizing his solidarity with the United States, but he worried about "the unity of the international community, and particularly the members of the council." He said that he had spoken with French President Chirac, who had "strong personal doubts about our approach to Saddam Hussein." Blair entreated, "we will have to work very hard to keep the French with us, not to mention the Russians."[52] When Clinton called Blair the following week, he expressed similar concerns. He feared that they were losing popular support in Europe, and that there was considerable "popular sympathy in the Middle East for the people of Iraq."[53] Clearly the American-led coalition at the United Nations was on the defensive.

After temporarily backing off, Saddam continued to apply political and economic pressure to divide the Security Council. By February 1998, he was confident, as he explained to his advisors, that Iraq could manipulate the "personal interests" of officials in Russia, France, and China. "Because of what they will get out of this," Saddam believed, their "positions" would "be stronger in a second confrontation."[54]

The Iraqi regime continued to clash with the United Nations and as CNN reported, "the crisis over weapons inspections . . . brought the Gulf to the brink of war, with the United States sending a naval armada and 25,000 troops to the region to mount possible air strikes."[55] In response, Iraq mobilized its international networks to stop an American attack. In 1996, Iraq had exerted enough political pressure in the region to prevent the US military from launching attacks from local air bases. As a result, Washington had to call off its operation against the Iraqi military and instead to launch largely ineffective missile strikes on Baghdad.

In February 1998, Saddam adopted a similar strategy. One of his most effective weapons was to incite his supporters, especially Islamists, around the
region. As tensions between Iraq and the United States rose, Iraq convened a
Popular Islamic Conference in Baghdad. The event's message was: "the states
of infidelity and aggression are launching an unjust campaign and making
false allegations."[56] Conference delegates from around the Muslim world
marched through Baghdad. They set fire to American and Israeli flags outside the UN office and called for an end to "aggression against Iraq and its
people."[57]

The Iraqi regime coordinated the efforts of its sympathizers around the
region to coincide with the conference in Baghdad. In Egypt, the Muslim
Brotherhood's General Guide, Mustafa Mashhur, defended the Iraqi regime.
In an essay titled, "This Harassment of Iraq," he condemned the United States
and Britain. At the same time, the Islamist press covered what it termed
"mammoth" pro-Iraq demonstrations in Egypt.[58] Similarly, several thousand
Islamists took to the streets in Jordan to support Saddam during the conference. The demonstrations ended in a violent clash with Jordanian security
forces.[59] For authoritarian regimes, such events were as great a danger as any
diplomatic or economic threat.

Yet, after bringing the world to the brink of war in February 1998, Saddam
again backed down. This time, French President Chirac and UN Secretary
General Kofi Annan stepped in to quell the crisis. Annan travelled to
Baghdad to negotiate a compromise with Tariq Aziz. The Iraqis made two
key concessions. They allowed inspectors to enter presidential palaces, and
the regime gave up its insistence on setting an end date to the sanctions and
inspections regime. The French had worked behind the scenes to cement the
deal and Chirac saw it as a major victory for French diplomacy over the more
militarized American approach.[60]

Although Saddam backed down, Clinton and Blair worried that he continued to pose a real threat to peace and security. They also knew they were
losing the fight for global opinion. In a meeting at the White House on
February 5, Blair asserted, "We have to educate international opinion so they
see the real threat and choices we face."[61] A week later in a phone call with
Blair, Clinton feared that they looked "blood thirsty" to "European public
opinion and Arab public opinion."[62]

By the summer, Iraq was again confronting the inspectors. On August
3, Saddam once more attempted to sow division at the Security Council by
announcing that he was suspending the inspections until the teams were

reconfigured with fewer "Anglo-Saxons."[63] The UN inspection teams left Iraq. Washington and London prepared for military strikes.

As the military buildup continued in the fall, Saddam was clearly frustrated with the inspections and honestly skeptical about their intentions. He complained to his advisors in a private meeting, "they destroyed everything they wanted to destroy and said Iraq implemented 95 percent of the resolution ... As for the five percent, it might take another ten years without getting results." Concerned that he might have just given the wrong impression to his inner circle about the contents of the remaining five percent, he clarified that if any of "you might think we still have hidden chemical weapons, missiles and so forth. We have nothing; not even one screw."[64]

Nevertheless, as military strikes appeared imminent in November, Iraq backed down again. To many observers, Saddam seemed to be toying with the Americans. Clinton came under intense domestic pressure to deal with Iraq decisively. Ralph Peters, a former Army officer turned public intellectual, wrote, "Iraq just taught the world how to put the most powerful military in history on a leash: plant your vulnerable assets in cities, broadcast the misery of your people and convince America's leadership that political defeat will be the price of military victory."[65]

Mobilizing and then demobilizing every few months was not feasible for the United States financially or in terms of manpower. By mid-December, Clinton had reached the end of his patience. The Americans and the British launched an intense four-day operation that included hundreds of airstrikes and cruise missiles.[66]

The Iraqis again mobilized their international networks to apply political pressure on the United States, its Middle Eastern allies, and the Security Council. Across the Arab World, Iraqi Ba'thists worked with local allies to hold marches, publish articles, and protest at Western embassies.[67] Although these events were designed to appear as spontaneous expressions of rage by local populations, Baghdad supplied approved lists of slogans. They included: "The Arab masses will remain thorns in the eyes of Americans and their agents"; "Victory to the great Iraq, and to its leader Saddam Hussein"; "The evil blockade on Iraq will fall"; and "The banner of Iraq and the banner of *allah akbar* will remain high despite the Zionist-British-American terrorism." The last slogan contained a double meaning. The banner of *allah akbar* clearly conjured Islamic passions, but it also referred to the Iraqi flag, which had the words *allah akbar* written on it.[68]

In Europe, Iraqi influence operations targeted states such as Italy and Poland, which had rotating seats on the Security Council.[69] The Iraqis also organized demonstrations at the United Nations headquarters in Geneva. They pushed stories about how American intelligence agencies had infiltrated the UN inspection teams and how the real goal of the inspectors was to overthrow the regime rather than eliminate illicit weapons. Those allegations contained enough truth to garner a sympathetic hearing in the Western press.[70]

At the Security Council, Saddam's halting of inspections in August was such a blatant violation of binding resolutions that even Russia and France could not openly support Baghdad. They remained uncharacteristically quiet throughout the fall, but in private conversations with Clinton, the crisis in their relationships with the United States was deepening.

Part of the disagreement concerned differing interpretations of UN resolutions and the right to use force. The Security Council resolutions governing sanctions and inspections were part of the Gulf War's ceasefire agreement. The Americans and the British maintained that Iraqi violations put Baghdad in breach of the ceasefire and thus in a state of conflict. That conflict had already been authorized by the Security Council in 1991. As such the United States and United Kingdom did not believe they needed another Security Council resolution to attack Iraq. Russia and China disagreed with this interpretation. They felt another resolution was necessary. France had agreed with the United States and the United Kingdom earlier in the decade but had since switched to the Russian and Chinese position.

The Russians attempted to pressure Iraq back into compliance, and in early December, President Yeltsin wrote to Clinton to reassure him that Russia was cooperating. Yet, at the same time, Yeltsin admonished Clinton, "we should not overdramatize the situation."[71] As the month progressed and American military strikes became imminent, the relationship spiraled downward. Clinton and other world leaders with whom he spoke claimed that Yeltsin did not have strong personal feelings about the American actions, but that Yeltsin was under immense domestic pressure, and other Russian leaders were extremely upset.[72] After the American-led attacks began on December 16, an internal US National Security Council memo described Russian Foreign Minister Primakov as acting "very emotionally,"[73] and on December 18, Moscow recalled its ambassador to Washington for the first time since World War II.[74]

Clinton wrote Yeltsin, pleading, "the relationship between the United States and Russia that you and I have worked so hard to build is far too important and, to my mind, far too sound, to be subverted by Saddam Hussein."[75] Yet, on December 30, Yeltsin wrote back, clarifying that, indeed, "what is at stake is not just the person of Saddam Hussein but our relations with the US."[76] The Russian-American relations that harkened a new world order at the beginning of the decade were crumbling.

Of course, Iraq was not the only issue spoiling Russian-American relations. Russians had adopted the free-market principles that they associated with America and the West, but those policies had made a small group of oligarchs extraordinarily rich while leaving most of the country impoverished. As this reality became apparent in the late 1990s, many Russians soured on the United States. In August 1998, just as Iraq was challenging the "Anglo-Saxon" inspectors, Russia experienced a major financial crisis. Moscow devalued the Russian ruble and defaulted on its dept. The result was an economic meltdown that spread throughout Russia and to its neighbors as well.[77] Russians blamed Westernizing reforms and that context almost certainly affected Yeltsin's relationship with Clinton as the crisis in Iraq unfolded in the autumn. Yet, in the end, Russia finally recalled its ambassadors in Washington and London over Iraq, not economics, or other points of disagreement like NATO expansion or conflict in the Balkans.

Clinton's relationship with Chirac was more cordial, but they clearly disagreed. Chirac made the case over the course of multiple conversations that the American approach was self-defeating. As he told Clinton, "Saddam thinks . . . the best way to regain control of the people is to pretend to be a martyr." In other words, "what he's thinking is that if there is a military strike against him, he'll regain control of those people and public opinion in the Arab world." As such, "we find ourselves in a rather peculiar position. We have nothing to give, nothing to offer . . . But in truth I'm afraid we are working here with an unarmed gun. I think it's in his own interest to be bombed."[78]

Chirac made a strong argument and Clinton could not dispute his point about military strikes empowering Saddam. However, for Clinton, like Bush before him, a larger question of principle and world order was at stake. "What happens to countries when they pledge to complete an inspection regime and don't do it?" he asked Chirac.[79] If a state could simply ignore binding Security Council resolutions, the rule of law could not be upheld.

Clinton also thought that Chirac was feigning innocence about his relationship with Iraq. In a follow-on conversation, Clinton brought up the same point about the need to enforce resolutions. In reply Chirac asked whether Clinton thought Saddam would allow inspectors to return. Quite undiplomatically, Clinton quipped, "I think he might if the French Government asks him."[80] The obvious implication was that France had not done all it could to pressure Iraq.

Arab leaders supported Clinton in private conversations, but they were much more cautious in public. In October 1998, Saudi Arabia's de facto ruler, Crown Prince Abdullah, told Clinton that he would support military action if diplomacy failed. In November, Clinton called him back to state that diplomacy had indeed failed and to request Saudi support. The American Joint Chiefs of Staff and the Office of the Secretary of Defense pushed hard to base strike aircraft in the kingdom for an attack on Iraq, and Clinton sent Secretary of Defense William Cohen to discuss the matter with Abdullah. Although the crown prince supported Clinton in private, he did not allow any strike missions to be flown from bases in his country. The political cost was just too high.[81]

Even in the United States, the political landscape was changing. Congress pushed Clinton to be more aggressive in Iraq, but at the same time, pockets of discontent grew increasingly vocal in denouncing American policy there. The changing mood was perhaps most evident in February 1998 when CNN hosted Clinton's National Security Advisor Sandy Berger, Secretary of Defense Cohen, and Secretary of State Albright at Ohio State University for a televised townhall on the administration's Iraq policy. Much of the audience was openly hostile to US policy, and the large, raucous crowd repeatedly interrupted the speakers. Members of the audience shouted down points they did not like and frustrated the administration officials by accusing Clinton of trying to "send a message" to Saddam "with the blood of Iraqi men, women and children."[82]

The 1998 Iraq crisis unfolded as Clinton faced a domestic backlash surrounding an extramarital affair he had with the White House intern, Monica Lewinsky. Accusations that he lied about the affair under oath were leading to calls for his impeachment. His critics claimed that he had manufactured the conflict with Iraq to distract the public from his personal and political problems. A Republican Representative from New York, Gerald Solomon, claimed "It is obvious that he is doing this for political reasons." Senate Majority Leader Trent Lott averred, "While I have been assured by administration officials that there is no connection with the impeachment process . . . [b]oth the timing and the policy are subject to question." Even critics who accepted that Clinton acted in good faith, offered backhanded condemnations. *The Wall Street Journal* editorial board stated, "It is dangerous for an American president to launch a military strike, however justified, at a time when many will conclude he acted only out of narrow self-interest to forestall or postpone his own impeachment."[83]

More damning for the operation than the political blowback was its complete ineffectiveness in achieving its objective. It cost the United States half a billion dollars and was America's largest military operation since the Gulf War. Yet, it did not compel Saddam to allow inspectors back into Iraq.[84]

Stalemate in Postinspections Iraq

Far from quelling Saddam's obstinance, the December 1998 strikes on Iraq seemed to embolden him, and he confronted restrictions on Iraqi sovereignty even more forcefully. As an American Air Force officer, Paul White, claimed, following the operation, "overt Iraqi challenges in the no-fly zones quickly became an almost daily occurrence."[85] The Americans and the British responded in kind. The commander of Iraqi air defense, Lt. Gen. Shakir, reported that the allies flew 10,977 sorties against Iraq between the end of hostilities in December 1998 and August 1999. The Americans and the British fired over 1,000 missiles at 360 Iraqi targets during that period.[86] Yet, as White argued, the US Department of Defense "deliberately downplayed the continuing air strikes against Iraq in an effort to avoid antagonizing neighboring Arab countries who tacitly approved of the campaign but deplored the impact it was having on the Iraqi people."[87] As a result, some observers termed the period a "low-level war of attrition," the "forgotten war," or the "silent war."[88]

Yet, the UN inspectors did not return to Iraq and there was nothing that the United States or the United Nations could do about it. Saddam had sapped the power from the post–Cold War order to the point that it could no longer compel him into compliance. The Security Council struggled to deal with Iraq. Without inspectors on the ground, the United Nations had no way to monitor Iraqi weapons programs. Baghdad made clear that the UN Special Commission responsible for inspections would never be permitted to work in Iraq again. Members of the Security Council presented competing plans to return observers to the country, but they could not find a compromise. The process further frayed relationships between the permanent five members. Even Washington and London, which had been in lockstep on their approach to Iraq found themselves disagreeing. In public, they continued to present a unified front. However, in private, British attempts to bridge differences between Washington and Paris created tensions. Although the details of Blair's proposal remain classified and redacted, it clearly irked Clinton. During a private phone call in October 1999, Clinton told Blair bluntly that "the language your people worked out with the French crosses a red line because it suspends sanctions on Saddam Hussein before disarmament."[89]

Eventually, in December 1999, the Security Council passed a resolution creating the UN Monitoring, Verification, and Inspection Commission. It loosened the restrictions on Iraq considerably. However, even this new regime proved contentious. France, Russia, and China allowed it to pass, but they abstained rather than vote in favor of it. With the sharp divisions at the Security Council, Baghdad felt little pressure to cooperate. The Iraqis rejected the new program and continued to bar any UN inspectors.

The new monitoring program was also controversial in the United States, where political leaders in both major parties felt it was too lenient on Saddam's regime. In March 2000, US Senate hearings on Iraqi sanctions showed clear bipartisan disillusionment with the United Nations as well as the trans-Atlantic alliance that was supposed to underpin the post–Cold War system. Democratic Senator Joseph Biden argued "Saddam is the problem." However, Biden elaborated, "it is clear, on the part of the French and others, they would rather essentially normalize the relationship."[90] Clinton's Assistant Secretary of State for Near Eastern Affairs, Edward Walker, clarified, "the perception that [. . .] sanctions" were "responsible for the problems that the Iraqi people face" eroded the ability to enforce them. Biden agreed, adding, "I guess maybe that is what is wrong with the UN."[91] Ba'thist actions had helped to foreground global perceptions about Iraqi suffering, which as this episode demonstrated, had diluted trust in the United Nations for both opponents and proponents of sanctions. In Washington, as elsewhere, the unresolved situation in Iraq gnawed away at bilateral relations between individual states and also at trust in the post–Cold War system as a whole.

Conclusion

As the 1990s ended, Saddam had improved his geopolitical position considerably. He had split the once-united Security Council into competing factions. The oil-for-food program that went into effect in 1996 gave him the political and economic tools to ensure that it would never again unite against Iraq. He had used flexible tactics of confrontation and retreat to frustrate the Clinton administration, and eventually to expel UN inspectors. Then he weathered the intense but brief attacks, emerging even stronger in their aftermath. Thus, by the end of the decade, he had removed the inspectors, gained a steady source of revenue, and made important political allies that would safeguard Iraqi interests.

As Iraq emerged stronger in the new millennium, the dreams of a rules-based post–Cold War order were fraying. Norms of unity that had guided Security Council actions early in the 1990s were decaying. Russia, France, and China openly broke with the United States and the United Kingdom, at times even threatening to veto resolutions. The principle of enforcement, which was the backbone of the Security Council's power and the key to a century-long dream of a rules-based international order was giving way to economic manipulation and national interests. The once promising relationship between Washington and Moscow was in tatters, and Paris was increasingly disappointing its Western allies. London remained in lockstep with Washington publicly, but in private British officials had some reservations about aggressive American calls for regime change. The British also began to reconsider bedrock strategies such as the oil-for-food program and no-fly zones.[92]

As such, conflicts over Iraq were not just frustrating the United States, they were shaping international order. They would do so even more drastically in the years ahead and as a result, this period of Iraqi history would have lasting effects on issues far outside the Middle East and well after Saddam had lost power.

9

Normalization, 9/11, and the Road to War

On July 25, 2001, the British Joint Intelligence Committee produced a Top Secret assessment on Saddam's regime. "Iraq's isolation has diminished," the report asserted. The Iraqi regime garnered sympathy, especially in the Arab World, by "maintaining the illusion that UN sanctions inflict suffering on the Iraqi people." Russia blocked all attempts to reinvigorate sanctions at the Security Council and the Ba'thists were rebuilding economic and diplomatic ties. The report assessed that "Saddam judges his position to be the strongest since the Gulf War." It described him as "defiant" and "secure."[1]

Less than two months later, the September 11 attacks by al-Qaida in the United States made this assessment obsolete. Less than two years later, the Ba'thist regime fell. Saddam failed to grasp how the September 11 attacks changed American priorities and its strategy toward Iraq. By implication, he did not realize the danger to his regime or to himself until it was too late.

The Bush administration was motivated by concerns over American security following the September 11 attacks, but world order also featured heavily in debates about the Iraq War in 2003, just as it had in the 1991 Gulf War. In the new millennium, unlike in 1991, the world was sharply divided over the future of the international system. Saddam had helped sow the disunity and he had benefited from it tremendously. The discord and thus lack of strong coercion from the Security Council allowed him to normalize his economy and his diplomacy in the years prior to the war. Without decisive American action, it became increasingly obvious that the sanctions regime, and consequently the Gulf War ceasefire that was once seen as a pillar of a new world order, would atrophy and fail. That context is essential but often lacking in discussion about the 2003 Iraq War. Following the September 11 attacks, the George W. Bush administration was not willing to allow a rogue state like Iraq to escape its constraints. Tired of what it saw as the machinations of the international community, the new Bush administration launched a war to topple Saddam's regime despite the lack of any UN resolution explicitly authorizing regime change. In doing so, Bush recklessly undermined the norms and institutions, which, ironically, he said he was trying to save.

Iraq against the World. Samuel Helfont, Oxford University Press. © Oxford University Press 2023.
DOI: 10.1093/oso/9780197530153.003.0010

Normalizing Iraq at the turn of the Twenty-First Century

With the disillusionment of the anti-Iraq consensus at the United Nations, the Ba'thists pressed their international operations to break down the American-led order even further and to attempt to normalize Baghdad's diplomatic position. Their reports from this period were bold and confident about the strategic impacts of their actions. In Moscow they met regularly with "the heads of Russian political parties," organized demonstrations, published articles supporting Iraq in local newspapers. By their own account, they contributed to the "erosion of the American British position."[2] It was no coincidence that British diplomats reported Russia to be the most uncompromising supporter of Iraq on the Security Council.[3] The Ba'thists also capitalized on increased sympathy throughout the Arab World to undermine their adversaries. For example, they had sources within the Saudi diplomatic corps who fed them information.[4]

In an attempt to shape global political narratives and thus to further breakdown support for, and compliance with the UN sanctions regime, the Ba'thists expanded their presence considerably among international activists, especially in student and youth networks. As mentioned previously, the Iraqi regime had created the Non-Aligned Student and Youth Organization (NASYO) in April 1993. By the end of the decade, it had 97 chapters around the world. Its governing committee had assistant secretaries from Mauritius, Lebanon, and Libya; members from Egypt, Germany, and Japan; and regional centers in Italy, Britain, Brazil, Tunisia, Sudan, Jordan, Pakistan, and Malaysia.[5] In the spring of 2001, Huda Ammash took responsibility for the organization and the Central Office of Youth and Students to which it reported within the Iraqi Ba'th Party's Secretariat in Baghdad.

NASYO worked closely with organizations such as World Youth Council, International Union of Muslim Students, World Student Christian Federation, The Asian Youth Council, the Association of Asian Students, and the African Student Movement to raise awareness about Iraqi suffering under sanctions. Its literature reminded "world youth and students that the collective punishment regime directed against peoples, as manifested in imposition of total blockades, is a breach of civil and political rights."[6] "The new world order" one of its pamphlets argued in 2001, "did not come about as a result of legislative process of international will, or out of agreement by influential international parties, or to satisfy the people's needs for a new system of international relations." Instead, the pamphlet continued, "it was borne out of the ascendance and unilateralism of American power, and its hegemony over the world." Thus, far from the idealistic dreams of the end of history, the post–Cold War order was rooted in "brute force, and the imperialist tendency, based on domination, hegemony, blackmail, enslavement, and the expropriation of people['s] rights and freedoms."[7]

In the new century, a wide audience existed for such assertions among left wing international student and youth networks. At the 2001 World Festival of Youth and Students, which was the preeminent international gathering for young leftists and anti-Imperialists, NASYO gathered signatures from 122 students representing organizations from all over the world.[8]

This focus on Iraqi youth was not limited to student activism on university campuses. Often the Ba'thists were able to use it to influence policymakers in important states. Iraqi teachers, for example, were also seen as advocating for the youth. Thus, they made exceptionally effective envoys. In 2001, a delegation of Iraqi teachers traveled to France. It met local teachers at various levels and worked on "strengthening relations between French and Iraqi universities." The delegation also met an official at the French Foreign Ministry. The French official spoke about France's "hard work to lift the embargo irrespective [dun al-nazar] of Security Council resolutions." The Iraqi delegation reported to Huda Ammash that the French official felt that "in particular, culture and cultural exchanges are important frames for breaking the embargo." He emphasized the importance of French and Iraqi teacher unions in carrying out that work. And he promised that France would support it materially.[9]

This episode highlights how French-Iraqi cooperation to break the sanctions regime often relied on relief work, targeting populations like students and youth that would garner international sympathy. Another example of how the French supported these efforts occurred in September 2000. The Iraq Sanctions Committee at the UN Security Council required all passenger flights to Iraq to obtain the committee's approval. On September 21, 2000, France notified the committee that a civilian flight filled with doctors, artists, and sports personalities would depart for Iraq the morning of September 22. The French knew that gaining approval was impossible on such short notice. Peter van Walsum, the Dutch ambassador to the Security Council and the chairman of the Iraq Sanctions Committee from 1999 to 2001, requested that France delay the flight by twenty-four to thirty-six hours, but his request was denied. As van Walsum later recalled, "it did not pass unnoticed that France—not Russia, China, Malaysia, or any other country—had taken it upon itself to defy the sanctions committee's chair in a way that had not been seen before."[10]

Van Walsum claimed that throughout his tenure as chair of the Iraq Sanction Committee, "France played a leading role in the advocacy of Iraq's interest and the struggle against [its] isolation." He thought that French policy "risked giving the wrong signals to the Iraqi leadership, since it encouraged their noncompliance with international demands." In private meetings, he "detected some embarrassment" among French diplomats indicating that "the lengths to which France would go in its solidarity with Iraq were beginning to puzzle even its own insiders."[11]

Van Walsum was also deeply frustrated by the Iraqis. He knew that divisions among the permanent members of the Security Council meant that the Sanctions Committee was unlikely to accomplish much during his tenure as chairman. He decided to focus on small issues where he felt he could do some good. When he learned that Iraqis were unable to perform the *hajj*, he thought it well within his power to fix that problem. He worked with other committee members to meet all Iraqi demands. The Saudis even offered to pay the expenses of Iraqi pilgrims. Baghdad's response was twofold. First, it dismissed the plans as a violation of Iraqi dignity. Second, it blamed the sanctions for preventing Iraqis from performing their religious duty. In the end, using the *hajj* as a political weapon was more important for the Ba'thists than allowing Iraqis to perform it.[12]

Even more nefariously, Baghdad also rejected targeted nutrition programs for children and nursing mothers. Iraqi children suffered from malnutrition throughout this period. Yet, when a Dutch charity shipped 300,000 US dollars-worth of skimmed milk powder to Iraq, the Ba'thist regime arbitrarily changed the expiration dates to one year instead of the customary two years. It then rejected the milk as out of date. Subsequent checks in the Netherlands and a third country showed the milk was fine, but Iraq refused to change its decision. As van Walsum wrote, "I could not believe that a government would deliberately exacerbate the suffering of its own people in order to score a political point . . . but I came across more and more cases where the lack of Iraqi cooperation could not easily be explained otherwise." Iraqi suffering, according to van Walsum, was an important part of the Iraqi regime's strategy. "Iraqi diplomats in New York," he claimed, "began to display a serene confidence that the sanctions were becoming so untenable that their days were numbered."[13] Such claims were bolstered by the fact that the humanitarian situation in the Kurdish regions, where the oil-for-food program was run by the UN and the Americans, was far superior to Iraq proper, where it was controlled by Saddam's regime.[14]

The Iraqi regime had sophisticated programs to manipulate data on the humanitarian crisis in Iraq. The suffering in Iraq was quite acute and very real, but the Ba'thists managed to convince the world that the situation was even worse than the already abysmal reality. In 1999, the United Nations' Children Fund (UNICEF) published a report showing that death rates of children under five years old had doubled since 1990. The data were reviewed by an expert panel and published in the well-respected medical journal, *The Lancet*. These findings set off alarm bells among humanitarians around the globe and put significant pressure on governments to end the sanctions. Yet, after the fall of the Ba'thist regime in 2003, the United Nations and various independent demographers reexamined such claims in light of fuller access to Iraqi census data. They concluded that no such spike in child mortality had occurred and that the Iraqi regime had somehow duped UNICEF. It is still unclear how they did so, but it is now almost certain that UNICEF's study resulted from a complex and well-orchestrated information operation designed to shape international opinion and make the sanctions politically intolerable.[15]

Baghdad's position on issues like the *hajj* and the suffering of Iraqi children played well politically in the Middle East. Iraq even began to normalize its relationship with its erstwhile adversaries in Syria and Iran. Baghdad and Damascus exchanged several high-level delegations in 1998 and 1999. Senior officials like Tariq Aziz and Foreign Minister Muhammad al-Sahhaf visited Syria. Numerous trade deals were penned, and Syria became an important avenue to export Iraqi goods and smuggle Iraqi oil onto global markets.[16]

As a sign of just how confident the Iraqis had become, they changed their approach to the oil-for-food program. In the early years of the program, Baghdad had prioritized gaining political support from key states, even if Iraq lost money. Yet, by 2000, Iraq's goal of breaking up the American-led coalition at the Security Council had largely succeeded, and it turned to making money from illicit surcharges on oil sales. Iraq sold its oil in exchange for humanitarian goods to contractors at prices that allowed the contractors to profit beyond the market value. Then the contractors paid a surcharge as a kickback in cash to an Iraqi embassy or through Iraq's State Oil Marketing Organization accounts in Jordan or Lebanon.

Iraq's shifting approach to the oil-for-food program required overcoming several obstacles. The contractors who were willing and able to trade oil for political influence were not always the same contractors that were willing to pay blatantly illegal kickbacks. French companies in particular were skittish about the new scheme.[17] Finding ways to deliver the money to Iraq also presented some practical obstacles. Iraqi embassies in Greece, Egypt, Switzerland, Italy, Malaysia, Turkey, Austria, Yemen, and Syria collected illegal surcharges in cash. However, in most states, these transactions had to be handled secretly.

Russia, which was willing to turn a blind eye, and may have even facilitated these efforts, became an important hub for collecting payments.[18] The commercial counselor at the Iraqi embassy in Moscow collected cash and receipts. Then he arranged for the money to be delivered to Baghdad in red canvas diplomatic bags that could hold up to 1.5 million dollars in 100-dollar bills. The Iraqis chartered airplanes from the company AVM Air to fly Iraqi diplomats to and from Baghdad with the bags of money. Baghdad allocated five million barrels of oil to the President of AVM to ensure that the flights proceeded smoothly and discretely.[19]

The Iraqis also bribed Benon Sevan, who served as the UN Under-Secretary General and Executive Director of the United Nations Office of the Iraq Programme. In that role he was responsible for managing the oil-for-food program. In private conversations, Saddam and Tariq Aziz discussed his "compensation money."[20] The independent inquiry into the oil-for-food program found that "Sevan corruptly solicited and received oil allocations" from Iraq between 1998 and 2001. In return, he turned a blind eye to Iraqi schemes.[21]

The oil-for-food program began to provide Iraq with a steady stream of income in the early 2000s. Over a two-year period from 2000 to 2002, Iraq gained more than 1.5 billion US dollars from this process.[22] This money combined with other illicit revenue that was facilitated by the breakdown in the United Nations' ability to enforce its resolutions. Iraq opened an oil pipeline to Syria, which Damascus used for its own energy needs and then sold the rest on international markets. As Tariq Aziz later recalled, "Iraq's economy was back by the end of 2000."[23] Regular flights occurred between Saddam International Airport and Jordan, Syria, and Lebanon. According to a British reporter focusing on Iraq, "trade was flourishing" and "for the first time in more than twenty years signs of prosperity had returned to the streets of Baghdad."[24] Not only was Iraq breaking its isolation diplomatically; it was also recovering economically.

George W. Bush and Iraq

The George W. Bush administration inherited this problem when it came to office in 2001. Yet, a war to overthrow Saddam was not one of Bush's initial priorities. Unlike his father, the younger President Bush had little foreign policy experience. Despite his elite family and his education at Yale and Harvard, he relied on his background in Texas to present a rustic, down-homey persona to voters. He wanted to focus on the everyday concerns of Americans, not the high politics of diplomacy and world order.

To the extent he considered the world beyond the American shores, Bush hoped to distinguish himself from his predecessor's liberal internationalism. During the Clinton administration, some American conservatives had turned against humanitarian intervention and nation building in places like Africa and the Balkans. In a fall 2000 presidential election debate that focused on international affairs, Bush repeatedly insisted that "interests" should be the guiding principle of foreign policy and argued, "I don't think our troops ought to be used for what's called nation-building." He stated rather bluntly that "I'm not so sure the role of the United States is to go around the world and say this is the way it's got to be" and then, even more forcefully, "one way for us to end up being viewed as the ugly American is for us to go around the world saying, we do it this way, so should you."[25] Bush's positions during the campaign became the foundation of what he referred to as a "humble" foreign policy. The United States would act when its interests were threatened but it would not impose American values abroad. If a people were oppressed in some far-off corner of the world, those people were obliged to do something about it, not the United States.

This restrained outlook was welcomed in Baghdad, where Ba'thists saw themselves as the victims of American attempts to fashion a new world order. Though the Iraqi regime felt that ultimately Bush would be hostile, the Iraqi Intelligence Service developed a "Media Strategy" to target the new administration. Iraqi intelligence officers used sympathetic international media to influence coverage of Iraq in the United States. The Iraqi Intelligence Service recommended that "Iraqi media should refrain from attacking the American administration leadership as individuals as they are currently formulating a new policy towards Iraq." The Iraqis also thought they could sway the new administration by highlighting that American policies toward Iraq did not align with American interests. Ba'thists argued that the US approach was dividing it from its Arab allies and its economic interests.[26] In private conversations, Saddam and his advisors even mused that Bush's connections to the oil industry might allow them to influence him.[27]

Following September 11, the Bush administration transformed its approach to foreign policy. In an increasingly interconnected world, Americans were not immune to problems festering overseas, however far away they might seem. Threats that had appeared manageable prior to the attacks on New York and Washington suddenly seemed too dangerous to ignore. Iraq quickly gained renewed attention. Technically, Bush had maintained a policy of regime change in Iraq since his first day in office. However, like Clinton before him, Bush was not inclined to carry it out militarily. The September 11 attacks created new possibilities to rally domestic support around more muscular strategies to implement the existing regime change policy.[28]

Bush and his team began to paint Iraq as an unacceptable threat, arguing that it possessed weapons of mass destruction which it could provide to terrorists like the ones who had recently struck the United States. The containment regime that the United Nations had imposed on Iraq had broken down. There were no weapons inspectors in the country; Iraq's economy was recovering, and its diplomacy was normalizing. In some of their more zealous moments, members of the Bush administration even attempted to link Saddam to the September 11 attacks or to the al-Qaida operatives who carried them out.[29]

Senior members of the Bush administration also came to believe that the restrained foreign policy that they had touted during the campaign and their first few months in office was ill-equipped to handle the threats they faced. While the Bush administration appears to have been propelled toward war in Iraq by fear, it also fell back into some of the arguments about liberalism and world order that had typified its predecessors.

On February 26, 2003, with the invasion of Iraq less than a month away, Bush addressed the American Enterprise Institute in Washington to outline his justifications for the coming war. As one might expect, he spoke of "a dictator" in Iraq who was "building and hiding weapons." Furthermore, Bush declared "this same tyrant has close ties to terrorist organizations, and could supply them with the terrible means to strike this country." He then launched into a long discussion about history and world order reminiscent of the idealistic rhetoric that defined the end of the Cold War. "There was a time" he insisted, "when many said that the cultures of Japan and Germany were incapable of sustaining democratic values. Well, they were wrong." Then he moved on to the issue at hand: "Some say the same of Iraq today.

They are mistaken. The nation of Iraq—with its proud heritage, abundant resources and skilled and educated people—is fully capable of moving toward democracy and living in freedom." Tied up in such statements was a deep confidence in the notion that liberal democracy was humanity's natural state. "Human cultures can be vastly different," Bush continued, "Yet the human heart desires the same good things everywhere on Earth. In our desire to be safe from brutal and bullying oppression, human beings are the same." For these "fundamental reasons," Bush concluded, "freedom and democracy will always and everywhere have greater appeal than the slogans of hatred and the tactics of terror." Accordingly, "Any future the Iraqi people choose for themselves will be better than the nightmare world that Saddam Hussein has chosen for them."[30]

These points could have been taken straight from the "end of history" thesis. If there were any doubt that Bush was tapping into Fukuyama's ideas, it was dispelled later in 2003, when Bush gave an important address to the US Chamber of Commerce. In his speech, Bush offered a brief history of democratization beginning in the early 1970s. He listed cases of democratic transitions in Spain, Greece, Latin America, Korea, Taiwan, and South Africa in almost the identical order that Fukuyama had listed them at the beginning of Chapter 2 in his book on the end of history. Then Bush, like Fukuyama, ended with a discussion of Nelson Mandela's election following his release from prison.[31] The implication of such an analysis was clear. Bush would take the lessons that Fukuyama had imbibed at the end of the Cold War and apply them to twenty-first century Iraq.

Despite his adoption of these liberal principles, Bush's thought differed in several important ways from the liberalism that had defined his predecessors' terms. Liberal theorists of international relations have even argued that Bush's justifications for war owed more to a power hungry, realist push for American hegemony than it did to any form of liberal internationalism.[32] Bush was more openly unilateral than either his father or Clinton. His administration trusted what it considered to be the righteousness of American power.

Bush's view of American power as inherently good and legitimate led him to argue that customary legal restrictions on it were obsolete. Both Bush's father and Clinton approved covert programs to topple Saddam, but neither had openly launched a war for regime change. The UN Security Council had never provided such a mandate. The senior President Bush had attempted to push UN policy in that direction following the Gulf War. However, he failed to gain enough support and his administration backed down.

In addition to breaking free of such legal constraints by pushing for a war of regime change without a clear Security Council authorization, the George W. Bush administration also adopted the provocative concept of preventative war. Bush laid out his thinking in a speech to the graduating class of West Point in June 2002. "For much of the last century, America's defense relied on the Cold War doctrines of deterrence and containment." However, "new threats also require new thinking. Deterrence—the promise of massive retaliation against nations—means nothing against shadowy terrorist networks with no nation or citizens to defend." Thus, "if we wait for threats to fully materialize, we will have waited too long . . . We must take the battle to the enemy, disrupt his plans, and confront the worst threats before they emerge."[33]

The related concept of preemption, in which a state goes to war to stop an *imminent* threat, is generally considered legitimate under theories of just war. Bush's promotion of prevention, in which a state goes to war because an adversary might be a threat at some unknown point in the future, has never been accepted.[34] The precedent it set would allow strong states to topple their weaker adversaries on even the weakest evidence about some future and still unmanifested ill intent. Such thinking could easily lead to the might-makes-right nightmares that had exploded international politics in the first half of the twentieth century and it proved extremely controversial in the early twenty-first century even among some of America's closest allies.

Diplomatic Breakdown

Bush pursued his new, more muscular international strategy with the zeal of a convert. Yet, he quickly ran into several diplomatic obstacles. France and Russia had disagreed with previous American approaches to Iraq, and Bush's aggressiveness made them even more uneasy. In the fall of 2002, the Russians said they opposed a new war and would not participate in it. France maintained a more nuanced view. In a long and highly publicized interview with the *New York Times* on September 9, 2002, French President Chirac stated that he had "great reservations" about Bush's doctrine of preventative war, and that he was "totally against unilateralism." Distinguishing France from other opponents of war, Chirac did not rule out French participation in an American led attack on Iraq. Yet, he insisted, "if a military action is to be undertaken, it must be the responsibility of the international community, via a decision by the Security Council." And he made clear that "the Security Council has decided that Iraq must not have weapons of mass destruction; it did not say that a regime change was necessary."[35]

Chirac wanted to prevent an ill-conceived war. However, some claims that France was simply following a "legalistic approach that Paris had defended for years" or that France simply wanted "the UN process to follow its course" give him too much credit.[36] Much of Chirac's rhetoric reflected political posturing rather than a commitment to principle. After all, at his direction, France had spent the previous few years undermining and circumventing the Security Council resolutions on Iraq that he now claimed were sacrosanct. Chirac's promise to go along with a war if it passed a Security Council vote was a useful position diplomatically because it pressured Saddam to comply with UN demands, but Bush and everyone else knew that it was a meaningless gesture. France could simply veto any Security Council resolution that authorized war.

When Bush began to make the case for war publicly in 2002, he did not believe he needed a new Security Council resolution to overthrow Saddam's regime. The Security Council had authorized the use of force in the Gulf War. Saddam was preventing UN inspections, which were a key feature of the 1991 Gulf War ceasefire. The ceasefire agreement was itself embedded in yet another binding Security Council resolution. Since the end of the Gulf War, the United States had consistently argued that if Iraq violated the ceasefire, then the Gulf War resolution on the use of force was still valid. George H. W. Bush and then Clinton had used this reasoning to attack Iraq in 1993, 1996, and 1998. The 2003 invasion rested on the same legal justification, reasoning that the only way to rid Iraq of elicit weapons as require by the UN cease fire was to topple Saddam.[37]

France actually went along with American logic about the use of force when it joined the 1993 air strikes in Iraq without a new Security Council resolution. However, it had never approved regime change and it had since changed its position on the use of force. Russia and China had opposed American arguments about attacks on Iraq since the end of the Gulf War. In 2002 and 2003, Germany also emerged as a fierce opponent of the war and of American plans to launch one without explicit Security Council approval.

America's international allies and some domestic constituents pressured Bush to work through the United Nations. London had also been moving away from Washington on the need for a new resolution to authorize a war to remove Saddam. The British had supported military action to enforce

binding UN resolutions in Iraq, but there was no resolution calling for regime change. In October 2000, officials in the British Foreign Office had
conducted an internal policy review, where they considered a war for regime change. In addition to numerous other problems, they stated bluntly, "It
would also be illegal."[38]

On September 12, 2002—a year and a day after al-Qaida's attacks on
New York and Washington—Bush addressed the United Nations General
Assembly in an attempt to allay the fears of his allies and secure international
support. He fell back on many of the arguments that his father and Clinton
had advanced in the 1990s. Despite his reputation for unilateralism, the
younger Bush claimed to be committed to the United Nations and its principles. He noted that the United States had been one of the founders of the
United Nations, and it "created the United Nations Security Council, so that,
unlike the League of Nations, our deliberations would be more than talk, our
resolutions would be more than wishes." The fecklessness of the League and
its members' unwillingness to enforce its decisions had led to the calamity of
World War II. Bush, then rattled off a long list of binding Security Council
resolutions that Iraq had violated and continued to disregard. As such, Bush
insisted, "The conduct of the Iraqi regime is a threat to the authority of the
United Nations, and a threat to peace." He continued, "All the world now faces
a test, and the United Nations a difficult and defining moment. Are Security
Council resolutions to be honored and enforced, or cast aside without con-
sequence? Will the United Nations serve the purpose of its founding, or will
it be irrelevant?"[39] He could have easily added his father's new world order
rhetoric about the rule of law versus the law of the jungle. For the younger
Bush, the post–Cold War order hung in the balance.

This was not simply a line of reasoning that Bush paraded out at the United
Nations. It was a common theme that ran through his speeches even when
he addressed less internationalist audiences. In February 2003, for example,
he spoke to sailors at a Navy base in Mayport, Florida. It was not a widely
publicized speech and certainly not meant to target international audiences,
yet as Bush laid out his reasoning for the coming war, he told the mostly en-
listed sailors that the United Nations needed "to decide, if you lay down a
resolution, does it mean anything?" He then clarified that he felt the war was
a test of the international system: "The United Nations Security Council can
now decide if it has the resolve to enforce its resolutions."[40]

For all the praise one might rightly heap on France or Russia for
attempting to avoid war in 2003, it should not be forgotten that those same

states had spent the previous years attempting to normalize Iraq's violations of binding Security Council resolutions. Such resolutions were at the heart of a peaceful post–Cold War order. World order was not Bush's primary reason for launching the Iraq War. Yet, French and Russian actions and the frustrations they generated in Washington were clearly one of the many factors that pushed him in that direction. For Bush, the international system had failed. The United Nations had never authorized regime change in Iraq, but as twisted as the logic may seem, Bush saw a war for regime change as his attempt to enforce the United Nations' authority and uphold world order.

Iraqi Miscalculations

Saddam never fully understood how the September 11 attacks had changed the United States or the danger that these changes posed for his regime. Afterall, he had nothing to do with the attacks.[41] Despite his pragmatic cooperation with Islamists, he saw his regime as the ideological enemy of groups such as al-Qaida. Saddam also reveled in the breakdown of an international system that he had fought so hard to weaken. The Ba'thists felt their strategy to divide the international community and raise popular opposition to American policies was working and that it would protect Iraq from American aggression. Tariq Aziz argued that prior to the war, "France and Russia each secured millions of dollars worth of trade and service contracts in Iraq, with the implied understanding that their political posture with regard to sanctions on Iraq would be pro-Iraq." Of course, these countries would oppose war. Aziz insisted that the French wanted "to safeguard their trade and service contracts in Iraq. Moreover, they wanted to prove their importance in the world as members of the Security Council; that they could use their veto to show they still had power."[42]

Similarly, in October 2002, the Iraqi ambassador to Moscow wrote to Baghdad that "our friends [in Russian intelligence] have told us that President Putin has given very clear instructions to the Ministry of Foreign Affairs vis-à-vis Iraq." Russian President Vladimir Putin, according to the ambassador, "will not allow the new resolution to include any intention that would allow the use of force against Iraq."[43]

In addition to these official positions, Saddam put considerable weight on the fact that opposition to another war against Iraq inflamed popular opinion around the world. Mass protests began in the fall of 2002. Between January and April 2003, these ballooned into the largest wave of protests in global history. More than 35 million protestors participated in nearly 3,000 separate protests in 90 countries. The largest single protest in history occurred on February 15, 2003. Over 10 million people gathered at almost 900 separate events in 78 countries.[44]

Iraqi Ba'thists had embedded themselves in the antiwar networks that coordinated these protests and they helped to organize them. Of course, there were numerous reasons for the protests, many of which would have existed without Ba'thist involvement. The George W. Bush administration's hubris alienated global audiences. The Bush administration's glib attitude toward anyone who disagreed with it—even close allies—inflamed anti-American and anti-Western sentiment around the world. The Ba'thists channeled and amplified those sentiments. They connected disparate groups and ideologies, and they linked large networks, which allowed activists to coordinate protests across time and space.

These networks did not suddenly materialize in 2002 and 2003. The Ba'thists had spent over a decade knitting them together, often with Iraqis playing covert and clandestine roles at key nodes. The Iraqis did not only focus on the great powers. They had also carried out operations designed to shape global opinion more broadly in places like Europe and the Middle East. A good example of a Ba'thist campaign in a lesser power, and thus as an indicator of broader global operations, could be seen in Sweden. Chapter 7 offered a granular look at Ba'thist operations to influence Sweden during the earl-to-mid 1990s and picking up that thread here provides an opportunity to show how Ba'thists helped to transform Iraq's place in the politics of a European state.

As discussed in Chapter 7, the Ba'thists began to make inroads into a previously hostile Swedish political landscape in the early 1990s. By 2002, they worked covertly through organizations like the Left Party, which held about 10 percent of the seats in parliament, as well as sympathetic Arab and Muslim groups and their own proxies to organize protests in Stockholm and Malmo. These were the largest protests in the country since World War II, and they grew even bigger as 2002 turned to 2003.[45]

Over the course of a decade, the Ba'thists in Sweden had helped to transform how the Swedish media depicted Iraq. In the early 1990s, the Swedish press concentrated on the Iraqi regime's misdeeds—its flagrant violations of international law and the atrocities that it committed. As the decade progressed, those frames began to shift. One of the Ba'thists' favorite techniques for shaping media coverage was to hold protests or demonstrations and then gin up news coverage about them. Doing so focused the media's attention away from the actions of the Iraqi regime and toward the protesters' grievances—usually the humanitarian crisis in Iraq or American aggression. As war approached in 2002–2003, the Swedish media had adopted the preferred Ba'thist frames.[46]

It would be a gross overstatement to claim that Ba'thist operations in Sweden were the sole cause of the Swedish media's shifting coverage of Iraq. The Ba'thists may not have even been the primary reason for this shift. However, it is equally difficult to believe that Iraqi actions had no effect. The combination of organizing demonstrations, networking through proxies, and planting stories helped steer the Swedish press in directions that Baghdad preferred. Viewed through Saddam's populist worldview, he was winning in places like Sweden.

Throughout the 1990s, similar transformations took place all over the world. In the early 1990s, the political frames through which global audiences understood Iraq focused on Saddam's atrocities and Iraq's assaults on neighbors. By the early 2000s, those political frames had shifted to focus on the humanitarian crisis and what many understood as the danger of unchecked American power. The unprecedented global protests against the Iraq War in 2002 and 2003 both fed and were fed by these narratives. The protests created more press coverage. Then press coverage further inflamed popular passions, causing even more protests in a self-reenforcing cycle. In Saddam's worldview, bottom-up, mass protests like those that occurred in the buildup to the Iraq War were a driving force in international politics. Not only would they create pressure to break down the sanctions regime that had pinned the Iraqi regime in, but when combined with the diplomatic support from Paris and Moscow, most senior Iraqi officials thought they made war unlikely.

Saddam also felt that the United States was a paper tiger. Iraq, Saddam told his advisors in early 2003, suffered more casualties in the battle of al-Faw during the Iran–Iraq War than the United States suffered in the entire Vietnam War. Since Vietnam, the Americans became even more gun-shy. In Somalia, a handful of casualties forced the vaunted United States military to withdrawal. Saddam's narrative about the Gulf War was either that the Iraqis had halted the coalition or that the Americans stopped their assault to avoid paying the heavy price that a march on Baghdad would require. Since the Gulf War, Saddam noted that the United States relied on air rather than ground forces not only in Iraq but in places like the Balkans too. He thought that the

Americans and the British lacked the stomach for ground combat, especially against Iraqis, whom he was convinced were naturally good fighters.[47]

In the 1990s, the Iraqi regime had learned to push the boundaries that the world—and the United States—would accept, and then to back off at the last moment to avert attacks. It adopted a similar approach in 2002. After intense debates and negotiations, the Security Council passed a unanimous resolution in November 2002, demanding that Baghdad allow UN weapons inspectors to return to Iraq. The French and Russians ensured that the resolution contained no language authorizing the use of force. As US ambassador to the Unite Nations John Negroponte stated, the resolution contained no "hidden triggers" or "automaticity" that would prompt a war. However, he also clarified that the resolution did "not constrain any Member State from acting to defend itself against the threat posed by Iraq or to enforce relevant United Nations resolutions and protect world peace and security."[48] Moreover, the resolution determined that "Iraq has been and remains in material breach of its obligations under relevant resolutions," which is all the justification that the Bush administration felt it needed to launch a war.[49] In the face of these clear threats, Saddam allowed the inspectors back into the country and promised to cooperate fully.

Iraq produced a dossier on its weapons programs and the inspectors went to work. The dossier did not come clean on the regime's denial and deception program in the early 1990s, but the only way Saddam could have satisfied Bush's demands would have been to turn over weapons that he did not have. As the inspectors made progress but failed to find any illicit weapons, the French, Russians, and Germans argued that they needed more time.

Meanwhile the Bush administration had deployed a large military force to the Persian Gulf. Spring was approaching and would bring scorching temperatures. The Americans and British had surged their troops to the region, and they could not leave them there indefinitely. If they were going to launch a war, they needed to do it in the first few months of 2003. The British and other American allies wanted a Security Council resolution explicitly authorizing force, but American diplomats could not muster the votes and France threatened to veto it even if they could. The United States and its flimsy "coalition of the willing" invaded Iraq on March 20, 2003. It quickly toppled the Ba'thist regime.

How Saddam and his regime miscalculated so badly in 2003 is difficult to understand, especially considering how adeptly they had tapped into the pulse of global politics over the previous decade. The Iraqi regime never seemed to comprehend the Bush administration's determination following the September 11 attacks. Even with coalition troops assembling in the region, the Iraqis felt that the United States could not march on Baghdad in the face of overwhelming diplomatic and popular opposition. Even if the American-led coalition invaded, the Iraqis believed that it would stall once the casualties began to mount.

In a damning indictment on the Ba'thist understanding of international politics, the Bush administration pushed ahead despite everything. The American-led military coalition quickly dispatched the Iraqi military and sacked Baghdad, ending over three decades of entrenched Ba'thist rule. After the downfall of the regime, several senior Iraqi officials spoke about their misperceptions prior to the invasion. Incredibly, the then former Chief of Staff of the Iraqi Armed Forces stated, "No Iraqi leaders had believed Coalition forces would ever reach Baghdad." The Commander of the Iraqi Air and Air Defense Forces said, "We thought this would be like 1991. We figured that the United States would conduct some operations in the south and then go home." The Director General of the Republican Guard's General Staff similarly claimed, "We thought the Coalition would go to Basrah, maybe to Amarah, and then the war would end." When an American debriefer asked the Director of Iraqi Military Intelligence, "What did you think was going to happen with the Coalition invasion?" He responded, "We were more interested in Turkey and Iran."[50]

For all the successes that Saddam felt he had achieved with influence operations and manipulative statesmanship, these strategies proved no match for a determined adversary willing to use overwhelming military power.

Beyond the damage the war caused in Iraq, the new world order also fell victim to the conflict. The war inflamed political rifts across the globe. Most states rejected the American logic of preventative war. They viewed Bush's decision to overthrow Saddam's regime without a new UN resolution explicitly authorizing regime change as a blatant violation of international law. If the United States was not willing to abide by the rules, why should anyone else. Thus, the war drove a stake into the cooperative norms that internationalists hoped would define the post-Cold War system. Any lingering talk of the new world order ended.

Conclusion

For its proponents, the post-Cold War order was meant to hold aggressive states at bay; to prevent the powerful from attacking the weak just because they could. Instead, international disputes were supposed to be resolved through a system of rules, implemented by legitimate international institutions. Throughout the 1990s, the leading states in the post–Cold War order soured on this deal. When their interests clashed, the Ba'thist pushed, prodded, and persuaded them to act. Each side accused each other of breaking the rules and failing to work within the accepted system. Prior to the September 11 attacks in 2001, the Ba'thist strategy seemed to be working and Iraq seemed poised to break free of the UN-imposed constraints. Al-Qaida's attacks on New York and Washington changed the calculus in Washington and put the Bush administration on a war path. Whatever remaining checks the international order put on states were strained and proved unable to prevent the 2003 Iraq War.

Saddam was a master at manipulating the international system and eventually defeating it. Yet, in a bitter irony, the breakdown in global order that he worked so hard to accomplish also untethered the American power that ultimately overthrew his regime. Saddam's highly politicized view of international politics biased him to see mass public opinion and diplomacy as the drivers of international relations. This view blinded him to the raw power of military force when backed by a determined leader. The result was a tragedy for Iraq and for the world.

Conclusion and Afterword
Saddam's Iraq and Twenty-First Century Disorder

On December 30, 2006, Saddam Hussein was hanged after having been convicted of crimes against humanity in an Iraqi court. His executioners were not the liberal democrats of George W. Bush's fevered imagination. They were adherents of a brand of militant Shi'i Islamism known as Sadrism and they taunted the former Iraqi president with their Islamist slogans as he faced his gruesome end. The world these Sadrists wished to build was neither liberal nor peaceful. They were committed to militant politics, and they fed the rivers of blood that flowed through Iraq in the mid-2000s. The Bush administration's assumption that once freed from Saddam's totalitarianism most Iraqis would embrace liberal democracy proved incorrect.

This was not the only liberal assumption that died in Iraq. Frustrations over the clash with Iraq fostered a changing political discourse on foreign policy in the West, especially in the United States. Dreams of liberalism and the rule of law, which were discussed so hopefully at the end of the Cold War, gave way to talk of power and interests. The latter forces had sunk the world into chaos and bloodshed during the first half of the twentieth century. However, the norms, institutions, and tools that had propped up the post–Cold War order and that were supposed to act as a check on such revisionism were battered after a decade of confrontation with Saddam. The 2003 Iraq War delivered a decisive blow.

America's clash with Saddam is a topic that refuses to die. It continues to shape how intellectuals and statesmen discuss foreign policy and how electorates choose their leaders. It has earned an enduring place in twenty-first century debates about international politics, foreign policy, and history. Here, it is worth documenting the legacy of Iraq's fight against the world, how it undermined the case for liberalism, and then breathed new life into arguments for realism and restraint. Along the way, it will be necessary to investigate how a state like Iraq could and could not influence global politics.

Iraq against the World. Samuel Helfont, Oxford University Press. © Oxford University Press 2023.
DOI: 10.1093/oso/9780197530153.003.0011

Liberal Internationalism Reconsidered

The great scholar of liberal internationalism, G. John Ikenberry, watched the fall of the Soviet Union and the dawn of a new era from his perch at Princeton University's Woodrow Wilson School.[1] He then spent the following decades applying theoretical rigor to Wilson's internationalism for the new epoch. In the thirty years since the fall of the Soviet Union, he has emerged as perhaps the most lucid theorist of the liberal ideas that propped up the post–Cold War order.[2]

Ikenberry argued that following major wars, the victors attempt to cement their gains as leaders of the international system. The end of the Cold War, he stated, was no different in that respect from the end of the Napoleonic Wars, World War I, and World War II. In each case, he maintained, the victors developed a new international order to govern the world. In doing so, they imposed constraints on all states in the international system through what Ikenberry called "institutional bargains." The victors did so not out of altruism but because it was beneficial for all sides. "The leading state," Ikenberry wrote, wanted "to lock other states into the order" with it at the top. "The weaker and secondary states," he continued, wanted "rules and institutions as protections against the possibility that the leading state will become a despotic hegemon."[3]

Through its first decade, the post–Cold War order fitted neatly into Ikenberry's theory. George H. W. Bush clearly stated that he wished to build something akin to what Ikenberry theorized. Bush worked through the United Nations instead of acting unilaterally. He spoke openly about the need to unite the great powers and to create broad consensus among less powerful states. He also discussed how the system would constrain the powerful. He promised "A world where the strong respect the rights of the weak."[4] Indeed, while Bush pushed for regime change in the aftermath of the Gulf War, American policy and strategy was constrained by the lack of support at the Security Council. Clinton doubled down on this project following his election in 1992, making it the centerpiece of his foreign policy.

However, Ikenberry later admitted that he overestimated the liberal order's robustness. In particular, he underestimated the George W. Bush administration's ability to break institutional bargains and to act outside of their constraints, most notably in a war for regime change in Iraq.[5] So why did the system break down, as Ikenberry claimed, over Iraq in 2002–2003? Of course, cynics argue that Bush and Clinton never really meant what they said. Such critics argue that the new world order was nothing more than rhetoric designed to appeal to an unsophisticated and gullible public. Others have offered structural explanations for the breakdown in order. Prominent political scientists have since theorized that the concentration of power inherent in a unilateral world order annuls the systemic constraints described by Ikenberry and others.[6] While such theoretical analysis can be insightful, this book has focused on more concrete, historical explanations for the breakdown in the post–Cold War system.

Confrontations over Iraq, along with disillusionment over globalization and disagreements in places like the Balkans made it increasingly difficult for the Security Council to find consensus. In the early 1990s, strong norms of unity and cooperation were indeed emerging at the Council, especially among the five permanent members. These states were reluctant to express differences publicly and they tried to vote as a bloc. Yet, by the early twenty-first century, Iraq was one of several issues—and perhaps the most important of them—that pushed these states to disagree openly. In a significant break from the spirit of the early post–Cold War, these states threatened to veto each other's initiatives.

Saddam used a savvy combination of influence operations, economic interests, and manipulative statesmanship to drive a wedge between the United States and the United Kingdom on one side, and France, Russia, and China on the other. Of course, there were limits to what the Iraqis could accomplish. They could neither create nor change the fundamental nature of international politics. Ba'thist influence campaigns needed to flow within existing political trends. Therefore, when the Ba'thists attempted to push against the political grain, they failed.[7]

Relatedly, the Ba'thists, like their predecessors in the Cold War and their successors today, were most effective when they were ideologically agile. At what this book describes as the operational level—in other words, building a network of supporters in key positions around the world—Iraqi attempts to impose Ba'thist dogma on international audiences was largely a fruitless endeavor. The Ba'thists were much more successful when they allied with people or groups that shared Baghdad's desire to end sanctions or prevent military attacks on Iraq even if those groups disliked Saddam and his regime. The Ba'thists were also more successful when relying on local actors and groups that had developed organically in foreign states. They were less effective when they attempted to create such actors themselves.

Combining influence campaigns based on moral and political arguments with economic interests proved remarkably productive in transforming operational gains into influence at the strategic level, which impacted the national policies of important states. However, this type of highly politicized strategy also had limits. Most importantly, influence campaigns were no match for a determined adversary who was willing to use overwhelming military force.

By acting within broader political trends, the Ba'thists coaxed several states on the Security Council into breaking or at least undermining their own resolutions on the embargo against Iraq. The permanent members of the Security Council also disagreed over laws for using force in Iraq, leading them to accuse each other of breaking the rules. All this rule breaking, and perceived rule breaking, weakened norms about a rules-based system. The Security Council never recovered its unity. The stigma against military operations without a Security Council resolution, or even breaking international law more generally, faded at least partly due to Iraq.

Restraint and the Return of Power Politics

With these blows to the post–Cold War order, other political theories that were more skeptical of liberal internationalism gained momentum, and then accelerated rapidly in the wake of the Iraq War in 2003. The realist school of international relations saw the sharpest gains. Realists assert that material interests and security, rather than norms, ideology, or institutions drive international politics. They insist that a balance of power, rather than international institutions or a rules-based order, creates political stability. This was the type of analysis that liberals had blamed for the chaos of the twentieth century and which they were trying to move past in the post–Cold War period.

Indeed, realist theories initially proved problematic in the post–Cold War period. In the early 1990s, when realists disregarded norms, institutions, or the appeal of liberalism itself, their analysis failed. For example, prominent realists had predicted that the end of the Cold War would lead many of Washington's allies to band together in opposition to American power. Yet, that type of "balancing" did not occur other than in some "soft" instances.[8] Moreover, the United States, which was the most important actor in the international system, behaved in accordance with liberal rather than realist assumptions in places like the Balkans and Eastern Europe in the 1990s, and in the Middle East after September 11, 2001. The United States undertook humanitarian interventions in places where it had few vital national interests; it expanded its alliances based on ideological commitments rather than security requirements; and it forcefully promoted liberal democracy.

Realists, as their name implies, pride themselves on detailing the harsh realities of international politics. They scoff at idealists for theorizing about how states *ought* to act. Yet, in the post–Cold War period, these same realists argued that America's commitment to international liberalism was a mistake, and they called for "restraint" in American foreign policy.[9] Those arguments failed to describe the reality of American foreign policy and instead made claims about what American foreign policy ought to be. These were exactly the type of prescriptive assertions that the realist school claimed to reject. As such, international statesmen and intellectuals in the 1990s regularly described realist assumptions as outdated and atavistic.

Just as the realists seemed to have less and less to offer, the 2003 Iraq War appeared to vindicate them. Realists argued that misplaced morality and liberalism had prevented Washington from living with a tyrant such as Saddam, even though it was in the American interest to do so. These realists presented the invasion of Iraq as the architype of the democracy-promoting, world-shaping foreign adventure that their theories warned against. As debates about a new war in Iraq began to boil in the fall of 2002, a group of thirty-three academics, consisting of the who's-who of realist scholars, bought an advertisement in the *New York Times*. The headline read "War with Iraq Is Not in America's National Interest." In line with their theory, realists argued that the war was tied to foolhardy dreams of liberal world order and that it was unaligned with American interests. They insisted that such idealism could only end in a strategic disaster. Their argument contained internal inconsistencies, but they were right about the war not aligning with American interest.[10] It cost far more in terms of blood and treasure than could ever be justified.

Many of the signatories of the advertisement have been understandably proud of their vindication. Writing in *The Atlantic*, the journalist Robert Kaplan profiled John Mearsheimer, who is perhaps the most prominent living realist. Kaplan claimed that the advertisement was Mearsheimer's "finest hour."[11] Another signatory, Brandeis University's Robert Art, hung a copy of it on his office wall.[12]

Rightly or wrongly, the Bush administration's post–September 11 foreign policies were often associated with neoconservatism, which rejected the realists' amoral power politics, and promoted a type of militarized, unilateral liberalism. Thus, even though their thoeries had often floundered in the post-Cold War period, the realists had little trouble positioning themselves as the antidote to the Bush administration's folly. They gloated that they had tried to warn the country.

When American leaders began to reassess their foreign policy after their failures in Iraq, they turned to these realists and their ideas. The US Congress, for example, assembled "The Iraq Study Group" in 2006. This bipartisan collection of elder statesmen was led by Republican former Secretary of State James Baker and former Democratic Congressman Lee Hamilton. After a decade of frustration in which Washington was unwilling to live with Saddam's Iraq, leading to a debacle in 2003, the group recommended that the United States reverse course in the Middle East—for example, by reaching out to Syria and Iran, which were both accused of being rogue regimes and impediments to a rules-based system in the region. The *Washington Post* argued that the resulting report "might well be titled 'The Realist Manifesto.'"[13] Realist academics such as Mearsheimer and Harvard's Stephen Walt, who had opposed the invasion of Iraq, also capitalized on its failure. Their explanation of what had gone wrong in US foreign policy—and their naming of a scapegoat—propelled them into the status of public intellectuals. This new standing garnered lucrative speaking and book contracts.[14] A string of other realist books became best sellers in international relations in the first two decades of the twenty-first century.[15]

Of course, not all political leaders and intellectuals abandoned liberalism in response to the Iraq War. Some even fought back against what they saw as decidedly antiliberal trends. Left-wing intellectuals such as Paul Berman and Christopher Hitchens in the United States, as well as Nick Cohen in the United Kingdom defended American foreign policy, and more controversially, the Iraq War, on liberal grounds. They presented Saddam as an unrepentant fascist and accused the realists and others of rehashing the same type of apologist policies that had failed in the 1930s.[16]

Similarly, in 2006, a group of prominent left-wing British intellectuals released what they called the Euston Manifesto. They asserted, "It is vitally important for the future of progressive politics that people of liberal, egalitarian and internationalist outlook should now speak clearly." And they insisted, "We must define ourselves against those for whom the entire progressive-democratic agenda has been subordinated to a blanket and simplistic 'anti-imperialism' and/or hostility to the current US administration."[17]

The meat of the manifesto was fairly banal. It took a firm stand in support of democracy, equality, and freedom of thought. Its authors insisted on "no apology for tyranny" and they opposed all forms of racism. The *New York Times* called it "a manifesto from the left too sensible to ignore."[18] Yet, in the aftermath of the Iraq War, even this basic statement of liberal principles faced a torrent of criticism. Detractors could remember how American leaders had weaponized these ideas to argue for sanctions and then war in Iraq. The Manifesto's opponents claimed it justified imperialism and American aggression.[19]

Francis Fukuyama, whose end of history thesis drove early debates about post–Cold War politics, also felt the need to intervene against what he saw as gathering illiberal trends. In February 2006, he began an essay in *New York Times Magazine* by asserting "it seems very unlikely that history will judge either the intervention [in Iraq] itself or the ideas animating it kindly."[20] This was a stunning assertion considering that Fukuyama had been an early proponent of the war and that Bush had invoked Fukuyama's ideas to justify it.[21] In this and several other high-profile pieces he published in the following years, Fukuyama critiqued the growing influence of realism and retrenchment. He distanced himself from the Iraq War and attempted to distinguish his concept of the end of history from the ideas of the Bush administration. Fukuyama asserted that that he had "presented a kind of Marxist argument for the existence of a long-term process of social evolution, but one that terminates in liberal democracy rather than communism." He insisted that "the neoconservative position . . . was, by contrast, Leninist; they believed that history can be pushed along with the right application of power and will."[22]

Fukuyama hoped to rescue the concepts of liberalism and democracy as universal forces from critics of the Bush administration who, he claimed, were throwing the baby out with the bath water.[23] As he wrote in 2006, Bush's policies in his first term "led many critics to simply desire the opposite of whatever he wants."[24]

It should not be forgotten that Saddam's Ba'thists had helped knit together the global coalitions that, as Fukuyama argued, almost automatically rejected Bush's policies. For over a decade prior to the 2003 war, Ba'thists had laid the groundwork both organizationally and intellectually to oppose the forms of liberalism that Bush appropriated to justify his policies in Iraq. In that sense, Saddam's operations in the decade before his demise helped redraw the lines of global politics that influenced world order long after he was gone. Neither

Fukuyama nor other liberal intellectuals could turn back time. The norms, taboos, and coalitions which had shaped the post–Cold War moment were shadows of their former selves.

Indeed, while Barack Obama relied on the slogan "hope and change" in his campaign to replace Bush in 2008, his foreign policy instincts were most often described as realist. "I . . . believe that the world is a tough, complicated, messy, mean place, and full of hardship and tragedy," he argued. The United States must "recognize that there are going to be times where the best that we can do is to shine a spotlight on something that's terrible, but not believe that we can automatically solve it."[25]

By the end of Obama's presidency in 2016, skepticism about liberal internationalism reached new heights, even in the Anglo states which had been at the core of the post–Cold War order. Iraq was certainly not the only or even the primary reason for illiberal developments like Brexit or Trumpism since 2016. However, any narrative about their origins which ignore Iraq would be incomplete. Neither Trump nor his British counterparts were political sorcerers who convinced their electorates to vote against their own instincts. These leaders tapped into existing skepticism about liberalism that had been growing among segments of their populations. At least some of that skepticism grew out of the failures of liberalism in Iraq.

Much of Trump's appeal was rooted in domestic American racial tensions and the economic challenges of deindustrialization, but foreign policy and Iraq in particular, also played a role in his rise to power. Trump attacked the "globalist" alliances and institutions that had propped up liberal internationalism for over a half century. He stirred up populist sentiment about the cost America paid to uphold world order while adversaries and unappreciative allies took a free ride. This line of reasoning had always existed as an undercurrent in American politics, but no American presidential candidate in generations had so openly opposed a liberal world order. While Trump's arguments were broader than critiques of America's approach to Saddam's Iraq, he often cited it as a key example of where traditional American foreign policy had gone astray. Echoing the realist critiques of liberal internationalism, Trump argued during a debate with his Republican rivals that "obviously the war in Iraq was a big fat mistake . . . we should have never been in Iraq. We have destabilized the Middle East."[26]

Trump's arguments in favor of retrenchment were not isolated to the fringe of the American right. In fact, Trump repeated what had previously been left wing criticisms of American foreign policy. In his debate with

George W. Bush's brother, Jeb, about the Iraq War, Trump accosted his opponent: "They lied! They said there were weapons of mass destruction. There
were none and they knew there were none."[27] The magazine, *Politico*, ran the
headline, "Trump Goes Code Pink on George W. Bush," referring to the left-
wing antiwar group that regularly hurled similar critiques.[28]

In the third decade of the twenty-first century one can find powerful
voices arguing for retrenchment in almost every political camp in the United
States. Perhaps the most influential and well-funded foreign policy think
tank to emerge in the last few years is the Quincy Institute for Responsible
Statecraft, which was founded in 2019 with substantial grants from George
Soros's left-wing Open Society Foundation, and the right-wing Koch
Foundation.[29] The think tank was named after John Quincy Adams, who famously argued America "goes not abroad in search of monsters to destroy."[30]
Saddam is the unstated archetype of a monster that gives this saying such
power, and America's disastrous confrontation with him has transformed it
into a mantra for American proponents of restraint and retrenchment. The
election of Joseph Biden in 2020 and the Russian Ukraine War in 2022 may
have slowed America's retreat from the liberal post–Cold War order, but it
certainly did not reverse the momentum. Lingering in the background of all
these events and debates, even now, twenty years later, is the American confrontation with Iraq and the desire not to repeat it.

Here, one must note that a more restrained American foreign policy
makes sense for a number of reasons that have little to do with Ba'thist Iraq.
The post–Cold War order was built on institutions designed after World War
II. At that time, the United States accounted for roughly half of the world's
gross domestic product and very few countries had the political, military,
or economic power to shape international relations. Institutions built for
that world were unlikely to endure as other powers emerged. The post–Cold
War period saw the rise of the United States as the sole superpower and the
world's undisputed hegemon, but it also heralded the emergence of countries like India, China, Brazil, and a reunified Germany. The so-called Asian
Tigers flourished as did economies in Latin America and Africa. These trends
would have led to what the political commentator Fareed Zakaria called the
"post-American world" with or without the conflicts in Iraq, and the rise of
"the rest" makes American attempts to dominate the world increasingly difficult both economically and militarily.[31]

Yet, America's clash with Iraq from 1990 onward left the United States
more skeptical of its allies and of international institutions such as the

United Nations. The Ba'thists frustrated American policies, chipped away at American alliances, and diluted American ambitions for the post–Cold War order. Ba'thist actions humbled proponents of a liberal international order and empowered its critics. American support for international liberalism stumbled and Americans became less willing to play a leading role in organizing a liberal world order. As a result, the post-American world is less likely to emerge within and through liberal internationalist institutions, and more likely to emerge in conflict with them. Budding great powers will be less constrained and feel less pressure to conform to norms of a rules-based system. Saddam's Iraq was certainly not the only factor that shaped these trends, but historians have given it far less attention than it deserves.

Notes

Introduction

1. George H. W. Bush, *Address Before a Joint Session of the Congress on the Persian Gulf Crisis and the Federal Budget Deficit*, September 11, 1990, *George H. W. Bush Presidential Library and Museum* https://bush41library.tamu.edu/archives/public-papers/2217.

2. Charles Krauthammer, "The Unipolar Moment," *Foreign Affairs* 70, no. 1 (Winter 1990/1991): 23–33; Francis Fukuyama, *The End of History and the Last Man* (New York: The Free Press, 1992); Hal Brands, *Making the Unipolar Moment: U.S. Foreign Policy and the Rise of the Post-Cold War Order* (Ithaca, NY: Cornell University Press, 2016).

3. Michael Mandelbaum, *The Rise and Fall of Peace on Earth* (New York: Oxford University Press, 2019), xii, 7.

4. Mark Mazower, *Governing the World: The History of an Idea, 1815 to the Present* (New York: Penguin Books, 2012), xi.

5. Amy Chua, *Day of Empire: How Hyperpowers Rise to Global Dominance – and Why They Fall* (New York: Random House, 2007).

6. Paul A. Volcker et al., "Management of the United Nations Oil-for-Food Programme," *Independent Inquiry Committee into the United Nations Oil-for-Food Programme* Vol 1. (2005): 39.

7. "محضر اجتماع هيأع مكتب الامانة العامة" [Proceedings of the meeting of the General Secretariat Group], *BRCC*, 026-5-5 (207), February. 15, 1989.

8. The Ba'th Party archives contain thousands of pages on the party's influence operations in the 1990s and early 2000s. In addition to sources cited above and below, see the following for a small sampling: "مقترح" [Recommendation], From: The Director of the Office of the Secretariat of the Region, To: The Presidential Diwan, *BRCC*, 2837_0002 (585), April 1992; "برنامج عمل" [Work Plan], From: The Secretary General of the Central Office of Students and Youth, To: The Office of the Secretariat of the Region, *BRCC*, 2749_0000 (567), December 22, 1991; and "نشاطات" [Activities], From: The Assistant to the Secretary General of the Founding Leader Branch Command, To: The Regional Command of Iraq/Office of the Secretariat of the Region, *BRCC*, 2099_0003 (505), February 24, 1999.

9. Sun Tzu, *The Art of War*, trans. Samuel B. Griffith (New York: Oxford University Press, 1963), 77.

10. William Shakespeare, *Coriolanus*, act 3, scene 2; Discussed in, Paul A Smith, *On Political War* (Washington, DC: National Defense University Publications, 1989), 61.

11. Lawrence Freedman, *Strategy: A History* (New York: Oxford University Press, 2013), 250.
12. Freedman, *Strategy*, 268–9.
13. Justin Hart, *Empire of Ideas: The Origins of Public Diplomacy and the Transformation of U.S. Foreign Policy* (New York: Oxford University Press, 2013), 1–14.
14. Hannah Arendt, *The Origins of Totalitarianism* (New York: Harcourt, Brace and World Inc. Original Copyright: 1951. This is the 1966 edition), 306–16.
15. Thomas Rid, *Active Measures: The Secret History of Disinformation and Political Warfare* (New York: Farrar, Straus and Giroux, 2020); For American influence Operations in the early Cold War, see, Hart, *Empire of Ideas*, and George Herring, *From Colony to Superpower: U.S. Foreign Relations since 1776* (New York: Oxford University Press, 2017), 660–8.
16. George Kennan, Policy Planning Staff Memorandum, Washington, May 4, 1948. A copy can be downloaded at: http://academic.brooklyn.cuny.edu/history/johnson/65ciafounding3.htm.
17. Christopher Andrew, *The Sword and the Shield: The Mitrokhin Archive and the Secret History of the KGB* (New York: Basic Books, 1999), 20; For good examples of Soviet influence operations, also see pp. 94, 230–1, 290–3, and 326 as well as Jonathan Haslam, *Near and Distant Neighbors: A New History of Soviet Intelligence* (New York: Farrar, Straus and Giroux, 2015), 52.
18. Andrew, *The Sword and the Shield*.
19. Clint Watts, *Messing with the Enemy* (New York: Harper Collins, 2018); and Linda Robinson et al., "Modern Political Warfare," *RAND Corporation* (2008),
20. "X" (George F. Kennan), "The Sources of Soviet Conduct," *Foreign Affairs*, July 1947. https:// www.for eign affa irs.com/ artic les/ russ ian- fed erat ion/ 1947- 07- 01/ sour ces- sov iet- cond uct; "George Kennan's 'Long Telegram,'" February 22, 1946, History and Public Policy Program Digital Archive, National Archives and Records Administration, Department of State Records (Record Group 59), Central Decimal File, 1945– 1949, 861.00/ 2- 2246; reprinted in US Department of State, ed., *Foreign Relations of the United States, 1946*, Volume VI, Eastern Europe; The Soviet Union (Washington, DC: United States Government Printing Office, 1969), 696– 709. https://digitalarchive.wilsoncenter.org/document/116178.
21. Con Coughlin, *Saddam: His Rise and Fall* (New York: Ecco, 2005), 177.
22. وقائع المؤتمر الإسلامي الشعبي الثاني [Proceedings of the Second Popular Islamic Conference] (Baghdad: Ministry of Endowments and Religious Affairs, 1986). 385–90.
23. Taha Yasin Ramadan, "Continuous Popular Mobilization," *CRRC*, SH-MISC-D-001-446, January 28, 1999.
24. For a general description of this argument pertaining to postcolonial states, see, Ian S. Lustick, "The Absence of Middle Eastern Great Powers: Political "Backwardness" in Historical Perspective," *International Organization* 51, no. 4 (1997), 653–83; and Francis Fukuyama, *Political Order and Political Decay: From the Industrial Revolution to the Globalization of Democracy* (New York: Farrar, Straus and Giroux, 2014), 538–48; Daniel Neep, "War, State Formation, and Culture," *International Journal of*

Middle East Studies 45 (2013), 795–7; and Dina Rizk Khoury, "The Government of War," *International Journal of Middle Eastern Studies* 46, no. 4 (2014), 791–3; Ariel I. Ahram, "War-Making, State-Making, and Non-State Power In Iraq," *Yale Program on Governance and Local Development*, Working Paper No.1 2015. The Middle Eastern context can be contrasted with European state formation, about which Charles Tilly famously stated "War made the state and the state made war." See, Charles Tilly, "Reflections on the History of European State-Making," in *The Formation of National States in Western Europe*, ed. Charles Tilly (Princeton, NJ: Princeton University Press, 1975), 42.

25. Malcom Kerr, *The Arab Cold War: Gamal 'Abd al- Nasir and His Rivals* (New York: Oxford University Press, 1971); Samuel Helfont, "Islam in Saudi Foreign Policy: The Case of Ma'ruf al- Dawalibi," *International History Review* 42 (2020): 449–64.

26. For the emergence and evolution of the post–Cold War international order, see Robert Service, *The End of the Cold War, 1985–1991* (New York: Public Affairs Books, 2015); G John Ikenberry, Nuno P Monteiro, and William C Wohlforth, eds., *International Relations Theory and the Consequences of Unipolarity* (New York: Cambridge University Press, 2011); Nuno P Monteiro, *Theory of Unipolar Politics* (New York: Cambridge University Press, 2014); Joseph Nye, *Is the American Century Over?* (Cambridge: Polity, 2015); Michael Mandelbaum, *Mission Failure: America and the World in the Post-Cold War Era* (New York: Oxford University Press, 2016); Brands, *Making a Unipolar Moment*; Hal Brands, *From Berlin to Baghdad: America's Search for Purpose in the Post-Cold War World* (Lexington, KY: University Press of Kentucky, 2008); Jeffrey A. Engel, *When the World Seemed New: George H. W. Bush and the End of the Cold War* (New York: Houghton Mifflin Harcourt, 2017).

27. Rid, *Active Measures: The Secret History of Disinformation and Political Warfare*, 156.

28. On the end of the Cold War in Saddam's calculous, see the forthcoming dissertation by Daniel Chardell at Harvard University.

29. On "wedging" as a strategy in international relations, see, Timothy W. Crawford, "Preventing Enemy Coalitions: How Wedge Strategies Shape Power Politics," *International Security* 35, no. 4 (Spring 2011): 155–189, and Alexander Cooley and Daniel Nexon, *Exit from Hegemony: The Unraveling of the American Global Order* (New York: Oxford University Press, 2020), 59–61.

30. On institutional bargains in liberal international relations theory, see, G John Ikenberry, *After Victory: Institutions, Strategic Restraint, and the Rebuilding of Order After Major Wars* (Princeton, NJ: Princeton University Press, 2019), xvi.

31. These expectations clearly met the generally agreed definition of norms "as a standard of appropriate behavior for actors with a given identity." See, Martha Finnemore and Kathryn Sikkink, "International Norm Dynamics and Political Change," *International Organization* 52, no. 4 (Autumn 1998): 891, 900. For a more recent overview of the literature on norms, see, Matthew J. Hoffmann, "Norms and Social Constructivism in International Relations," *Oxford Research Encyclopedias*, December 22, 2017. https:// oxfor dre.com/ inter nati onal stud ies/ view/ 10.1093/ acref ore/ 978019 0846 626.001.0001/acrefore-9780190846626-e-60.

32. In the language of constructivists, the norms never fully "internalized" and thus failed to develop "a taken- for- granted quality." Finnemore and Sikkink, "International Norm Dynamics and Political Change," 895–6.

33. Fanar Haddad, "Essential Readings: Iraq," *Jadaliyya*, September 18, 2018. http:// www.jadali yya.com/ Deta ils/ 38016/ Essent ial- Readi ngs- Iraq; For examples, see, Joseph Sassoon, *Saddam Hussein's Ba'ath Party: Inside an Authoritarian Regime* (Cambridge: Cambridge University Press, 2012); Aaron Faust, *The Ba'thification of Iraq: Saddam Hussein's Totalitarianism* (Austin: University of Texas Press, 2015); Dina Rizk Khoury, *Iraq in Wartime: Soldiering, Martyrdom and Remembrance* (Cambridge: Cambridge University Press, 2013); Samuel Helfont, *Compulsion in Religion: Saddam Hussein, Islam, and the Roots of Insurgency in Iraq* (New York: Oxford University Press, 2018); Lisa Blaydes, *State of Repression: Iraq under Saddam Hussein* (Princeton, NJ: Princeton University Press, 2018). Alissa Walter, *The Ba'th Party in Baghdad: State- Society Relations through Wars, Sanctions, and Authoritarian Rule, 1950–2003* (PhD Dissertation, Georgetown University, 2018).

34. The main exception is the excellent yet unpublished dissertation of Kate Tietzen. See Katelyn Karly Tietzen, *The Iraqi Quest for Autonomy through Military and Diplomatic Interventions, 1968–2003* (PhD Dissertation, Kansas State University, 2019).

35. For a sample of this literature, see: Williamson Murray and Kevin Woods, *The Iran– Iraq War: A Military and Strategic History* (Cambridge: Cambridge University Press, 2014); Kevin Woods, *The Mother of All Battles: Saddam Hussein's Strategic Plan for the Persian Gulf War* (Washington, DC: Institute for Defense Analysis, 2008); Kevin Woods et al., *A Review of Iraqi Freedom from Saddam's Senior Leadership* (Washington, DC: Institute for Defense Analysis, 2008); Hal Brands and David Palkki, "Conspiring Bastards: Saddam's Strategic View of the United States," *Diplomatic History* 36, no. 3 (2012): 625– 59; Hal Brands, "Inside the Iraqi State Records: Saddam Hussein, 'Irangate,' and the United States," *Journal of Strategic Studies* 34, no. 1 (2011): 95–118; Hal Brands and David Palkki, "Saddam, Israel, and the Bomb: Nuclear Alarmism Justified?" *International Security* 36, no. 1 (2011): 133– 66; Gregory D. Koblentz, "Saddam Versus the Inspectors: The Impact of Regime Security on the Verification of Iraq's WMD Disarmament," *Journal of Strategic Studies* 41, no. 3 (2018): 372–409.

36. Erez Manela, "International Society as a Historical Subject," *Diplomatic History* 44, no. 2 (2020): 185–6.

37. United Nations Security Council archives are available at, Dag Hammarskjöld Library, https:// resea rch.un.org/ en/ docs/, hereafter, *UNSC Records*; American archives include the George H. W. Bush Presidential Library and Museum, Texas A&M, College Station, TX, https://bush41 library.tamu.edu/; The William J. Clinton Presidential Library and Museum, Little Rock, AK, https://www.clintonlibrary.gov/ research, hereafter *Clinton Library*; The James Baker III Papers, Princeton University, Princeton, NJ; The Boutros Boutros- Ghali Papers, Hoover Library and Archives, Stanford University, Stanford, CA; British files used for this book were released through the Iraq Inquiry, also known as the Chilcot Inquiry, https://webarchive.natio nalarchives.gov.uk/ ukgwa/ 20130809094300/http://www.iraqinquiry.org.uk/, here- after, *UK Iraq Inquiry Documents*.

38. On ethics, see Christopher Darnton, "The Provenance Problem: Research Methods and Ethics in the Age of WikiLeaks," *American Political Science Review* (released online 2021; print edition forthcoming); Alissa Walter, "The Repatriation of Iraqi Ba'th Party Archives: Ethical and Practical Considerations," *Journal of Contemporary Iraq & the Arab World* 16, nos. 1 & 2 (2022).

39. Conflict Records Research Center, National Defense University, Washington, DC. Hereafter, *CRRC*. For a time, the author had access to the complete set of records behind the government firewall and helped the CRRC to identify some records for release to the general public.

40. Kevin M. Woods, David D. Palkki, and Mark E. Stout, eds., *The Saddam Tapes: The Inner Workings of a Tyrant's Regime 1978–2001* (New York: Cambridge University Press, 2011) [hereafter, *The Saddam Tapes*]. Kevin M. Woods, *Iraqi Perspectives Project, Saddam and Terrorism: Emerging Insights from Captured Iraqi Documents* (Washington, DC: Institute for Defense Analysis, 2007), vols. 1–5.

41. Ba'th Party Regional Command Collection. Hereafter, *BRCC*. The collection can be found within the Hizb al-Ba'th al-'Arabi al-Ishtiraki in Iraq [Ba'th Arab Socialist Party of Iraq] records at Hoover Library and Archives, Stanford University.

Chapter 1

1. John Nixon, *Debriefing the President: The Interrogation of Saddam Hussein* (New York: Random House, 2018), 91–2; Efraim Karsh and Inari Rautsi, *Saddam Hussein: A Political Biography* (New York: Grove Press, 2002), 13–15;

2. On this period of Saddam's life, see, Coughlin, *Saddam*, Chapters 2–3.

3. Saddam discusses the details of the meeting and the video in, "Saddam Hussein Talks to the FBI: Twenty Interviews and Five Conversations with "High Value Detainee # 1" in 2004," *National Security Archive* [hereafter "Saddam Interrogation"], Session 9. https://nsarchive2.gwu.edu/NSAEBB/NSAEBB279/09.pdf; See, also, Coughlin, *Saddam*, 155–63.

4. Hal Brands, "Why Did Saddam Invade Iran? New Evidence on Motives, Complexity, and the Israeli Factor," *Journal of Military History* 75, no. 3 (July 2011).

5. Anthony H Cordesman, *Iraq's Military Forces: 1988–1993* (Washington, DC: CSIS Middle East Dynamic Net Assessment, 1994), 77.

6. Helfont, *Compulsion in Religion*, 76.

7. Géraldine Chatelard, "Migration from Iraq between the Gulf and the Iraq Wars (1990–2003): Historical and Socio-Spatial Dimensions," University of Oxford, *Centre on Migration, Policy and Society,* Working Paper No. 68 (2009): 11.

8. Aaron Terrazas, "Iraqi Immigrants in the United States in 2007," *Migration Policy Institute, Migration Information Source Spotlight* (March 5, 2009), https://www.migrationpolicy.org/article/iraqi-immigrants-united-states-2007.

9. See *BRCC* box files 022-1-17 from 1989 and 033-4-2 from 1992.

10. "معوقات" [Barriers], From: The Director of the Office of the General Secretariat, To: The Head of the Presidential Diwan, *BRCC*, 006-2-2 (0352). February 12, 1985.

11. For the responses from the ambassadors, see files titled "معوقات" [Barriers], *BRCC*, 006-2-2 (0340-0350), February to September 1985.

12. "محضر اجتماع هيأع مكتب الامانة العامة" [Proceedings of the meeting of the General Secretariat Group], *BRCC*, 026-5-5 (0207), February 15, 1989.

13. Faust, *The Ba'thification of Iraq*.

14. Coughlin, *Saddam*, 55–8. Saddam discusses the incident, in Saddam Interrogation, Session 6, pp 2–5. https://nsarchive2.gwu.edu/NSAEBB/NSAEBB279/06.pdf

15. Saddam discusses the incident, in Saddam Interrogation, Session 6, pp. 6–7. https://nsarchive2.gwu.edu/NSAEBB/NSAEBB279/06.pdf

16. Karsh and Rautsi, *Saddam Hussein: A Political Biography*, 31, 48–49.

17. Muhammad al-Mashat, كنت سفيرا للعراق في واشنطن: حكايتي مع صدام في غزو الكويت [*I was Iraq's Ambassador in Washington: My story with Saddam during the invasion of Kuwait*] (Beirut: The Iraqi Institute for Research and Publishing, 2008), 14, 103–5.

18. al-Mashat, كنت سفيرا للعراق في واشنطن : حكايتي مع صدام في غزو الكويت [*I was Iraq's Ambassador in Washington: My story with Saddam during the invasion of Kuwait*], 103–5.

19. Abd al-Malik Ahmad al-Yasin, ذكريات ومحطات حتى لا تضيع الحقيقة [*Memories and Stages: For the Sake of not Losing the Truth*] (Amman: Dar al-Amana for Publishing and Distribution, 2013), 84–90.

20. Samuel Helfont, "Authoritarianism beyond Borders: The Iraqi Ba'th Party as a Transnational Actor," *The Middle East Journal* 72, no. 2 (Spring 2018).

21. "محضر اجتماع هيأع مكتب الامانة العامة" [Proceedings of the meeting of the General Secretariat Group], *BRCC*, 026-5-5 (0208), February 15, 1989.

22. al-Mashat, كنت سفيرا للعراق في واشنطن: حكايتي مع صدام في غزو الكويت [I was Iraq's Ambassador in Washington: My story with Saddam during the invasion of Kuwait], 39–40.

23. Sassoon, *Saddam Hussein's Ba'th Party*, 268–74.

24. Hanna Batatu, *The Old Social Classes and the Revolutionary Movements of Iraq: A Study of Iraq's Old Landed and Commercial Classes and of Its Communists, Ba'thists and Free Officers* (Princeton, NJ: Princeton University Press, 1978), 731.

25. Batatu, *The Old Social Classes*, 1125 and 742.

26. Ofra Bengio, *Saddam's Word: Political Discourse in Iraq* (New York: Oxford University Press, 1998), 50–1.

27. Batatu, *The Old Social Classes*, 1120.

28. For a list of countries in which the student union had branches, see untitled list from 1993, BRCC, 033-4-2 (0605).

29. "فرع الإتحاد الوطني في روسيا" [The National Union branch in Russia], *BRCC*, 2383_0002 (0183), June 24, 2002.

30. "منشورات معادية" [Hostile publications], *BRCC*, 3796_ 0001 (573), July 9, 1986; "نشاطات فروع الاتحاد خارج القطر" [Activities of the branches of the union outside the region], *BRCC*, 3796_0001 (0464-0530), August 23, 1986.

31. For a list of the foreign chapters as of 1993, see "معلومات" [Information], *BRCC*, 033-4-2 (0561-0564), January 30, 1993.

32. Elaine Sciolino, "The Big Brother: Iraq Under Saddam Hussein," *New York Times Magazine*, February. 3, 1985. https://www.nytimes.com/1985/02/03/magazine/the-big-brother-iraq-under-saddam-hussein.html.

33. Faust, 124; Sassoon, *Saddam Hussein's Ba'th Party*, 253–8. Sassoon quotes Marion Faruq Sluglett using the term about the Iraqi regime in her 1993 essay, "Liberation or Repression? Pan- Arab Nationalism and the Women's Movement in Iraq," in *Iraq: Power and Society*, St. Anthony's Middle East Monographs, ed. Derek Hopwood, Habib Ishow, and Thomas Koszinowski (Reading: Ithaca Press, 1993), 68–9.

34. See, for example, "مقترح" [Recommendation], *BRCC*, 2997_0000 (0279), September 25, 1996.

35. Five out of eighteen foreign chapters in 1993 were headed by the wives of the ambassador. "معلومات" [Information], *BRCC*, 033-4-2 (0561-0564), January 30, 1993.

36. "نشاط اجتماعي" [Social activity], *BRCC*, 2383_0002 (0177), October 5, 2002.

37. "ترشيح" [Nomination], From: The Special Secretary for Party Matters, To: The Regional Command—Office of the Secretariat of the Region, *BRCC* 022-1-7 (0101), December 24, 1988.

38. "ترشيح" [Nomination], From: The Special Secretary for Party Matters, To: The Regional Command—Office of the Secretariat of the Region, *BRCC* 022-1-7 (0098), June 18, 1989.

39. "مقترحات" [Recommendations]. From: The Director General of the Office of the Secretariat of the Region, To: The Regional Office of Foreign Relations and the Office of the Bureau of Iraqis outside of Iraq. *BRCC*, 022-1-7 (0008), September 19, 1989.

40. Kanan Makiya, *Cruelty and Silence: War, Tyranny, Uprising, and the Arab World* (New York: Norton, 1993), 112.

41. Harvey Morris, "Saddam's Enemies in Exile," *The Independent* (London), September 11, 1990; and, Patrick Mcgowan, "Britain Treats Iraqi Poisoned by Saddam," *Evening Standard* (London), February 1, 1995.

42. "A Safe Haven will be Hard to Find," *The Herald* (Scotland), August 27, 1996. https://www.heraldscotland.com/news/12033008.a-safe-haven-will-be-hard-to-find/.

43. Samir al- Khalil, *The Republic of Fear: The Politics of Modern Iraq* (Berkeley, CA: University of California Press, 1989).

44. These essays can be found in, Michel Aflaq, في سبيل البعث [In the Way of the Ba 'th] (Beirut: Dar al-Tali'a, 1963).

45. Michel Aflaq, "ذكرى الرسول العربي" [Memory of the Arab Messenger], 52.

46. Michel Aflaq, "ذكرى الرسول العربي".[Memory of the Arab Messenger], 60.

47. Michel Aflaq, "نظرتنا إلى الدين" [Our View Toward Religion],128.

48. For Alfaq's assertions about Islam being more appropriate for Arabs, see, Michel Aflaq"ذكرى الرسول العربي" [Memory of the Arab Messenger], 55, 58.

49. Saddam Hussein, *On History, Heritage, and Religion*, Translated by Naji al- Hadithi. (Baghdad: Translation and Foreign Language Publishing House, 1981), 26–7.

50. التقرير المركزي للمؤتمر القطري التاسع [The Central Report of the Ninth Regional Conference] (Baghdad: Hizb al-Ba'th al-'Arabi al-Ishtiraki, 1983), 263–304.

51. Ma'ruf al-Dawalibi, "Background on Ma'ruf al-Dawalibi Given" *Al-Majallah* (London), May, 14 1982, *Joint Publications Research Service*, Near East/North Africa Report No. 2583, July 16, 1982.

52. Muhammad Ma'ruf al-Dawalibi, مذكرات الدكتور معروف الدواليبي [The Memoirs of Doctor Ma'ruf al-Dawalibi] (Riyadh: Maktabat al-'Ubaykan, 2005), 193–4.

53. On al-Dawalibi's career in this period, see, al-Dawalibi, مذكرات, 193–225; Helfont, "Islam in Saudi Foreign Policy."

54. وقائع المؤتمر الإسلامي الشعبي: وثائق وقرارات [Proceedings of the Popular Islamic Conference: Documents and Resolutions] (Baghdad: al-Najaf al-Ashraf, 1983); وقائع المؤتمر الإسلامي الشعبي الثاني [Proceedings of the Second Popular Islamic Conference] (Baghdad: Ministry of Endowments and Religious Affairs, 1986). For the role of these conferences in Iraqi foreign policy, see Samuel Helfont, "Saddam and the Islamists: The Ba'thist Regime's Instrumentalization of Religion in Foreign Affairs," *The Middle East Journal* 68, no. 3 (Summer 2014): 352–66.

55. "قرارات المؤتمر الشعبي الإسلامي الثاني" [Decisions of the Second Popular Islamic Conference], *BRCC*, 3591_0002 (0444), April 28, 1985.

56. "Saddam and Ba'ath Party Members Discussing the Status of the Party in the Arab World and Potential Cooperation with the Muslim Brotherhood," *CRRC*, SH-SHTP-A-001-167, July 24, 1986.

57. "Iraqi Leader's Address to Baghdad Islamic Conference on Iranian Arms, the War," Voice of the Masses, Baghdad. February 20, 1987. *BBC Worldwide Monitoring*; Ofra Bengio, "Iraq," in *Middle East Contemporary Survey: Volume XI, 1987*, ed. Itamar Rabinovich and Haim Shaked (Boulder, CO: Westview Press), 438.

58. "تقرير عن جامعة صدام للدراسات الإسلامية: حاجات وطموحات" [Report on the Saddam University for Islamic Studies: Needs and Aspirations], *BRCC*, 3493_0001 (0025-0033), September 19, 1992.

59. "مقترح" [Suggestion], *BRCC*, 3260_0002 (0214-0219), October 1992.

60. [Islamic College of the University], *BRCC*, 029-1-6 (0076), August 11, 1988.

Chapter 2

1. Daniel P. Moynihan, "The United States in Opposition," *Commentary* (March 1975); Mark Mazower, *Governing the World: The History of an Idea* (New York: Penguin Books, 2012), 305–42.

2. Boutros Boutros-Ghali, "Introduction," *The United Nations and the Iraq-Kuwait Conflict 1990–1996*, The United Nations Blue Books Series, vol. IX, Department of Public Information United Nations, New York, 1996.

3. Saddam Interrogation, Session 14, 1. https://nsarchive2.gwu.edu/NSAEBB/NSAEBB 279/14.pdf.

4. "Five Days after Invading Kuwait, the Revolutionary Command Council Votes on Unification with Kuwait and Whether to Demarcate Kuwait's Border with Saudi

Arabia. Saddam Discusses the Need to Crush Kuwaiti Opposition," August 7, 1990. *The Saddam Tapes*, 172.

5. "Five Days after Invading Kuwait, the Revolutionary Command Council Votes on Unification with Kuwait and Whether to Demarcate Kuwait's Border with Saudi Arabia. Saddam Discusses the Need to Crush Kuwaiti Opposition," August 7, 1990. *The Saddam Tapes*, 171–2.

6. Saddam Interrogation, Session 3, 5. https://nsarchive2.gwu.edu/NSAEBB/NSAEBB 279/03.pdf

7. Kevin M. Woods, *Um Al-Ma'arik (The Mother of All Battles): Operational and Strategic Insights from an Iraqi Perspective* (Washington, DC: Institute for Defense Analysis, 2008). 69–85.

8. "Saddam Appraises American and International Reactions to the Invasion of Kuwait," August 7, 1990, *The Saddam Tapes*, 176; Saddam Interrogation, Session 9. https://nsa rchive2.gwu.edu/NSAEBB/NSAEBB279/10.pdf.

9. Daniel Chardell is currently completing his dissertation at Harvard University on this topic.

10. For example, Stephen M Walt, "WikiLeaks, April Glaspie, and Saddam Hussein," *Foreign Policy*, January 9, 2011. https://foreignpolicy.com/2011/01/09/wikile aks-april-glaspie-and-saddam-hussein/; and, Coughlin, Saddam, 562–4.

11. "Interview with Tariq 'Aziz by Ali Al-Dabagh," *Al-Arabiyya*, Summer, 2010, formerly available through *CRRC*.

12. George H. W. Bush and Brent Scowcroft, *A World Transformed* (New York: Vintage, 1999), 311; Engel, *When the World Seemed New*, 381–3.

13. "Saddam Appraises American and International Reactions to the Invasion of Kuwait," August 7, 1990, *The Saddam Tapes*, 176.

14. Woods, *Um Al-Ma'arik*, 69–84; Hal Brands and David Palkki, "Conspiring Bastards," 625–659; "Saddam Appraises American and International Reactions to the Invasion of Kuwait," August 7, 1990, *The Saddam Tapes*, 175.

15. Joseph Sassoon and Alissa Walter, "The Iraqi Occupation of Kuwait: New Historical Perspectives," *The Middle East Journal* 71, no. 4 (2017): 609.

16. Sassoon and Walter, 615.

17. A brief and digestible version of Hegel's ideas can be found in Georg Wilhelm Friedrich Hegel, *Introduction to the Philosophy of History* (Indianapolis, IN: Hackett Publishing Company, 1988).

18. Francis Fukuyama, "The End of History?" *National Interest* (Summer, 1989).

19. John Mueller, *Retreat from Doomsday: The Obsolescence of Major War* (New York: Basic Books, 1989).

20. John Keegan, *A History of Warfare* (New York, Robert F. Knopf, 1993), 48–9.

21. John Lewis Gaddis, "Toward the Post-Cold War World," *Foreign Affairs* 70, no. 2 (Spring, 1991): 103.

22. Gaddis, "Toward the Post-Cold War World," 104. It should be noted that Gaddis's analysis does not suppose that the forces of integration will succeed, or even that they should.

23. Sarah Snyder, *Human Rights Activism and the End of the Cold War: A Transnational History of the Helsinki Network* (New York: Cambridge University Press, 2011).

24. Dan Goodgame, "What If We Do Nothing?" *Time Magazine* 137, no. 1, January 7, 1991.

25. Jeffrey A. Engel, *When the World Seemed New*, 386.

26. Bush and Scowcroft, *A World Transformed*, 317–8.

27. Engel, *When the World Seemed New*, 396.

28. Joshua R Itzkowitz Shifrinson, "George H. W. Bush: Conservative Realist as President," *Orbis* 62, no. 1 (2018).

29. George H. W. Bush, January 20, 1989: Inaugural Address, Miller Center, University of Virginia, https://millercenter.org/the-presidency/presidential-speeches/january-20-1989-inaugural-address; and Engel, *When the World Seemed New*, 73–4.

30. Memorandum of Conversation: The President's Meeting with President Gorbachev of the Soviet Union, September 9, 1990, 1–2. *George H. W. Bush Presidential Library and Museum*, https://bush41library.tamu.edu/files/memcons-telcons/1990-09-09--Gorbachev%20[1].pdf.

31. Bush and Scowcroft, *A World Transformed*, 364.

32. Bush, "Address Before a Joint Session of the Congress."

33. Shifrinson, "George H. W. Bush: Conservative Realist as President"; Paul Lewis, "Fighting in Panama: United Nations; Security Council Condemnation of Invasion Vetoed," *The New York Times*, December 24, 1989; Victoria Graham, "General Assembly Condemns Panama Invasion 75-20," *Associated Press*, December 29, 1989.

34. George H. W. Bush, *National Security Directive 45*, August 20, 1990, *George H. W. Bush Presidential Library and Museum*, https://bush41 library.tamu.edu/files/nsd/nsd45.pdf; George H. W. Bush, *National Security Directive 54*, January 15, 1991, *George H. W. Bush Presidential Library and Museum*, https://bush41 library.tamu.edu/files/nsd/nsd54.pdf; *Conduct of the Persian Gulf War: Final Report to Congress* (Washington, DC: Department of Defense, April 1992), 38. https://apps.dtic.mil/dtic/tr/fulltext/u2/a249270.pdf.

35. The most forceful— and influential— member of this camp was Fred Halliday, who insisted that the "war had little or nothing to do with something called 'a New International Order.'" Fred Halliday, "The Gulf War 1990– 1991 and the Study of International Relations," *Review of International Studies* 20, no. 2 (April 1994): 110. See also, Hal Brands, *Berlin to Baghdad*, 80–96.

36. Paul Kennedy, *The Parliament of Man: The Past, Present, and Future of the United Nations* (New York: Vintage Books, 2006), 3– 50; Mueller, *Retreat from Doomsday*, 33–36. Oona A. Hathaway, and Scott J. Shapiro, *The Internationalists: How a Radical Plan to Outlaw War Remade the World* (New York: Simon & Schuster, 2017) 101–130.

37. Kennedy, *The Parliament of Man*, 33.

38. United Nations: Sanctions Against Rhodesia, *Time Magazine*, December 23, 1966. http://content.time.com/time/subscriber/article/0,33009,840760,00.html.

39. Moynihan, "The United States in Opposition"; Mazower, *Governing the World*, 305–342.

40. Brands, *Making of a Unipolar Moment*.

41. Kennedy, *The Parliament of Man*, 64.

42. Memorandum of Conversation: Telephone Call to President Turgut Ozal of Turkey, August 4, 1990, *George H. W. Bush Presidential Library and Museum*, 2 https://bush41 library.tamu.edu/files/memcons-telcons/1990-08-04--Ozal.pdf.

43. Intervention by North Atlantic Council Ministerial Meeting. NATO HQ, Brussels Belgium, September 10, 1990, Box 109, Folder 5 number 12. James A Baker III Papers, Princeton University.

44. Notes from 9/7/90 remarks to USAF personnel stations at Ta'if, Saudi Arabia, September 7, 1990. Box 109 Folder 5, Number 16. James A Baker III Papers, Princeton University.

45. Boutros-Ghali, "Introduction," 21–3.

46. Memorandum of Conversation: Meeting with Prime Minister Toshiki Kaifu of Japan, September 29, 1990, *George H. W. Bush Presidential Library and Museum*, 2. https:// bush41library.tamu.edu/files/memcons-telcons/1990-09-29--Kaifu.pdf.

47. See, Resolution 670, S/RES/670, September 25 1990, *UNSC Records*, and, Boutros Boutros-Ghali, "Introduction," 21–3.

48. Mazower, *Governing the World*, 379.

49. "غلق سفارات وقنصليات" [Closing of Embassies and Consulates], From: The Director General of the Office of the Secretariat of the Region, To: The President of the Republic / Secretary of the President of the Republic for Party Matters, BRCC, 2827_ 0001 (0525), November 20, 1990.

50. "نشاط منظمة" [Activities of the Organization], From: The Director General of the Office of the Secretariat of the Region, To: The President of the Republic / Secretary of the President of the Republic for Party Matters, BRCC, 2827_0001 (0492), November 28, 1990.

51. "معلمات" [Information], From: The Director General of the Office of the Secretariat of the Region, To: The President of the Republic / Secretary of the President of the Republic for Party Matters, BRCC, 2827_0001 (0542), November 5, 1990.

52. "موقف نضالي" [Militant Position], From: The Secretary General of the Office of the Bureau of Iraqis outside the Region, To: All the Organizations of Iraqis outside the Region. BRCC, 2827_ 0001 (0417- 0418). Date: October 13, 1990; "ابعاد رفاق" [Deporting Comrades], From: The Director General of the Office of the Secretariat of the Region, To: The President of the Republic / Secretary of the President of the Republic for Party Matters. BRCC, 2827_0001 (0383), September 24, 1990.

53. "Letter from the (British) Immigration and Nationality Department," BRCC, 2827_ 0001 0698, September 17, 1990.

54. "معلمات" [Information], From: The Director General of the Office of the Secretariat of the Region, To: The President of the Republic / Secretary of the President of the Republic for Party Matters. BRCC, 2827_0001 (0449), November 5, 1992.

55. "معلمات" [Information], From: The Director General of the Office of the Secretariat of the Region, To: The President of the Republic / Secretary of the President of the Republic for Party Matters. BRCC, 2827_0001 (0513), November 5, 1990.

56. "تقرير" [Report], From: Secretary General of the Central Office for the Popular and Professional Bureau, To: The Office of the Secretariat of the Region. *BRCC*, 2211_0000 (0722-0725), September 24, 1990.

57. "الطلبة المبعدون في الجارج" [Deported Students Abroad], *BRCC*, 2211_0000.

58. "مذكرات" [Recollections], From: Secretary General of the Central Office for the Popular and Professional Bureau, To: The Office of the Secretariat of the Region. *BRCC*, 2211_0000 (0665), October 13, 1990.

59. "تقرير" [Report], From: Secretary General of the Central Office for the Popular and Professional Bureau, To: The Office of the Secretariat of the Region. *BRCC*, 2211_0000 (0685-0696), October 7, 1990.

60. "موقف نضالي" [Militant Position], From: The Secretary General of the Office of the Bureau of Iraqis outside the Region, To: All the Organizations of Iraqis outside the Region. *BRCC*, 2827_0001 (0419). October 13, 1990.

61. "معلومات] [Information], From: The Director of the office of the Bureau of Iraqis outside the Region, To the Regional Command / Office of the Secretariat of the Region. *BRCC*, 2211_0000 (0643-0642), October 30, 1990.

62. Al- Mashat, كنت سفيرا للعراق في واشنطن: حكايتي مع صدام في غزو الكويت [*I was Iraq's Ambassador in Washington: My story with Saddam during the invasion of Kuwait*], 21–30.

63. Al-Mashat, كنت سفيرا للعراق في واشنطن: حكايتي مع صدام في غزو الكويت [*I was Iraq's Ambassador in Washington: My story with Saddam during the invasion of Kuwait*], 179–208.

64. "برقية جفرية" [Cable] From the Command of the office of Iraqis outside of the Region, To: The Organizations of Iraqis outside of the region. *BRCC*, 2827_0001 (0482-0483), December 26, 1990.

65. "توجهات" [Directives] From: The Secretary General of the office of the tanzim of Iraqis outside the region, To: All Organizations of Iraqis outside the region. *BRCC*, 2827_0001 (0294), August 4, 1990; "نشاطات" [Activities], From: The Secretary General of the Office of the Bureau of Iraqis outside the Region, To: All Organizations of Iraqis outside the Region. *BRCC*, 2827_0001 (0297), August 9, 1990.

66. Memorandum of Telephone Conversation: Telephone Conversation with King Hassan of Morocco, August 7, 1990, *George H. W. Bush Presidential Library and Museum*, 2. https://bush41 library.tamu.edu/files/memcons-telcons/1990-08-07-- Hassan.pdf

67. "Students Stage Pro-Iraqi Demonstrations," *Iraqi News Agency*, August 8 1990, World News Connection.

68. "Students Form Brigade to Hit US Interests," *Al-Ra'y* (Jordan), September 9 1990. World News Connection.

69. "Express Solidarity with Iraq," *Omdurman Domestic Service*, August 11 1990. World News Connection.

70. "Over 200,000 March to Show Support for Iraq," *Khartoum SUNA*, August 13 1990. World News Connection.

71. "نشاطات" [Activities], From: The Director General of the Office of the Secretariat of the Region, To: The President of the Republic / Secretary of the President of the Republic for Party Matters. *BRCC*, 2827_0001 (0395), October 2, 1990.

72. Jerry M. Long, *Saddam's War of Words: Politics, Religion, and the Iraqi invasion of Kuwait* (Austin: University of Texas Press, 2004), 130–1.

73. "برقية" [Cable], From: The Director General of the Office of the Secretariat of the Region, To: The President of the Republic / Secretary of the President of the Republic for Party Matters. *BRCC*, 2827_0001 (0391), September 18, 1990.

74. Peter Applebome, "War in the Gulf: Antiwar Rallies," *The New York Times*, January 27, 1991; Barbara Epstein, "The Antiwar Movement During the Gulf War," *Social Justice*, Vol. 19, No. 1 (Spring 1992), 115–37.

75. Alan Riding, "Confrontation in The Gulf; Crowds in European Cities Protest a War in Gulf Area" *The New York Times*, January 13, 1991.

76. Nick Cohen, *How the Left Lost its Way* (New York: Harper Perennial, 2007), 5.

77. Kanan Makiya, *Republic of Fear: The Politics of Modern Iraq* (University of California Press, 1998).

78. Edward W. Said, "Edward Said, an American and an Arab, Writes on the Eve of the Iraqi-Soviet Peace Talks," *London Review of Books* 13, no. 5 (1991) https://www.lrb.co.uk/the-paper/v13/n05/edward-said/edward-said-an-american-and-an-arab-writes-on-the-eve-of-the-iraqi-soviet-peace-talks.

79. Edward W. Said, "Behind Saddam Hussein's Moves," *The Christian Science Monitor* (1990) https://www.csmonitor.com/layout/set/amphtml/1990/0813/esaid.html

80. Said, "Behind Saddam Hussein's Moves."

81. For Said's claims, see, Said, "Edward Said, an American and an Arab, Writes on the Eve of the Iraqi-Soviet Peace Talks"; For a thorough debunking of the Army War College report, see, Douglas V. Johnson II and Stephen C. Pelletiere, reply by Edward Mortimer, "Iraq's Chemical Warfare," *The New York Review of Books*, November 22, 1990. https://www.nybooks.com/articles/1990/11/22/iraqs-chemical-warfare/.

82. See Said's interview with Barbara Harlow. Barbara Harlow, "The Intellectuals and the War," *Middle East Report* 171 (July/August 1991).

83. On this shift, see Nick Cohen, *What's Left*. See also, Makiya, *Cruelty and Silence*, 346 endnote 11.

84. "توجيهات" [Guidance] From: The Secretary General of the Office of the Bureau of Iraqis outside the Region, To: All Organizations of Iraqis outside the Region. *BRCC*, 2827_0001 (0313-0314), August 21, 1990.

85. A full text of this speech can be found in: Saddam Husayn, "Call For Jihad, 5 Sep 1990" in Ofra Bengio, ed., *Saddam Speaks on the Gulf Crisis: A Collection of Documents* (Tel Aviv: Moshe Dayan Center for Middle Eastern and African Studies, Tel Aviv University, 1992), 136–43.

86. "Miscellaneous Information Regarding the Iraqi Invasion of Kuwait and the American Operation to Liberate Kuwait," *CRRC*, SH-GMID-D-000-998, September-October 1990.

87. Long, *Saddam's War of Words*, 120.

88. Helfont, *Compulsion in Religion*.

89. "Saddam Hussein Meeting with Advisors Regarding the American Ground Attack During First Gulf War –Garnering Arab and Iraqi Support –and a Letter to Gorbachev," *CRRC*, SH-SHTP-A-000-931, February 24, 1991.

90. For example, see the list of participants in: وقائع المؤتمر الإسلامي الشعبي: وثائق وقرارات [Proceedings of the Popular Islamic Conference: Documents and Resolutions].

91. "نشاط منظمة" [Activities of the Organization], From: The Director General of the Office of the Secretariat of the Region, To: The President of the Republic / Secretary of the President of the Republic for Party Matters, *BRCC*, 2827_ 0001 (0492), November 28, 1990; "معلومات" [Information], From: The Director General of the Office of the Secretariat of the Region, To: The President of the Republic / Secretary of the President of the Republic for Party Matters, *BRCC*, 2827_ 0001 (0542), November 5, 1990.

92. "Blockade of Iraq by America and its Allies," From Jamiat- ul- Ulama- i- Islam Pakistan, To the Iraqi Ambassador in Pakistan, *BRCC*, 2827_ 0001 (0380), September 1990.

93. "نشاطات" [Activities] From: The Director General of the Office of the Secretariat of the Region, To: The President of the Republic / Secretary of the President of the Republic for Party Matters, *BRCC*, 2827_0001 (0335), September 5, 1990.

94. Martin Kramer, "Islam in the New World Order," in *Middle East Contemporary Survey: Volume XV, 1991*, ed. Ami Ayalon (Boulder, CO: Westview Press, 1993), 173.

95. "Executive Council of the Popular Islamic Conference," in *Islamic Conferences Held in the Kingdom of Saudi Arabia in the Course of the Arab Gulf Incidents* (The Kingdom of Saudi Arabia Ministry of Information, Saudi Press Agency, No Date), 177.

96. James Piscatori, "Religion and Realpolitik," in *Islamic Fundamentalisms and the Gulf Crisis*, ed. James Piscatori (Chicago: American Academy of Arts and Sciences with the Fundamentalism Project, 1991).

97. Gehad Auda, "An Uncertain Response: The Islamic Movement in Egypt," in *Islamic Fundamentalisms and the Gulf Crisis*, ed. James Piscatori (Chicago: American Academy of Arts and Sciences with the Fundamentalism Project, 1991), 118.

98. Mona El- Ghobashy, "The Metamorphosis of the Egyptian Muslim Brothers," *International Journal of Middle Eastern Studies* 37, no. 3 (2005): 379; Martin Kramer, "Islam in the New World Order," in *Middle East Contemporary Survey 1991*, 173.

99. Beverley Milton- Edwards, "A Temporary Alliance with the Crown: The Islamic Response in Jordan," in *Islamic Fundamentalisms and the Gulf Crisis*, ed. James Piscatori (Chicago: American Academy of Arts and Sciences with the Fundamentalism Project, 1991), 93–98.

100. "Correspondence within the General Military Intelligence Directorate Concerning Information on the Movements of the Coalition Forces in the Gulf Area," *CRRC*, SH-GMID-D-000-957, November 2, 1990.

101. "Open Letter to President George Bush of USA (sic)" From "the Armed Battalions Revolutionary Party" *BRCC*, 2827_0001 (0529-0530) November 1, 1990.

102. "Open Letter to President George Bush of USA (sic)" From "the Armed Battalions Revolutionary Party" *BRCC*, 2827_0001 (0529-0530) November 1, 1990.

103. The best overview of the war can be found in Michael R. Gordon and General Bernard E Trainor, *The Generals' War: The Inside Story of the Conflict in the Gulf* (New York: Little, Brown and Company, 1995).

104. Personal Letter. From Egyptian Ambassador to the US, El Sayed Abdel Rauf El Reedy, To: Secretary of State James Baker III, June 8, 1992, Box 102, Number 3, James A Baker III Papers, Princeton University.

105. Katelyn Karly Tietzen, *The Iraqi Quest for Autonomy through Military and Diplomatic Interventions, 1968–2003* (PhD Dissertation, Kansas State University, 2019), 251.

106. Coughlin, *Saddam*, 259.

107. "برقية جفرية" [Cable] From the Command of the office of Iraqis outside of the Region, To: The Organizations of Iraqis outside of the region, *BRCC* (0482-0483), December 26, 1990.

108. "Miscellaneous information regarding the Iraqi invasion of Kuwait and the American operation to liberate Kuwait," *CRRC*, SH-GMID-D-000-998, September–October 1990.

109. "Commando (Fedayeen) Volunteers," IISP-2003-00029003, October 11, 1990, in Kevin M Woods, ed., *Iraqi Perspectives Project Primary Source Materials for Saddam and Terrorism: Emerging Insights from Captured Iraqi Documents*, Volume 3, 162–3.

110. For an overview of these actions, see, "IIS Research Study on the Rebellion of 1991 Refugee Camp and a Volunteered Fedayeen Saddam Member." IISP-2003-00029003, December 4, 1991, in Kevin M Woods, ed., *Iraqi Perspectives Project Primary Source Materials for Saddam and Terrorism: Emerging Insights from Captured Iraqi Documents*, vol. 3, 117–65.

111. Pesach Malovany, *Wars of Modern Babylon: A History of the Iraqi Army from 1921 to 2003* (Lexington, KY: The University Press of Kentucky, 2017), 549.

112. Charles Duelfer, *Hide and Seek: The Search for Truth in Iraq Hardcover* (New York: Public Affairs, 2009), 71–2.

113. Malovany, *Wars of Modern Babylon*, 556–63.

114. Woods, *Um Al-Ma'arik*, 26.

115. "Oral History: Richard Cheney," PBS Front Line, January 1996, https://www.pbs.org/wgbh/pages/frontline/gulf/oral/cheney/1.html.

116. "Discussion Following the First Gulf War," *CRRC*, SH-SHTP-A-000-835, 1991. I would like to thank Michael Brill for pointing me toward sources that were beneficial in this section of the article.

117. "World Reacts to Shelter Bombing," *Xinhua*, February 15, 1991, *FBIS*; "Civilian Casualties Increase" *TASS*, February 14, 1991, *FBIS*.

118. "Arafat Condemns 'Heinous' Baghdad Bombing," *Voice of Palestine (Algiers)*, February 14, 1991. *FBIS*; "King Husayn on US Glaring Violation," *Xinhua*, February 14, 1991, *FBIS*.

119. "World Reacts to Shelter Bombing," *Xinhua*, February 15, 1991. *FBIS*; "Rognoni Says Bombing Iraqi Cities Intolerable," *Agence France Presse*, February 15, 1991, *FBIS*; David Malone, *The International Struggle Over Iraq: Politics in the UN Security Council 1980-2005* (New York: Oxford University Press, 2006), 73.

120. Gordan and Trainor, *The General's War*, 326.

121. Interview with Jon Alpert by phone. April 19, 2017.

122. Robert A. Pape, *Bombing to Win: Air Power and Coercion in War* (Ithaca, NY: Cornell University Press, 1996), 211–53; Daryl G. Press, "The Myth of Air Power in the Persian Gulf War and the Future of Warfare," *International Security* 26, no. 2 (Fall 2001): 5–44.

123. Williamson Murray et al., *Gulf War Air Power Survey, Vol. 2: Operations and Effectiveness* (Washington, DC, U.S. Government Printing Office, 1993), 304–5.

124. Nuha al- Radi, *Baghdad Diaries: A Woman's Chronicle of War and Exile* (New York: Vintage, 2003), 29.

125. Al-Radi, *Baghdad Diaries*, 31.

126. "النظام الدولي الجديد و كارثة اطفال العراق" [The New World Order and the Disaster of the Iraqi Children], *BRCC*, 2749_0000 (0667-0656), 1991.

Chapter 3

1. "النظام الدولي الجديد وكارثة اطفال العراق" [The New World Order and the Disaster of the Iraqi Children], *BRCC*, 2749_0000 (0667-0656), 1991.

2. The White House, *National Security Strategy of the United States* (Washington, DC: The White House, August 1991), v.

3. On the fallout from the Gulf War, see, Samuel Helfont, "The Gulf War's Afterlife: Dilemmas, Missed Opportunities, and the Post-Cold War Order Undone," *The Texas National Security Review* 4, no. 2 (Spring 2021), 26–47.

4. Boutros-Ghali, "Introduction," 29.

5. Provisional Record of the 2981st Meeting, UN Security Council, S/PV. 2981, April 3, 1991. *UNSC Records*, 111–2; Boutros Boutros-Ghali, "Introduction," 33–4.

6. Provisional Record of the 2981st Meeting, UN Security Council, S/PV. 2981, April 3, 1991. *UNSC Records*, 99.

7. Provisional Record of the 2981st Meeting, UN Security Council, S/PV. 2981, April 3, 1991. *UNSC Records*, 82.

8. Provisional Record of the 2981st Meeting, UN Security Council, S/PV. 2981, April 3, 1991. *UNSC Records*, 93; Boutros Boutros-Ghali, "Introduction," 33–4.

9. Provisional Record of the 2981st Meeting, UN Security Council, S/PV. 2981, April 3, 1991. *UNSC Records*.

10. "The Unfinished War: The Legacy of Desert Storm," *CNN*, January 5, 2001, http://transcripts.cnn.com/TRANSCRIPTS/0101/05/cp.00.html.

11. For an overview of these events, and the myths that surround them, see Fanar Haddad, *Sectarianism in Iraq: Antagonistic Visions of Unity* (London: Hurst & Company, 2011), 13, 65– 84, 117– 32. Makiya, *Republic of Fear*, xxx– i; Khoury, *Iraq in Wartime*, 135– 6; Charles Tripp, *A History of Iraq* (Cambridge: Cambridge University Press, 2002), 264–71; Helfont, *Compulsion in Religion*, 121–6.

12. Scott Peterson, "Kurds Say Iraq's Attacks Serve as a Warning," *Christian Science Monitor*, May 13, 2002.

13. Bush, "Address before a Joint Session of the Congress."

14. Provisional Record of the 2981st Meeting, UN Security Council, S/PV. 2982, April 5, 1991. *UNSC Records*. 53.

15. Tietzen, *The Iraqi Quest for Autonomy through Military and Diplomatic Interventions, 1968-2003*, 254.

16. Provisional Record of the 3059th Meeting, UN Security Council, S/PV.3059, March 11, 1992. *UNSC Records*, 51.

17. Boutros Boutros-Ghali, "An Agenda for Peace Preventive Diplomacy, Peacemaking and Peace-Keeping," Report of the Secretary General pursuant to the statement adopted by the Summit Meeting of the Security Council on January 31, 1992, https://digitallibrary.un.org/record/145749?ln=en.

18. Boutros Boutros-Ghali, *Unvanquished: A U.S.-UN Saga* (New York: Random House, 1999), 24.

19. Boutros Boutros-Ghali, *Unvanquished*, 24.

20. "Notes of the Secretary General's meeting with Mr. Max van der Stoel, Human Rights Rapporteur for Iraq," April 30, 1992. *Boutros Boutros-Ghali Papers*, Box 62, Folder 5.

21. Malone, *The International Struggle Over Iraq*, 98.

22. Provisional Record of the 3105th Meeting, UN Security Council, S/PV.3105, August 11, 1992. *UNSC Records*, 51.

23. Malone, *The International Struggle Over Iraq*, 86.

24. For an overview of Chinese concerns at the United Nations during this period, see, "Notes of the Meeting of the Secretary-General and then Minister of Foreign Affairs of the People's Republic of China," April 15, 1992. *Boutros Boutros-Ghali Papers*, Box 62, Folder 4.

25. Quoted in Tietzen, *The Iraqi Quest for Autonomy through Military and Diplomatic Interventions, 1968–2003*, 253.

26. For an example of this language, see "Notes of the Secretary-General's meeting with the Permanent Representative of the United States of America," December 19, 1992. *Boutros Boutros-Ghali Papers*, Box 66, Folder 1.

27. Provisional Record of the 3059th Meeting, UN Security Council, S/PV.3059, March 11, 1992. *UNSC Records*, 34.

28. Provisional Record of the 3059th Meeting, UN Security Council, S/PV.3059, March 11, 1992. *UNSC Records*, 52–3.

29. "Notes of the Secretary-General's meeting with the Executive Chairman of the United Nations Special Commission," February 18, 1992. *Boutros Boutros-Ghali Papers*, Box 62, Folder 2.

30. "Report to the Secretary-General on humanitarian needs in Kuwait and Iraq in the immediate post-crisis environment by a mission to the area led by Mr. Martti Ahtisaari, Under-Secretary-General for Administration and Management," March 20, 1991, in *The United Nations and the Iraq-Kuwait Conflict 1990-1996*, pg. 187.

31. Paul Lewis, "After the War; UN Survey Calls Iraq's War Damage Near-Apocalyptic," *New York Times*, March 22, 1991.

32. Lewis, "After the War."

33. Provisional Record of the 2981st Meeting, UN Security Council, S/PV. 2981, April 3, 1991. *UNSC Records*, 93.

34. "Harvard Study Team Report: Public Health in Iraq after the Gulf War" May 1991. A copy of this report can be found in: *BRCC*, 2749_0000 (0311-0388). Quote found on page 0312.

35. Lewis, "After the War"; Barton Gellman, "Allied Air War Struck Broadly in Iraq," *Washington Post*, June 23, 1991.

36. Gellman, "Allied Air War Struck Broadly in Iraq."

37. Joseph David Steib, *The Regime Change Consensus: Iraq in American Politics 1990– 2003* (PhD Dissertation, University of North Carolina, 2019), 104.

38. Notes from 4/17/91 EC Ministerial Working Dinner, Luxembourg, Luxembourg, April 17, 1991. Box 110, Folder 2, Number 14. James A Baker III Papers, Princeton University.

39. Peter Jennings Reporting, "Unfinished Business: The CIA and Saddam Hussein," *ABC* (Television), June 27, 1997.

40. "Oral History: Richard Cheney," PBS Frontline, January 1996, https://www.pbs.org/ wgbh/pages/frontline/gulf/oral/cheney/1.html. For analysis, see Donald Stoker, *Why America Loses Wars: Limited War and US Strategy from the Korean War to the Present* (New York: Cambridge University Press, 2019), 195–6.

41. James Gerstenzang, "Bush Airs Thoughts on End of Gulf War," *Los Angeles Times*, January 15, 1996, https://www.latimes.com/archives/la-xpm-1996-01-15-mn-24868- story.html; and Bush and Scowcroft, *A World Transformed*, 487. For analysis of un- clear objectives in the war, see Stoker, *Why America Loses Wars*, 195–6.

42. Meir Litvak, "Iraq (*Al- Jumhuriyya al- 'Iraqiyya*)," in *Middle East Contemporary Survey: Volume XV, 1991*, ed. Ami Ayalon (Boulder, CO: Westview Press, 1993), 440–1.

43. Provisional Record of the 2995th Meeting, UN Security Council, S/PV.2995, June 26, 1991, *UNSC Records*; Provisional Record of the 3004th Meeting, UN Security Council, S/PV 3004, August 15, 1991, *UNSC Records*; Litvak, "Iraq (*Al-Jumhuriyya al-'Iraqiyya*)," 440–1.

44. "Report to the Secretary-General Dated 15 July 1991 on Humanitarian Needs in Iraq Prepared by Mission Led by Sadruddin Aga Khan, Executive Delegate of the Secretary General," July 15, 1991, 11.

45. Ibid., 13.

46. Ibid., 12.

47. Ibid., 13.

48. Ibid., 16.

49. Ibid., 17.

50. Ibid., 16.

51. Provisional Record of the 3004th Meeting, UN Security Council, S/PV 3004, August 15, 1991, *UNSC Records*, 98.

52. Ibid., 81.

53. Ibid., 56, 81–2, 98, 101.

54. See for example, Boutros Boutros- Ghali, "Document 77. Letter to Jose Luis Jesus, President of the Security Council," July 15, 1992, in *The Papers of United Nations Secretary- General Boutros Boutros- Ghali*, vol. 1, ed. Charles Hill (New Haven, CT: Yale University Press, 2003), 173–6; and Boutros Boutros-Ghali, "Document 88. Letter to Tariq Aziz, Deputy Prime Minister, Republic of Iraq," August 4, 1992, in *The Papers of United Nations Secretary-General Boutros Boutros-Ghali*, vol.1, ed. Charles Hill (New Haven, CT: Yale University Press, 2003), 193–4.

55. Boutros Boutros-Ghali, *Unvanquished*, 210.

56. "تصريحات" [Comments], From: Official of the Branch of the Bureau of Iraqis outside the Region, To: The Regional Command / Office of the Secretariat of the Region. *BRCC*, 3835_0000 (0445-0447). February 20, 1992.

57. "معلومات" [Information], From: Official of the Branch of the Bureau of Iraqis outside the region, To: The Regional Command / Office of the Secretariat of the Region. *BRCC*, 3835_0000 (0209-0213). March 10, 1992.

58. "معلومات" [Information], From: The Official of the Branch of the Bureau of Iraqis outside the Region, To: The Regional Command/ Office of the Secretariat of the Region. *BRCC*, 3203_0003 (0307). January 23, 1992.

59. Makiya, *Cruelty and Silence*, 224–5.

60. "معلومات" [Information], From: The Official of the Branch of the Bureau of Iraqis outside the Region, To: The Regional Command of Iraq / Office of the Secretariat of the Region. *BRCC*, 2721_0000 (0352). September 27, 1992.

61. "مطبوعات معادية" [Hostile Publications], From: Official of the Branch of the Bureau of Iraqis outside the Region, To: The Regional Command / Office of the Secretariat of the Region. *BRCC*, 3835_0000 (172). March 24, 1992.

62. "مطبوعات معادية" [Hostile Publications], From: Official of the Branch of the Bureau of Iraqis outside the Region, To: The Regional Command / Office of the Secretariat of the Region. *BRCC*, 3835_0000 (0475). February 18, 1992.

63. "معلومات" [Information], From: The Official of the Branch of the Bureau of Iraqis outside the Region, To: The Regional Command of Iraq / Office of the Secretariat of the Region. *BRCC*, 2721_0000 (0348). September 27, 1992.

64. "الصحف العراقية" [Iraqi Newspapers], From: Official of the Branch of the Bureau of Iraqis outside the Region, To: The Regional Command / Office of the Secretariat of the Region. *BRCC*, 3835_0000 (0503). November 25, 1991.

65. "الصحف العراقية" [Iraqi Newspapers], From: The Minister of Information and Culture, To: The Office of the Secretariat of the Region. *BRCC*, 3835_0000 (0429). February 18, 1992.

66. "وضع شعبة رعاية مصالح العراق في واشنطن" [Situation of the section for Iraqi interests in Washington], From: Official of the Organization of Iraqis in America, To: The Regional Command of Iraq— Branch of the Bureau of Iraqis outside the Region. *BRCC*, 3733_0000 (0520-0521). February 27, 1992.

67. "وضع الطلبة" [Status of Students], From: The Official of the Branch of the Bureau of Iraqis outside the Region, To: The Regional Command / Office of the Secretariat of the Region. *BRCC*, 3835_0000 (0057). March 10, 1992; "تسهيل عودة الطلبة" [Facilitating the Return of Students], From: Official of the Branch of the Bureau of Iraqis outside the Region, To: The Regional Command / Office of the Secretariat of the Region. *BRCC*, 2071_0002 (0286). August 31, 1992.

68. "معلومات" [Information], From: Official of the Branch of the Bureau of Iraqis outside the Region, To: The Regional Command / Office of the Secretariat of the Region. *BRCC*, 3835_0000 (0256). August 21, 1991; "معلومات" [Information], From: Official of the Branch of the Bureau of Iraqis outside the Region, To: The Regional Command / Office of the Secretariat of the Region. *BRCC*, 3835_0000 (0256). March 9, 1992.

69. "معلومات" [Information], From: Official of the Branch of the Bureau of Iraqis out-side the Region, To: The Regional Command / Office of the Secretariat of the Region. *BRCC*, 2071_0002 (0276). August 20, 1992.

70. "النظام الدولي الجديد وكارثة اطفال العراق" [The New World Order and the Disaster of the Iraqi Children], *BRCC*, 2749_0000 (0667-0656).

71. "مقترحات لرفع الحصار الاقتصادي عن القطر" [Recommendations for Lifting the Economic Embargo on the Region], From: Head of the Presidential Diwan, To: The Foreign Ministry / Office of the Minister. *BRCC*, 3203_0003 (0348). December 22, 1991.

72. "جمعيات وشخصيات" [Associations and People], From: The Official of the Branch of the Bureau of Iraqis outside the Region, To: The Regional Command/ Office of the Secretariat of the Region. *BRCC*, 3203_0003 (0360-0361). December 16, 1991.

73. "Letter dated 1978/10/28 from Nizar Hamdun to Saddam Hussein Regarding Iraqi and Syrian Ba'ath Party Commitments and Relations," *CRRC*, SH-SPPC-D-000-639, October 28, 1978; "Two handwritten letters addressed to Saddam Hussein from Nizar Hamdun," *CRRC*, SH-SPPC-D-000-795, August 1976.

74. "Saddam Hussein's Response to Ambassador Nizar Hamdun's Criticisms of the Regime," *CRRC*, SH-SPPC-D-000-498, November 1999.

75. "مقترحات لرفع الحصار الاقتصادي عن القطر" [Recommendations for Lifting the Economic Embargo on the Region], From: Head of the Presidential Diwan, To: The Foreign Ministry / Office of the Minister. *BRCC*, 3203_0003 (0348). December 22, 1991.

76. "مقترح" [Recommendation], From: The Director of the Office of the Secretariat of the Region, To: The Presidential Diwan. *BRCC*, 2837_0002 (0585). April 1992.

77. "تقييم الوفود" [Establishing Delegations], From: The Foreign Minister (Muhammad Said al-Sahaf), To: The Arab Socialist Baath Party/ Office of the Secretariat of the Region. *BRCC*, 2071_0002 (0628). July 17, 1992.

78. "مقترح" [Recommendation], From: [author note: cut off], To: The Presidential Diwan. *BRCC*, 2837_0002 (0583). March 30, 1992.

79. For the regime's strategy and plans on instituting Ba'thification, see: "A Project Plan for Working toward Coordination between the Party and the Mass Organizations in the Field of the Ba'thification of Society." *BRCC*, 025-5-5 (0476-0497). No date but from 1988 or earlier. See Sassoon, *Saddam Hussein's Ba'ath Party*, and Faust, *The Ba'thification of Iraq*.

80. Brands and Palkki, "Conspiring Bastards."

81. For example, of the regime's international political strategies during the Iran Contra scandal, see *BRCC* box file, 027-2-3, 1986.

82. "الحصار الظالم" [Unjust Siege], From: The Director of the Office of the Secretariat of the Region, To: The Central Office for the Professional and Popular Bureau. *BRCC*, 2837_0002 (0584). January 28, 1992.

83. "A Call" [in English], *BRCC*, 2749_0000 (0604). No date.

84. "فعاليات" [Activities], From: The General Secretary of the Central Office of Professional and Popular Bureau, To: The Office of Comrade Taha Yasin Ramadan, Vice President of the Republic. *BRCC*, 2749_0000 (0597-0598). December 16, 1991.

85. "العامة لخطة العمل وآلية التنفيذ لعام ١٩٩٢" [General Indicators for the Work Plan and Implementation Mechanisms for 1992], *BRCC*, 2749_0000 (133-142).

86. "تسهيل عودة الطلبة" [Facilitating the Return of Students], From: Official of the Branch of the Bureau of Iraqis outside the Region, To: The Regional Command / Office of the Secretariat of the Region. *BRCC*, 2071_0002 (0286). August 31, 1992.

87. " برنامج عمل" [Work Plan], From: The Secretary General of The Central Office of Students and Youth, To: The Office of the Secretariat of the Region. *BRCC*, 2749_0000 (0568). December 22, 1991.

88. One need look no further than the American strategy and policy document for the Gulf War, NSD 54.

89. " برنامج عمل" [Work Plan], From: The Secretary General of The Central Office of Students and Youth, To: The Office of the Secretariat of the Region. BRCC, 2749_0000 (0568). December 22, 1991.

90. " برنامج عمل" [Work Plan], From: The Secretary General of The Central Office of Students and Youth, To: The Office of the Secretariat of the Region. BRCC, 2749_0000 (0567-0573). December 22, 1991.

91. " برنامج عمل" [Work Plan], From: The Secretary General of The Central Office of Students and Youth, To: The Office of the Secretariat of the Region. BRCC, 2749_0000 (0570). December 22, 1991.

92. " برنامج عمل" [Work Plan], From: The Secretary General of The Central Office of Students and Youth, To: The Office of the Secretariat of the Region. BRCC, 2749_0000 (0571). December 22, 1991.

93. " برنامج عمل" [Work Plan], From: The Secretary General of The Central Office of Students and Youth, To: The Office of the Secretariat of the Region. BRCC, 2749_0000 (0572). December 22, 1991.

94. " بطاقة تهنئة" [Greeting Card], From: The Secretary General of The Central Office of Students and Youth, To: The Office of the Secretariat of the Region. *BRCC*, 2749_0000 (0516-0517). January 7 1992.

95. For example, see, "نشاطات الاتحاد للتعبئة العربية والدولية ليوم ١٢/٢" [Activities of the Union for Arab and International Mobilization for December 2], From: The Head of the National Union for Iraqi Students, To: The Central Office of Students and Youth. *BRCC*, 2749_0000 (0631-0637). December 3, 1991.

96. "تضامن عربي ودولي" [Arab and International Solidarity], From: The Secretary General of the Central Office of Students and Youth, To: The Office of the Secretariat of the Region. *BRCC*, 2749_0000 (0623-0626). December 10, 1991.

97. "رسالة" [Message], From: The Secretary General of The Central Office of Students and Youth, To: The Office of the Secretariat of the Region. BRCC, 2749_0000 (0530-0533). December 30, 1991.

98. "تضامن عربي ودولي" [Arab and International Solidarity], From: The Secretary General of the Central Office of Students and Youth, To: The Office of the Secretariat of the Region. *BRCC*, 2749_0000 (0623-0626). December 10, 1991.

99. "تضامن عربي ودولي" [Arab and International Solidarity], From: The Secretary General of the Central Office of Students and Youth, To: The Office of the Secretariat of the Region. *BRCC*, 2749_0000 (0623-0626). December 10, 1991.

100. "رسالة" [Message], From: The Secretary General of The Central Office of Students and Youth, To: The Office of the Secretariat of the Region. *BRCC*, 2749_0000 (0512-0514). January 5, 1992. [My note: letter itself is dated December 18, 1992.]

101. *BRCC*, 2749_0000 (0177).

102. "تضامن عربي وعالمي" [Arab and World Solidarity], From: The Secretary General of The Central Office of Students and Youth, To: The Office of the Secretariat of the Region. *BRCC*, 2749_0000 (0493- 0494). January 5, 1992; "تضامن عربي وعالمي" [Arab and World Solidarity], From: The Secretary General of The Central Office of Students and Youth, To: The Office of the Secretariat of the Region. BRCC, 2749_0000 (0447-0448). January 14, 1992.

103. "نداء" [Call], From: The Secretary General of The Central Office of Students and Youth, To: The Office of the Secretariat of the Region. *BRCC*, 2749_0000 (0616). December 12, 1991.

104. "نشر مقالات في الصحف العربية" [Publishing Articles in Arab Newspapers], From: The President of the National Union of Iraqi Students, To: Central Office of Students and Youth. *BRCC*, 2749_0000 (0257). January 11, 1992.

105. From: Helen Kinsey from the Middle East Department of the Foreign and Commonwealth Office, To: Unions and Organizations of Arab Students and Youth in India. *BRCC*, 2749_0000 (0178-0179). October 24, 1991.

106. "معلومات" [Information], From: the Secretary General of the Central Office of Students and Youth, To: The Secretariat of the Region. *BRCC*, 2749_0000 (0442). January 12, 1992.

107. "مؤتمر اتحاد الطلاب العالمي" [World Student Union Conference], From: The Secretary General of the Central Office of Students and Youth, To: The Office of the Secretariat of the Region. *BRCC*, 2749_0000 (0196-204). February 11, 1992.

Chapter 4

1. "جمعيات وشخصيات" [Associations and People], From: The Official of the Branch of the Bureau of Iraqis outside the Region, To: The Regional Command/ Office of the Secretariat of the Region. *BRCC*, 3203_0003 (0360-0361). December 16, 1991.

2. "المرصد. ينشر رسالة حول فساد في سفارات عراقية" [Observatory Publishes Letter on Corruption in Iraqi Embassies], *Iraqi Media Observatory in Cairo*, June 12, 2007, http://iraqegypt.blogspot.com/2007/06/blog-post_12.html.

3. For statements in the press, see, "Iraq blocks UN inspectors in Baghdad," *Associated Press*, July 7, 1992.

4. See, for example, "معلومات" [Information], From: The Director of the Office of the General Secretariat, To: The Office of the Secretariat of the Region, *BRCC*, 039-4-1 (0133-0135), April 4, 1993; "نشرة التحدي" [The Publication The Challenge], From: Official of the Organization of Iraqis in America, To: The Regional Command of Iraq – Branch of the Bureau of Iraqis outside the Region. *BRCC*, 039-4-1 (0207). July 13, 1993; "الهيئة الادارية لفرع الاتحاد الوطني" [The Administrative Board for the Branch of the National Union], From: Official of the Branch of the Bureau of Iraqis Outside the Region, To: The Regional Command / Office of the Secretariat of the Region. *BRCC*, 2071_0002 (0652). July 18, 1992.

5. "Maryland Man Pleads Guilty to Conspiracy to Act as an Iraqi Agent," *US Department of Justice*, December 22, 2008. https://www.justice.gov/archive/opa/pr/2008/Decem ber/08-nsd-1141.html; "معلومات" [Information], From: The Official of the Branch of the Bureau of Iraqis outside the Region, To: The Regional Command / Office of the Secretariat of the Region. *BRCC*, 039-4-1 (0168). August 20, 1993.

6. For examples of such reports, see, *BRCC*, 3402_0000 (0259-0300).

7. Melinda Liu, "What 'Mrs. Anthrax' Told Me," *Newsweek*, December 21, 2005. https://www.newsweek.com/what-mrs-anthrax-told-me-114077; "'Chemical Sally' Captured Says US," *The Irish Times*, May 5, 2003. https://www.irishtimes.com/news/ chemical-sally-captured-says-us-1.475414.

8. "مقترح" [Recommendation], From: Huda Salih Mahdi Ammash, Member of the Branch of the Bureau of Iraqis outside the Region, To: The Official of the Branch. *BRCC*, 2721_0000 (0082). October 18, 1992.

9. "جمعيات وشخصيات" [Associations and People], From: The Official of the Branch of the Bureau of Iraqis outside the Region, To: The Regional Command/ Office of the Secretariat of the Region. *BRCC*, 3203_0003 (0360-0361). December 16, 1991.

10. "مقترح" [Recommendation], From: Huda Salih Mahdi Ammash, Member of the Branch of the Bureau of Iraqis outside the Region, To: The Official of the Branch. *BRCC*, 2721_0000 (0082-0071). October 18, 1992.

11. Susan King, "Still Trying to Shake Things Up: For Kris Kristofferson, Politics Is Always on His Mind," *Los Angeles Times*, October 3, 1993. https://www.latimes.com/ archives/la-xpm-1993-10-03-tv-41616-story.html.

12. Untitled, From: Member of the Branch, Official of the Territory, To: Official of the Branch [of the Bureau of Iraqis outside the Region.], *BRCC*, 3835_ 0000 (0369). March 7, 1992.

13. John Lewis Gaddis, *On Grand Strategy* (New York: Penguin Press, 2018); Hal Brands, *What Good Is Grand Strategy?: Power and Purpose in American Statecraft from Harry S. Truman to George W. Bush* (Ithaca, NY: Cornell University Press, 2014).

14. Information and papers on the American-Iraqi Friendship Federation. *BRCC*, 3835_ 0000 (0165-0169).

15. "Obituary for Ali Hossaini," *Richmond Times-Dispatch*, August 7, 2015, https:// richmond.com/obituaries/hossaini-ali/article_2a0180e5-126f-53da-9f8f-a303a59ce 08b.html.

16. Sharon Cohen, "Tense Days of Waiting for Iraqi-Americans," *Midland Daily News*, March 21, 2003. https://www.ourmidland.com/news/article/Tense-Days-of-Wait ing-for-Iraqi-Americans-7202954.php.

17. Information and papers on the American-Iraqi Friendship Federation. *BRCC*, 3835_ 0000 (0165-0169).

18. Information and papers on the American-Iraqi Friendship Federation. *BRCC*, 3835_ 0000 (0148-0149).

19. "جمعية الصداقة العراقية - لاميركية" [American-Iraqi Friendship Federation], From: Comrade Sameer al-Nima, To: The Regional Command Branch of the Bureau of Iraqis outside the Region. *BRCC*, 3835_0000 (0135). February 22, 1992.

20. "انشطة" [Activities], From: Comrade Sameer al-Nima, To: The Regional Command Branch of the Bureau of Iraqis outside the Region. *BRCC*, 3835_0000 (0049). March 30, 1992.

21. "جمعية الصداقة العراقية - لاميركية" [American-Iraqi Friendship Federation], From: The Director of the Regional Office of Foreign Relations, To: Office of the Secretariat of the Region. *BRCC*, 3835_0000 (0128-0130). March 14, 1992.

22. "لجنة انقاذ اطفال العراق" [Committee to Save the Children of Iraq], From: Sameer al-Nima, Official of the Organization of Iraqis in America, To: The Regional Command of Iraq – Branch of the Bureau of Iraqis outside the Region. *BRCC*, 2837_0002 (0288-0290). April 22, 1992.

23. Nadine Brozan, "Chronicle," *The New York Times*, October 4, 1993. https:// www.nytimes.com/1993/10/04/nyregion/chronicle-513793.html?auth=link-dismiss-goo gle1tap.

24. "انشطة" [Activities], From: Comrade Sameer al-Nima, To: The Regional Command Branch of the Bureau of Iraqis outside the Region. *BRCC*, 3835_0000 (0049). March 30, 1992.

25. "الهيئة الادارية لفرع الاتحاد الوطني" [The Administrative Board of the Branch of the National Union], From: Official of the Branch of the Bureau of Iraqis outside the Region, To: The Regional Command / Office of the Secretariat of the Region. *BRCC*, 2071_0002 (0652). July 18, 1992.

26. "انشطة" [Activities], From: Comrade Sameer al-Nima, To: The Regional Command Branch of the Bureau of Iraqis outside the Region. *BRCC*, 2071_0002 (0619-0620). August 8, 1992.

27. "المقاطعة المفروضة على العراق والجهد المضاد لها" [The Boycott Imposed on Iraq and the Efforts to Counteract it.], From: Sameer al-Nima. Official of the Organization of Iraqis in America, To: The Regional Command of Iraq – Branch of the Bureau of Iraqis outside the Region. *BRCC*, 2837_0002 (0349-50). April 22, 1992.

28. "المقاطعة المفروضة على العراق والجهد المضاد لها" [The Boycott Imposed on Iraq and the Efforts to Counteract it.], From: Sameer al-Nima. Official of the Organization of Iraqis in America, To: The Regional Command of Iraq – Branch of the Bureau of Iraqis outside the Region. *BRCC*, 2837_0002 (0349-50). April 22, 1992.

29. "المنظمات غير الحكومية" [Nongovernmental Organizations], From: The Official of the Branch of the Bureau of Iraqis outside the Region, To: The Regional Command of Iraq / Office of the Secretariat of the Region. *BRCC*, 2837_0002 (0355). April 16, 1992.

30. Untitled, From: Member of the Branch, Official of the Territory, To: Official of the Branch [of the Bureau of Iraqis outside the Region]. *BRCC*, 3835_0000 (0273). March 7, 1992.

31. Untitled, From: Member of the Branch, Official of the Territory, To: Official of the Branch [of the Bureau of Iraqis outside the Region]. *BRCC*, 3835_0000 (0303). March 7, 1992.

32. "احتجاج ضد المقاطعة والحصار" [Protest against Boycott and Sanctions], From: Comrade Sameer al-Nima, To: The Regional Command Branch of the Bureau of Iraqis outside the region. *BRCC*, 3835_0000 (0370). February 17, 1992.

33. Provisional Record of the 2981st Meeting, UN Security Council, S/PV. 2981, April 3, 1991. *UNSC Records*, 93.

34. Provisional Record of the 2981st Meeting, UN Security Council, S/PV. 2981, April 3, 1991. *UNSC Records*, 93; Boutros Boutros-Ghali, "Introduction," 33–4.

35. "جمعيات وشخصيات" [Associations and People], From: The Deputy Prime Minister, Tariq Aziz, To: The Regional Command/ Office of the Secretariat of the Region. *BRCC*, 3203_0003 (0355-0366). December 22, 1991.

36. "جمعيات وشخصيات" [Associations and People], From: The Official of the Branch of the Bureau of Iraqis outside the Region, To: The Regional Command/ Office of the Secretariat of the Region. *BRCC*, 3203_0003 (0360-0361). December 16, 1991.

37. "امر" [Order], From: Taha Yassin Ramadan, Vice President of the Republic, Head of the Committee for Mobilizing the Masses. *BRCC*, 2071_0002 (0066-0067). September 30, 1992.

38. "انشطة" [Activities], From: The Official of the Branch of the Bureau of Iraqis outside the Region, To: The Regional Command/ Office of the Secretariat of the Region. *BRCC*, 3203_0003 (0254). February 6, 1992; "نشاطات لجنة الارتباط" [Activities of the Liaison Committee], From: The Official of the Branch of the Bureau of Iraqis outside the Region, To: The Regional Command / Office of the Secretariat of the Region. *BRCC*, 3835_0000 (0080). March 1, 1992.

39. "تقرير ايفاد" [Dispatch Report], From: Head of the National Union of Iraqi Student, To: The Central Office of Students and Youth. *BRCC*, 2749_0000 (0468 – 0474). December 27, 1991.

40. "اعلام" [Advertisement], From: The Official of the Branch of the Bureau of Iraqis outside the Region, To: The Regional Command / Office of the Secretariat of the Region. *BRCC*, 3835_0000 (0074- 0077). March 1, 1992; "صحيفة" [Newspaper], From: The Official of the Branch of the Bureau of Iraqis outside the Region, To: The Regional Command / Office of the Secretariat of the Region. *BRCC*, 3835_0000 (0095). March 1, 1992; "اعلان معادي" [Hostile Announcement], From: The Official of the Branch of the Bureau of Iraqis outside the Region, To: The Regional Command / Office of the Secretariat of the Region. *BRCC*, 3835_0000 (0099). March 1, 1992.

41. "معلومات" [Information], From: The Official of the Branch of the Bureau of Iraqis outside the Region, To: The Regional Command of Iraq / Office of the Secretariat of the Region. *BRCC*, 2721_0000 (0358). August 26, 1992; "معلومات" [Information], From: The Official of the Branch of the Bureau of Iraqis outside the Region, To: The Regional Command/ Office of the Secretariat of the Region. *BRCC*, 3203_0003 (0307). January 23, 1992.

42. "حول وضع الطلاب الدراسي" [On the Status of Studying Students], From: The Official of the Branch of the Bureau of Iraqis outside the Region, To: The Regional Command / Office of the Secretariat of the Region. *BRCC*, 3203_0003 (0261). January 28, 1992.

43. Al- Mashat, كنت سفيرا للعراق في واشنطن: حكايتي مع صدام في غزو الكويت [*I was Iraq's Ambassador in Washington: My story with Saddam during the invasion of Kuwait*], 179–203.

44. "شريط فيديو" [Video Tape], From: Official of the Branch of the Bureau of Iraqis outside the Region, To: The Regional Command / Office of the Secretariat of the Region. *BRCC*, 3835_0000 (0307). March 9, 1992.

45. "شريط فيديو" [Video Tape], From: Official of the Branch of the Bureau of Iraqis outside the Region, To: The Regional Command / Office of the Secretariat of the Region. *BRCC*, 3835_0000 (0307). March 9, 1992.

46. "حزب الخضر النمساوي" [The Austrian Green Party], From: Official of the Branch of the Bureau of Iraqis outside the Region, To: The Regional Command / Office of the Secretariat of the Region. *BRCC*, 3835_0000 (0323). March 9, 1992.

47. No Subject, Letter in English, From: International Youth Federation for Environmental Studies and Conservation. Signed: Mohan Mathews. Denmark, To: The Executive Board of the National Union of Iraqi Students and Youth. *BRCC*, 2749_0000 (0694). October 10, 1991.

Chapter 5

1. Provisional Record of the 2981st Meeting, UN Security Council, S/PV. 2981, April 3, 1991. *UNSC Records*, 99.

2. "التقرير السياسي السنوي لعام 1992" [The Annual Political Report for the Year 1992], From: The Ambassador [to Russia], To: The Foreign Ministry / Third Political Department. *BRCC*, 033-4-2 (0663-0665). January 1, 1993.

3. "التقرير السياسي السنوي لعام 1992" [The Annual Political Report for the Year 1992], From: The Ambassador [to Russia], To: The Foreign Ministry / Third Political Department. *BRCC*, 033-4-2 (0663-0665). January 1, 1993.

4. "التقرير السياسي السنوي لعام 1992" [The Annual Political Report for the Year 1992], From: The Ambassador [to Russia], To: The Foreign Ministry / Third Political Department. *BRCC*, 033-4-2 (0663-0665). January 1, 1993.

5. See Tietzen, *The Iraqi Quest for Autonomy through Military and Diplomatic Interventions, 1968–2003*, 267.

6. "التقرير السياسي السنوي لعام 1992" [The Annual Political Report for the Year 1992], From: The Ambassador [to Russia], To: The Foreign Ministry / Third Political Department. *BRCC*, 033-4-2 (0663-0665). January 1, 1993.

7. "التقرير السياسي السنوي لعام 1992" [The Annual Political Report for the Year 1992], From: The Ambassador [to Russia], To: The Foreign Ministry / Third Political Department. *BRCC*, 033-4-2 (0663-0665). January 1, 1993.

8. Marc Trachtenberg, "The United States and the NATO Non-extension Assurances of 1990: New Light on an Old Problem?" *International Security*, Vol. 45. No. 3. (2021).

9. "بحث" [Research], From: Official of the Branch of the Bureau of Iraqis outside the Region, To: The Regional Command / Office of the Secretariat of the Region. *BRCC*, 2071_0002 (0166). September 23, 1992.

10. "مطبوعات معادية" [Hostile publications], From: Official of the Branch of the Bureau of Iraqis outside the Region, To: The Regional Command / Office of the Secretariat of the Region. *BRCC*, 3835_0000 (0475). February 18, 1992; "معلومات" [Information], From: Official of the Branch of the Bureau of Iraqis outside the Region, To: The Regional Command / Office of the Secretariat of the Region. *BRCC*, 3835_0000 (0183). January 27, 1992; "معلومات" [Information], From: The Director of the Office of the Bureau of Iraqis outside the Region, To: The Regional Command / Office of the Secretariat of the Region. *BRCC*, 3835_0000 (0019). May 25, 1991.

11. CRRC, SH-MISC-D-000-870 undated- after Persian Gulf War.

12. See, for example, "معلومات" [Information], From: The Official of the Branch of the Bureau of Iraqis outside the Region, To: The Regional Command / Office of the Secretariat of the Region. *BRCC*, 3835_0000 (0118-0122). March 24, 1992; "نشاطات" [Activities], From: Official of the Branch of the Bureau of Iraqis outside the Region, To: The Regional Command / Office of the Secretariat of the Region. *BRCC*, 2071_0002 (0263-0264). September 24, 1992; "اشرطة كاسيت" [Cassette Tapes], From: Official of the Branch of the Bureau of Iraqis outside the Region, To: The Regional Command / Office of the Secretariat of the Region. *BRCC*, 3835_0000 (0024). March 7, 1992.

13. "ندوة" [Seminar], From: The Director of the Office of the Secretariat of the Region, To: The Ministry of Culture and Information/ Office of the Minister. *BRCC*, 2749_ 0000 (0040). May 18, 1992.

14. "برقية" [Cable], From: The Official of the Branch of the Bureau of Iraqis outside the Region, To: The Regional Command of Iraq / Office of the Secretariat of the Region. *BRCC*, 2837_0002 (0387). April 22, 1992.

15. "زيارة وفد تونسي" [A Tunisian Delegation Visit], From: President of the National Union of Iraqi Students, To: The Central Office for Students and Youth. *BRCC*, 2749_ 0000 (0577-0579). December 12, 1991.

16. "برقية" [Cable], From: The Official of the Branch of the Bureau of Iraqis outside the Region, To: The Regional Command of Iraq / Office of the Secretariat of the Region. *BRCC*, 2721_0000 (0179). June 8, 1992.

17. Memorandum of Telephone Conversation: Telephone Call to President Turgut Ozal of Turkey, September 10, 1990, pg 2, *George H.W Bush Presidential Library and Museum*. https://bush41library.tamu.edu/files/memcons-telcons/1990-09-10--Ozal.pdf.

18. Provisional Record of the 3004th Meeting, UN Security Council, S/PV 3004, August 15, 1991, *UNSC Records*; and Provisional Record of the 3059th Meeting, UN Security Council, S/PV.3059, March 11, 1992. *UNSC Records*, 75–9.

19. "المقاطعة المفروضة على العراق والجهد المضاد لها" [The Boycott Imposed on Iraq and the Efforts to Counteract it], From: Sameer al-Nima. Official of the Organization of Iraqis in America, To: The Regional Command of Iraq – Branch of the Bureau of Iraqis outside the Region. *BRCC*, 2837_0002 (0349-50). April 22, 1992.

20. "نشاطات" [Activities] From: Official of the Branch of the Bureau of Iraqis outside the Region, To: The Regional Command / Office of the Secretariat of the Region. *BRCC*, 3835_ 0000 (0202- 0188). March 17, 1992; "تظاهرة" [Demonstration], From: The Official of the Branch of the Bureau of Iraqis outside the Region, To: The Regional Command/ Office of the Secretariat of the Region. *BRCC*, 3835_0000 (0192). January 7, 1992.

21. "World Islamic Organisation Calls for End to Blockade; Condemns Iran," *Iraqi News Agency*, June 1, 1991. *BBC Worldwide Monitoring*.

22. "World Islamic Organisation Calls for End to Blockade; Condemns Iran," *Iraqi News Agency*, June 2, 1991. *BBC Worldwide Monitoring*.

23. "World Islamic Organisation Calls for End to Blockade; Condemns Iran," *Iraqi News Agency*, June 2, 1991. *BBC Worldwide Monitoring*.

24. David Schenker, *Dancing with Saddam: The Strategic Tango of Jordan-Iraq Relations* (New York: Lexington Books, 2003), 29–37.

25. On domestic drivers of Jordanian foreign policy, see Curtis R Ryan, *Inter- Arab Alliances: Regime Security and Jordanian Foreign Policy* (Gainesville: University of Florida Press, 2009); also see, Samuel Helfont and Tally Helfont, "Jordan: Between the Arab Spring and the Gulf Cooperation Council," *Orbis* 56, no. 1 (2012).

26. "Notes of the Secretary- General's meeting with H. E. Mr. J. Danford Quayle, Vice- President of the United States," *Boutros Boutros- Ghali Papers*, Box 62, Folder 5; Schenker, *Dancing with Saddam: The Strategic Tango of Jordan-Iraq Relations*, 44–8.

27. Schenker, *Dancing with Saddam: The Strategic Tango of Jordan-Iraq Relations*, 66.

28. "نشاطات" [Activities], From: The Official of the Branch of the Bureau of Iraqis outside the Region, To: The Regional Command/ Office of the Secretariat of the Region. *BRCC*, 3203_ 0003 (0421). January 13, 1992; "بيان مشتلك" [Joint Proclamation], From: The Secretary General of the Officer of the Central Office of the Popular Professional Bureau, To: The Office of Taha Yasin Ramadan / Vice President of the Republic. *BRCC*, 2749_0000 (0672-0673). December 3, 1991; Schenker, *Dancing with Saddam: The Strategic Tango of Jordan-Iraq Relations*, 69.

29. "مقترح" [Recommendation], From: Official of the Branch of the Bureau of Iraqis outside the Region, To: The Regional Command / Office of the Secretariat of the Region. *BRCC*, 3835_0000 (0179). March 4, 1992.

30. "تقرير" [Report], From: The Official of the Branch of the Bureau of Iraqis outside the Region, To: The Command of the Iraqi Region / Office of the Secretariat of the Region. *BRCC*, 3402_0000 (0463). July 2, 1992.

31. See, for example, one such thread about aiding Iraqi professors in Jordan that begins at, *BRCC*, 2071_0002 (0248).

32. For example, see, "نشاطات" [Activities], From: The Official of the Branch of the Bureau of Iraqis outside the Region, To: The Command of the Iraqi Region / Office of the Secretariat of the Region. *BRCC*, 3402_0000 (0368). July 6, 1992.

33. "نشاطات" [Activities], From: The Official of the Branch of the Bureau of Iraqis outside the region, To: The Regional Command/ Office of the Secretariat of the Region. *BRCC*, 3403_0003 (0421). January 13, 1992.

34. On the evolution of Jordanian foreign policy, see, Ryan, *Inter-Arab Alliances*.

35. "التقرير السياسي لعام 1991" [Political Report for the year 1991], "From: The Official of the Branch of the Bureau of Iraqis outside the Region, To: The Regional Command of Iraq / Office of the Secretariat of the Region. *BRCC*, 3402_0000 (0563). February 21, 1992.

36. Hal Brands, *From Berlin to Baghdad*, 49–56.

37. "التقرير السياسي لعام 1991" [Political Report for the year 1991], "From: The Official of the Branch of the Bureau of Iraqis outside the Region, To: The Regional Command of Iraq / Office of the Secretariat of the Region. *BRCC*, 3402_0000 (0560-0561). February 21, 1992.

38. "التقرير السياسي لعام 1991" [Political Report for the year 1991], "From: The Official of the Branch of the Bureau of Iraqis outside the Region, To: The Regional Command

of Iraq / Office of the Secretariat of the Region. *BRCC*, 3402_0000 (0584). February 21, 1992.

39. "التقرير السياسي لعام 1991" [Political Report for the year 1991], "From: The Official of the Branch of the Bureau of Iraqis outside the Region, To: The Regional Command of Iraq / Office of the Secretariat of the Region. *BRCC*, 3402_0000 (0561-0563). February 21, 1992.

40. See, for example, "Saddam Hussein meeting with the Revolutionary Council Command and State Command," *CRRC*, SH-RVCC-A-001-774, January 1, 1995.

41. "التقرير السياسي لعام 1991" [Political Report for the year 1991], "From: The Official of the Branch of the Bureau of Iraqis outside the Region, To: The Regional Command of Iraq / Office of the Secretariat of the Region. *BRCC*, 3402_0000 (0550-0552). February 21, 1992.

42. "التقرير السياسي لعام 1991" [Political Report for the year 1991], "From: The Official of the Branch of the Bureau of Iraqis outside the Region, To: The Regional Command of Iraq / Office of the Secretariat of the Region. *BRCC*, 3402_0000 (0574). February 21, 1992.

43. "التقرير السياسي لعام 1991" [Political Report for the year 1991], "From: The Official of the Branch of the Bureau of Iraqis outside the Region, To: The Regional Command of Iraq / Office of the Secretariat of the Region. *BRCC*, 3402_0000 (0561-0562). February 21, 1992.

44. "شريط كاسيت" [Cassette Tape], From: Official of the Branch of the Bureau of Iraqis outside the Region, To: The Regional Command / Office of the Secretariat of the Region. *BRCC*, 3835_0000 (0269). March 10, 1992.

45. "التقرير السياسي لعام 1991" [Political Report for the year 1991], "From: The Official of the Branch of the Bureau of Iraqis outside the Region, To: The Regional Command of Iraq / Office of the Secretariat of the Region. *BRCC*, 3402_0000 (0552). February 21, 1992.

46. "التقرير السياسي لعام 1991" [Political Report for the year 1991], "From: The Official of the Branch of the Bureau of Iraqis outside the Region, To: The Regional Command of Iraq / Office of the Secretariat of the Region. *BRCC*, 3402_0000 (0572- 0575). February 21, 1992. At times, the Iraqis misunderstood some of these projects. For example, they thought that al-Udeid would be a naval base rather than an air base. The confusion is understandable. Al-Udeid is an estuary on the Qatari coast and the Iraqis quite reasonably thought that it would be a naval base. Instead, the United States and Qatar built an air base named al-Udeid in the Qatari interior.

47. "التقرير السياسي لعام 1991" [Political Report for the year 1991], "From: The Official of the Branch of the Bureau of Iraqis outside the Region, To: The Regional Command of Iraq / Office of the Secretariat of the Region. *BRCC*, 3402_0000 (0575). February 21, 1992.

48. "التقرير السياسي لعام 1991" [Political Report for the year 1991], "From: The Official of the Branch of the Bureau of Iraqis outside the Region, To: The Regional Command of Iraq / Office of the Secretariat of the Region. *BRCC*, 3402_0000 (0575). February 21, 1992.

Chapter 6

1. Brands, *What Good Is Grand Strategy?*, 14.
2. Barry R Posen, *Restraint: A New Foundation for U.S. Grand Strategy* (Ithaca, NY: Cornell University Press, 2014), 1.
3. Brands, *What Good Is Grand Strategy?*, 147.
4. "Statement by President- Elect Clinton," December 22, 1992. *Warren Christopher Papers*, Box 8, Folder 3; Clinton discusses the reasons for elevating Albright's position to a Cabinet post in his memoir, Bill Clinton, *My Life* (New York: Vintage, 2005), 318–9.
5. Anthony Lake, *Confronting Backlash States* (Washington, DC: U.S. Government, 1994).
6. Madeline Albright, *Madame Secretary: A Memoir* (New York: Harper Perennial, 2013), 139.
7. Kenneth Pollak, *The Threatening Storm: The Case for Invading Iraq* (New York: Random House, 2002), 55–112; and Warren Christopher, *Chances of a Lifetime: A Memoir* (New York: Scribner, 2001).
8. Albright, *Madame Secretary*, 227.
9. Albright, *Madame Secretary*, see Chapter 17, which she titled "Migraine Hussain."
10. "Saddam and Top- Level Ba'ath Officials Discuss the Causes and Consequences of Clinton's Election Victory and Potential for Improved Relations," circa November 4th, 1992, *The Saddam Tapes*, 41. For a similar statement by Huda Ammash, see, [No Subject], From: Huda Salih Mahdi Ammash, Member of the Branch of the Bureau of Iraqis outside the Region, To: The Secretary General of the Branch Command. *BRCC*, 2721_0000 (0307). November 25, 1992.
11. "Saddam and Top- Level Ba'ath Officials Discuss the Causes and Consequences of Clinton's Election Victory and Potential for Improved Relations," circa November 4, 1992, *The Saddam Tapes*, 44.
12. "Saddam and Top- Level Ba'ath Officials Discuss the Causes and Consequences of Clinton's Election Victory and Potential for Improved Relations," circa November 4, 1992, *The Saddam Tapes*, 44.
13. "Saddam and Senior Advisers Discuss Clinton's Desire for Talks with Iraq and Impediments to Improved Relations," January 13, 1993, *The Saddam Tapes*, 44–5.
14. "Saddam and Top- Level Ba'ath Officials Discuss the Causes and Consequences of Clinton's Election Victory and Potential for Improved Relations," circa November 4, 1992, *The Saddam Tapes*, 42; Kevin M. Woods and Mark E. Stout, "Saddam's Perceptions and Misperceptions: The Case of 'Desert Storm,'" *The Journal of Strategic Studies* 33, no. 1 (2010): 25–6.
15. "برقية جفرية" [Cable], From: The Secretary General of the Branch of the Bureau of Iraqis outside the Region, To: The Regional Command of Iraq / Office of the Secretariat of the Region. *BRCC*, 033-4-2 (0766). November 23, 1992.
16. "برقية جفرية" [Cable], From: The Secretary General of the Branch of the Bureau of Iraqis outside the Region, To: The Regional Command of Iraq / Office of the Secretariat of the Region. *BRCC*, 033-4-2 (0717). December 19, 1992.

17. "برقية جفرية" [Cable], From: Aid to the Director General of the Office of the Secretariat of the Region, To: The Command of the Branch of the Bureau of Iraqis outside the Region. *BRCC*, 033- 4- 2 (0755). December 6, 1992; "رسائل" [Letters], From: The Secretary General of the Branch of the Bureau of Iraqis outside the Region, To: The Regional Command of Iraq / Office of the Secretariat of the Region. *BRCC*, 033-4-2 (0825). December 30, 1992.

18. "رسائل" [Letters], From: The Official of the Organization of Iraqis in India, To: The Branch Command / Iraqis outside the Region. *BRCC*, 033- 4- 2 (0821). December 5, 1992.

19. "برقية جفرية" [Cable], From: The Foreign Ministry, To: The Iraqi Regional Command for the Arab Socialist Baath Party / Office of the Secretariat of the Region. *BRCC*, 033-4-2 (0740). January 11, 1993.

20. "الجالية اللبنانية في امريكا" [The Lebanese Community in America], From: The Secretary General of the Branch of the Bureau of Iraqis outside the Region, To: The Secretary General of the Branch. *BRCC*, 2721_0000 (0131). November 21, 1992; "برقية جفرية" [Cable], From: The Secretary General of the Branch of the Bureau of Iraqis outside the Region, To: The Regional Command of Iraq / Office of the Secretariat of the Region. *BRCC*, 2721_0000 (0130). November 25, 1992.

21. "Q&A: Oil-for-Food Scandal," *BBC*, September 7, 2005. http://news.bbc.co.uk/2/hi/4232629.stm; Duelfer, *Hide and Seek*, 229.

22. "Saddam and His Advisers Discuss the Decline of the United Sates and the Possibility of Rapprochement with the Incoming Clinton Administration," circa January 14, 1993, *The Saddam Tapes*, 47–50.

23. [No Subject], From: Huda Salih Mahdi Ammash, Member of the Branch of the Bureau of Iraqis outside the Region, To: The Secretary General of the Branch Command. *BRCC*, 2721_0000 (0307). November 25, 1992.

24. "مقترحات" [Recommendations], From the Secretary General of the Branch of the Bureau of Iraqis outside the Region, To: The Regional Command of Iraq/Office of the Secretary General of the Region. *BRCC*, 3187_0001 (484–87). February 10, 1993.

25. Ofra Bengio, "Iraq," *Middle East Contemporary Survey: Volume XIX: 1995*, ed. Bruce Maddy-Weitzman (Boulder CO: Westview Press, 1997), 221–2.

26. "مقترحات" [Recommendations]. *BRCC*, 3187_0001 (484-87). February 10, 1993.

27. "مقترحات" [Recommendations]. *BRCC*, 3187_ 0001 (0469- 0375). February - October, 1993.

28. Quil Lawrence, *Invisible Nation: How the Kurds' Quest for Statehood Is Shaping Iraq and the Middle East* (New York: Walker Books, 2009), 94.

29. *BRCC*, 033-4-2 (0557). This is a letter from Ramsey Clark, Jon Alpert, Maryanne De Leo, and Abdul Kadir Al Kaysi on behalf of HBO. It is on HBO letterhead. It is to Saddam Hussein. It was delivered to the regional secretariat in January 1993; Author Interview with John Alpert by phone April 19, 2017.

30. Letter from Ramsey Clark, Jon Alpert, Maryanne De Leo, and Abdul Kadir Al Kaysi, *BRCC*, 033-4-2 (0557); Author Interview with John Alpert by phone April 19, 2017.

31. Letter from Ramsey Clark, Jon Alpert, Maryanne De Leo, and Abdul Kadir Al Kaysi, *BRCC*, 033-4-2 (0557); Author Interview with John Alpert by phone April 19, 2017.

For footage of Alpert's program, see, https://www.democracynow.org/2007/1/3/exclusive_democracy_now_airs_rare_interview. [Democracy Now incorrectly stated that the interview occurred in 1992. The interview discussed Clinton already being in office and Bush being out of office, so it had to be early 1993.]

32. "عناوين" [Address], From: The Secretary General of the Branch of the Bureau of Iraqis outside the Region, To: The Regional Command of Iraq / Office of the Secretariat of the Region. *BRCC*, 033-4-2 (0004-0031). March 14, 1993.

33. "بريد منظمة امريقا" [Mail of the Organization in America], From: Secretary General of the Branch of the Bureau of Iraqis outside the Region, To: The Regional Command / Office of the Secretariat of the Region. *BRCC*, 039-4-1 (0637). July 22, 1993.

34. "مقترح" [Recommendation], From: Huda Salih Mahdi Ammash, Member of the Branch Command / Official of the Territory, To: The Secretary General of the Branch. *BRCC*, 039-4-1 (0557). March 17, 1993.

35. "تقرير" [Report], From: The Secretary General of the Branch of the Bureau of Iraqis outside the Region, To: The Regional Command of Iraq / Office of the Secretariat of the Region. *BRCC*, 033-4-2 (0059-0061). March 14, 1993.

36. For example, "وضع شعبة رعاية مصالح العراق في واشنطن" [Situation of the section for Iraqi interests in Washington], From: Official of the Organization of Iraqis in America, To: The Regional Command of Iraq – Branch of the Bureau of Iraqis outside the Region. *BRCC*, 3733_0000 (0520-0521). February 27, 1992.

37. "اعتقال مؤيد" [Arrest of a supporter], From: The Secretary General of the Branch of the Bureau of Iraqis outside the Region, To: The Regional Command of Iraq/ Office of the Secretary General of the Region. *BRCC*, 3187_0001 (0685). September 29, 1993.

38. "تنظيم الجالية" [Community Organization], From: The Secretary General of the Bureau of Iraqis outside the Region, To: The Regional Command of Iraq / Office of the Secretariat of the Region. *BRCC*, 3733_0000 (0539). March 20, 1993.

39. "معلومات" [Information], From: The Director of the office of the General Secretariat, To: The Office of the Secretariat of the Region. *BRCC*, 039-4-1 (0133-0135). April 4, 1993; "معلومات عن عبد القادر القيسي" [Information on Abd al-Qadir al-Qiyasi], From: From: Sameer al-Nima. Official of the Organization of Iraqis in America, To: The Regional Command of Iraq – Branch of the Bureau of Iraqis outside the Region. *BRCC*, 039-4-1 (0124). April 30, 1993.

40. "معلومات" [Information], From: The Director of the office of the General Secretariat, To: The Office of the Secretariat of the Region. *BRCC*, 039-4-1 (0133-0135). April 4, 1993.

41. "عبد القادر القيسي" [Abd al-Qadir al-Qiyasi], From: From: Official of the Organization of Iraqis in America, To: The Regional Command of Iraq – Branch of the Bureau of Iraqis outside the Region. *BRCC*, 039-4-1 (0114). August 17, 1993.

42. "معلومات" [Information], From: The Director of the office of the General Secretariat, To: The Office of the Secretariat of the Region. *BRCC*, 039-4-1 (0133-0135). April 4, 1993.

43. "معلومات عن عبد القادر القيسي" [Information on Abd al-Qadir al-Qiyasi], From: Official of the Organization of Iraqis in America, To: The Regional Command of Iraq – Branch of the Bureau of Iraqis outside the Region. *BRCC*, 039-4-1 (0124). April 30, 1993.

44. "معلومات" [Information], From: The Director of the Mukhabarat, To the Office of the Secretariat of the Region. *BRCC*, 039-4-1 (0149). January 8, 1991; "معلومات عن عبد القادر القيسي" [Information on Abd al-Qadir al-Qiyasi], From: From: Sameer al-Nima. Official of the Organization of Iraqis in America, To: The Regional Command of Iraq – Branch of the Bureau of Iraqis outside the Region. *BRCC*, 039-4-1 (0124). April 30, 1993.

45. "معلومات عن عبد القادر القيسي" [Information on Abd al-Qadir al-Qiyasi], From: Official of the Organization of Iraqis in America, To: The Regional Command of Iraq – Branch of the Bureau of Iraqis outside the Region. *BRCC*, 039-4-1 (0124). April 30, 1993.

46. On Soviets using this tactic, see, Andrew, *The Sword and the Shield*, 326.

47. Letter from Arab American Press Guild, *BRCC*, 033-4-2 (0036). March 1993.

48. "نشرة التحدي" [The publication The Challenge], From: Official of the Organization of Iraqis in America, To: The Regional Command of Iraq – Branch of the Bureau of Iraqis outside the Region. *BRCC*, 039-4-1 (0207). July 13, 1993.

49. "رئيس تحرير جريدة الوطن" [Head Editor of the Newspaper Al-Watan], From: Official of the Organization of Iraqis in America, To: The Regional Command of Iraq – Branch of the Bureau of Iraqis outside the Region. *BRCC*, 3733_0000 (0134). February 17, 1993.

50. Mark Matthew and Lyle Denniston, "Author doesn't want articles on Saudis reprinted," *The Baltimore Sun*, November 30, 1993, https://www.baltimoresun.com/news/bs-xpm-1993-11-30-1993334031-story.html; Ahmed Fouad Anwar, "Can the Muslim Brotherhood regain influence in Oman?," *The Arab Weekly*, January 26, 2020, https://thearabweekly.com/can-muslim-brotherhood-regain-influence-oman.

51. "ندوة في جامعة برنستون حول الدستور العراقي المستقبلي" [Seminar in Princeton University on the Future Iraqi Constitution], From: Assistant Secretary General of the Branch of the Bureau of Iraqis outside the Region, To: The Regional Command of Iraq – Office of the Secretariat of the Region. *BRCC*, 2847_0002 (0094). December 19, 1994.

52. "اللاجئون الهاربون العراقيون" [Iraqi Refugees Fleeing], From: The Secretary General of the Branch of the Bureau of Iraqis outside the Region, To: The Regional Command of Iraq / Office of the Secretariat of the Region. *BRCC*, 033-4-2 (0091). March 8, 1993; "اللاجئون الهاربون" [Escaping Refugees], From: The Secretary General of the Branch of the Bureau of Iraqis outside the Region, To: The Regional Command of Iraq / Office of the Secretariat of the Region. *BRCC*, 033-4-2 (0055). March 14, 1993; "الهاربون العراقيون في الولايات المتحدة اللاجئون" [Iraqi Refugees Fleeing in the United States], From: From: Official of the Organization of Iraqis in America, To: The Regional Command of Iraq – Branch of the Bureau of Iraqis outside the Region. *BRCC*, 3733_0000 (0638). February 27, 1993.

53. "عناوين" [Address], From: The Secretary General of the Branch of the Bureau of Iraqis outside the Region, To: The Regional Command of Iraq / Office of the Secretariat of the Region. *BRCC*, 033-4-2 (0004-0031). March 14, 1993.

54. "جمعية بابل العراقية" [Iraqi Babylon Committee, Inc.], *BRCC*, 2847_0002 (0627). October 28, 1993.

55. "نيو يورك" [New York], From: Secretary General for the Organization of Friendship Peace and Solidarity in Iraq, To: Brother and Sister Members of the Iraqi Babylon Committee. *BRCC*, 2847_0002 (0619). February 7, 1994; "رسائل" [Letters], From: The Assistant Secretary General of the Branch of the Bureau of Iraqis outside the Region, To: The Regional Command of Iraq – Officer of the Secretariat of the Region. *BRCC*, 2847_ 0002 (0614). March 20, 1994; "تظاهرة" [Demonstration], From: Assistant Secretary General of the Branch of Iraqis Outside the Region, To: The Region Command of Iraq / Office of the Secretariat of the Region. *BRCC*, 2847_0002 (0513). October 10, 1994.

56. [Letter to Bill Clinton]. *BRCC*, 2847_0002 (0596). November 12, 1993.

57. [Untitled Letter], From: Abdul Z. Aldulaimi, President, Iraqi- American Cultural Society, To: President William Jefferson Clinton. *BRCC*, 2166_0000 (0067). March 15, 1993.

58. [No title. No date.], From: Bill Clinton, To: Abdul Z. Aldulaimi, *BRCC*, 2166_0000 (0066).

59. For more on the Iraqi-American Cultural Society, see, Robert E. Tomasson, "Future Events Parties With a Purpose," *The New York Times*, December 2, 1984. https://www.nyti mes.com/ 1984/ 12/ 02/ style/ fut ure- eve nts- part ies- with- a- purp ose.html; and Shawn Ewald, "Endorse the Call to Action about Iraq," *A- Info*, February 12, 1998. http://www.ainfos.ca/98/feb/ainfos00220.html.

60. [Letter on White House Letterhead], From: Alice J. Pushkar, Director of Communications for the First Lady, To: Mr. Mohammad Mostafa, Iraqi Babylon Committee, Inc. *BRCC*, 2847_0002 (0592). January 22, 1994.

61. A letter on White House letterhead signed in ink by Bill Clinton, From: Bill Clinton, To: The Iraqi Babylon Committee, Inc. *BRCC*, 2847_0002 (0591). 1994.

62. Christopher, *In the Steam of History*, 11, 28.

63. Letter from James C West to William J Clinton, January 13, 1993. *Warren Christopher Papers*, Box 18, Folder 1.

64. Speech to American- Arab Anti- Discrimination Committee, April 23, 1993. *Warren Christopher Papers*, Box 18, Folder 4

65. Kenneth M. Pollack, *The Threatening Storm*, 56.

66. Paul K. White, *Crisis after the Storm: An Appraisal of U.S. Airpower in Iraq since 1991* (Washington, DC: Washington Institute for Near East Policy, 1999), 19–20.

67. White, *Crisis after the Storm*, 26–7.

68. Memorandum for: The President. From: Clifton Wharton, Jr., Acting [Deputy Secretary of State] Subject: Meeting with Prime Minister John Major of Great Britain, February 18, 1993. National Security Council and Records Management Office, "Declassified Documents concerning John Major," *Clinton Library*, https:// clin ton. presidentiallibraries.us/items/show/36622, 46.

69. Ofra Bengio, "Iraq," in *Middle East Contemporary Survey: Volume XVII, 1993*, ed. Ami Ayalon (Boulder, CO: Westview Press, 1995), 396.

70. Albright, *Madame Secretary*, 275.

71. Provisional Record of the 3245th Meeting, UN Security Council, S/PV.3245, June 27, 1993. *UNSC Records*. Quotes taken from pp. 16–7.

72. David Malone, *The International Struggle Over Iraq*, 169.

73. Duelfer, *Hide and Seek*, 79.

74. Charles Duelfer, Comprehensive Report of the Special Advisor to the DCI on Iraq's WMD, Vol. 1-3, *Central Intelligence Agency*, 2004.

75. "Misreading Intentions: Iraq's Reaction to Inspections Created Picture of Deception," *Central Intelligence Agency*, January 5, 2006, 16. National Security Archive.

76. Koblentz, "Saddam versus the inspectors."

77. Målfrid Braut- Hegghammer, "Cheater's Dilemma: Iraq, Weapons of Mass Destruction, and the Path to War," *International Security* 45, no. 1 (2020): 51–89.

78. "Points to be made on Iraq," October 11, 1994., National Security Council, Speechwriting Office, and Antony Blinken, "Clinton—Iraq/Haiti Insert 10/13/94 for National Association of Broadcasters,'" *Clinton Library*, 13. https://clinton.presidenti allibraries.us/items/show/9074.

79. Memorandum for: The President. From: Clifton Wharton, Jr., Acting [Deputy Secretary of State] Subject: Meeting with Prime Minister John Major of Great Britain, February 18, 1993. National Security Council and Records Management Office, "Declassified Documents concerning John Major," *Clinton Library*, 38 https://clinton. presidentiallibraries.us/items/show/36622.

80. Peter Jennings Reporting, Unfinished Business: The CIA and Saddam.Hussein, ABC (Television), June 27, 1997. David Ignatius, "The CIA and the Coup that Wasn't," *The Washington Post*, May 16, 2003. https:// www.was hing tonp ost.com/ arch ive/ opini ons/2003/05/16/the-cia-and-the-coup-that-wasnt/0abfb8fa-61e9-4159-a885-89b8c 476b188/.

81. Ofra Bengio, "Iraq," in *Middle East Contemporary Survey: Volume XX, 1996*, ed. Bruce Maddy-Weitzman (Boulder, CO: Westview Press, 1998), 331

82. Malone, *The International Struggle over Iraq*, 121.

83. *Comprehensive Report of the Special Advisor to the DCI on Iraq's WMD*, September 2004, vol. 1, 61.

84. See file ISGZ- 2004- 018948, "Fedayeen Saddam Instructions on Planning and Preparing for Operations from 1999, steps that were to be carried out in selection of personnel, as well as mission planning and coordination steps, assassinations, bombings, etc.," May 25, 1999, in In Kevin M Woods, ed., *Iraqi Perspectives Project Primary Source Materials for Saddam and Terrorism: Emerging Insights from Captured Iraqi Documents*, vol. 4, 263–4.

85. File, ISGQ-2003-00005228, "A plot to liquidate Ahmad Al-Jalabi, one of the Iraqi op-position leaders in London" April 23, 2000," in Kevin M. Woods, ed., *Iraqi Perspectives Project Primary Source Materials for Saddam and Terrorism: Emerging Insights from Captured Iraqi Documents*, vol. 3, 261–80.

86. "مذكر" [Memo], From: Huda Salih Mahdi Ammash—Branch Member—Responsible for the Territory, To: Comrade Secretary General of the Branch. BRCC, 2847_0002 (0577). July 31, 1994.

87. For example, Francis Fukuyama turned his thesis on the end of History into a book, which he published in 1992. Francis Fukuyama, *The End of History and the Last Man* (New York: Free Press, 1992).

88. Samuel P. Huntington, "The Clash of Civilizations?," *Foreign Affairs* 72, no. 3 (Summer, 1993), 22–49; Henry Kissinger, *Diplomacy* (New York: Simon and Schuster, 1994).

89. Michael S Serrill "Under Fire," *Time*, January 18, 1993. http://content.time.com/time/subscriber/article/0,33009,977515-5,00.html

90. "Iraq Sanctions Cannot Be Forever," *The New York Times*, August 1, 1994. https://www.nytimes.com/1994/08/01/opinion/iraq-sanctions-cannot-be-forever.html.

Chapter 7

1. Jorn Leonhard, *Pandora's Box: A History of the First World War*, trans. Patrick Camiller (Boston: Harvard University Press), 836.

2. Ofra Bengio, "Iraq," in *Middle East Contemporary Survey: Volume XIX, 1995*, ed. Bruce Maddy-Weitzman (Boulder, CO: Westview Press, 1997), 332–3.

3. Nora Boustany, "A Religious Revival, With Iraq's Blessing; Baghdad Finds Piety Good for Morale," *The Washington Post*, April 5, 1998, *BBC World Monitor*.

4. Haddad, *Sectarianism in Iraq*, 93; and: Jo Abraham, "Baghdad Diary," *The Guardian*, March 3, 1997. *BBC World Monitor*.

5. Memorandum for: The President. From: Clifton Wharton, Jr., Acting [Deputy Secretary of State] Subject: Meeting with Prime Minister John Major of Great Britain, February 18, 1993. National Security Council and Records Management Office, "Declassified Documents concerning John Major," Clinton Library, https://clinton.presidentiallibraries.us/items/show/36622, 46.

6. Thomas Friedman, *The Lexus and the Olive Tree: The Lexus and the Olive Tree: Understanding Globalization* (New York: Farrar, Straus and Giroux, 2000), Chapter XXX.

7. "To Paris, U.S. Looks Like a 'Hyperpower,'" *International Herald Tribune*. February 5, 1999. https://www.nytimes.com/1999/02/05/news/to-paris-us-looks-like-a-hyperpower.html.

8. David Stayn, *France and Iraq: Oil, Arms and French Policy Making in the Middle East* (New York: I.B. Tauris, 2006), 183. Ofra Bengio, "Iraq," *Middle East Contemporary Survey: Volume XVII, 1993*, ed. Ami Ayalon (Boulder, CO: Westview Press, 1995), 398.

9. National Security Council, Speechwriting Office, and Robert Boorstin, "Declassified Documents concerning Robert Boorstin, NSC Speechwriter," Clinton Library, accessed March 15, 2020, https://clinton.presidentiallibraries.us/items/show/36625, 105.

10. Cable: FM AMEMBASSY PARIS, SUBJ: PRESIDENTIAL CALL TO PM BALLADUR, ORIG: AMEMBASSY PARIS TO: SECSTATE WASHDC, Date: 21 OCT 94. National Security Council, National Security Advisor, and Anthony Lake, "Declassified documents concerning Rwanda," Clinton Library, https://clinton.presidentiallibraries.us/items/show/47967, 62–3.

11. Styan, *France and Iraq*, 184–5.

12. Styan, *France and Iraq*, 184–5.

13. National Security Council, Speechwriting Office, and Robert Boorstin, "Declassified Documents concerning Robert Boorstin, NSC Speechwriter," Clinton Library, accessed March 15, 2020, https:// clin ton.presid enti alli brar ies.us/ items/ show/ 36625, 105.

14. Ofra Bengio, "Iraq," in *Middle East Contemporary Survey: Volume XVIII, 1994,* eds. Ami Ayalon and Bruce Maddy- Weitzman (Boulder, CO: Westview Press, 1996), 357–8.

15. Stayn, *France and Iraq*, 183; Ofra Bengio, "Iraq," *Middle East Contemporary Survey, 1995,* 337.

16. Provisional Record of the 3059th Meeting, UN Security Council, S/PV.3059, March 11, 1992. *UNSC Records*, 34.

17. Frédéric Bozo, "'We Don't Need You': France, the United States, and Iraq, 1991–2003," *Diplomatic History* 41, no. 1 (January 2017): 188–9.

18. Bengio, "Iraq," *Middle East Contemporary Survey: 1995,* 337; Bengio, "Iraq," *Middle East Contemporary Survey, 1996,* 352.

19. "معلومات" [Information], From: The Official of the Organization [in Sweden], To: The Regional Command of the Bureau of Iraqis outside the Region. *BRCC*, 3733_0000 (0341-0342). March 18, 1993; "معلومات" [Information], From: The Secretary General of the Bureau of Iraqis outside the Region, To: The Regional Command of Iraq / Office of the Secretariat of the Region. *BRCC*, 3733_0000 (0340). April 8, 1993.

20. Proposed Agenda for Meeting with President, February 19, 1992. Box 115, Folder 9, Number 2. James A Baker III Papers, Princeton University.

21. "Notes of the Secretary- General's meeting with the Prime Minister of Sweden," February 13, 1992. BBG Papers, Box 62, Folder 1.

22. "نشاطات اللجنة الخاصة" [Activities of the Special Committee], From: The Official of the Organization in Sweden, To: The Branch Command of the Bureau of Iraqis outside the Region. *BRCC*, 3187_0001 (0592). May 28, 1993.

23. "نشاطات اللجنة الخاصة" [Activities of the Special Committee], From: The Official of the Organization in Sweden, To: The Branch Command of the Bureau of Iraqis outside the Region. *BRCC*, 3187_0001 (0592). May 28, 1993.

24. "مقترحات" [Recommendations], From: The Director General of the Office of the Secretariat of the Region, To: The Regional Office of External Relations. *BRCC*, 3187_0001 (0810). April 12, 1993; "مقترحات" [Recommendations], From: The Central Office for the Popular and Professional Bureau, To: The Office of the Secretariat of the Region. *BRCC*, 3187_0001 (0800). July 5, 1993; For outside verification of the incident, see, Amnesty International, *Amnesty International Report 1994 - Iraq*, January 1, 1994; and "Notes of the Secretary-General's meeting with the Minister for Foreign Affairs of Sweden and the Chairperson- in- Office of the CSCE," January 14, 1993, *Boutros Boutros-Ghali Papers*, Box 66, Folder 3.

25. Memorandum For: Acting Director for Central Intelligence; Subject: Serbia and the Russian Problem, From: Roger Z. George, National Intelligence Officer for Europe and George Kolt, National Intelligence Officer for Russia and Eurasia, 1993-01-25, NIC Memo re Serbia and the Russian Problem," January 25, 1993. Clinton Library, https://clinton.presidentiallibraries.us/items/show/12300.

26. Russia's Yugoslav Policy Reaching Critical Juncture; Intelligence Memorandum Office of Slavic and Eurasian Analysis 27 January 1993 "1993-01-27B, Office of Slavic and Eurasian Analysis re Moscow's Yugoslav Policy Reaching Critical Juncture," 4. Clinton Library, https://clinton.presidentiallibraries.us/items/show/12302.

27. "تطورات الوضع في روسيا" [Developments of the situation in Russia], From: The Director General of the Office of the Regional Secretariat, To: The Regional Office of Foreign Relations. *BRCC*, 3733_0000 (0355). April 11, 1993.

28. "معلومات" [Information], From: The Secretary General of the Branch of the Bureau of Iraqis outside the Region, To: The Regional Command of Iraq / Office of the Secretariat of the Region. *BRCC*, 2166_0000 (0578-580). July 5, 1993.

29. "رسائل احتجاج" [Protest Letters], From: The Secretary General of the Branch of the Bureau of Iraqis outside the Region, To: The Regional Command of Iraq / Office of the Secretariat of the Region. *BRCC*, 033-4-2 (0657). January 24, 1993.

30. Bengio, "Iraq," *Middle East Contemporary Survey, 1993*, 399.

31. Duelfer, *Hide and Seek*, 102, 129.

32. Quote taken from an Iraqi Intelligence Service file, see, "Correspondence between the Iraqi embassy in Moscow, the Ministry of Foreign Affairs, and the Iraqi Intelligence Service regarding Russian-Iranian relations," *CRRC*, SH- IISX- D- 000- 148, 1996. Pg 10; National Security Council, Speechwriting Office, and Robert Boorstin, "Declassified Documents concerning Robert Boorstin, NSC Speechwriter," 105. Clinton Library, https://clinton.presidentiallibraries.us/items/show/36625; Bengio, "Iraq," *Middle East Contemporary Survey, 1994*, 356-7.

33. See, "Notes on the Secretary- General's Meeting with the President of the Security Council," September 19, 1994. *Boutros Boutros-Ghali Papers*, Box 74.

34. "Notes on the Secretary-General's Meeting with H.E. Mr. Andrei V. Kozyrev, Minister for Foreign Affairs of the Russian Federation," October 5, 1994. *Boutros Boutros-Ghali Papers*, Box 74.

35. "Saddam Says That He Had Deployed Republican Guard Divisions to the South with the Hope of Creating a Crisis," circa October 9-10, 1994. *The Saddam Tapes*, 266-7.

36. "Noes of the Meeting of the Secretary-General with the Permanent Representative of the United States," October 10, 1994. Boutros Boutros-Ghali Papers, Box 74.

37. *The United Nations and the Iraq-Kuwait Conflict 1990-1996*, Document 197, Letter from the Representatives of Iraq and of the Russian Federation transmitting the text of a joint communique containing Iraq's announcement that it had withdrawn its troops to rearguard positions on October 12, 1994, S/1994/1173, October 15, 1994, 695.

38. Provisional Record of the 3439th Meeting, UN Security Council, S/PV.3439, October 17, 1994. *UNSC Records*, 3.

39. Provisional Record of the 3439th Meeting, UN Security Council, S/PV.3439, October 17, 1994. *UNSC Records*, 94, 4–5.

40. Provisional Record of the 3439th Meeting, UN Security Council, S/PV.3439, October 17, 1994. *UNSC Records*, 6.

41. United Nations Security Council Resolution 949, S/ RES/ 949, October 15, 1994. *UNSC Records*.

42. "Notes on the Secretary-General's Meeting with H.E. Mr. Andrei V. Kozyrev, Minister for Foreign Affairs of the Russian Federation," October 5, 1994. *Boutros Boutros-Ghali Papers*, Box 74.

43. Provisional Record of the 3059th Meeting, UN Security Council, S/PV.3059, March 11, 1992. *UNSC Records*, 52–3.

44. Bengio, "Iraq," *Middle East Contemporary Survey, 1993*, 357.

45. "Correspondence between the Iraqi embassy in Moscow, the Ministry of Foreign Affairs, and the Iraqi Intelligence Service regarding Russian-Iranian relations," *CRRC*, SH-IISX-D-000-148, 1996, 11.

46. See for example, "معلومات" [Information], From: The Secretary General of the Branch of the Bureau of Iraqis outside the Region, To: The Regional Command of Iraq / Office of the Secretariat of the Region. *BRCC*, 033-4-2 (0784-0786). January 4, 1993; "التقرير السياسي" [Political Report], From: The Secretary General of the Branch of the Bureau of Iraqis outside the Region, To: The Regional Command of Iraq / Office of the Secretariat of the Region. *BRCC*, 033-4-2 (0790). January 4, 1993; "الاعلام الخارجي العراقي" [Foreign Iraqi Media], From: The Secretary General of the Branch of the Bureau of Iraqis outside the Region, To: The Regional Command of Iraq / Office of the Secretariat of the Region. *BRCC*, 033-4-2 (0541). January 4, 1993.

47. "الكتابة والنشر" [Writing and publishing], From: Secretary General of the Branch of the Bureau of Iraqis outside the Region, To: The Regional Command / Office of the Secretariat of the Region. *BRCC*, 039-4-1 (0427). August 4, 1993; "بولند اجويد والحظر الاقتصادي على القطر" [Bülent Ecevit and the economic embargo on the region], From: Secretary General of the Branch of the Bureau of Iraqis outside the Region, To: The Regional Command / Office of the Secretariat of the Region. *BRCC*, 039-4-1 (0284). August 17, 1993; Bengio, "Iraq," *Middle East Contemporary Survey, 1994*, 358.

48. "مقترح" [Recommendation], From: The Secretary General of the Branch of the Bureau of Iraqis outside the Region, To: The Regional Command of Iraq / Office of the Secretariat of the Region. *BRCC*, 033-4-2 (0478). January 31, 1993; [No Title], From: The Director General of the Office of the Secretariat of the Region, To: The Deputy Secretary General of the Regional Command of Iraq. *BRCC*, 033-4-2 (0106). January 11, 1993.

49. "Islamic Popular Conference Leader: Iraq Ready for Any Cooperation with Russia," *RIA News Agency (Russia)*. June 8, 2000. *BBC Worldwide Monitoring*; On al-Sa'di's background and career, see the regime's file on him: Information on Doctor 'Abd-al-Razzaq 'Abd-al-Rahman Al-Sa'di, *CRRC*, SH-MISC-D-001-446, 2000. Also see, his correspondences: "Letters from Dr. 'Ahd-al-Razzaq 'Abd-al-Rahman Al Sa'di of the General Secretariat of Popular Islamic Conference Organization in Baghdad to Many Oganizations in Different Countries all over the World," *CRRC*, SH-MISC-D-001-445.

50. For membership and meeting of the Popular Islamic Conference's Executive Council, see, "Meeting Minutes of the Executive Council," *CRRC*, SH-MISC-D-001-446, 1995. For more on Farrakhan's relationship with the Ba'thist regime, see, "'Islamic Popular Conference' Issues Final Statement," *Iraqi News Agency*, September 16, 1999, *FBIS*; and: "Awqaf Minister Meets With Farrakhan," Iraqi News Agency, February 15, 1996, *FBIS*.

51. "Iraqi Efforts to Cooperate with Saudi Opposition Groups and Individuals," *CRRC*, SH-MISC-D-000-503, 1997.

52. "Iraqi Efforts to Cooperate with Saudi Opposition Groups and Individuals," *CRRC*, SH-MISC-D-000-503, 1997.

53. "Iraqi Efforts to Cooperate with Saudi Opposition Groups and Individuals," *CRRC*, SH-MISC-D-000-503, 1997

54. "Iraqi Efforts to Cooperate with Saudi Opposition Groups and Individuals," *CRRC*, SH-MISC-D-000-503, 1997

55. "Report on the Saddam University for Islamic Studies: Needs and Aspirations," *BRCC*, 3493_0001 (0025-0033). September 19, 1992.

56. Syed Saleem Shahzad, "A 'third force' awaits US in Iraq," *Asia Times*, March 1, 2003, http://www.atimes.com/atimes/Middle_East/EC01Ak04.html; On the regime's religious policies and especially the Faith Campaign, see, Helfont, *Compulsion in Religion*; and Samuel Helfont and Michael Brill. "Saddam's ISIS? The Terrorist Group's Real Origin Story," *Foreign Affairs*, January 12, 2016. https://www.foreignaffairs.com/articles/iraq/2016-01-12/saddams-isis.

57. Phillip Smucker, "Iraq Builds 'Mother of all Battles' Mosque in Praise of Saddam." *Sunday Telegraph* (London), July 29, 2001, *BBC World Monitor*.

58. For the regime's discovery and reaction to such activities, see, "معلومات" [Information], *BRCC*, 3342_0003 (0235). April 23, 1993; and "معلومات" [Information], *BRCC*, 3342_0003 (0236). March 20, 1993.

59. See: "Saddam and Military Officials Discussing Reorganizing the Intelligence Service," *CRRC*, SH-SHTP-A-001-219, January 14, 2001. Cited in Woods et al., *The Saddam Tapes*. 84.

60. For more on NASYO's founding and early operations, see, "معلومات" [Information], From: Seif al-Din Muhammad Al-Mashhadni, [illegible title] General Federation of Iraqi Youth, To: The Central Office of Students and Youth. *BRCC*, 3634_0001 (0388). January 13, 1993; "مؤتمر طلب وشباب عدم الانحياز" [The Non-Aligned Student and Youth Conference], From: The Secretary General of the Central Office of Students and Youth, To: The Office of the Secretariat of the Region. *BRCC*, 3634_0001 (0356). March 28, 1993; as well numerous other files in the binder.

61. Michael M. Gunter, "The KDP-PUK Conflict in Northern Iraq," *Middle East Journal* 50, no. 2 (Spring, 1996): 224–41.

62. Robert Baer, *See No Evil: The True Story of a Ground Soldier in the CIA's War on Terrorism* (New York: Three Rivers Press, 2003), 169–214.

63. Kanan Makiya, *Cruelty and Silence*.

64. Albright, *Madam Secretary*, 280.

65. White, *Crisis after the Storm*, 40.

66. White, *Crisis after the Storm*, 40.

67. Boutros Boutros-Ghali, *Unvanquished*, 327.

68. White, *Crisis after the Storm*, 48.

69. Bengio, "Iraq," *Middle East Contemporary Survey, 1996*, 352.

70. Bengio, "Iraq," *Middle East Contemporary Survey, 1996*, 352.

71. Bengio, "Iraq," *Middle East Contemporary Survey, 1996*, 352.

72. Stayn, *France and Iraq*, 182; Bozo, " 'We Don't Need You': France, the United States, and Iraq, 1991-2003," 188–9.
73. Bengio, "Iraq," *Middle East Contemporary Survey, 1996*, 348.
74. Bengio, "Iraq," *Middle East Contemporary Survey, 1996*, 349–50.

Chapter 8

1. Julian Corbett, *Some Principles of Maritime Strategy* (Annapolis, MD: United States Naval Institute, 1988), 15–6.
2. Gary Sick "Rethinking Dual Containment" *Survival* 40, no. 1 (1998), 11.
3. "60 Minutes," *CBS*, May 12, 1996. A clip of the exchange can be seen here: https://www.youtube.com/watch?v=FbIX1CP9qr4.
4. Albright, *Madam Secretary*, 276.
5. Luis Ayllon, "Spain Prepares To Reestablish Diplomatic Presence in Iraq," *Foreign Broadcast Information Service Report*, February 27, 1995; "Swiss Sources: Iraq Trying To Revive Arms Deals With Brazil," *Al-Sharq Al-Aswat*, March 17, 1995, *FBIS*.
6. Provisional Record of the 3519th Meeting, UN Security Council, S/PV.3519, April 14, 1992. *UNSC Records*, 2.
7. Malone, *The International Struggle over Iraq*, 117.
8. "Notes of the meeting of the Secretary-General with the Deputy Prime Minister of Iraq," June 12, 1992. *Boutros Boutros-Ghali Papers*, Box 63, Folder 4.
9. See UN Security Council Resolution 986. For analysis, see Malone, *The International Struggle over Iraq*. 117–8.
10. "Meeting between President Saddam Hussein and his Cabinet talking about the 706 decision to Pumping the Oil in Exchange for Medicine and Foodstuffs and the UN stance for the Kurdish and Shia case," *CRRC*, SHTP-A-000-774. Unknown date, 8.
11. Meeting between President Saddam Hussein and his Cabinet talking about the 706 decision to Pumping the Oil in Exchange for Medicine and Foodstuffs and the UN stance for the Kurdish and Shia case," *CRRC*, SHTP-A-000-774. Unknown date, 4–5.
12. Meeting between President Saddam Hussein and his Cabinet talking about the 706 decision to Pumping the Oil in Exchange for Medicine and Foodstuffs and the UN stance for the Kurdish and Shia case," *CRRC*, SHTP-A-000-774. Unknown date, 7.
13. Meeting between President Saddam Hussein and his Cabinet talking about the 706 decision to Pumping the Oil in Exchange for Medicine and Foodstuffs and the UN stance for the Kurdish and Shia case," *CRRC*, SHTP-A-000-774. Unknown date, 11.
14. Volcker et al., "Management of the United Nations Oil-for-Food Programme," 39.
15. "مقترح" [Recommendation], From: The Director General of the Office of the Secretariat of the Region, To: The Presidential Diwan. *BRCC*, 2099_0003 (0672-0673). November 24, 1998; "مقترح" [Recommendation], From: The Assistant to the Head of the Presidential Diwan, To: The Office of the Secretariat of the Region. *BRCC*, 2099_0003 (0671). January 23, 1999; Volcker et al., "Management of the United Nations Oil-for-Food Programme," 16–7.

16. "مقترح" [Recommendation], From: The Director General of the Office of the Secretariat of the Region, To: The Presidential Diwan. *BRCC*, 2099_0003 (0672-0673). November 24, 1998.

17. "مقترح" [Recommendation], From: The Assistant to the Secretary General of the Founding Leader Branch Command, To: The Regional Command of Iraq / Office of the Secretariat of the Region. *BRCC*, 2099_0003 (0032). July 15, 1999.

18. "مقترح" [Recommendation], From: The Assistant to the Secretary General of the Founding Leader Branch Command, To: The Regional Command of Iraq / Office of the Secretariat of the Region. *BRCC*, 2099_0003 (0020). July 15, 1999.

19. "معلومات" [Information], From: The Director of the Office of the General Secretariat, To: The Office of the Secretariat of the Region. *BRCC*, 039-4-1 (0133-0135). April 4, 1993; "شاكر الخفاجي وعبد القادر القيسي" [Shakir al-Khafaji and Abd al-Qadir al-Qaysi], From: Secretary General of the Branch of the Bureau of Iraqis outside the Region, To: The Regional Command / Office of the Secretariat of the Region. *BRCC*, 039-4-1 (0119-0120). May 16, 1993.

20. See Chapter 4.

21. "شاكر الخفاجي وعبد القادر القيسي" [Shakir al- Khafaji and Abd al- Qadir al- Qaysi], From: Secretary General of the Branch of the Bureau of Iraqis outside the region, To: The Regional Command / Office of the Secretariat of the Region. *BRCC*, 039-4-1 (0119-0120). May 16, 1993.

22. Volcker et al., "Management of the United Nations Oil-for-Food Programme," 118.

23. Volcker et al., "Management of the United Nations Oil-for-Food Programme," 122–3.

24. Volcker et al., "Management of the United Nations Oil-for-Food Programme," 103–5.

25. "South Africa: Protesters Call for Lifting UN Sanctions Against Iraq," *South African Press Association*, June 30 1997, *FBIS*.

26. Volcker et al., "Management of the United Nations Oil-for-Food Programme," 105–8.

27. Volcker et al., "Management of the United Nations Oil-for-Food Programme," 103.

28. Volcker et al., "Management of the United Nations Oil- for- Food Programme," 108–10.

29. Volcker et al., "Management of the United Nations Oil-for-Food Programme," 103–5.

30. Volcker et al., "Management of the United Nations Oil-for-Food Programme," 103–5.

31. "Hinweise auf Öl-Geld von Saddam schon 2004" (Hints of Oil Money From Saddam already in 2004), *Die Presse*, August 9, 2010, http://diepresse.com/home/innenpoli tik/586527/Hinweise-auf-OelGeld-von-Saddam-schon-2004?from=suche.intern. portal.

32. Volcker et al., "Management of the United Nations Oil- for- Food Programme," 79; Tim Castle, "Galloway Iraq Fund Had Illicit Oil Cash: Regulator," *Reuters*, June 7, 2007, https://www.reuters.com/article/us-britain-galloway/galloway-iraq-fund-had-illicit-oil-cash-regulator-idUSL0783566820070607.

33. Volcker et al., "Management of the United Nations Oil-for-Food Programme," 9.

34. Volcker et al., "Management of the United Nations Oil-for-Food Programme," 16.

35. Volcker et al., "Management of the United Nations Oil-for-Food Programme," 22–3.

36. Volcker et al., "Management of the United Nations Oil-for-Food Programme," 29.

37. Volcker et al., "Management of the United Nations Oil-for-Food Programme," 49.

38. Stayn, *France and Iraq*, 186.

39. David Shucosky, "Former French UN ambassador admits taking oil-for-food bribes," November 18, 2005, https://www.jurist.org/news/2005/11/former-french-un-ambassador-admits/; Volcker et al., "Management of the United Nations Oil-for-Food Programme," 49–51.
40. "France's Total Fined for Graft in UN's Iraq Aid Program," *DW*, February 27, 2016, https://www.dw.com/en/frances-total-fined-for-graft-in-uns-iraq-aid-program/a-19078619; "Volvo Agrees to Penalty over Iraq Oil-for-Food," *Reuters*, March 20, 2008, https://www.reuters.com/article/volvo-iraq/volvo-agrees-to-penalty-over-iraq-oil-for-food-idUKWBT008625200803 20; Volcker et al., "Management of the United Nations Oil-for-Food Programme," 47–78.
41. Braut-Hegghammer, "Cheater's Dilemma."
42. Trachtenberg, "History Teaches," *Yale School of Journal Affairs* 7, no. 2 (September 2007): 32, endnote 16. *Comprehensive Report of the Special Advisor to the DCI on Iraq's WMD*, September 2004, vol. 1, 61.
43. Provisional Record of the 3768th Meeting, UN Security Council, S/PV.3768, April 16, 1997, *UNSC Records*; Ofra Bengio, "Iraq," in *Middle East Contemporary Survey: Volume XXI, 1997*, ed. Bruce Maddy-Weitzman (Boulder, CO: Westview Press, 2000), 390–1.
44. Saddam interrogation. Session 23. Page 1. https://nsarchive2.gwu.edu/NSAEBB/NSAEBB279/23.pdf.
45. Provisional Record of the 3826th Meeting, UN Security Council, S/PV 3826, October 23, 1997, *UNSC Records*, 5.
46. Western European states that held rotating seats on the council tended to vote with the United States and the United Kingdom in this period. Provisional Record of the 3826th Meeting, UN Security Council, S/PV 3826, October 23, 1997, *UNSC Records*, 9; Peter Van Walsum, "The Iraq Sanction's Committee," in *The UN Security Council: From the Cold War to the 21st Century*, ed. David Malone (Boulder, CO: Lynne Rienner Publishers, 2004), 186–7.
47. "Saddam Orders Iraqis to Resist and Intimidate UN Inspectors," July 1992, *The Saddam Tapes*, 264.
48. "Security Council Condemns Iraq for Attempt to Dictate Terms of Cooperation with Special Commission," Press Release, SC/6434, October 29, 1997, *UNSC Records*; "Security Council Imposes Travel Ban on Iraqi Officials," November 12, 1997, Press Release, SC/6441, *UNSC Records*; "Security Council Condemns Iraq's Expulsion of Special Commission Members," November 13, 1997, Press Release, SC/6442, *UNSC Records*.
49. Yevgeny Primakov, *Russia and the Arabs: Behind the Scenes in the Middle East from the Cold War to the Present* (New York: Basic Books, 2009), 318–9.
50. James Goldgeier, "Bill and Boris: A Window into a Most Important Post-Cold War Relationship," *Texas National Security Review* 1, no. 4 (August 2018).
51. Subject: Message to President Yeltsin. From: The White House. To: AMEMBASSY Moscow (eyes only for Amb Collins). November 27, 1997, "Declassified Documents concerning Russia," Clinton Library, accessed March 11, 2020, 2–4. https://clinton.presidentiallibraries.us/items/show/16205.

52. Untitled Cable from British Cabinet Office to the White House, November 8, 1997. National Security Council and Records Management Office, "Declassified documents concerning Tony Blair," 38–9. Clinton Library, accessed March 15, 2020, https://clin ton.presidentiallibraries.us/items/show/47973.

53. "Telcon with British Prime Minister Tony Blair," November 15, 1997, National Security Council and Records Management Office, "Declassified documents concerning Tony Blair," Clinton Library, accessed March 12, 2020, 52–55. https://clinton. presidentiallibraries.us/items/show/48779.

54. "Iraqi Leadership Discusses the Memorandum of Understanding with Kofi Annan to Allow Inspections of Iraq's Presidential Sites. Taha Mentions Iraq's Agreement on Compensations with Benon Sevan and Predicts That Iraqi Bribery Will Lead to Increased Support from Russia, France, and China," circa February 23, 1998. *Saddam Tapes*, 290–1.

55. "Annan, Iraq Sign Weapons-Inspection Deal," *CNN*, February 23, 1998. https://web. arch ive.org/ web/ 202 0092 6003 121/ http:// www.cnn.com/ WORLD/ 9802/ 23/ iraq. deal.update.4am/index.html.

56. "Men of Religion Visit Presidential Palace," *Baghdad Television Network*, February 10, 1998, *FBIS*.

57. "Protesters in Baghdad Set Fire to US, Israeli Flags," *Baghdad Television Network*, February 18, 1998, *FBIS*.

58. *Al-Sha'b* (Egypt), February 10, 1998, *FBIS*. Large numbers of Egyptian security forces were deployed, but it is unclear how large these demonstrations actually were. What is important is that the Brotherhood attempted to pressure the Egyptian regime into supporting Iraq.

59. Rula Amin, "Jordanian Police Attack Pro-Iraqi Demonstrators," *CNN*, February 13, 1998. http://edition.cnn.com/WORLD/9802/13/iraq.amman.protest/index.html.

60. "Annan, Iraq Sign Weapons-Inspection Deal,"; Stayn, *France and Iraq*, 186.

61. "Meeting with Tony Blair, Prime Minister of the United Kingdom," February 5, 1998, National Security Council and Records Management Office, "Declassified documents concerning Tony Blair," 64–77. Clinton Library, accessed March 12, 2020, https://clin ton.presidentiallibraries.us/items/show/48779.

62. Telcon with British Prime Minister Blair, February 16, 1998. National Security Council and Records Management Office, "Declassified documents concerning Tony Blair," 80. Clinton Library, accessed March 12, 2020, https://clinton.presidentiallibrar ies.us/items/show/48779, 80.

63. White, *Crisis after the Storm*, 56.

64. "Saddam Discusses Areas in which Iraq Should Continue Refusing UN Disarmament Demands and the Possibility of War with the United States," circa late November 1998, *Saddam Tapes*, 293.

65. Ralph Peters, "How Saddam Won this Round," *Newsweek*, November 30, 1998. Also, White, *Crisis After the Storm*, 58.

66. White, *Crisis after the Storm*, 59–60.

67. For example, "نشاطات" [Activities], From: The Assistant to the secretary general of the Founding Leader Branch Command, To: The Regional Command of Iraq / Office

of the Secretariat of the Region. *BRCC*, 2099_0003 (0368). March 18, 1999; and "نشاطات" [Activities], From: The Assistant to the Secretary General of the Founding Leader Branch Command, To: The Regional Command of Iraq / Office of the Secretariat of the Region. *BRCC*, 2099_0003 (0368). March 18, 1999; and "نشاطات" [Activities], From: The Assistant to the Secretary General of the Founding Leader Branch Command, To: The Regional Command of Iraq / Office of the Secretariat of the Region. *BRCC*, 2099_0003 (0566). February 11, 1999.

68. For a list of the approved slogans, see, *BRCC*, 2099_0003 (0568-0578).

69. "تظاهرة" [Demonstration], From: The Assistant to the Secretary General of the Founding Leader Branch Command, To: The Regional Command of Iraq / Office of the Secretariat of the Region. *BRCC*, 2099_0003 (0520). February 17, 1999; "مقابلة صحفية" [Newspaper Interview], From: The Assistant to the Secretary General of the Founding Leader Branch Command, To: The Regional Command of Iraq / Office of the Secretariat of the Region. *BRCC*, 2099_0003 (0482). March 6, 1999.

70. "نشاطات" [Activities], From: The Assistant to the Secretary General of the Founding Leader Branch Command, To: The Regional Command of Iraq / Office of the Secretariat of the Region. *BRCC*, 2099_0003 (0466). March 3, 1999.

71. Translation of a letter from Yeltsin to Clinton, December 2, 1998, National Security Council and Records Management Office, "Declassified Documents concerning Iraq," 79–80. Clinton Library, accessed March 11, 2020, https://clinton.presidentialli braries.us/items/show/16192.

72. Memorandum of Telephone Conversation between Presidents Clinton and Chirac. December 17, 1998. National Security Council and Records Management Office, "Declassified Documents concerning Iraq," 53–6. Clinton Library, accessed March 11, 2020, https://clinton.presidentiallibraries.us/items/show/16192.

73. "Memorandum for Samuel Berger, Subject: Letter to. President Yeltsin on Iraq," December 17, 1998. National Security Council and Records Management Office, "Declassified Documents concerning Iraq," 70. Clinton Library, accessed March 11, 2020, https://clinton.presidentiallibraries.us/items/show/16192.

74. Ian Jeffries, *The New Russia: A Handbook of Economic and Political Developments* (New York: Routledge, 2013), 587.

75. "Message to President Yeltsin," December 18, 1998. National Security Council and Records Management Office, "Declassified Documents concerning Iraq," 66–7. Clinton Library, accessed March 11, 2020, https:// clin ton.presid enti allibrar ies.us/ items/show/16192.

76. "Telephone Conversation with Russian President Yeltsin," December 30, 1998. National Security Council and Records Management Office, "Declassified Documents concerning Iraq," 72–6, Clinton Library, accessed March 11, 2020, https://clin ton. presidentiallibraries.us/items/show/16192.

77. Homi Kharas, Brian Pinto, and Sergei Ulatov, *An Analysis of Russia's 1998 Meltdown: Fundamentals and Market Signals* (Washington, DC: Brookings Institution, 2001).

78. "Telcon with President Chirac of France." November 4, 1998. National Security Council and Records Management Office, "Declassified Documents concerning

Iraq," 17–8. Clinton Library, accessed March 11, 2020, https://clinton.presidentialli braries.us/items/show/16192.

79. "Telcon with President Chirac of France." November 4, 1998. National Security Council and Records Management Office, "Declassified Documents concerning Iraq," 17–8. Clinton Library, accessed March 11, 2020, https://clinton.presidentialli braries.us/items/show/16192.

80. Memorandum of Telephone Conversation with President Jacques Chirac of France, December 17, 1998. National Security Council and Records Management Office, "Declassified Documents concerning Iraq," 53–6. Clinton Library, accessed March 11, 2020, https://clinton.presidentiallibraries.us/items/show/16192.

81. "Briefing Memo for POTUS Call to Crown Prince Abdullah of Saudi Arabia," November 2, 1998, National Security Council and Records Management Office, "Declassified Documents concerning Iraq," 2–7. Clinton Library, accessed March 11, 2020, https://clinton.presidentiallibraries.us/items/show/16192; "Memorandum of Telephone Conversation with the Crown Prince Abdullah of Saudi Arabia, December 15, 1998. National Security Council and Records Management Office, "Declassified Documents concerning Iraq," 41–3. Clinton Library, accessed March 11, 2020, https://clinton.presidentiallibraries.us/items/show/16192;

82. For a transcript, see, Remarks at Town Hall Meeting, Ohio State University, Columbus, Ohio, February 18, 1998. *U.S. Department of State Archive.* https://1997-2001.state.gov/www/statements/1998/980218.html.

83. For these and other critiques, see, William Saletan, "Wag the Doubt," *Slate*, December 20, 1998. https://slate.com/news-and-politics/1998/12/wag-the-doubt.html.

84. White, *Crisis after the Storm*, 60.

85. White, *Crisis after the Storm*, 59–60, 62.

86. Ofra Bengio, "Iraq," in *Middle East Contemporary Survey: Volume XXIII, 1999*, ed. Bruce Maddy-Weitzman (Syracuse, NY: Syracuse University Press, 2002), 282–3.

87. White, *Crisis after the Storm*, 64.

88. Bengio, "Iraq," *Middle East Contemporary Survey: Volume XXIII, 1999*, 282.

89. Telcon with British Prime Minister Blair, October 13, 1999, "National Security Council and Records Management Office, "Declassified documents concerning Tony Blair," 423–438. Clinton Library, accessed March 12, 2020, https://clinton.presidenti allibraries.us/items/show/48779.

90. "Saddam's Iraq: Sanctions and U.S. Policy," Hearing Before the Subcommittee on Near Eastern and South Asian Affairs of the Committee on Foreign Relations United States Senate, One Hundred Sixth Congress, Second Session, March 22, 2000, 5. https:// www.govi nfo.gov/ cont ent/ pkg/ CHRG- 106sh rg67 659/ html/ CHRG- 106sh rg67 659.htm.

91. "Saddam's Iraq: Sanctions and U.S. Policy," 19.

92. "McKane to Sawers minute and attachment," February 15, 2001, *UK Iraq Inquiry Documents.* https:// web arch ive.natio nala rchi ves.gov.uk/ 201 3080 9094 640/ http:// www.iraq inqu iry.org.uk/ tran scri pts/ decla ssif ied- docume nts.aspx; "McKane to Sawers minute," April 6, 2001, *UK Iraq Inquiry Documents.* https:// web arch ive. natio nala rchi ves.gov.uk/ 201 3080 9095 438/ http:// www.iraq inqu iry.org.uk/ media/

50488/McKanetoSawers-6April2001-minute.pdf; "Letter from John Sawers - (Prime Minister's Private Secretary) to Sherard Cowper-Coles (FCO) re Iraq: new policy framework," March 7, 2001 *UK Iraq Inquiry Documents*. https://webarchive.nationala rchives.gov.uk/20130809094640/http://www.iraqinquiry.org.uk/transcripts/decla ssified-documents.aspx

Chapter 9

1. "Iraq: Continuing Erosion of Sanctions," *United Kingdom Joint Intelligence Committee Assessment*, July 25, 2001. *UK Iraq Inquiry Documents*. https://webarchive.nationala rchives.gov.uk/2017112 3124 012/ http:/ www.iraqinquiry.org.uk/ media/ 203 196/ 2001-07-25-jic-assessment-iraq-continuing-erosion-of-sanctions.pdf.
2. "نشاطات" [Activities], From: The Assistant to the Secretary General of the Founding Leader Branch Command, To: The Regional Command of Iraq / Office of the Secretariat of the Region. BRCC, 2099_0003 (0505). February 24, 1999.
3. "Testimony of Sir Jeremy Greenstock," *UK Iraq Inquiry Documents*, May 26, 2010, 3. https:// web arch ive.natio nala rchi ves.gov.uk/ 201 3080 9094 729/ http:// www.iraq inquiry.org.uk/media/50162/greenstock-20100526-declassified.pdf.
4. "زيارة ولي عهد ملك السعودية الى اليبان" [Visit of the Saudi Crown Prince to Japan], From: The Assistant to the Secretary General of the Founding Leader Branch Command, To: The Regional Command of Iraq / Office of the Secretariat of the Region. *BRCC*, 2099_0003 (0529). February 16, 1999.
5. Untitled information sheet. *BRCC*, 2699_0000 (0244-0245).
6. "NASYO at the 15th World Festival of Youth and Students 2001, Algeria." *BRCC*, 2699_0000 (0228-0229).
7. "NASYO at the 15th World Festival of Youth and Students 2001, Algeria." *BRCC*, 2699_0000 (0236-0237).
8. "NASYO at the 15th World Festival of Youth and Students 2001, Algeria." *BRCC*, 2699_0000 (0160-0173).
9. "تقرير" [Report], From: Huda Salih Mahdi Ammash, Secretary General of the Central office of Students and Youth, To: The Office of the Secretariat of the Region. *BRCC*, 2699_0000 (0325-0333). July 3, 2001.
10. Van Walsum, "The Iraq Sanctions Committee," 192.
11. Van Walsum, "The Iraq Sanctions Committee," 191–2.
12. Van Walsum, "The Iraq Sanctions Committee," 189–90.
13. Van Walsum, "The Iraq Sanctions Committee," 189–90.
14. Steib, *Regime Change Consensus*, 252.
15. Tim Dyson, "New Evidence on Child Mortality in Iraq," *Economic and Political Weekly* 44, no. 2 (January, 2009): 56–9.
16. Ofra Bengio, "Iraq," in *Middle East Contemporary Survey: Volume XXII, 1998*, ed. Bruce Maddy-Weitzman (Boulder, CO: Westview Press, 2001), 402; Bengio, "Iraq," *Middle East Contemporary Survery: Volume XXIII, 1999*, 287.

17. Volcker, 13.
18. Volcker, 38.
19. Volcker, 41.
20. Iraqi Leadership Discusses the Memorandum of Understanding with Kofi Annan to Allow Inspections of Iraq's Presidential Sites. Taha Mentions Iraq's Agreement on Compensations with Benon Sevan and and Predicts That Iraqi Bribery Will Lead to Increased Support from Russia, France, and China," circa, February 23, 1998. *Saddam Tapes*, 291–2.
21. Volcker, 519.
22. Volcker, 4.
23. Duelfer, *Hide and Seek*, 182.
24. Coughlin, *Saddam*, 313–4.
25. "October 11, 2000 Debate Transcript," *Commission on Presidential Debates*, October 11, 2000. http://www.debates.org/?page=october-11-2000-debate-transcript.
26. "Report from IIS News and Media Bureau Office about a New Media Policy against the United States," *CRRC*, SH-IISX-D-000-147, January 2001.
27. "Saddam and His Advisers Discuss the Environment with the New Bush Administration," December 29, 2000–January 6, 2001, *The Saddam Tapes*, 57–8.
28. Melvyn P. Leffler, "Foreign Policies of the George W. Bush Administration: Memoirs, History, Legacy," *Diplomatic History* 37, no. 2 (2013): 190–216.
29. "The Vice President Appears on NBC's Meet the Press," George W. Bush White House Archives, December 9, 2001. https://georgewbush-whitehouse.archives.gov/vicepresident/news-speeches/speeches/print/vp20011209.html.
30. George W. Bush, "President Discusses the Future of Iraq," Washington DC, February 26, 2000. http://georgewbush-whitehouse.archives.gov/news/releases/2003/02/20030226-11.html.
31. For an analysis, pointing out the similarities between the speech and Chapter 2 of Fukuyama's book, see Andrew Moore, "History, Freedom and Bureaucracy," in *The Wire and America's Dark Corners: Critical Essays*, ed. Arin Keeble and Ivan Stacy (Jefferson, NC: McFarland and Company Inc. 2015), 17–8. To compare Bush's speech with Fukuyama's work, see: George W. Bush, "Remarks by the President at the 20th Anniversary of the National Endowment for Democracy," November 6, 2003. http://georgewbush-whitehouse.archives.gov/news/releases/2003/11/20031106-2.html; and, Fukuyama, *The End of History and the Last Man*, 13–5.
32. Daniel Deudney and G. John Ikenberry, "Realism, Liberalism and the Iraq War," *Survival* 59, no. 4 (2017): 7–26.
33. "President Bush Delivers Graduation Speech at West Point," United States Military Academy, West Point, New York, June 1, 2002. https://georgewbush-whitehouse.archives.gov/news/releases/2002/06/20020601-3.html.
34. Franklin Eric Wester, "Preemption and Just War: Considering the Case of Iraq," *Parameters* (Winter 2004–05).
35. "Interview With Jacques Chirac," *New York Times*, September 9, 2002. https://www.nytimes.com/2002/09/09/international/europe/interview-with-jacques-chirac.html.

36. Frédéric Bozo, *A History of the Iraq Crisis: France, the United States, and Iraq, 1991–2003* (New York: Columbia University Press, 2016), 112.

37. Sean D. Murphy, "Assessing the Legality of Invading Iraq," *George Washington University Law School Scholarly Commons* (2004), 4–6. https://scholarship.law.gwu.edu/cgi/viewcontent.cgi?article=1898&context=faculty_publications.

38. "Goulty to McKane 20 October 2000 letter and attachment 'Iraq Future Strategy,'" *UK Iraq Inquiry Documents*, https://webarchive.nationalarchives.gov.uk/20130809100018/http://www.iraqinquiry.org.uk/media/50470/2000-10-20%20goulty%20to%20mckane%20letter%20and%20attachment%20iraq%20future%20strategy.pdf.

39. "President's Remarks at the United Nations General Assembly," September 12, 2002. https://georgewbush-whitehouse.archives.gov/news/releases/2002/09/20020912-1.html.

40. "Defense Issues." C-SPAN video, February 13, 2003. https://www.c-span.org/video/?175080-1/defense-issues.

41. See, for example, Duelfer, *Hide and Seek*, 200–1.

42. Kevin Woods et al., *View of Operation Iraqi Freedom from Saddam's Senior Leadership* (Washington, DC: Institute for Defense Analysis, 2006), 28–9.

43. Woods, *View of Operation Iraqi Freedom from Saddam's Senior Leadership*, 28–9.

44. Dominique Reynié, "Does a 'European Public Opinion' Exist?," *Forum Constitutionis Europae*, Humboldt University, Germany, September 2009, 12–3, https://www.rewi.hu-berlin.de/de/lf/oe/whi/FCE/archiv/rede-reynie-engl.pdf.

45. "نشاطات" [Activities], From: Official of the Organization, To: The Founding Leader Branch Command. *BRCC*, 2383_ 0002 (0085). September 29, 2002; "نشاطات" [Activities], From: Official of the Organization of Iraqis in Sweden, To: The Founding Leader Branch Command. *BRCC*, 2383_0002 (0030-0031). November 30, 2002.

46. Daniela V. Dimitrova and Jesper Strömbäck, "Mission Accomplished? Framing of the Iraq War in the Elite Newspapers in Sweden and the United States," *Gazette: The International Journal for Communication Studies* 67, no. 5 (2005), 410.

47. Woods, *View of Operation Iraqi Freedom from Saddam's Senior Leadership*, 15–6, 30.

48. Provisional Record of the 4644th Meeting, UN Security Council, S/ PV. 4644, November 8, 2002, *UNSC Records*, 3; Boutros Boutros-Ghali, "Introduction," 33–4.

49. Resolution 1441, S/RES/1441, November 8, 2002, *UNSC Records*, 3.

50. Quotes taken from, Woods, *View of Operation Iraqi Freedom from Saddam's Senior Leadership*, 25, 31. See also, Duelfer, *Hide and Seek*, 10.

Conclusion and Afterword

1. In 2020, the school changed its name the Princeton School of Public and International Affairs.

2. For an overview of his work, see, Ikenberry, *After Victory*; G. John Ikenberry, *Liberal Order and Imperial Ambition: American Power and International Order* (New York: Polity Press, 2005); G. John Ikenberry, *Liberal Leviathan: The Origins,*

Crisis, and Transformation of the American System (Princeton: Princeton University Press, 2011); G. John Ikenberry, *A World Safe for Democracy: Liberal Internationalism and the Crises of Global Order* (New Haven: Yale University Press, 2020).

3. Ikenberry, *After Victory*, xvi.

4. George H. W. Bush, *Address Before a Joint Session of the Congress on the Persian Gulf Crisis and the Federal Budget Deficit*, September 11, 1990, *George H. W. Bush Presidential Library and Museum* https://bush41library.tamu.edu/archives/public-papers/2217.

5. Ikenberry, *After Victory*, xvi–xix.

6. Stephen G. Brooks and William C. Wohlforth, *World Out of Balance: International Relations and the Challenge of American Primacy* (Princeton: Princeton University Press, 2008)

7. Samuel Helfont, "Iraq's Real Weapons of Mass Destruction were 'Political Operations,'" *War on the Rocks*, February 26, 2018, https://warontherocks.com/2018/02/iraqs-real-weapons-mass-destruction-political-operations.

8. See for example, John J. Mearsheimer, "Back to the Future: Instability in Europe after the Cold War," *International Security* 15, no. 1 (Summer, 1990): 5–56; John J. Mearsheimer, "Why We Will Soon Miss the Cold War," *The Atlantic Monthly* 266, no. 2 (August 1990): 35–50. On soft balancing, see cluster of articles under the title "Balancing Act," in, *International Security* 30, no. 1 (Summer, 2005).

9. Posen, *Restraint*.

10. As an example of an inconsistency, realists asserted that because states act in accordance with their national interests, many traditional American fears were overblown. For example, as the *New York Times* advertisement read, "Even if Saddam Hussein acquired nuclear weapons, he could not use them without suffering massive U.S. or Israeli retaliation." Such a massive retaliation was not in Saddam's interests, the logic went, and therefore Iraq would not use nuclear Iraq weapons even if it had them. However, the whole point of the advertisement was that a war in Iraq was not in America's national interests, but that Bush might do it anyway. And, of course, the United States did launch the war, showing that states do not always act in accordance with their national interests. Sometimes leaders inflict disaster on themselves, and Saddam's regime was no different.

11. Robert D. Kaplan, "Why John J. Mearsheimer Is Right (About Some Things)," *The Atlantic Monthly* (January/February 2012). https://www.theatlantic.com/magazine/archive/2012/01/why-john-j-mearsheimer-is-right-about-some-things/308839/.

12. "They Got It Right: (1) Robert J. Art," *Radio Open Source*, October 19, 2007, https://radioopensource.org/they-got-it-right-1-robert-j-art/

13. Glenn Kessler and Thomas E. Ricks, "The Realists' Repudiation of Policies for a War, Region," *The Washington Post*, December 7, 2006. http://www.washingtonpost.com/wp-dyn/content/article/2006/12/06/AR2006120601482.html.

14. The book deal they signed to write "The Israel Lobby" reportedly came with a 750,000 dollar advance. See: Christopher L Ball, ed., *The Israel Lobby and U.S. Foreign*

Policy: Roundtable Review, H-Diplo Roundtables 8, no. 18 (2007): 3. http://h-diplo. org/roundtables/PDF/IsraelLobby-Schoenbaum.pdf.

15. For example, Posen, *Restraint*; Stephen M. Walt, *The Hell of Good Intentions: America's Foreign Policy Elite and the Decline of U.S. Primacy* (New York: Farrar, Straus and Giroux, 2018); John J Mearsheimer, *The Great Delusion: Liberal Dreams and International Realities* (New Haven: Yale University Press, 2019).

16. Paul Berman, *Terror and Liberalism* (New York: W. W. Norton and Company, 2003); Christopher Hitchens, *A Long Short War: The Postponed Liberation of Iraq* (New York: Plume, 2003); Nick Cohen, *What's Left?*

17. *Euston Manifesto for a Renewal of Progressive Politics* (2006). https://eustonmanifesto. org/the-euston-manifesto/.

18. Roger Cohen, "A Manifesto From the Left Too Sensible to Ignore," *The New York Times*, December 30, 2006 https://archive.nytimes.com/www.nytimes.com/iht/2006/ 12/30/ world/ IHT- 30gl obal ist.html?n= Top%252FN ews%252FWo rld%252F Colu mns%252FRoger%2520Cohen.

19. John Farley, "A New Pro-Imperialist 'Left' Manifesto" *Counterpunch*, May 27, 2006. https:// www.count erpu nch.org/ 2006/ 05/ 27/ a- new- pro- impe rial ist- quot- left-quot- manife sto/; Geoffrey Wheatcroft, "They Should Come Out as Imperialist and Proud of It," *The Guardian*, May 9, 2006. https://www.theguardian.com/commentisf ree/ 2006/ may/ 10/ foreig npol icy.comm ent; Daniel Davies, "Next Stop Euston. This Manifesto Terminates Here," *The Guardian*, April 14, 2008. https://www.theguardian. com/ commen tisfree/ 2008/ apr/ 14/ nextst opis eust onwh erethis; Martin Shaw, "Why I Didn't Sign the Euston Manifesto," *Democratiya*, Autumn 2006. https:// www.diss entmagazine.org/democratiya_article/why-i-didnt-sign-the-euston-manifesto.

20. Francis Fukuyama, "After Neoconservatism," *New York Times Magazine*, February 19, 2006. http:// www.nyti mes.com/ 2006/ 02/ 19/ magaz ine/ neo.html?pag ewan ted= all&_r=1&.

21. Samuel Helfont, "Catalyst of History: Francis Fukuyama, the Iraq War, and the Legacies of 1989 in the Middle East" in Piotr Kosicki and Kyrill Kunakhovich eds., *The Long 1989: Decades of Global Revolution* (Central European University Press, 2019).

22. Fukuyama, "After Neoconservatism," and, Francis Fukuyama, *America at the Crossroads: Democracy, Power, and the Neoconservative Legacy* (New Haven: Yale University Press, 2006), 55.

23. Fukuyama, "After Neoconservatism."

24. Fukuyama, *America at the Crossroads*, 47.

25. Quoted in, Thomas Juneau, "The Obama Administration, Defensive Realism, and American Foreign Policy in the Middle East," *Comparative Strategy* 39, no. 4 (2020): 385.

26. "Donald Trump attacks George W. Bush on 9/11, Iraq," *CBS News*, February 13, 2016. https://www.youtube.com/watch?v=H4ThZcq1oJQ

27. "Donald Trump attacks George W. Bush on 9/11, Iraq."

28. Michael Grunwald, "Trump Goes Code Pink on George W. Bush," *Politico*, February 14, 2016. https:// www.polit ico.com/ magaz ine/ story/ 2016/ 02/ trump- code- pink-bush-iraq-9-11-213630.

29. Stephen Kinzer, "In an Astonishing Turn, George Soros and Charles Koch Team up to end US 'Forever Far' Policy." *Boston Globe*, June 30, 2019. https://www.bostonglobe.com/opinion/2019/06/30/soros-and-koch-brothers-team-end-forever-war-policy/WhyENwjhG0vfo9Um6Zl0JO/story.html.
30. The Quincy Institute. https://quincyinst.org/about/.
31. Fareed Zakaria, *The Post-American World* (New York: Norton, 2008).

Bibliography

Archives and Collections

Boutros Boutros-Ghali Papers, Hoover Library and Archives, Stanford University, Stanford, CA.

Conflict Records Research Center (CRRC), National Defense University, Washington, DC.

George H. W. Bush Presidential Library and Museum, Texas A&M, College Station, TX, https://bush41library.tamu.edu/

Hizb al- Ba'th al- 'Arabi al- Ishtiraki in Iraq [Ba'th Arab Socialist Party of Iraq], Ba'th Regional Command Collection (BRCC), Hoover Library and Archives, Stanford University, Stanford, CA.

James A Baker III Papers, Princeton University, Princeton, NJ.

National Security Archive, https://nsarchive.gwu.edu/.

United Kingdom Iraq Inquiry Documents (Chilcot Inquiry), https://web arch ive.natio nalarchives.gov.uk/ukgwa/20130809094300/http:/www.iraqinquiry.org.uk/.

United Nations Security Council archives, Dag Hammarskjöld Library, https://research. un.org/en/docs/.

Warren Christopher Papers, Hoover Library and Archives, Stanford University, Stanford, CA.

William J. Clinton Presidential Library and Museum, Little Rock, AK, https:// www.cli ntonlibrary.gov/research,

International Press Databases

BBC Worldwide Monitoring

World News Connection

Foreign Broadcast Information Service (FBIS)

Published Sources

"A Safe Haven will be Hard to Find," *The Herald* (Scotland), August 27, 1996.

Aflaq, Michel. في سبيل البعث [In the Way of the Ba'th]. Beirut: Dar al-Tali'a, 1963.

Ahram, Ariel I. "War-Making, State-Making, and Non-State Power In Iraq," *Yale Program on Governance and Local Development*, Working Paper No. 1 (2015).

al-Dawalibi, Ma'ruf. "Background on Ma'ruf al-Dawalibi Given," *Al-Majallah* (London), May, 14 1982, *Joint Publications Research Service*, Near East/North Africa Report No. 2583, July 16, 1982.

al-Dawalibi, Muhammad Ma'ruf. مذكرات الدكتور معروف الدواليبي [The Memoirs of Doctor Ma'ruf al-Dawalibi]. Riyadh: Maktabat al-'Ubaykan, 2005.

al-Mashat, Muhammad. كنت سفيرا للعراق في واشنطن: حكايتي مع صدام في غزو الكويت [*I was Iraq's Ambassador in Washington: My story with Saddam during the invasion of Kuwait*]. Beirut: The Iraqi Institute for Research and Publishing, 2008.

al-Khalil, Samir. *The Republic of Fear: The Politics of Modern Iraq*. Berkeley, CA: University of California Press, 1989.

al- Radi, Nuha. *Baghdad Diaries: A Woman's Chronicle of War and Exile*. New York: Vintage, 2003.

al- Yasin, Abd al- Malik Ahmad. ذكريات ومحطات حتى لا تضيع الحقيقة [*Memories and Stages: For the Sake of not Losing the Truth*]. Amman: Dar al-Amana for Publishing and Distribution, 2013.

Albright, Madeline. *Madame Secretary: A Memoir*. New York: Harper Perennial, 2013.

Amin, Rula. "Jordanian Police Attack Pro-Iraqi Demonstrators," *CNN*, February 13, 1998. http://edition.cnn.com/WORLD/9802/13/iraq.amman.protest/index.html.

"Annan, Iraq Sign Weapons-Inspection Deal," *CNN*, February 23, 1998. https://web.arch ive.org/web/20200926003121/http://www.cnn.com/WORLD/9802/23/iraq.deal.upd ate.4am/index.html.

Andrew, Christopher. *The Sword and the Shield: The Mitrokhin Archive and the Secret History of the KGB*. New York: Basic Books, 1999.

Anwar, Ahmed Fouad. "Can the Muslim Brotherhood Regain Influence in Oman?," *The Arab Weekly*, January 26, 2020, https://thearabweekly.com/can-muslim-brotherhood-regain-influence-oman.

Applebome, Peter. "War in the Gulf: Antiwar Rallies," *The New York Times*, January 27, 1991.

Arendt, Hannah. *The Origins of Totalitarianism*. New York: Harcourt, Brace and World Inc. 1966.

Auda, Gehad. "An Uncertain Response: The Islamic Movement in Egypt." In *Islamic Fundamentalisms and the Gulf Crisis*, ed. James Piscatori. Chicago: American Academy of Arts and Sciences with the Fundamentalism Project, 1991.

Ball, Christopher L. ed., "The Israel Lobby and U.S. Foreign Policy: Roundtable Review," *H-Diplo Roundtables*, 8, no. 18 (2007), 3. http://h-diplo.org/roundtables/PDF/IsraelLo bby-Schoenbaum.pdf.

Baer, Robert. *See No Evil: The True Story of a Ground Soldier in the CIA's War on Terrorism*. New York: Three Rivers Press, 2003.

Batatu, Hanna. *The Old Social Classes and the Revolutionary Movements of Iraq: A Study of Iraq's Old Landed and Commercial Classes and of Its Communists, Ba'thists and Free Officers*. Princeton, NJ: Princeton University Press, 1978.

Bengio, Ofra. "Iraq." In *Middle East Contemporary Survey: Volume XI, 1987*, ed. Itamar Rabinovich and Haim Shaked. Boulder, CO: Westview Press.

Bengio, Ofra. "Iraq." In *Middle East Contemporary Survey: Volume XVII, 1993*. ed. Ami Ayalon. Boulder, CO: Westview Press, 1995.

Bengio, Ofra. "Iraq." In *Middle East Contemporary Survey: Volume XVIII, 1994*, eds. Ami Ayalon and Bruce Maddy-Weitzman. Boulder, CO: Westview Press, 1996.

Bengio, Ofra. "Iraq." In *Middle East Contemporary Survey: Volume XIX: 1995*, ed. Bruce Maddy-Weitzman. Boulder, CO: Westview Press, 1997.

Bengio, Ofra. "Iraq." In *Middle East Contemporary Survey: Volume XX, 1996*, ed. Bruce Maddy-Weitzman. Boulder, CO: Westview Press, 1998.

Bengio, Ofra. "Iraq." In *Middle East Contemporary Survey: Volume XXI, 1997*, ed. Bruce Maddy-Weitzman. Boulder, CO: Westview Press, 2000.

Bengio, Ofra. Iraq." In *Middle East Contemporary Survey: Volume XXII, 1998*, ed. Bruce Maddy-Weitzman. Boulder, CO: Westview Press, 2001.

Bengio, Ofra. "Iraq." In *Middle East Contemporary Survey: Volume XXIII, 1999*, ed. Bruce Maddy-Weitzman. Syracuse, NY: Syracuse University Press, 2002.

Bengio, Ofra. *Saddam Speaks on the Gulf Crisis: A Collection of Documents*. Tel Aviv: Moshe Dayan Center for Middle Eastern and African Studies, Tel Aviv University, 1992.

Bengio, Ofra. *Saddam's Word: Political Discourse in Iraq*. New York: Oxford University Press, 1998.

Berman, Paul. *Terror and Liberalism*. New York: W. W. Norton and Company, 2003.

Blaydes, Lisa. *State of Repression: Iraq under Saddam Hussein*. Princeton, NJ: Princeton University Press, 2018.

Boutros-Ghali, Boutros. "An Agenda for Peace Preventive Diplomacy, Peacemaking and Peace-Keeping," Report of the Secretary-General pursuant to the statement adopted by the Summit Meeting of the Security Council on January 31, 1992, https://www.un.org/ruleoflaw/files/A_47_277.pdf.

Boutros-Ghali, Boutros. *The United Nations and the Iraq-Kuwait Conflict 1990–1996*, The United Nations Blue Books Series, Vol. IX, Department of Public Information United Nations, New York, 1996.

Boutros-Ghali, Boutros. *Unvanquished: A U.S.– U.N. Saga*. New York: Random House, 1999.

Brands, Hal. *From Berlin to Baghdad: America's Search for Purpose in the Post-Cold War World*. Lexington, KY: University Press of Kentucky, 2008.

Brands, Hal. "Inside the Iraqi State Records: Saddam Hussein, 'Irangate,' and the United States," *Journal of Strategic Studies* 34, no. 1 (2011): 95–118.

Brands, Hal. *Making the Unipolar Moment: U.S. Foreign Policy and the Rise of the Post-Cold War Order*. Ithaca, NY: Cornell University Press, 2016.

Brands, Hal. *What Good Is Grand Strategy?: Power and Purpose in American Statecraft from Harry S. Truman to George W. Bush*. Ithaca, NY: Cornell University Press, 2014.

Brands, Hal. "Why Did Saddam Invade Iran? New Evidence on Motives, Complexity, and the Israel Factor," *Journal of Military History* 75, no. 3 (July 2011): 861–85.

Bozo, Frédéric. *A History of the Iraq Crisis: France, the United States, and Iraq, 1991–2003*. New York: Columbia University Press, 2016.

Bozo, Frédéric. "'We Don't Need You': France, the United States, and Iraq, 1991–2003," *Diplomatic History* 41, no. 1 (January 2017): 183–208.

Brooks, Stephen G., and William C. Wohlforth. *World Out of Balance: International Relations and the Challenge of American Primacy*. Princeton, NJ: Princeton University Press, 2008.

Brands, Hal, and David Palkki. "Conspiring Bastards: Saddam's Strategic View of the United States," *Diplomatic History* 36, no. 3 (2012), 625–59.

Brands, Hal, and David Palkki. "Saddam, Israel, and the Bomb: Nuclear Alarmism Justified?," *International Security* 36, no. 1 (2011): 133–66.

Braut-Hegghammer, Målfrid. "Cheater's Dilemma: Iraq, Weapons of Mass Destruction, and the Path to War," *International Security* 45, no. 1 (2020): 51–89.

Brozan, Nadine. "Chronicle," *The New York Times*, October 4, 1993. https://www.nytimes.com/1993/10/04/nyregion/chronicle-513793.html?auth=link-dismiss-google1tap.

Bush, George H. W., and Brent Scowcroft. *A World Transformed*. New York: Vintage, 1999.

Bush, George W. "President Discusses the Future of Iraq," Washington, DC, February 26, 2000. http://georgewbush-whitehouse.archives.gov/news/releases/2003/02/20030226-11.html.

Bush, George W. "Remarks by the President at the 20th Anniversary of the National Endowment for Democracy," November 6, 2003. http:// geor gewb ush- whi teho use.archives.gov/news/releases/2003/11/20031106-2.html.

Castle, Tim. "Galloway Iraq Fund Had Illicit Oil Cash: Regulator," *Reuters*, June 7, 2007, https://www.reuters.com/article/us-britain-galloway/galloway-iraq-fund-had-illicit-oil-cash-regulator-idUSL0783566820070607.

Chatelard, Géraldine. "Migration from Iraq between the Gulf and the Iraq Wars (1990–2003): Historical and Socio- Spatial Dimensions," University of Oxford, *Centre on Migration, Policy and Society*, Working Paper No. 68 (2009).

Clinton, Bill. *My Life*. New York: Vintage, 2005.

Cohen, Nick. *How the Left Lost its Way*. New York: Harper Perennial, 2007.

Cohen, Roger. "A Manifesto From the Left Too Sensible to Ignore," *The New York Times*, December 30, 2006 https:// arch ive.nyti mes.com/ www.nyti mes.com/ iht/ 2006/ 12/ 30/ world/ IHT- 30gl obal ist.html?n= Top%252FN ews%252FWo rld%252F Colu mns%252FRoger%2520Cohen.

Cohen, Sharon. "Tense Days of Waiting for Iraqi- Americans," *Midland Daily News*, March 21, 2003. https://www.ourmidland.com/news/article/Tense-Days-of-Waiting-for-Iraqi-Americans-7202954.php.

Conduct of the Persian Gulf War: Final Report to Congress. Washington, DC: Department of Defense, April 1992.

Cooley, Alexander, and Daniel Nexon. *Exit from Hegemony: The Unraveling of the American Global Order*. New York: Oxford University Press, 2020.

Corbett, Julian. *Some Principles of Maritime Strategy*. Annapolis, MD: United States Naval Institute, 1988.

Cordesman, Anthony H. *Iraq's Military Forces: 1988–1993*. Washington, DC: CSIS Middle East Dynamic Net Assessment, 1994.

Coughlin, Con. *Saddam: His Rise and Fall*. New York: Ecco, 2005.

"'Chemical Sally' Captured Says US," *The Irish Times*, May 5, 2003. https:// www.iri shti mes.com/news/chemical-sally-captured-says-us-1.475414.

Christopher, Warren. *Chances of a Lifetime: A Memoir*. New York: Scribner, 2001.

Chua, Amy. *Day of Empire: How Hyperpowers Rise to Global Dominance—and Why They Fall*. New York: Random House, 2007.

Crawford, Timothy W. "Preventing Enemy Coalitions: How Wedge Strategies Shape Power Politics," *International Security* 35, no. 4 (Spring 2011): 155–89.

Darnton, Christopher. "The Provenance Problem: Research Methods and Ethics in the Age of WikiLeaks," *American Political Science Review* 116, no. 3 (2022): 1110–25.

Davies, Daniel. "Next stop Euston. This Manifesto Terminates Here," *The Guardian*, April 14, 2008. https://www.theguardian.com/commentisfree/2008/apr/14/nextstopiseust onwherethis.

"Defense Issues." C-SPAN video, February 13, 2003. https://www.c-span.org/video/?175 080-1/defense-issues.

Deudney, Daniel, and G. John Ikenberry. "Realism, Liberalism and the Iraq War," *Survival* 59, no. 4 (2017): 7–26.

Dimitrova, Daniela V. and Jesper Strömbäck. "Mission Accomplished? Framing of the Iraq War in the Elite Newspapers in Sweden and the United States," *Gazette: The International Journal for Communication Studies* 67, no. 5 (2005): 399–417.

"Donald Trump attacks George W. Bush on 9/11, Iraq," *CBS News*, February 13, 2016.

Duelfer, Charles. "Comprehensive Report of the Special Advisor to the DCI on Iraq's WMD," Vol. 1-3, *Central Intelligence Agency*, 2004.

Duelfer, Charles. *Hide and Seek: The Search for Truth in Iraq Hardcover*. New York: Public Affairs, 2009.

Dyson, Tim. "New Evidence on Child Mortality in Iraq," *Economic and Political Weekly* 44, no. 2 (January, 2009): 56–9.

El- Ghobashy, Mona. "The Metamorphosis of the Egyptian Muslim Brothers," *International Journal of Middle Eastern Studies* 37, no. 3 (2005): 373–95.

Engel, Jeffrey A. *When the World Seemed New: George H. W. Bush and the End of the Cold War*. New York: Houghton Mifflin Harcourt, 2017.

Epstein, Barbara. "The Antiwar Movement During the Gulf War," *Social Justice* 19, no. 1 (Spring 1992): 115–37.

Ewald, Shawn, "Endorse the Call to Action about Iraq," *A-Info*, February 12, 1998. http://www.ainfos.ca/98/feb/ainfos00220.html.

Euston Manifesto for a Renewal of Progressive Politics (2006). https://eustonmanifesto.org/the-euston-manifesto/.

"Executive Council of the Popular Islamic Conference," in *Islamic Conferences Held in the Kingdom of Saudi Arabia in the Course of the Arab Gulf Incidents*. The Kingdom of Saudi Arabia Ministry of Information, Saudi Press Agency, No Date.

Faust, Aaron. *The Ba'thification of Iraq: Saddam Hussein's Totalitarianism*. Austin, TX: University of Texas Press, 2015.

Farley, John. "A New Pro- Imperialist 'Left' Manifesto" *Counterpunch*, May 27, 2006. https://www.counterpunch.org/2006/05/27/a-new-pro-imperialist-quot-left-quot-manifesto/.

Finnemore, Martha, and Kathryn Sikkink. "International Norm Dynamics and Political Change," *International Organization* 52, no. 4 (Autumn 1998): 887–917.

"France's Total Fined for Graft in UN's Iraq Aid Program," *DW*, February 27, 2016, https://www.dw.com/en/frances-total-fined-for-graft-in-uns-iraq-aid-program/a-19078619.

Freedman, Lawrence. *Strategy: A History*. New York: Oxford University Press, 2013.

Friedman, Thomas. *The Lexus and the Olive Tree: The Lexus and the Olive Tree: Understanding Globalization*. New York: Farrar, Straus and Giroux, 2000.

Fukuyama, Francis. "After Neoconservatism," *New York Times Magazine*, February 19, 2006. http://www.nytimes.com/2006/02/19/magazine/neo.html?pagewanted=all&_r=1&.

Fukuyama, Francis. *America at the Crossroads: Democracy, Power, and the Neoconservative Legacy*. New Haven, CT: Yale University Press, 2006.

Fukuyama, Francis. *Political Order and Political Decay: From the Industrial Revolution to the Globalization of Democracy*. New York: Farrar, Straus and Giroux, 2014.

Fukuyama, Francis. "The End of History?," *National Interest* (Summer, 1989).

Fukuyama, Francis. *The End of History and the Last Man*. New York: The Free Press, 1992.

Gaddis, John Lewis. *On Grand Strategy*. New York: Penguin Press, 2018.

Gaddis, John Lewis. "Toward the Post-Cold War World," *Foreign Affairs* 70, no. 2 (Spring, 1991): 102–22.

Gellman, Barton. "Allied Air War Struck Broadly in Iraq," *Washington Post*, June 23, 1991.

Gerstenzang, James. "Bush Airs Thoughts on End of Gulf War," *Los Angeles Times*, January 15, 1996, https://www.latimes.com/archives/la-xpm-1996-01-15-mn-24868-story.html.

Goldgeier, James. "Bill and Boris: A Window into a Most Important Post- Cold War Relationship," *Texas National Security Review* 1, no. 4 (August 2018): 42–54.

Goodgame, Dan. "What If We Do Nothing?," *Time Magazine* 137, no. 1, January 7, 1991: 22–6.

Gordon, Michael R, and General Bernard E Trainor. *The Generals' War: The Inside Story of the Conflict in the Gulf*. New York: Little, Brown and Company, 1995.

Graham, Victoria. "General Assembly Condemns Panama Invasion 75-20," *Associated Press*, December 29, 1989.

Grunwald, Michael. "Trump Goes Code Pink on George W. Bush," *Politico*, February 14, 2016. https://www.politico.com/magazine/story/2016/02/trump-code-pink-bush-iraq-9-11-213630.

Gunter, Michael M. "The KDP-PUK Conflict in Northern Iraq," *Middle East Journal* 50, no. 2 (Spring, 1996): 224–41.

Halliday, Fred. "The Gulf War 1990-1991 and the Study of International Relations," *Review of International Studies* 20, no. 2 (April 1994): 109–30.

Herring, George. *From Colony to Superpower: U.S. Foreign Relations since 1776*. New York: Oxford University Press, 2017.

Haddad, Fanar. "Essential Readings: Iraq," *Jadaliyya*, September 26, 2018. https://www.jadaliyya.com/Details/38016.

Haddad, Fanar. *Sectarianism in Iraq: Antagonistic Visions of Unity*. London: Hurst & Company, 2011.

Hart, Justin. *Empire of Ideas: The Origins of Public Diplomacy and the Transformation of U.S. Foreign Policy*. New York: Oxford University Press, 2013.

Haslam, Jonathan. *Near and Distant Neighbors: A New History of Soviet Intelligence*. New York, Farrar, Straus and Giroux, 2015.

Hathaway, Oona A. and Scott J. Shapiro. *The Internationalists: How a Radical Plan to Outlaw War Remade the World*. New York: Simon & Schuster, 2017.

Hegel, Georg Wilhelm Friedrich. *Introduction to the Philosophy of History*. Indianapolis, Indiana: Hackett Publishing Company, 1988.

Helfont, Samuel. "Authoritarianism beyond Borders: The Iraqi Ba'th Party as a Transnational Actor," *The Middle East Journal* 72, no. 2 (Spring 2018): 229–45.

Helfont, Samuel. "Catalyst of History: Francis Fukuyama, the Iraq War, and the Legacies of 1989 in the Middle East." In Piotr Kosicki and Kyrill Kunakhovich eds., *The Long 1989: Decades of Global Revolution* (Central European University Press, 2019).

Helfont, Samuel. *Compulsion in Religion: Saddam Hussein, Islam, and the Roots of Insurgency in Iraq*. New York: Oxford University Press, 2018.

Helfont, Samuel. "Iraq's Real Weapons of Mass Destruction were 'Political Operations,'" *War on the Rocks*, February 26, 2018, https://warontherocks.com/2018/02/iraqs-real-weapons-mass-destruction-political-operations.

Helfont, Samuel. "Islam in Saudi Foreign Policy: The Case of Ma'ruf al-Dawalibi," *International History Review* 42 (2020).

Helfont, Samuel. "Saddam and the Islamists: The Ba'thist Regime's Instrumentalization of Religion in Foreign Affairs," *The Middle East Journal* 68, no. 3 (Summer 2014): 352–66.

Helfont, Samuel. "The Gulf War's Afterlife: Dilemmas, Missed Opportunities, and the Post-Cold War Order Undone," *The Texas National Security Review* 4, no. 2 (Spring 2021): 25–47.

Helfont, Samuel, and Michael Brill. "Saddam's ISIS? The Terrorist Group's Real Origin Story," *Foreign Affairs*, January 12, 2016. https://www.foreignaffairs.com/articles/iraq/2016-01-12/saddams-isis.

Helfont, Samuel, and Tally Helfont. "Jordan: Between the Arab Spring and the Gulf Cooperation Council," *Orbis* 56, no. 1 (2012): 82–95.

Hitchens, Christopher. *A Long Short War: The Postponed Liberation of Iraq.* New York: Plume, 2003.

Hoffmann, Matthew J. "Norms and Social Constructivism in International Relations," *Oxford Research Encyclopedias*, December 22, 2017. https:// oxfor dre.com/ inter nati onal stud ies/ view/ 10.1093/ acrefore/ 9780190846626.001.0001/ acrefore- 9780190846 626-e-60.

Hill, Charles. *The Papers of United Nations Secretary-General Boutros Boutros-Ghali* 1–3. New Haven: Yale University Press, 2003.

"Hinweise auf Öl-Geld von Saddam schon 2004" (Hints of Oil Money From Saddam aln ready in 2004), *Die Presse*, August 9 2010 http://diepresse.com/home/innenpolitik/586 527/Hinweise-auf-OelGeld-von-Saddam-schon-2004?from=suche.intern.portal.

Huntington, Samuel P. "The Clash of Civilizations?," *Foreign Affairs* 72, no. 3 (Summer, 1993): 22–49.

Hussein, Saddam. *On History, Heritage, and Religion,* Translated by Naji al- Hadithi. Baghdad: Translation and Foreign Language Publishing House, 1981.

Ignatius, David. "The CIA and the Coup that Wasn't," *The Washington Post*, May 16, 2003. https:// www.was hing tonp ost.com/ arch ive/ opini ons/ 2003/ 05/ 16/ the- cia- and- the-coup-that-wasnt/0abfb8fa-61e9-4159-a885-89b8c476b188/.

Ikenberry, G. John. *A World Safe for Democracy: Liberal Internationalism and the Crises of Global Order.* New Haven: Yale University Press, 2020.

Ikenberry, G. John. *After Victory: Institutions, Strategic Restraint, and the Rebuilding of Order After Major Wars.* Princeton, NJ: Princeton University Press, 2019.

Ikenberry, G. John. *Liberal Leviathan: The Origins, Crisis, and Transformation of the American System.* Princeton, NJ: Princeton University Press, 2011.

Ikenberry, G. John. *Liberal Order and Imperial Ambition: American Power and International Order.* New York: Polity Press, 2005.

Ikenberry, G John, Nuno P Monteiro, and William C Wohlforth, eds., *International Relations Theory and the Consequences of Unipolarity.* New York: Cambridge University Press, 2011.

"Interview With Jacques Chirac," *The New York Times*, September 9, 2002. https://www. nytimes.com/2002/09/09/international/europe/interview-with-jacques-chirac.html.

"Iraq blocks U.N. inspectors in Baghdad," *Associated Press*, July 7, 1992.

"Iraq Sanctions Cannot Be Forever," *The New York Times*, August 1, 1994. https://www. nytimes.com/1994/08/01/opinion/iraq-sanctions-cannot-be-forever.html.

Jeffries, Ian. *The New Russia: A Handbook of Economic and Political Developments.* New York: Routledge, 2013.

Johnson II, Douglas V, and Stephen C Pelletiere, reply by Edward Mortimer, "Iraq's Chemical Warfare," *The New York Review of Books*, November 22, 1990. https://www. nybooks.com/articles/1990/11/22/iraqs-chemical-warfare/.

Juneau, Thomas. "The Obama Administration, Defensive Realism, and American Foreign Policy in the Middle East," *Comparative Strategy* 39, no. 4 (2020): 385–400.

Kaplan, Robert D. "Why John J. Mearsheimer Is Right (About Some Things)," *The Atlantic Monthly* (January/ February 2012). https:// www.thea tlan tic.com/ magaz ine/ arch ive/ 2012/01/why-john-j-mearsheimer-is-right-about-some-things/308839/.

Karsh, Efraim, and Inari Rautsi. *Saddam Hussein: A Political Biography.* New York: Grove Press, 2002.

Keegan, John. *A History of Warfare.* New York: Robert F. Knopf, 1993.

Kennedy, Paul. *The Parliament of Man: The Past, Present, and Future of the United Nations.* New York: Vintage Books, 2006.

Kerr, Malcom. *The Arab Cold War: Gamal 'Abd al-Nasir and His Rivals.* New York: Oxford University Press, 1971.

Kessler, Glenn, and Thomas E. Ricks. "The Realists' Repudiation of Policies for a War, Region," *The Washington Post,* December 7, 2006. http://www.washingtonpost.com/wp-dyn/content/article/2006/12/06/AR2006120601482.html.

Kharas, Homi, Brian Pinto, and Sergei Ulatov, *An Analysis of Russia's 1998 Meltdown: Fundamentals and Market Signals.* Washington, DC: Brookings Institution, 2001.

Khoury, Dina Rizk. *Iraq in Wartime: Soldiering, Martyrdom and Remembrance.* Cambridge, UK: Cambridge University Press, 2013.

Khoury, Dina Rizk. "The Government of War," *International Journal of Middle Eastern Studies* 46, no. 4 (2014): 791–93.

King, Susan. "Still Trying to Shake Things Up: For Kris Kristofferson, Politics Is Always on His Mind," *Los Angeles Times,* October 3, 1993. https://www.latimes.com/archives/la-xpm-1993-10-03-tv-41616-story.html.

Kinzer, Stephen "In an Astonishing Turn, George Soros and Charles Koch Team up to end US 'Forever Far' Policy." *Boston Globe,* June 30, 2019. https://www.bostonglobe.com/opinion/2019/06/30/soros-and-koch-brothers-team-end-forever-war-policy/WhyENwjhG0vfo9Um6Zl0JO/story.html.

Kissinger, Henry. *Diplomacy.* New York: Simon and Schuster, 1994.

Koblentz, Gregory D. "Saddam Versus the Inspectors: The Impact of Regime Security on the Verification of Iraq's WMD Disarmament," *Journal of Strategic Studies* 41, no. 3 (2018): 372–409.

Kramer, Martin. "Islam in the New World Order." In *Middle East Contemporary Survey: Volume XV, 1991,* ed. Ami Ayalon. Boulder, CO: Westview Press, 1993.

Krauthammer, Charles. "The Unipolar Moment." *Foreign Affairs* 70, no. 1 (Winter 1990/1991): 23–33.

Lawrence, Quil. *Invisible Nation: How the Kurds' Quest for Statehood Is Shaping Iraq and the Middle East.* New York: Walker Books, 2009.

Lake, Anthony. *Confronting Backlash States.* Washington, DC: U.S. Government, 1994.

Leffler, Melvyn P. "Foreign Policies of the George W. Bush Administration: Memoirs, History, Legacy," *Diplomatic History* 37, no. 2 (2013): 190–216.

Leonhard, Jorn. *Pandora's Box: A History of the First World War,* trans. Patrick Camiller. Boston: Harvard University Press.

Lewis, Paul. "After the War; U.N. Survey Calls Iraq's War Damage Near-Apocalyptic," *New York Times,* March 22, 1991.

Lewis, Paul. "Fighting in Panama: United Nations; Security Council Condemnation of Invasion Vetoed," *The New York Times,* December 24, 1989.

Litvak, Meir. "Iraq (Al-Jumhuriyya al-'Iraqiyya)." In *Middle East Contemporary Survey: Volume XV, 1991,* ed. Ami Ayalon. Boulder, CO: Westview Press, 1993.

Liu, Melinda. "What 'Mrs. Anthrax' Told Me," *Newsweek,* December 21, 2005. https://www.newsweek.com/what-mrs-anthrax-told-me-114077.

Long, Jerry M. *Saddam's War of Words: Politics, Religion, and the Iraqi invasion of Kuwait.* Austin, TX: University of Texas Press, 2004.

Lustick, Ian S. "The Absence of Middle Eastern Great Powers: Political 'Backwardness' in Historical Perspective," *International Organization* 51, no. 4 (1997): 653–83.

Makiya, Kanan. *Cruelty and Silence: War, Tyranny, Uprising, and the Arab World.* New York: Norton, 1993.

Makiya, Kanan. *Republic of Fear: The Politics of Modern Iraq.* Berkeley, CA: University of California Press, 1998.

Malone, David. *The International Struggle Over Iraq: Politics in the UN Security Council 1980–2005.* New York: Oxford University Press, 2006.

Malovany, Pesach. *Wars of Modern Babylon: A History of the Iraqi Army from 1921 to 2003.* Lexington KY: The University Press of Kentucky, 2017.

Mandelbaum, Michael. *Mission Failure: America and the World in the Post-Cold War Era.* New York: Oxford University Press, 2016.

Mandelbaum, Michael. *The Rise and Fall of Peace on Earth.* New York: Oxford University Press, 2019.

Manela, Erez. "International Society as a Historical Subject," *Diplomatic History* 44, no. 2 (2020): 184–209.

"Maryland Man Pleads Guilty to Conspiracy to Act as an Iraqi Agent," *US Department of Justice,* December 22, 2008. https://www.justice.gov/archive/opa/pr/2008/December/08-nsd-1141.html.

Matthew, Mark, and Lyle Denniston, "Author Doesn't Want Articles on Saudis Reprinted," *The Baltimore Sun,* November 30, 1993, https:// www.balti more sun.com/ news/ bs-xpm-1993-11-30-1993334031-story.html.

Mazower, Mark. *Governing the World: The History of an Idea* (New York: Penguin Books, 2012.

Mearsheimer, John J. "Back to the Future: Instability in Europe after the Cold War," *International Security* 15, no. 1 (Summer, 1990): 5–56.

Mearsheimer, John J. *The Great Delusion: Liberal Dreams and International Realities.* New Haven: Yale University Press, 2019.

Mearsheimer, John J. "Why We Will Soon Miss the Cold War," *The Atlantic Monthly* 266, no. 2 (August 1990): 35–50.

Mcgowan, Patrick. "Britain Treats Iraqi Poisoned by Saddam," *Evening Standard* (London), February 1, 1995.

Milton-Edwards, Beverley. "A Temporary Alliance with the Crown: The Islamic Response in Jordan." In *Islamic Fundamentalisms and the Gulf Crisis,* ed. James Piscatori. Chicago: American Academy of Arts and Sciences with the Fundamentalism Project, 1991.

Monteiro, Nuno P. *Theory of Unipolar Politics.* New York: Cambridge University Press, 2014.

Moore, Andrew. "History, Freedom and Bureaucracy." In Arin Keeble and Ivan Stacy, eds., *The Wire and America's Dark Corners: Critical Essays.* Jefferson, NC: McFarland and Company Inc., 2015.

Morris, Harvey. "Saddam's Enemies in Exile," *The Independent* (London), September 11, 1990.

Moynihan, Daniel P. "The United States in Opposition," *Commentary* (March 1975).

Mueller, John. *Retreat from Doomsday: The Obsolescence of Major War.* New York: Basic Books, 1989.

Murphy, Sean D. "Assessing the Legality of Invading Iraq," *George Washington University Law School Scholarly Commons* (2004).

Murray, Williamson, *Gulf War Air Power Survey, Vol. 2: Operations and Effectiveness.* Washington, DC: U.S. Government Printing Office, 1993.

Murray, Williamson, and Kevin Woods, *The Iran–Iraq War: A Military and Strategic History*. Cambridge: Cambridge University Press, 2014.

National Security Strategy of the United States. Washington, DC: The White House, August, 1991.

Neep, Daniel. "War, State Formation, and Culture," *International Journal of Middle East Studies* 45, no. 4 (2013): 795–7.

Nixon, John. *Debriefing the President: The Interrogation of Saddam Hussein*. New York: Random House, 2018.

Nye, Joseph. *Is the American Century Over?* Cambridge: Polity, 2015.

"October 11, 2000 Debate Transcript," *Commission on Presidential Debates*, October 11, 2000. http://www.debates.org/?page=october-11-2000-debate-transcript.

"المرصد ينشر رسالة حول فساد في سفارات عراقية" [Observatory Publishes Letter on Corruption in Iraqi Embassies], *Iraqi Media Observatory in Cairo*, June 12, 2007, http://iraqegypt.blogspot.com/2007/06/blog-post_12.html.

"Obituary for Ali Hossaini," *Richmond Times-Dispatch*, August 7, 2015, https://richmond.com/obituaries/hossaini-ali/article_2a0180e5-126f-53da-9f8f-a303a59ce08b.html.

"Oral History: Richard Cheney," PBS Front Line, January 1996, https://www.pbs.org/wgbh/pages/frontline/gulf/oral/cheney/1.html.

Pape, Robert A. *Bombing to Win: Air Power and Coercion in War*. Ithaca, NY: Cornell University Press, 1996.

Peter Jennings Reporting, "Unfinished Business: The CIA and Saddam Hussein," *ABC* (Television), June 27, 1997.

Peterson, Scott. "Kurds Say Iraq's Attacks Serve as a Warning," *Christian Science Monitor*, May 13, 2002.

Piscatori, James. "Religion and Realpolitik." In *Islamic Fundamentalisms and the Gulf Crisis*, ed. James Piscatori. Chicago: American Academy of Arts and Sciences with the Fundamentalism Project, 1991.

Pollak, Kenneth. *The Threatening Storm: The Case for Invading Iraq*. New York: Random House, 2002.

Posen, Barry R. *Restraint: A New Foundation for U.S. Grand Strategy*. Ithaca, NY: Cornell University Press, 2014.

"President Bush Delivers Graduation Speech at West Point," United States Military Academy, West Point, New York, June 1, 2002. https://georgewbush-whitehouse.archives.gov/news/releases/2002/06/20020601-3.html.

"President's Remarks at the United Nations General Assembly," September 12, 2002. https:// geor gewb ush- whi teho use.archi ves.gov/ news/ relea ses/ 2002/ 09/ 20020 912-1.html.

Press, Daryl G. "The Myth of Air Power in the Persian Gulf War and the Future of Warfare," *International Security* 26, no. 2 (Fall 2001): 5–44.

Primakov, Yevgeny. *Russia and the Arabs: Behind the Scenes in the Middle East from the Cold War to the Present*. New York: Basic Books, 2009.

وقائع المؤتمر الإسلامي الشعبي: وثائق وقرارات [*Proceedings of the Popular Islamic Conference: Documents and Resolutions*]. Baghdad: al-Najaf al-Ashraf, 1983.

وقائع المؤتمر الإسلامي الشعبي الثاني [*Proceedings of the Second Popular Islamic Conference*]. Baghdad: Ministry of Endowments and Religious Affairs, 1986.

"Q&A: Oil-for-Food Scandal," *BBC*, September 7, 2005. http://news.bbc.co.uk/2/hi/4232629.stm.

"Remarks at Town Hall Meeting," Ohio State University, Columbus, Ohio, February 18, 1998. *U.S. Department of State Archive.* https://1997-2001.state.gov/www/statements/1998/980218.html.

Reynié, Dominique. "Does a "European Public Opinion" Exist?" *Forum Constitutionis Europae,* Humboldt University, Germany, September 2009, 12–3, http://www.whi-berlin.eu/documents/Rede-Reynie-engl.pdf.

Rid, Thomas. *Active Measures: The Secret History of Disinformation and Political Warfare.* New York: Farrar, Straus and Giroux, 2020.

Riding, Alan. "Confrontation in The Gulf; Crowds in European Cities Protest a War in Gulf Area." *The New York Times,* January 13, 1991.

Robinson, Linda. "Modern Political Warfare," *RAND Corporation* (2008).

Ryan, Curtis R. *Inter- Arab Alliances: Regime Security and Jordanian Foreign Policy.* Gainesville, FL: University of Florida Press, 2009.

"Saddam's Iraq: Sanctions and U.S. Policy," Hearing Before the Subcommittee on Near Eastern and South Asian Affairs of the Committee on Foreign Relations United States Senate, One Hundred Sixth Congress, Second Session, March 22, 2000, 5. https://www.govinfo.gov/content/pkg/CHRG-106shrg67659/html/CHRG-106shrg67659.htm.

Said, Edward W. "Behind Saddam Hussein's Moves," *The Christian Science Monitor* 0813 (1990). https://www.csmonitor.com/layout/set/amphtml/1990/0813/esaid.html.

Said, Edward W. "Edward Said, an American and an Arab, Writes on the Eve of the Iraqi-Soviet Peace Talks," *London Review of Books* 13, no. 5 (1991): 7–8.

Saletan, William. "Wag the Doubt," *Slate,* December 20, 1998. https://slate.com/news-and-politics/1998/12/wag-the-doubt.html.

Sassoon, Joseph. *Saddam Hussein's Ba'ath Party: Inside an Authoritarian Regime.* Cambridge: Cambridge University Press, 2012.

Sassoon, Joseph and Alissa Walter. "The Iraqi Occupation of Kuwait: New Historical Perspectives," *The Middle East Journal* 71, no. 4 (2017): 607–28.

Schenker, David. *Dancing with Saddam: The Strategic Tango of Jordan- Iraq Relations.* New York: Lexington Books, 2003.

Sciolino, Elaine. "The Big Brother: Iraq Under Saddam Hussein," *New York Times Magazine,* February. 3, 1985.

Service, Robert. *The End of the Cold War, 1985- 1991.* New York: Public Affairs Books, 2015.

Serrill, Michael S. "Under Fire," *Time,* January 18, 1993. http://content.time.com/time/subscriber/article/0,33009,977515-5,00.html.

Shakespeare, William. *Coriolanus.* New York: Oxford University Press, 1994.

Shahzad, Syed Saleem. "A 'third force' awaits US in Iraq," *Asia Times,* March 1, 2003, http://www.atimes.com/atimes/Middle_East/EC01Ak04.html.

Martin Shaw, "Why I didn't Sign the Euston Manifesto," *Democratiya,* Autumn 2006. https://www.dissentmagazine.org/democratiya_article/why-i-didnt-sign-the-euston-manifesto.

Shifrinson, Joshua R. Itzkowitz. "George H.W. Bush: Conservative Realist as President," *Orbis* 62, no. 1 (2018): 56–75.

Shucosky, David. "Former French UN Ambassador Admits Taking Oil-For-Food Bribes," November 18, 2005, https://www.jurist.org/news/2005/11/former-french-un-ambassador-admits/.

Sick, Gary. "Rethinking Dual Containment" *Survival* 40, no. 1 (1998): 5–32.

Sluglett, Marion Faruq. "Liberation or Repression? Pan- Arab Nationalism and the Women's Movement in Iraq." In Derek Hopwood, Habib Ishow, and Thomas Koszinowski, eds., *Iraq: Power and Society*, St. Anthony's Middle East Monographs. Reading: Ithaca Press, 1993.

Stayn, David. *France and Iraq: Oil, Arms and French Policy Making in the Middle East*. New York: IB Tauris, 2006.

Stoker, Donald. *Why America Loses Wars: Limited War and US Strategy from the Korean War to the Present*. New York: Cambridge University Press, 2019.

Smith, Paul A. *On Political War*. Washington, DC: National Defense University Publications, 1989.

Snyder, Sarah. *Human Rights Activism and the End of the Cold War: A Transnational History of the Helsinki Network*. New York: Cambridge University Press, 2011.

Steib, Joseph David. *The Regime Change Consensus: Iraq in American Politics 1990–2003*. PhD Dissertation, University of North Carolina, 2019.

Sun Tzu. *The Art of War*, trans. Samuel B Griffith. New York: Oxford University Press, 1963.

Terrazas, Aaron. "Iraqi Immigrants in the United States," *Migration Policy Institute, Migration Information Source Spotlight* (March 5, 2009), www.migrationpolicy.org/arti cle/iraqi-immigrantsunited-states.

"The Unfinished War: The Legacy of Desert Storm," *CNN*, January 05, 2001, http://tran scripts.cnn.com/TRANSCRIPTS/0101/05/cp.00.html.

التقرير المركزي للمؤتمر القطري التاسع [The Central Report of the Ninth Regional Conference]. Baghdad: Hizb al-Ba'th al-'Arabi al-Ishtiraki, 1983.

"The Vice President Appears on NBC's Meet the Press," George W Bush White House Archives, December 9, 2001. https://georgewbush-whitehouse.archives.gov/vicepr esident/news-speeches/speeches/print/vp20011209.html.

"They Got It Right: (1) Robert J. Art," *Radio Open Source*, October 19, 2007, https://radi oopensource.org/they-got-it-right-1-robert-j-art/.

Tietzen, Katelyn Karly. *The Iraqi Quest for Autonomy through Military and Diplomatic Interventions, 1968–2003*. PhD Dissertation, Kansas State University, 2019.

Tilly, Charles. "Reflections on the History of European State-Making." In *The Formation of National States in Western Europe*, ed. Charles Tilly. Princeton, NJ: Princeton University Press, 1975.

"To Paris, U.S. Looks Like a 'Hyperpower,'" *International Herald Tribune*. February 5, 1999. https://www.nytimes.com/1999/02/05/news/to-paris-us-looks-like-a-hyperpo wer.html.

Tomasson, Robert E, "Future Events Parties With a Purpose," *The New York Times*, December 2, 1984. https://www.nytimes.com/1984/12/02/style/future-events-parties-with-a-purpose.html.

Trachtenberg, Marc. "The United States and the NATO Non- extension Assurances of 1990: New Light on an Old Problem?," *International Security* 45. no. 3 (2021): 162–203.

Tripp, Charles. *A History of Iraq*. Cambridge: Cambridge University Press, 2002.

United Nations. "Sanctions Against Rhodesia," *Time Magazine*, December 23, 1966.

Van Walsum, Peter. "The Iraq Sanction's Committee." In *The UN Security Council: From the Cold War to the 21st Century*, ed. David Malone. Boulder, CO: Lynne Rienner Publishers, 2004.

Volcker, Paul A. "Management of the United Nations Oil- for- Food Programme," *Independent Inquiry Committee into the United Nations Oil- for- Food Programme* (2005).

"Volvo Agrees to Penalty over Iraq Oil-for-Food," *Reuters*, March 20, 2008, https://www. reut ers.com/ arti cle/ volvo- iraq/ volvo- agr ees- to- pena lty- over- iraq- oil- for- food- idUKWBT00862520080320.

Walt, Stephen M. *The Hell of Good Intentions: America's Foreign Policy Elite and the Decline of U.S. Primacy*. New York: Farrar, Straus and Giroux, 2018.

Walt, Stephen M. "WikiLeaks, April Glaspie, and Saddam Hussein," *Foreign Policy*, January 9, 2011. https://foreignpolicy.com/2011/01/09/wikileaks-april-glaspie-and-saddam-hussein/.

Walter, Alissa. "The Repatriation of Iraqi Ba'th Party Archives: Ethical and Practical Considerations," *Journal of Contemporary Iraq & the Arab World*, Vol. 16, No. 1 & 2 (2022): 117–36.

Walter, Alissa. *The Ba'th Party in Baghdad: State-Society Relations through Wars, Sanctions, and Authoritarian Rule, 1950–2003*. PhD Dissertation, Georgetown University, 2018.

Wester, Franklin Eric. "Preemption and Just War: Considering the Case of Iraq," *Parameters* (Winter 2004–05).

Wheatcroft, Geoffrey. "They Should Come Out as Imperialist and Proud of It," *The Guardian*, May 9, 2006. https://www.theguardian.com/commentisfree/2006/may/10/foreignpolicy.comment.

White, Paul K. *Crisis after the Storm: An Appraisal of U.S. Airpower in Iraq since 1991*. Washington DC: Washington Institute for Near East Policy, 1999.

Woods, Kevin M. *A Review of Iraqi Freedom from Saddam's Senior Leadership*. Washington, DC: Institute for Defense Analysis, 2008.

Woods, Kevin M. *Iraqi Perspectives Project, Saddam and Terrorism: Emerging Insights from Captured Iraqi Documents*. Washington, DC: Institute for Defense Analysis, 2007, Volumes 1–5.

Woods, Kevin M. *The Mother of All Battles: Saddam Hussein's Strategic Plan for the Persian Gulf War*. Washington, DC: Institute for Defense Analysis, 2008.

Woods, Kevin M. *Um Al- Ma'arik (The Mother of All Battles): Operational and Strategic Insights from an Iraqi Perspective*. Washington, DC: Institute for Defense Analysis, 2008.

Woods, Kevin M. *View of Operation Iraqi Freedom from Saddam's Senior Leadership*. Washington, DC: Institute for Defense Analysis, 2006.

Woods, Kevin M, David D. Palkki, and Mark E. Stout, eds., *The Saddam Tapes: The Inner Workings of a Tyrant's Regime 1978–2001*. New York: Cambridge University Press, 2011.

Woods, Kevin M, and Mark E Stout, "Saddam's Perceptions and Misperceptions: The Case of 'Desert Storm,'" *The Journal of Strategic Studies* 33, no. 1 (2010): 5–41.

Watts, Clint. *Messing with the Enemy*. New York: Harper Collins, 2018.

"X" (George F Kennan), "The Sources of Soviet Conduct," *Foreign Affairs*, July 1947.

Zakaria, Fareed. *The Post-American World*. New York: Norton, 2008.

Index

For the benefit of digital users, indexed terms that span two pages (e.g., 52–53) may, on occasion, appear on only one of those pages.